PSALMS OF A SAIVA SAINT

PSALMS OF A SAIVA SAINT

BEING SELECTIONS FROM THE WRITINGS OF TAYUMANASWAMY. TRANSLATED INTO ENGLISH

T. ISAAC TAMBYAH

WITH AN INTRODUCTION AND NOTES

GYAN

Published by

Gyan Publishing House
5, Ansari Road
Daryaganj, New Delhi-110002
Phone: 011-47034999, 9811692060
E-mail: books@gyanbooks.com

Distribution Network
gyanbooks.com
India, USA, Canada, UK, Australia, France

ISBN : 978-81-212-3925-7 (PB)
First Published, 1925

2nd Impression 2020

Printed at: Gyan Press, Delhi.

Psalms of A Saiva Saint
Author: T. Isaac Tambyah

To

My Wife

But for Whose Sustained Sympathy

And Stimulus

This Book

Would not have been completed.

புல்லா எழுத்திற் பொருளில் வறுங்கோட்டி
கல்லா ஒருவன் உரைப்பவுங் கண்ணோடி
நல்லார் வருந்தியுங் கேட்பரே மற்றவன்
பல்லாரு ணாணல் பரிந்து.

— நாலடியார்.

PREFACE

THIS book is a Christian layman's endeavour to understand a great Hindu poet-saint. My Christian prepossessions will, I believe, be found to be evenly balanced, if not altogether neutralized, by that bias which belongs to my being a Tamil. In my interpretation of S. Tāyumānavar I have striven, it is for the reader to say with what success, to maintain the historic sense and the literary judgment undimmed by either religious inclinations or racial sympathy, by keeping down prepossessions at the lowest level of the safest minimum. The production of this book has cost me over fifteen years' study. A faultless work—well, who is faultless? What is? Faultlessness is the frailty of the few: the many must make mistakes. One merit I may courageously claim for this work—it is the very first of its kind, the precursor of better ones.

The *Introduction* was planned on a small scale, but it had stealthily grown under my hands into one hundred and eighty-nine pages. I do not regret the length, considering the variety of subjects that called for necessary discussion. The treatment of some of them has been accorded an amount of fulness needed for a just appreciation of the poet. And so, I wonder if the reader will really rejoice to have what, in all good faith, is intended for his help, boiled down to the barrenness of superficial brevity. For myself, should the opportunity for re-writing the *Introduction* be ever mine, I would rather add somewhat to it.

Thus, the discussion of the subject of Part I of the *Introduction* might be supplemented with a notice of Professor S. Krishnasamy Aiyengar's views as expressed in his two books.[1] He, perhaps induced by pro-Aryan predilections to belittle the antiquity of Tamil literature and to make the Tamil language dependant on Sanscrit, is for trailing old heresies across

[1] *Some Contributions of South India to Indian Culture*, Calcutta, 1923. *Beginnings of South Indian History*, Madras, 1918.

the track of scientific research. Against the conclusions of the learned Aiyengar may be noted the recent illuminative interpretation of Dravidian Antiquity by Mr. S. Srinivasachari in *The Young Men of India* of December 1923. Dr. Slater's *Dravidian Element in Indian Culture*, London, 1924, is a work of singular merit except for its lapse into the fanciful and the frivolous at p. 20 on Tamil women. The writer on the whole supports the position strongly opposed to Prof. K. S. Aiyengar. The passing references to the Tamils in Colonel T. C. Hodson's *Primitive Culture of India*, London, 1922, are not sufficient for ascertaining the learned author's opinions on points of Tamilian antiquity and culture. The late Dr. Vincent A. Smith's work[1] of rare insight and ripe scholarship is one untainted by Aryan antipathies. Some of its conclusions are among the settled verdicts of history. Dr. Smith notices a 'distinct Dravidian civilization'[2] with its golden age of literature in the first three centuries of the Christian era,[3] while 'the most ancient Tamil literature, dating from the early centuries of the Christian era or even earlier, was composed on Dravidian lines and independent of Sanscrit models.'[4] He rightly deplores[5] that 'hitherto most historians of ancient India have written as if the South did not exist'.

Let us now pass from the secular to the sacred, supplementing a little what is said in Part VIII, which begins at p. cxliv. With reference particularly to pp. cliii and cliv, I desire to add that Dewan Bahadur A. S. Appasamy Pillay's most stimulating spiritual autobiography[6] had not come to my knowledge till March, 1925, when a copy was very kindly presented to me by his distinguished son, Judge Paul Appasamy Pillai. The honor I accord to Sadhu Sunder Singh as 'the first Indian Christian' with an experience of visions has to be shared

[1] *Oxford History of India*, Oxford, 1919.
[2] *Ibid.*, p. 14.
[3] *Ibid.*, p. 14.
[4] *Ibid.*, p. 13.
[5] *Ibid.*, p. 15.
[6] *Fifty Years' Pilgrimage of a Convert*, London and Madras, 1924.

by the devout Dewan Bahadur A. S. Appasamy Pillai.[1] A work by another distinguished member of the Appasamy family is in preparation—*Christianity as Bhakti Marga*, by Dr. A. J. Appasamy, M.A., B.D., D.Phil. The Right Rev. Bishop H. Pakenham Walsh, D.D., Principal of Bishop's College, Calcutta, has given us (with the courteous approval of Dr. Appasamy himself) a summary, in *The Guardian* (Calcutta) of September 4 and 11, 1924, of some of the main thoughts of the forthcoming book, which is a study of Johannine mysticism with special reference to Indian thought. The Bishop's articles are a very readable forecast of Dr. Appasamy's *bhakti* study to which all lovers of mysticism look forward with eagerness. There is one point in the Bishop's presenting of Dr. Appasamy's study of *bhakti* about which I venture to make a cautionary comment. Our Lord's 'Come unto Me and I will give you rest' is paralleled[2] with Sri Krishna's 'Come unto Me and I will deliver thee from all sins.' Now, a non-Christian reader is likely to forget[3] the transmigrational setting of the *Gita* sayings when he finds their verbal parallels in the Gospels. Again, the ἀνάπαυσις of Mt. xi. 28, 29, 30 does not shut out the sense, provable from classical Greek and the papyri, of a temporary refreshing and resting to fit one for *further labour and service*.[4]

To what I have said at p. clxii on the *Song of Songs* I would add, by way of reference for study, the late Rev. Jesse Brett's *Via Mystica* (London, 1925).

One more item by way of addendum. With particular reference to the fifth foot-note at p. clxxii, and supplementing the Bernard passage at pp. 189 and 190 in the Notes, may be given this passage from S. Bernard's *De Diligendo Deo, c. 10*:—

> As iron made hot and glowing, becometh very like fire itself, and seemeth to put off its own position and proper form; and as the air suffused with the light of the same is transferred into light with all its brilliancy, and seemeth to be not so much illuminated as illumination

[1] *Pilgrimage*, pp. 106–26.

[2] *Guardian*, September 4, 1924, p. 128.

[3] See my *Foregleams of God*, p. 223.

[4] See Moulton and Milligan, *Vocabulary of the Greek New Testament*, p. 36.

itself; so is it that with saintly souls every human affection in a certain ineffable manner melteth away and is transfused entirely into the will of God.[1]

About the plan of this book itself, it may be thought by some that the printing of the Tamil text of the psalms side by side with the English is likely to be useful. I have advisedly not chosen to do so, for the purpose of encouraging or stimulating those who know enough Tamil to read the psalms to read them in the N.M.[2] or other good Tamil edition *in the context of those not translated here.* The Tamil first lines are given to help those who wish to read the original.[3] All translations in the *Introduction*, and in the *Notes*, of Tāyumānavar's psalms incidentally quoted and of passages from the writings of other Tamil authors are mine, except where it is otherwise indicated.

The total number of psalms translated is 366, out of the 1452 given in most editions of the Tamil. Various renderings of a few psalms are given. The numbering is explained at p. 4.

I have said a little in the *Introduction*[4] about the construction of my renderings. To that little may be added the assertion that *every line of the translation scans.* In the use of words I have not availed myself much of the devices of poetic license, and have studiously avoided the frequency (if not indeed the occurrence at all) of the 'do, didst, did, dost' expedients with which some people seek to signalize their versifyings. Wherever I could say 'he came' I have eschewed 'he did come', and so 'he did do' and the like. This may be a defect, and seem 'unpoetic'—well, I plead guilty. The coining of words is more than poetic license; it is quite a great thing. On a small scale I have striven after such greatness by, perhaps, the use of 'bodiment', 'undifferent', 'unrooted', 'non-different', 'non-dual', etc. The words *non-dual, undifferent, non-different* had to be employed to make the Siddhanta implications of the Tamil equivalents clear to the reader. It would be

[1] Grimley's translation in his *Selections from Saint Bernard*, pp. 219 and 220.

[2] See *Introduction*, p. clxxx.

[3] *Index* ii.

[4] p. clxxxvii.

sheer nonsense to write for the above three 'one', 'same', 'alike'. Concerning words suggestive of Christian thought—e.g., paradise, save, salvation, alleluia, manna, grace, and the like—the reader is referred to p. clxxxviii of the *Introduction* for one explanation and, if need be, excuse. The context, setting, and contents of each equivalent in the original are sufficient safeguards against a confusion of ideas (where there is any) by the use of terms.[1]

An apology is due to the reader for the paging of the book. The Text and the Notes, etc., having been printed first in order, monopolised the Arabic numerals. The *Introduction*, written next in order, and having to be placed naturally before the Text, used up the Roman numerals. The title-page, preface, etc., written later than, but entitled to precedence over, the *Introduction*, had to be decorated with the somewhat odd marks they are now content to bear. The reader will sympathize with the inured pages and share their dignified contentment.

From apologies to whom apology is due let me turn with pleasure to mete out gratitude to whom gratitude is indeed due. To Mr. Kenneth, the Superintendent of the Diocesan Press, Madras, most affable of Superintendents, and to his intelligent staff I am very much obliged, for their care and despatch in seeing this work through the press. They had a very difficult task in not only deciphering my handwriting (I am of course not at all convinced that my handwriting is so bad as some people say it is) but in following, with remarkable alertness, intelligence and patience, the vicissitudes of my corrections, alterations, re-correctings, re-alterings, revisions, re-revisings, through a whole course of diverse changes and re-changings till the fatal 'strike' order settled author, proof-reader and printer into a much-desired calm and quiet. Not, perhaps, the author—for I feel I can effect fresh changes here and there, but it is too late now, and may be in time for the next edition!

In a way, the writing of a book is not very hard work: the harder and more arduous labour is the preparation of the

[1] See *Introduction*, p. cxix.

indexes. The toil of the task has been greatly lightened for me by Mr. J. A. R. Navaratnam of Bishop's College, Calcutta; Mr. T. R. P. Dawson of the Treasury, Penang; and Mr. T. A. Turaiappa Pillai, Principal of the Mahajana English School, Tellipalai. I thank them cordially.

The crowning of every piece of work, however small and of what little consequence, is not so much in its being acclaimed a success, as in its being accounted a contribution, of whatever degree, to the Glory of God. It has pleased Almighty God to enable me to complete this undertaking of many hard years. I render Him all praise, and I humbly pray that this book may in some measure exalt His Holy Name. *πάντα ἐις δόξαν Θεοῦ ποιεῖτε.*

T. ISAAC TAMBYAH.

'PENANG HOUSE', JAFFNA,
September, 1925.

CONTENTS

CONTENTS

PAGE

ERRATA

N.B.—The obvious is not covered by this list.

Page	ii.	Foot-note 2, read Madame Ragozin.
,,	vi.	,, 5, *for* Somasundaram *read* Ponnambalam.
,,	ix.	,, 3, read *Families of Speech.*
,,	xiii.	,, 3, read *Outline.*
,,	xvii.	,, 3, read Rev. R. Hoisington.
,,	xxii.	,, 3, applies only to p. 138.
,,	xxii.	,, 6, *read* Ananda K. Cumaraswamy. See p. xli.
,,	xxviii.	First paragraph, *read* ' Hearts . . . are.'
,,	xxix.	Last paragraph, *read* ' This is brought out.'
,,	xlvi.	Foot-note 6, *read* ' Rāmānantha.'
,,	xlviii.	,, 4, *before* 1265 supply N. M.
,,	lii.	,, 8, *for* at *read* cf.
,,	lxxi.	,, 5, read Mahādēva.
,,	lxxv.	Fifth line from top *read* Karnams.
,,	lxxvii.	Foot-note 6, second line, *read* Sutra I.
,,	lxxxiii.	Is misnumbered.
,,	lxxxv.	Ninth line from top, *read* removal *for* remoral.
,,	cxxii.	Foot-note 5, end, *for* 38.17 *read* 3.8.17.
,,	cxxvii.	,, 7, the reference is N. M. 961.
,,	cxxxi.	In the translation 4th from top, read Sivam.
,,	24.	Heading of verse, *read* Wilt *for* Will.
,,	60.	Line 187 of translation, delete the full stop.
,,	87.	Fifth line of last verse, *for* Life *read* Like.
,,	131.	Foot-note 4, the *K. Alangaram* passage is St. 73.
,,	156.	,, 6, *read* 118 *for* 134.
,,	166.	,, 4, *for* 38 *read* 98.
,,	172.	,, 2, the Brihad. reference is 2.1.19.
,,	172.	,, 3, the Brihad. reference is 4.3.20.
,,	192.	Top *for* page 65 *read* page 64.
,,	192.	Foot-note 5, the R. V. reference is x. 135.7.
,,	192.	,, 8, the Katha reference is i. 4.
,,	193.	,, 4, the page of the book quoted is 230.
,,	196.	,, 5, the Tiruvachagam section is L.
,,	199.	,, 5, *for* 30.31 *read* 27.28.
,,	200.	,, 3, the reference is Tiruvilangam's edition p. 73.
,,	203.	,, 6, *for* 43 *read* 42.
,,	219.	Note 218 read *jnānendriya.*
,,	221.	Foot-note 5, the work is *Nenjari Vilakkam.*

INTRODUCTION

PART I.—TAMIL

§ 1. Mr. J. W. McCrindle in his translation, published in 1878, of the *Periplus Maris Erythraei*,[1] observes, with reference to the anonymous Greek author's mention[2] of Limurikê, that, in the Indian segment of early Roman maps, the portion of India to which the name Limurikê is applied is called Damirikê, and, identifying the name with the Tamil country, he follows Bishop Caldwell[3] in considering it the earliest appearance of the name *Tamil* in any foreign document.[4] It is the name of a land, the name of a language, the name of a people. The land is *Tamil-agam* or the Tamil realm, the language is *Tamil*, and the people are *the Tamils.* The word 'Dravidian', from an ethnic name *Dravida* or *Dramida*, in Pali *Damila*, apparently identical in origin with the adjective *Tamil*, although strictly applicable to a single race, *the Tamils*, is often used to denote all the races of whom the Tamils are one.[5] Megasthenes, the Greek historian

[1] McCrindle dates the *Periplus* between A.D. 80 and 89. For a discussion of the date of the *Periplus* see J. Kennedy's notes in *J.R.A.S.*, October, 1916, pp. 829–37; W. H. Schoff's notes in *J.R.A.S.*, October, 1917, pp. 827–30; J. Kennedy's notes in *J.R.A.S.*, January, 1918, pp. 106–14.

[2] *Periplus*, ch. li.

[3] *Dravidian Grammar*, Introd., p. 14.

[4] McCrindle, *Periplus*, pp. 126, 127.

[5] L. D. Barnett, in *Camb. Hist. of India*, i. 593. In *Sen Tamil* xii. 30–50, 90–103 a thesis on *Tamil-Agam in Tamil Literature* by Mr. S. S. Parathiar, M.A., B.L. (Madras) is given a Tamil translation. The learned author holds, on his view of the evidence afforded by Tamil writings, that the Tamils did not enter India from outside. Mr. Duraisamy, on the other hand, gives reasons (*Tamil Literature*, p. 5) for a contrary opinion, the one more acceptable. On *Tamil-Agam* see, for modern Tamil views, Duraisamy's *Tamil Lit.*, c. i. § 2, and articles in *Sen Tamil Chelvie* (a monthly magazine distinct from the older *Sen Tamil*) i. p. 42. 74. As to the evolution of the word தமிழ் *Tamil* out of திராவிடம் *Dravidam* it must be confessed that, although I have given above Dr. Barnett's endorsement of that evolution, I am in favour of the contention that தமிழ் is not so evolved, it is an indigenous Tamil word of pure Tamil origin. The late Rai Bahadur

of about 300 B.C., refers in his account of India to Tamil-agam and about half a century later the Emperor Asoka in one of his rock inscriptions, mentions, the Tamils among those who had accepted Buddhism. The overlords of the Tamil-agam were the Tamils in the strict sense of the word.[1] The kingdoms of Tamil-agam, to merit any notice as early as the fourth century before Christ, must have been of some importance. Kātyāyana, the commentator of the grammarian Panini, in the fourth century before Christ names the Tamil kingdoms with their capitals at Mūdūr and Uriyūr.[2] It is reasonable to suppose that the notices in pre-Christian antiquity of Tamil-agam are not of kingdoms of savages but of men meriting external mention. The Tamils figure in history as invaders of Ceylon[3] after the time of Megasthenes's visit to India, and there is no warrant for the opinion entertained by some[4] that Tamil invasions of Ceylon were not organised military enterprises. Ceylon history shows the Tamils as conquerors and colonists. It is striking[5] that the

Kingsbury Tamothiram Pillai strongly protested against the Sanscrit source of the word தமிழ். A very convincing and scholarly presenting of the case for the Tamil origin of the name தமிழ் is to be found in learned articles on the subject in *Sen Tamil Chelvie*, i. pp. 19, 47, 98, 116, 147. The calm, judicious, balanced reasoning of the writer is supported by quotations from Tamil classics. See *Ārya Mitran*, April 1923, p. 13, and Duraisamy's *Tamil Lit.*, pp. i. 16.

[1] Barnett in *C. H. Ind.*, i. 596-7.

[2] R. W. Frazer, in *E.R.E.* 5, p. 21. Ūr (ஊர்) is the Tamil word for 'town'. In an able note on ஊர், in his article *Bharata Land* in *Tamilian Antiquary*, 19, Pandit Savariroyan sees an analogy between the Tamil Ūr and the Chaldaean *Ur*. He quotes Madam Ragazin (*Vedic India*, 305), in further support of Tamil and Chaldaean associations, as to the finding of South Indian teak among the ruins of Ūr of the Chaldees, a city founded over three thousand year before Christ. See Rawlinson, *India and the Western World*, 3.

[3] The dates of the three Tamil invasions of Ceylon are 257 B.C., 207 B.C., 103 B.C., In 50 B.C. a Tamil became the favourite of Queen Anula of Ceylon and was raised to the throne. See Turnour's *Mahavansa*, pp. 127, 128, 203, 209.

[4] E.G. by Osmond De Beauvoir Priaulx, in *J.R.A.S.* (O.S.) xviii. 359.

[5] A very convincing and scholarly study of the Tamil word ஆரியர் by the late Mr. V. J. Tamby Pillai in the *Tamilian Antiquary*, No. 1, p. 27 (*The Solar and the Lunar Races of India*) establishes, on linguistic grounds, that Arya ஆரிய is one of the ten Tamil words derived from the Tamil root ஆர் 'noble', 'rare', 'precious', and it is not of Sanscrit origin. See the same learned writer's *Origin of the Word Arya*, in *T.A.*, No. 2, p. 21.

Tamil Kings of Jaffna had the title *Arya*-Chakravartis. The last King of Ceylon, Sri Wickrema Rajah Singhe, was a Tamil.

§ 2. In enterprises of peace the Tamils are not less conspicuous than in war. In an embassy to the Court of the Cæsars in Rome about 27 B.C. or 20 B.C. it is possible that the interests of a Pandyan King were represented, but this has been doubted, the statement of Strabo notwithstanding.[1] The second embassy to Rome from Asiatics was in the reign of Claudius Cæsar, between A.D. 40 and A.D. 54. It was from Ceylon. It was a Tamil embassy. The ambassador-in-chief was a Tamil of Jaffna, in Ceylon, as his name, Rasaiah, indicates.[2] Sir Emerson Tennent thinks[3] that Rasaiah was the representative to Rome of the Rajah of Jaffna. The Roman galley of a freedman of one Annius Plocamus had been driven by a gale in the Red Sea into Hippuros[4] a port of Ceylon. During his sojourn in Hippuros for some months prior to his departure for Rome, the master of the ship communicated information of Rome to the King, and Rasaiah,[5] having acquired sufficient information of Rome, and a working knowledge of the language of Rome, went to Rome.

The commerce of Tamil-agam with the outside world is thus described by a modern Indian scholar:

> Babylonia, Assyria and Egypt traded with India. The land flourished; the people of the South grew richer and thrived better than their brethren in the North. They enjoyed the blessings of continued peace and held a very influential position among the then civilized nations on account of their maritime pursuits and commercial enterprise.[6]

---

[1] See Osmond De Beauvoir Priaulx's, *Indian Embassy to Augustus* in *J.R.A.S.* (O.S.), xvii. 317. The principal classical references to the embassy are noted by the writer.

[2] For an account of this embassy, and for the references to Pliny, *N. Hist.* vi. 24 and other classical sources of information, see the article of M. Osmond De Beauvoir Priaulx in *J.R.A.S.* (O.S.), xviii. 345. It is doubtful if the learned author is right in supposing that till 543 B.C., his date for the conquest of Ceylon by Wijayo, the inhabitants of Ceylon were 'a barbarous and unimprovable race . . . as their descendants, the Veddhas, still are' (*Ibid.*, 350). What he says does not apply to the inhabitants of Tamil-agam.

[3] Tennent's *Ceylon*, ii. 539.

[4] Hippuros, whether Kudiramalai, Horse-Mount, or not, is believed to be a port of North Ceylon.

[5] I have rendered 'Rachias' of the embassy by 'Rasaiah'.

[6] Pandit Savariroyan in *Tamilian Antiquary*, No. 1, p. 18. See Rawlinson's *Intercourse between India and the Western World*, p. 7, and Kennedy's *Early Commerce of India with Babylon* in *J.R.A.S.*, 1898, p. 241

It has been suggested that Tamil trade extended even to the kingdom of Solomon, the merchant sailors being Tamils. The suggestion is based upon finding in the words of the Hebrew Bible[1] for 'ivory, apes, peacocks,' three Tamil words.[2] A great deal of conjecture has gathered round the words 'Tarshish' and 'Ophir' of the Bible.[3] It is the judgment of modern Biblical scholarship that the expression 'ships of Tarshish' does not mean ships going to, coming from, made at, or harboured in, any place called Tarshish but 'a large class of vessels similar to those which went to Tarshish'[4] 'a certain class of specially strong and large ships destined for longer voyages.'[5] If so, 1 Kings ix. 22 does not mean an expedition to Tarshish or that 'ivory, apes and peacocks' came from Tarshish. The nautical expression 'ships of Tarshish' had been misunderstood very early.[6] It is not necessary therefore to identify Tarshish with Galle in Ceylon.[7] As we are not told where 'ivory, apes and

[1] 1 Kings x. 22; 2 Chron. ix. 21. The LXX translators, reading differently or finding the words unusual have 'wrought stones, hewn stones' *λίθων τορευτῶν καὶ πελεκητῶν*.

[2] The Tamil words are இபம், கபி, தோகை. The Hebrew words are Shenhabim, Kōpim, Tukkeeyyim. In *H.D.B.* there is (iv. 733) a very brief reference to the similarity of the Tamil தோகை to the Hebrew word for peacock. A writer in *H.D.B.*, ii. 469 refers to the Hebrew names for 'ivory, apes, peacocks' as acquired from India as the result of trade with that country. The Tamil இபம் is equivalent to the Sanscrit *Ibha*. See Dr. Leathe's remarks on 1 Kings x. 22 in *J.R.A.S.* (N.S.) xviii. 541 where he gives Sanscrit equivalents, and Mr. Senathi Rajah's observations in *J.R.A.S.* (N.S.) xix. 595 where he lays stress, rightly, on the pre-Sanscrit elements of Tamil.

[3] 1 Kings ix. 26; x. 22; 2 Chron. ix. 21; xx. 26; 1 Kings xxii. 48. See Rawlinson, *India and the Western World*, pp. 11-14.

[4] W. H. Bennett in *H.D.B.*, iv, 804, note.

[5] W. Max Müller, in *H.D.B.*, iv. 684.

[6] E.g. by the writers of 2 Chron. ix. 21; xx. 26.

[7] Tennent, *Ceylon*, ii. 102; i. 554. My friend Mudaliyar C. Rasanayagam of Colombo would locate the source of Solomon's 'ivory, apes and peacocks' and gold in Matota, Kadiramalai and Kayts in 'the kingdom of Jaffna' in North Ceylon. See his learned paper read before the Ceylon Branch of the Royal Asiatic Society on October 23, 1922, summarized in the *Ceylon Daily News* of October 24, 1922. In the same paper Ophir is 'the land of the Oriyar' in Matotā in Ceylon. The LXX translators of the Old Testament render Ophir by *Σωφηρα* and it has been since thought that Supera in the Bombay Presidency is intended. Pandit Savariroyan (*T. Antiq.*, No. 1, p. 21) has much in favour of his Uvari (near Tuticorin in South India) once a seaport near Korkai, the

peacocks' came from it is unwarranted by the text of the Hebrew records to make them out to be products of Tarshish or Ophir, nor should it be forgotten that the records do not say that *all* the foreign products imported into Palestine came from the same place. *One fact is indubitable that Solomon's 'ivory, apes and peacocks' came from a Tamil country*, to judge from the Tamil names preserved in the Hebrew.[1] We may safely assert that 'long before the beginning of the Christian era the Dravidian South had developed a considerable culture of its own, and its inhabitants had consolidated themselves into powerful kingdoms, some of which carried on a thriving trade with Western Asia, Egypt, and later with the Greek and Roman empires.'[2]

§ 3. If to the Tamils there is conceded an early possession of kingdoms, military prowess, and commercial enterprise there is furnished enough material wherewith to repel any suspicion of a suggestion that anterior to the Christian era they were savages. From the fact that a good many of the extant works in Tamil are, in the present state of literary evidence and research, fixed by European scholars as belonging to about the eighth or the ninth century of the Christian era, it has been inferred that prior to that period of literary activity the state of Tamil

capital of the Pandyan (Tamil-agam) kings till the ninth century B.C. He refers to Pope's *Naladiar*, p. 295 for the statement that gold was found in South India in abundance from pre-historic times and to a tradition in the modern Uvari that traces of gold mines are to be seen there to this day. The LXX Σωφηρα (Sophera) is the name says Mr. Rawlinson (*Ind. and the W.W. 11*) by which South India is known in the Coptic language.

[1] Just as the Greek words πέπερι, ὄρυζα, ζιγγίβερις, καρπεον preserve the Tamil [illegible], [illegible], [illegible], [illegible] respectively, meaning pepper, rice, ginger, cinnamon, and attest early Greek commerce with Tamil lands; The word πέπερι is found in Plutarch, and ὄρυζα in a Greek writer of about 322 B.C. In Herodotus (iii. 111) we read in an account of the mode in which the Arabs collect cinnamon, that birds were said to pick up *ταυτα τα καρφεα τα ἡμεἰς ἀπο φοινεκων μαδοντες κιννμαμωμον καλεομεν*, 'the rolls of bark which we, from the Phœnicians call *cinnamon*'. The word καρφος is thus earlier than κινναμωμον. The Hebrew Bible has in Exod. xxx. 23 *K[illegible]* which the LXX translators render κιννaμωμον.

[2] Dr. Barnett in *C.H. Ind.* i. 594. Pandit Savariroyan (*Tamil Antiquary*, No. 1, p. 23) finds in the *Rig-Veda* references to Dravidian sea-faring enterprise. See *Young Men of India*, November 1923, p. 523.

culture was not high. Such a low estimate of Tamil civilization assumes, in the case of Tamil literature, a degree of suddenness quite inconsistent with any possibility of progress or evolution.[1] The literary output of the sixth, seventh or eighth century after Christ surely presupposes literary beginnings, development and progress, and earlier effort, endeavour, travail, and production. There is positive and indubitable evidence that about 250 B.C., the Tamils were a literate people. Asoka's Edicts were proclaimed in Tamil-agam: it would have been meaningless to publish in a land what the people could not read. In the *Lalita Vistara*, a legendary Sanscrit biography of Gautama Buddha, translated into Chinese *in the first century* of the Christian era, the Buddha is represented as having studied, in his infancy, among other languages, *Dravida* or *Tamil.*[2] There is evidence for the high antiquity of the Tamil alphabet, and its priority to, and independence of, Sanscrit.[3] As in their caste system, so in their prosody the Tamils are independent of Aryan influence.[4] Even if we place the *Tolkappiam*, the oldest Tamil grammar extant, in the opening years of the Christian era we are compelled to presuppose the existence of a developed language and literature long, long prior to the framing of the first grammar.[5] In the *Tolkappiam*, the Tamil language

[1] 'These few centuries would seem to be a remarkable period in the history of the Tamil country, giving birth to all its literary treasures at once! And we would have this curious fact that the Tamil people, though possessing settled form of government and arts, etc., had not produced a single word worth mentioning for over a thousand years! Such literary barrenness cannot be thought of in the history of any nation.' (Mr. J. M. Nallaswamy Pillai, in *Tamilian Antiquary*, 1910, p. 7.) See Smith *Oxford History of India*, pp. 13-15, and 144.

[2] See Senathi Rajah's *Pre-Sanscrit Element in Tamil* in *J. R. A. S.* (N.S.), xix. 567.

[3] See Burnell, *S. Ind. Paleography*, 130-32, and J. M. Nallaswamy Pillai's remarks at p. 21 of *Tamilian Antiquary*, 1910. Reasoning from the *Tolkappiam* and the *Ten Idylls* the latter concludes, 'We may fairly lay claim to possessing one of the oldest scripts in the world.'

[4] 'Of all the races of India the only people who had a poetical literature independent of Sanscrit, which has survived to this day are the Tamils . . . Tamil alone has preserved her ancient metres . . . The ancient Tamil versification is purely Dravidian.' Senathi Rajah, *Glimpses of Ancient Dravidians*, *T. Antiq.*, ii. p. 7. Same writer in *J.R.A.S.* (N.S.), xix. 568.

[5] See Somasundaram Pillai's line of reasoning in the *Proceedings of the Third Saiva Conference*, 1912, p. 11. On *Tolkappiam* see Swamikannu Pillai's *Indian Ephemeries*, Part i, pp. 457-470.

is divided into a poetical form, a dramatical and a colloquial. Literature, especially poetic, precedes the formulation of grammatical rules:[1] long anterior to the *Tolkappiam* there must have existed works purely poetic, and dramatic, and those more popular and colloquial. It has been observed, with reference particularly to Tamil, that ancient Dravidian literature 'enshrines somewhat of the early history of the social organizations and religious conceptions of the pre-Aryan period'.[2] A Brahmin scholar, Professor K. V. Rengaswamy Aiyengar, comparing Aryan and Dravidian civilizations,[3] says that long before the beginnings of authentic history in India the Dravidians had a high civilization and were possessors of a refined and polished literature by the first century of the Christian era. Considerable literary activity must have preceded the first Christian century in Tamilagam. It is conceded by those who would assign the bulk of Tamil literature to the sixth Christian century or to the ninth or the thirteenth that the oldest extant Tamil classical romances, the *Manimēkhalai* and the *Silappadikāram*, belong to the second century after Christ.[4] Then, we are asked to believe, followed five, six, or seven centuries of literary indolence!

To suppose that a people who had commercial and sometimes political relations with Phœnicians, Greeks, Romans, Chinese and Arabs from very early times and who were in contact for centuries with one of the most refined of languages, the Sanscrit, and who had well organized kingdoms of their own, as historically attested from at least the sixth century B.C., to suppose, I repeat, that such people had no literature of their own till the ninth century A. D., seems to me, to say the least, to be running counter to all probability! It is difficult to believe that the kingdom of Pandiya, sung by poet and bard as the cradle of Sentamil, had continued to exist from before the sixth century B.C. and had produced no literature during its palmy days,

---

[1] See Senathi Rajah's *Pre-Sanscrit Element in Tamil* in *J.R.A.S.* (N.S.), xix. 559, 569. It is remarkable about the *Tolkappiam* that it devotes itself exclusively to the structure of those metres peculiar to ancient Tamil poetry, and there is not even a passing mention of the later metres adopted into Tamil such as *Kattalaikalitturai* and *Viruttam* (see Bavanandham Pillai's Preface, p. vi to his edition of *Yapparungalam*).

[2] R.W. Frazer in *E.R.E.*, v. 21.

[3] *History of India*, passim.

[4] Frazer, *E. R. E.* v. 23. See Coomaraswamy's papers in the Ceylon *J. R. A. S.*, 1893, xiii. No. 44, and 1894, xiii. No. 45. Dr. Pope's English translation of *Manimēkhalai* 'a great epic and one of the five great classics of Tamil' has no introduction dealing with the date of the work.

but only in its old age and decrepitude in the ninth century A.D., when there was nothing capable of giving it such an impulse.[1]

It seems to me that something more than mere prepossession in favour of late dates is needed to invalidate the clear reasoning of Mr. S. Krishnaswamy Aiyengar[2] leading, on evidence literary and historical, to the conclusion that the second century of the Christian era was the period of the greatest literary activity in Tamil-agam. Confirmation comes from the tradition—all allowance being made for the exaggeration incidental to tradition—of the Madura Sangam.[3] If, further, the greatest of Tamil ethical treatises, the *Kural*, belongs, as is allowed, to the second Christian century, then it is more conceivable that the age which produced the *Kural* was truly the Tamil Augustan age than the ninth century.

§ 4. A consideration which, since Bishop Caldwell and other early European scholars, has predisposed inquirers into the history of the Tamils in favour of late dates for the best period of Tamil literature is the belief in the very low ethnological affinities of the Tamils. Again, a matter of convenience became a factor of mischief: the application of the name *Dravida*, which is peculiar to the Tamils, to allied peoples in inferior grades of culture. The responsibility is Bishop Caldwell's.[4] The wrong done to those, to whom alone the name *Dravidian* belongs, is aggravated by employing a philological convention as an ethnological distinction. The Caldwell terminology is unscientific and unsatisfactory.[5] The basic blunder of Bishop Caldwell's thesis as to the Tamils was the

[1] Senathi Rajah (*Pre-Sanscrit Element in Tamil*), *J.R.A.S.* (N.S.), xix. 565. See Prof. Sundaram Pillai's *Mile Stones of Tamil Literature*, p. 14 for a severe but very scholarly criticism of Dr. Barnett's views.

[2] *The Augustan Age of Tamil Literature*. Such masterpieces of literary refinement as the *Kural* and the *Silappadigaram* are the products of the second century. Dr. R. Rost (*Encyclopædia Britannica*, xxvi. 390) follows Dr. Burnell in placing the *Kural* in the eighth century after Christ.

[3] On the *Sangam* see Purnalingam Pillai, *Tamil Literature*, pp. 8-10, and the very able discussion of probabilities by Mr. V. J. Tamby Pillai in his *An Old Tradition Preserved* in *Tam Antiq.*, ii. No. 1, p. 1, and the editorial contribution, *A Note on the Sangam Periods* at p. 13 of the same. See also discussions in *Sen Tamil*, xv. 1, xvii. 185, and xvii. 457.

[4] *Dravidian Grammar*, 4.

[5] See W. Crooke's comments in *E. R. E.*, v. p. 1.

assumption of the Turanian origin of the Dravidians. Let us put side by side two descriptions, one of the Dravidian tongues, the other of the Turanian people :

Grammatical gender has been more fully and systematically developed in the Dravidian tongues than in perhaps any other language in the world. . . . There is no such thing as gender in the Scythian language . . . There is a refinement of expressiveness in which the Dravidian languages appear to stand alone. Sanskrit is far less highly developed in this particular, so that if there were any borrowing the Dravidian family must have been the lender, not the borrower. [1]

It is not extravagant to say that in its poetic form the Tamil is more polished and exact than the Greek and more copious than the Latin. In its fulness and power it more resembles English and German than any other living languages.[2]

We may say generally that a large number of these [the Turanians] belong to the lowest palaeozoic strata of humanity—peoples whom no nation acknowledges as its kinsmen, whose language, rich in words for all that can be eaten or hunted, seems absolutely incapable of expressing the reflex conceptions of the intellect or the higher forms of consciousness; whose life seems confined to the gratification of the animal wants with no hope in the future and no pride in the past. They are for the most part people without a literature, and without a history, and many of them apparently as imperfectible as the Ainos of Jezzo or the Veddhas of Ceylon—people whose tongues in some instances have twenty names for murder, no name for love, no name for gratitude, no name for God.[3]

Can the Tamil language be said to be *Turanian*, or the Tamil people Turanians?

The advance of linguistic scholarship since Caldwell's days has put it beyond all doubt that the Tamils are not Turanians, nor are they of the so-called Scythian group of Turanians, and further it is no longer seriously maintained that Tamil and Australian are identical in origin.[4] Tamil is to Bishop Caldwell's

[1] Caldwell, *Dravidian Grammar*, 147.

[2] Winslow, *Tamil-English Dictionary*, Preface, ii. 'Tamil is one of the most copious, refined and polished languages spoken by man.' (Rev. W Taylor, Preface to part iv. of Dr. Rottler's *Tamil-English Dictionary*.)

[3] Farrar, *Families of Speeches*, 155. There are 44 demi-octavo pages of the *Nigandu* devoted to a list of the Tamil names for God!

[4] See Gover, *Folk Songs of Southern India*, Introduction, pp. 6, 7. Prof. Vinson of Paris (in *S. Deepika*, v. 193) calls the Turanian hypothesis 'absurd and inadmissible' and the Tamil-Australian hypothesis 'a stupid assertion, presented by some amateurs'. Thurston (*Castes and Tribes of South India*, vol. i, Introduction, pp. xix-xxxvi) gives summaries of various classifications, and theories of origin, of the Tamils and other 'Dravidians'.

other 'Dravidian' languages what Latin is to the Romance languages of Europe. There may be no confusion in calling the Spaniards and the Portuguese Latin races, but it is indefensible to call the Spanish and Portuguese languages Latin. The practice of calling the Telugu, Canarese and Malayalam languages Dravidian (= Tamil) is equally illogical.

§ 5. The Dravidians were *not* the aborigines of India. The Dravidians, meaning mostly, if not mainly, the Tamils, entered India from outside. From where? Not from Central Asia, nor from the submerged continent of Lemuria, but from Elam in Western Asia. They were Elamites, not Turanians, not Scythians, not Negritoid Mongols, not Australians. They had affinities with perhaps the Caucasians, and, more surely in language, with the Accadian-Chaldaeans.[1] The Tamils entered India by way of Baluchistan where a dialect of Tamil is to this day spoken by the Brahhuis.[2] It is more generally believed that there were at first in India a class of people who may be called pre-Dravidians, then came people who may be called proto-Dravidians, and from the proto-Dravidians are sprung the Dravidians.

The Aryan entry into India is an event for which is claimed one of the earliest dates in history.[3] Whatever date may be assigned to the beginnings of Aryan settlement in India, the fact is indubitable that the Aryans, on their entry, found India already in the occupation of a people or some peoples who must have settled down in India *long before them*. In the *Rig Veda* which is, in all probability, the oldest Aryan book, we find frequent, and not always favourable or flattering, references to a people or peoples whom the Aryans called Dasyus, among other names. 'Around us is the Dasyu, void of sense, inhuman, keeping alien Laws. Baffle the weapons the Dasyu

[1] Pandit Savariroyan in *T. Antiq.*, pp. 7-9.

[2] Barnett, in C. H. Ind. i. 593, 594. The proto-Dravidians are described as a 'race higher in culture' than the pre-Dravidians. 'To the oldest stratum of pre-Dravidian blood probably belonged the savages . . .' (*Ibid.* 595). Mr. Roy's opinion (*The Oraons*, 18, 19) that the Dravidians did not at any time enter India from outside is not tenable, even if the learned author is right (p. 18) in the thesis that the Oraons are linguistically and ethnologically a Dravidian tribe.

[3] See present writer's *Foregleams of God*, pp. 46-50 for views on date.

wields.'[1] Like this are numerous prayers against the Dasyus. Let us note some of the many references to the Dasyus before we can draw any conclusion about the people. They are:

The ancient riteless ones. [2]
The godless. [3]
Those who offer up no gifts. [4]
Those who bring no sacrifice. [5]
Infidels. [6]
The prayerless. [7]
Those who practise godless arts of magic. [8]
Those who by magic fain would climb to heaven. [9]
Keepers of alien Laws. [10]

These foes of the Aryans are described further as wealthy,[11] of great courage,[12] numerous hosts, tribes and bands[13] who possess strong forts and castles almost impregnable.[14] Prayers are directed against enemies who are described as 'a dusky brood',[15] 'dwellers in the darkness,'[16] 'dwellers in the distance',[17] and 'dwellers in mountain heights'.[18] Contempt does not stop at painting them black: they are *anāsah,* that is, noseless *(a-nāsah)* or voiceless *(an-āsah)*.[19]

It has sometimes been thought that these references are to the Dravidians. Against such a view is the fact that *Rig Veda* Aryans had more than one people as their enemies. They feared, and prayed against, Dasas,[20] Dasyus,[21] Simyus,[22] Kritakas,[23] Asuras.[24] In one single passage, in the last book of the *Rik,* there is a grouping together of 'Vritras and enemies,

[1] *R.V.* ix. 22.8. [2] *R.V.* i. 33.4, ix. 22.8, ix. 41.2.
[3] *R.V.* v. 42.9, vi. 49.15, vii. 6.3, viii. 59.11.
[4] *R.V.* i. 81.9, i. 174.6, v. 7.10. [5] *R.V.* viii. 59.11.
[6] *R.V.* viii. 59.11. [7] *R.V.* iv. 16.9. [8] *R.V.* vii. 1.10, x. 73.7.
[9] *R.V.* viii. 14.14. [10] *R.V.* ix. 22.8. [11] *R.V.* i. 81.9.
[12] *R.V.* vi. 23.2. [13] *R.V.* vi. 25.2, vi. 49.15, ii. 20.7.
[14] *R.V.* i. 103.3, ii. 20.8, vii. 19.5, viii. 87.6, x. 47.4.
[15] *R.V.* i. 101.1, iv 16.12. [16] *R.V.* ii. 20.7. [17] *R.V.* i. 63.4.
[18] *R.V.* viii. 59.11. [19] *R.V.* v. 29.10. [20] *R.V.* i. 32.11.
[21] *R.V.* i. 33.4. In some places in *R.V.* the reference may be to demons.
[22] *R.V.* i. 100.18. [23] *R.V.* iii. 53.14.
[24] In *R.V.* vi. 22.4 Indra is 'the Asura-slayer.' Vritra (in *R.V.* i. 4.8 and other places) is the best-known of Asuras. Commentators think that 'Asura' refers to demons, 'ancient gods,' 'Lord God,' and hostile non-Aryans. Pandit Vedachalam in his learned Tamil dissertation, *Ancient Tamilian and Aryan,* p. 20 argues that Asurar (அசுரர்) was the Aryan corruption of Arasar (அரசர் = kings).

Dasyus, Asuras and foes.'[1] The Aryans had even Aryan foes.[2] If, however, it be urged that the people most hostile to the Aryans were the Dasyus, and the Dasyus be equated with the Dravidians, it is then well to remember that the inimical and naturally prejudiced Aryan references to the Dravidians bear unwilling testimony to a degree of Dravidian civilization which compelled the dread of the Aryans. The Dravidians (on the theory that they are the 'Dasyus' of the *Rik*) were found by the Aryans to be highly advanced in the art of warfare. Their system of fortifications[3] was a source of constant danger to Aryan safety. The Dravidians had kings who led great hosts to battle, and once there was a formidable confederacy of ten kings.[4] Dravidian wealth is abundantly attested in the *Rik*.[5] The picture of an enemy chieftain's wife bathing in milk while the Aryan lady had to be content with water, could she get it, is proof of Dravidian opulence.[6] The Aryans have left much unsaid.[7]

The psychology of abuse mav account for Chinese calling

[1] *R.V.* x. 170.2. [2] *R.V.* x. 83.1.

[3] See above § 3. The Pallava period of Dravidian architecture is placed (Jouyeau-Dubreuil, *Dravidian Architecture*, 36) at A.D. 600–800, but (p. 25) 'works in wood preceded works in stone.' For more than 13 centuries Dravidian architecture had remained pure. Dr. Sherring's article, *The Bhar Tribe* in *J.R.A.S.* (N. S.) v, 378 refers to traces of Bhar fortifications and irrigation works and to Bhar culture generally. He concludes that the Bhars in whose hands almost the whole of India was once have perished. I am inclined to accept the views of Pandit Savariroyan (*Tam. Antiq.*, 1913, p. 1) that the *Bharatas* were Tamils and that *Bharata* Land is 'Dravidian India.' In view of what has been said above (p. iv) about 'peacocks' it is noteworthy that the peacock was sacred to the 'Bhars,' and in Tamil religious literature the peacock is sacred to Siva of the Tamil religion. The mention by Prof. Hopkins (*Religions of India*, 525, 526, 536) of the Dravidians among 'Wild Tribes' of India belongs to an obsolete phase in the learning on the subject of Aryans and Dravidians.

[4] *R.V.* i. 53.9, vii. 83.6.7. [5] *R.V.* i 103.6. [6] *R.V.* i. 104.3.

[7] This was natural, for even post-Rik writers 'generally speak of the Dasyus and Asuras and all other non-Hindu [non-Aryan] races with superciliousness and contempt, and consequently rarely exhibit a particle of interest in their welfare' [Sherring, *J.R.A.S.*, (N.S.) v. 389]. At a late stage of Aryan association with the Dravidians the former adopted the manners and customs and even religious beliefs of the latter (Kennedy, *J.R.A.S.*, 1919, p. 523).

Europeans 'foreign devils', as much as it may explain the gradually developed contents of hate in the early Aryan references to non-Aryans as demons and monsters.[1] Such appellations do not mean much. However it may be, it is clear that the aborigines of India were not the Dravidians. The present-day hill tribes isolated in their mountain fastnesses are most probably the representatives of 'the dusky brood' aboriginal to Aryan India. The argument from colour is not a very secure one for connecting the Dravidian of to-day with the 'dusky' aborigines of the past. Against such an argument are three considerations :—

(1) There has been a considerable admixture of races in India, e.g., of Aryans with Dravidians, and of both with the aborigines. This may account for certain varieties of colour and features among Dravidians.

(2) All Dravidians are not dark.

(3) Even the *Rik* Aryans themselves were not the fairest of the fair, they were brunettes.[2]

Personally I am not for equating the Dasyus with the Dravidians since it is difficult to say from the ***Rig Veda*** which of the appellations of hate employed by the Aryans were specially levelled against their Dravidian enemies. Terms of scorn and opprobrium, moreover, cannot be given ethnological meaning.

§ 6. Without entering into particulars about the literature[3]

[1] See Pargiter, *Ancient Ind. Hist. Tradition*, 290-1.

[2] Kennedy, *J.R.A.S.*, 1919, p. 499. The modern Indian tribes of jungle-dwellers and hill-travellers, e.g., Kadirs, Paniyans, Scholigas, Karubas, Irulars, mostly very dark, short-statured and snub-nosed are the descendants of the aborigines? The late Mr. Tamby Pillai (*Tam. Antiq.*, 1913, pp. 32-3) has given good reasons for his theory that the Aryan foes claimed to be Aryans and were of the *same colour* as the Aryans. Flora Annie Steel in her *India Through the Ages*, p. 2, speaks of the Dasyus as '*reddish* or tawny'. On theories as to the primacy of colour in Aryo-Dravidian peoples see Kennedy in *J.R.A.S.*, 1920, p. 37. The whole article is worthy of study, in spite of the learned writer's adherence to views of 'Dravidian Sudras', 'Helot Dravidian,' 'the Dravidian herd.'

[3] See Purnalingam Pillai's *Tamil Literature*; Sundaram Pillai's *Some Milestones in Tamil Literature*; Chengalvaraya Pillai's *Tamil Prose Literature*; R. W. Frazer's *Literary History of India*; Kanagasabai Pillai's *Tamils 1800 Years Ago*; Farquhar's *Outlines of the Religious Literature of India*; Srinivasa Iyengar's *Tamil Studies*; Subramania Sastriar's (Tamil) *History of the Tamil*

of the Tamils it may be mentioned that religious and devotional writings occupy a considerable place in the poetic section of Tamil literature. Tamil devotional writers are many in number. No poet of Tamil India is so popularly known and so widely read as S. Tāyumānavar. He is the most melodious of the great poet-mystics of Tamil-agam. Kant in metre would be an uncouth experiment. Spinoza, or Hume, or Herbert Spencer, or Berkeley, or Haeckel in verse is simply unthinkable. Tāyumānavar has clothed the stern facts of the philosophy of the Siddhanta (see below, Part ii) in words the fascination of which never flags. It is not merely the elegance of language, the exquisite grace of diction, the musical inflow and infitting of syllable into syllable, and line into line, that charm and captivate the attention. There is something more. His words speak from the heart to the heart. The appeal is through the senses to the soul, from the æsthetic to the spiritual. Where in his lamentations and longings his words drop like tears, or they fall like flowers about the shrine of his adoration, in his praises and poems of rapture, we are driven to see the saint in the poet, the mystic seer in the mellifluous singer. The attention is drawn beyond the rhythm, the sweet cadences, the lilt and the swing, and the rush of metre to the raptures of one claiming to be familiar with the revelation of the Real. His psalms are indeed the 'word-garlands' he says they are, 'word-garlands woven' for the praise of God (see p. 116). No Tamil scholar can miss the traces of the poet's art in the structure of his lines. The artist with consummate care has covered his art with the mantle of an inimitable grace. The result is a clear impression of an unhalting, easy spontaneity of utterance. In many a place he is dealing with some of the great problems of Siddhanta philosophy, but every evidence of labour is rubbed out by a marvellous mastery of unrugged Tamil. A presentation of ponderous themes

Language; Casie Chetty's *Tamil Plutarch*; Arnold's (Tamil) *Galaxy of Tamil Poets*; Sheshagiri Sastri's *Essay on Tamil Literature*; Barnett's *Catalogue of Tamil Books in the British Museum*; Duraisamy's (Tamil) *Tamil Literature*. Sir Charles Eliot (*Hinduism and Buddhism*, ii, c. xxxviii) gives a short account of some Tamil writings and holds the view that the oldest Tamil literature belongs to the first three centuries of the Christian era.

in tolerably interesting verses is conceivable among a people, as the Tamils are, whose dictionaries, works on grammar and logic and mathematics, whose abstruse discourses and whose grand obscurities are in metre; but to write, as Tāyumānavar does, with melting grace and flawless charm, on the truths of religion and philosophy, is ascribable to something more than mere racial capacity for poetry; and we must believe that the poet had translated the theories of religion into the actualities of life's experiences and assimilated them to the soul's exalted aspirations. This alone can account for the living influence and immense popularity of the psalms of this great poet-mystic in all places where the Tamil language is spoken and read.

Part II.—The Siddhanta

§ 7. The psalms of Tāyumānaswamy belong to the large body of devotional literature of the religious philosophy known as the Siddhanta. Tamil writers use both the Tamil form ***Siddhāntam*** (சித்தாந்தம்) and the Sanscrit form ***Siddhānta*** (சித்தாந்த). The word means 'sure end', 'assured result', 'correct conclusion', 'the true end', 'the ultimate goal'. Certain astronomical works, of which there once were in India as many as eighteen,[1] are called ***Siddhantas.*** In Hindu logical systems the four kinds of conclusion are known as *Siddhantas.*[2] The word as applied to the religious philosophy which forms the environment of the writings of S. Tāyumānavar has the contents of 'a mathematical finding', 'a logical conclusion', 'a true end'. Hence it is popular Tamil teaching that 'Siddhanta' means 'the true end, the ultimate goal.'[3] 'Siddhanta' is 'the accomplished end, fixed or established truth.'[4] It is one of the six 'great ends' (*antas*) to which reference is made by Tāyumānavar who also speaks of a seventh.[5]

[1] V. Gopala Aiyer, *Chronology of Ancient India*, 62.

[2] Dasgupta, *History of Indian Philosophy*, i, 295.

[3] *Siddhanta Gnana Ratnavali*, Q. 23.

[4] Rev. J. E. Carpenter in *Hibbert Journal*, April 1920, p. 478. A very lucid exposition of the term may be found in *Siddhantam* (a Tamil monthly), January 1912, p. 1.

[5] See below, pp. 21, 170.

§ 8. If the theory propounded by Bishop Caldwell[1] and quoted without comment by Mr. William Crooke[2] be right that the religion of the early Dravidians consisted in a bare acknowledgment of the existence of God, whom they named *Kō* (கோ) and to whose honour they built a temple which they called *Kō-il* (கோயில்) 'the abode of God', and that they had no idea of 'heaven', 'hell', 'soul', 'sin', it is impossible to imagine that out of such a crude 'religion' there was evolved, the sublime religious philosophy of the Siddhanta. Caldwell is no more right about his *kō-il* conjecture than he is (see above, § 4) about the alleged Turanian affinities of the Tamils. The spread and prevalence of the Siddhanta (which Tamil writers equate with Saivism, Saivādvaita, Saivādvaita Saivaism) in Tamil lands are believed by some scholars to have begun from North India: the Kashmir Saivism of Abhinava Gupta of the eleventh Christian century extended southwards 'through various channels into the lands of the Dravidians for whose ancient cults it supplied a theological basis'.[3] But there must have been some 'theological basis' for the 'ancient cults' prior to the alleged Kashmir contribution. Apart from this, there is the claim put forward on behalf of Kashmir Saivism that 'although the Trika form of Saivism would seem to have made its first appearance in Kashmir at the beginning of the *ninth* or perhaps towards the end of the *eighth* century of the Christian era . . . *Saivism as such is far older than this date*'.[4] Saivism, whether of Kashmir or of S. India, is built upon the books known as *Agamas*.[5] This is an admitted fact. Now, the earliest Tamil religious writer who mentions the Agamas is Tirumūlar[6] and Tirumūlar's age is certainly *prior* to the ninth Christian century.[7] How long prior to the ninth century A. D.? This cannot be answered with much sureness of conviction, but it may be noted that he has been placed in the first century after

[1] *Dravidian Grammar*, 118. [2] *E. R. E.*, v, p. 1.

[3] Dr. Barnett, *J.R.A.S.*, 1910, p. 706. *Sidd. Deepika*, xi. 103; xi. 62–64.

[4] Chatterji, *Kashmir Shaivism*, 3, 23, 26. [5] See below, p. 139.

[6] See *Siddhanta Deepika*, iv. pp. 134–6.

[7] See a brief chronological statement in the Ripon Press edition of the *Tirumantram* of Tirumūlar, Introd., pp. 2, 3.

Christ.[1] Greater sureness attaches to the statement that Tirugnāna Sambandhar who flourished *after* Tirumūlar belongs to the sixth Christian century.[2] The Agamas, and Saivism based on the Agamas, did not originate with Tirumūlar: their existence is anterior to Tirumūlar's time, anterior to the sixth century A. D., at the least. Indeed, it is no exaggeration to state that Agamic beliefs may be ascribed to the period of the Brahmanas.[3] The evidence of inscriptions establishes the fact that Saivism was flourishing in Conjeevaram in the sixth century, and that there were men proficient in the system of the Saiva Siddhantas.[4] If we place the fierceness of the anti-Jain contests of Saivism and Vaishnavism in the Tamil country in the fourth and fifth Christian centuries,[5] we arrive very close to a reasonable probability that Saivism as a philosophical system of religion must have had its beginnings long before the fourth century of the Christian era. It is not a precarious proposition to state that the Siddhanta is of far greater antiquity than the thirteenth, eleventh or ninth Christian centuries, and the absence of early books on the Siddhanta may be easily accounted for by the suggestion that they have perished.[6]

§ 9. So far as Tamil is concerned the Siddhanta is based primarily upon fourteen treatises written by great Saivite teachers of accredited sanctity and scholarship. The fourteen 'sastras' are:

Sivagnāna Bōdham by Meykanda Devar.
Irupā Irupaktu by Arulnanti Sivācharyar.
Sivagnāna Siddhiyār by Arulnanti Sivācharyar.
Unmay Vilakkam by Manivāsagam Kadantār.
Tiru Untiār by Uyya Vanta Devar.
Tiru Kalittuppadiar by Uyya Vanta Devar.

---

[1] E.g. by Mr. M. K. Narayanaswamy Aiyar, quoted with approval by Mr. J. M. Nallaswami Pillai in his *Siddhiyar*, Introd., p. xv.

[2] Sundaram Pillai's *The Age of Tirugnana Sambandhar*, p. 52.

[3] Rev. J. Hoisington in his Introduction to *Sivagnana Bodham*.

[4] Bhandarkar, *Vaisnavism and Saivism*, pp. 141, 142.

[5] Bhandarkar, *V. S.*, 142.

[6] Mr. Ponnampalam Pillai, so supposes. See *Saiva Conference Addresses*, 1911, p. 144. Sir Charles Eliot (*Hinduism and Buddhism*, II, pp. 213–14) agrees with Tamil scholars in 'referring the oldest Tamil Literature to *the first three centuries of our era*.'

Tiru Arul Payan by Umāpati Sivācharyar.
Pöttippaktōdai by Umāpati Sivācharyar.
Vinā Venba by Umāpati Sivācharyar.
Kodikkavi by Umāpati Sivācharyar.
Unmai Neri Villakkam by Umāpati Sivācharyar.
Sangalpa Nirā Karanam by Umāpati Sivācharyar.
Nenju Vidu Tūtu by Umāpati Sivācharyar.
Siva Pragāsam by Umāpati Sivācharyar.

The authors of the above fourteen writings flourished in the thirteenth and fourteenth centuries of our era.[1] Among the fourteen 'sastras' the first place is assigned by Hindu writers to *Sivagnāna Bōdham* ('The Teaching as to the knowledge of God') and to its author Meykanda Devar ('The saint who had seen Truth'). The *Bōdham* is reckoned as revelation. A work by Arulnanti, a disciple of Meykanda, is *Sivagnāna Siddhiyār*, the authorized commentary on the *Bōdham*. It holds the second place among the fourteen works. Of the eight books written by Umāpati the most important are *Siva Pragāsam* ('The Splendour of God') and *Tiru Arul Payan* ('An exposition of Holy Grace'). Umāpati is the last of the four Santāna Achāryas ('Teachers in a line of succession'), the others in order being Meykanda Devar, Arulnanti, Maraignāna Sambandhar. They are 'expounders of Philosophy and Fathers of the Church'[2] as distinguished from *Samaya* Acharyas (writers of devotional works) such as Tirugnana Sambandhar, Vahisar, Sundarar, Manikka Vāchagar.' The fourteen 'sastras' are believed to exhaust the canonical presenting of the teachings of the Saiva Siddhanta, although one is free to consult for further information such extra-canonical writings as *Tatva-Vilakkam*, *Tukal Aru Bōdham*, *Tatva Pragāsam*, etc.

§ 10. I am disposed to think that all these fourteen writings are of pure Tamil origin in language and contents. In this opinion I feel confirmed by the absence of any suggested Sanscrit original of the 'sastras' except in the case of the *Bōdham*. It is usually believed that the *Bōdham*, in the part

[1] See Nalla, *Bōdham*, p. xv., *T.A.P.*, p. 2; Farquhar, *O.R.L.I.* 257; Barnett and Pope's *Catalogue of Tamil Books in the Library of the British Museum*, pp. v, vi.
[2] Nalla, *Bōdham*, p. xviii.

which is not commentary, is a Tamil rendering of the *Pāsa Vimōsana Padalam* (பாச விமோசன படலம் 'section relating to the getting rid of sin') of the Sanscrit *Kaurava Āgama.* On the other hand there is a great deal to be said in favour of the propositions :

1. That the *Pāsa Vimōsana Padalam* is probably an interpolation in the *Kaurava Āgama*.
2. That, whether it is so or not, it is not the original of the *Sivagnāna Bōdham*.
3. That the *Sivagnāna Bōdham* is an original work of Meykanda Devar in Tamil and the Sanscrit version of it is a translation from the Tamil.

I am indebted to the able dissertation [1] of Mr. T. Ponnambalam Pillai, M.R.A.S., for the following reasons in support of the Tamil originality of the *Bōdham* :

1. Long before the fourteenth Christian century, indeed before the age of the *Tolkappiam*,[2] the Tamils of Tamil-agam had begun to study, speculate upon, and discuss the great questions of God, Soul, Sin.

2. In old Tamil writings such as the *Silappadikāram* and *Kurral*[3] ideas of God (கடவுள்), (the indweller), soul (உயிர்), 'sin' or Pāsam (வினை) are found scattered.

3. Meykanda Devar collected and arranged in the form of a digest the doctrines that had existed from before his time, and his codification was at a time of irreligion and of foreign influence. This compendium was the *Bōdham.*

4. Had Meykanda Devar been a mere translator he would have said so, particularly if he were translating a section of an *Agama.*

   1. He is silent as to translation.
   2. Those who wrote Introductory verses to his book are silent as to translation.
   3. There is no reference anywnere as to the Bōdham being a translation.

5. In the Sanscrit version, the second line of the twelfth sloka is capable of meaning that the first line of that Sloka is from a treatise called *Sivagnāna Bōdham.* There is *no* such treatise in Sanscrit.

[1] *Third Saiva Conference Addresses*, pp. 4-59.
[2] See above § 3. [3] See above, p. viii.

6. A comparison of the Sanscrit with the Tamil of some of the slokas yields the following results :

1. In the first sloka the Tamil alone gives the cause of re-births *mala*.

2. In the second sloka the Tamil makes, rightly, the relationship of God to the soul 'an inseparable union.' The Sanscrit makes the 'command' of God inseparable from Him.

3. In the fourth sloka the Tamil alone has statements about the condition of the soul in 'darkness'[1] and about its 'unconsciousness' in *mala*. These are important tenets of the Saiva Siddhanta.

4. In the ninth sloka the Tamil alone has the statement that God is not to be seen by the physical senses, and the Tamil lays down that the contemplation of the sacred Five Letters is according to accepted rules.

5. The twelfth sloka in Sanscrit refers by name to the *Sivagnāna Bōdham*; the Tamil *does not* since it is itself the *Bōdham*.

6. The second part of the twelfth sloka treats of one subject in the Tamil and of another in the Sanscrit.

7. The Tamil of the twelfth sloka refers to the saints as 'God's beloved who have washed themselves from the soul's *mala*'. The Sanscrit speaks of 'sages', 'sadhus'.

Tayumanavar speaks[2] of Meykanda Devar in terms which exclude the supposition that Meykanda was merely a translator: 'The master who saw the Truth, the bliss of Advaita which was unknown to men dwelling in untruth.' The Advaita[3] according to the Saiva Siddhanta is not the same as anything analogous to it known to the non-Tamils. The first systematic expounder of the Advaita according to the Saiva Siddhanta deserves the praise Tayumanavar accords him: such praise would be ill-merited in a mere translator. Add to Tayumanavar's praise the tradition, be it true or false, which ascribes divinity and inspiration to the work of Meykanda Devar, and we must feel increasingly convinced of the utter unlikelihood of a translator of Sanscrit slokas (assuming they formed part of an old Agama) being accorded such high honour. With the utmost deference to scholars who think the other way, I venture to submit that the Saiva Siddhanta, as expounded in the fourteen 'sastras', is of purely Tamil origin and such origin is consistent with contact

[1] See below, p. 150.

[2] N.M., 1097. பொய்கண்டார் காணாப் புனிதமெனும் அத்துவித மெய்கண்ட நாதன் . . .
There is a play upon the word மெய்கண்ட 'Meykanda'.

[3] See below, *Introd.* part v., for fuller treatment of Advaita.

with, illumination from, and even development out of, non-Tamil material.[1]

§ 11. The fundamentals of the Siddhanta are treated with some amount of fulness in part iv., v., vi., vii. of this Introduction. It is needless, therefore, to do more than state very briefly here the chief heads of teaching of the system.

God is one. He is the *Pati*, பதி, 'President,' 'Lord'. There is not one soul but there are multitudes of souls, *Pasu*, பசு. God is 'the Lord of souls.'[2] Eternity is postulated both of God and of souls. A soul could co-exist with God for ever, as from eternity in indissoluble union, but for a third entity of which too eternity is postulated. It is *Pāsam*, பாசம், the power which keeps the soul in bondage. It is the discordant element in the soul's relationship to God. Its constant endeavour is to keep the soul apart from God. The soul would gravitate towards God but for the attraction of *Pāsam*. The power of *Pāsam* is wielded by means of *Ānavam*,[3] 'ignorance,' 'darkness of self-assertion', which prevents the soul from knowing itself and its Divine affinities. Coupled with *Anavam* are *Karma*, கன்மம், 'deeds' and *Maya*, மாயை, 'material cause and consciousness.' All souls are not subject to all the three aspects of *Pāsam*, but all are subject to *Anavam*; some to all three; some to *Anavam and Pāsam*, and others to *Anavam* only.[4] According to the extent of the 'bondage' is the soul 'born' on earth, and God permits a soul to be born in a body. The soul has a capacity of becoming that to which it is attached. It is the 'grace'[5] of God, 'grace' manifested to men out of compassion for souls, that frees the soul from its fetters, effects

[1] No Tamil scholar has put the case for the Sanscrit origin of the Saiva Siddhanta more strongly than Mr. J. M. Nallaswami Pillai. See his admirable *Studies in Saiva Siddhanta*, pp. 109-145, 224 and 244-315, and note his opinion at p. xi of his *Siddhiyar*: 'I should like to correct the notion that there is anything peculiarly Tamilian in Saiva Religion and Philosophy'. Yet, even that learned author is constrained to write (*S. S. Studies*, 67), 'The merit of expounding this beautiful view of *Advaita* must *in the first place* be accorded to S. Meykandan'.

[2] See below, pp. 10.162. [3] See below, p. 150. [4] See below, p. 167.

[5] 'Grace,' is not the same as the Christian word. See below, Introduction, part vii.

detachment and attaches it purified to God. This union (re-unicn) of the soul to God is *advaita*,[1] a relationship in which God and the soul, *Pati* and *Pasu*, are 'neither one, nor two, nor neither.'[2] This union is attainable in this life: in the life to come it is *Mukti*, Vēēdu, முத்தி, வீடு, 'home.'

§ 12. Readers of the poems of Tāyumānaswāmy have sometimes formed different opinions as to what exactly was the religion he professed. An early translator of the poet, the Rev. G. McKenzie Cobban,[3] wrote:[4]

> Fragments of Tayumanawar's poetry are quoted wellnigh everywhere. It is a charcteristic feature of Vedantam that its creed has been shot into the popular mind by means of short sentences which are summaries, i.e. remarks and fragments of Tayumanavar's poetry often greet us in this way.

This would seem to suggest that in Mr. Cobban's view the poet was a Vedanti. 'He is no Saivite, but a Vedantist,' says the Rev. G. E. Phillips.[5] The poet-saint, according to a more recent interpreter,[6] rose from 'the Saiva Siddhanta faith in which he was born to the Universalism of the Vedanta.' The writer of the article on Tamil in the *Encyclopædia Britannica*[7] speaks of Tayumanavar as a pantheist. A Tamil editor[8] of the psalms repudiates the imputation of monism and universalism to the poet. From the numerous heterodox views the poet may be proved to be refuting[9] we may reasonably infer he was not a holder of any of them. As any opinion about the poet's religion is sure to be wrong if it does not appeal to his utterances in support, we may usefully proceed to see what he says of himself.

[1] See below, Introduction, part v.

[2] *Irupā Irupaktū* . . . ஒன்றாகாமல், இரண்டாகாமல், ஒன்றுமிரண்டு மின்றாகாமல்.

[3] I regret that this name has been misspelled as 'Cobham' at pp. 132, 138.

[4] *Madras Christian College Magazine*, July 1884, p. 5.

[5] *Ibid.*, April 1910, p. 513.

[6] 'A.K.' (probably Dr. Ānanda Kumaraswami ?) in *Prabuddha Bharata*, July 1913, p. 131.

[7] Vol. 26 (11th edition) p. 390. The writer is Dr. Reinhold Rost.

[8] Nagalingam Mudaliar, Preface, p. 20. His edition of the text is the basis of the translation by the present writer, and it is referred to as N.M. See below, p. 1.

[9] See below, § 15 for heresies refuted.

(1) He clearly holds that the two great foundations of religion, according to Hinduism, namely the *Vedas* and the *Agamas* [1] are of one and the same origin.

Who spake the Vedas, Agamas who spake,
Grace of the Silence gives ;
And seen by saints beneath the banyan shade
First cause of all He lives.
Behold Him there : the vision puts to death
The fickle mind that spins
In giddiness of worldly greed and gain
And reels in pleasant sins.
And lo ! there spring within the soul eight powers
Of wonders of the will,
Nay Heaven itself is reached, the home of Good,
Where never comes an ill.[2]

---

[1] See above, § 8, and below, pp. xxiv, 130-138.

[2] N.M. 425. The English, like many other renderings in this book is a paraphrase-translation of the original. What is rendered in the English as 'eight powers of wonders of the will' is in the original எண்சித்தி, 'eight' psychic powers which belong to those who have reached the yogic stage of spirituality. Such persons are called சித்தர் (*Siddhar*) 'possessors of psychic power'. Our poet devotes a whole section of hymns, N.M. 57-66 to 'the company of *Siddhar*,' and in the hymns mention is made of the many miraculous powers of the *Siddhar*. That the mere possession of psychic powers apart from real religion, however possible, is useless is emphasized by the poet himself in N.M. 118. As a matter of fact the poet knew, and we know, that some of the so-called marvels are performed by jugglers, circus men and other common folk who do not, it must be said to their credit, lay claim to spiritual excellence. The words of the hymn N.M. 118 may however mean that feats mentioned are not performed by physical skill but by psychic influence only :

The wild-willed tusker breaking every bond
Is meekly led where'er I will ;
I bid : behold the mouths of bears are bound,
The cruel tiger's jaws are still ;
Lo ! on the lordly lion's back I ride ;
The serpent dances at my call ;
The metals five in mercury and fire
I turn to gold that buys me all ;
Unseen of men I move about on earth ;
The gods in heaven my behests heed ;
For ever young I may remain ; nay pass
Into other bodies at need ;
Upon the waters I may walk ; may sit
Unscathed amidst the flames of fire ;

Yet, from the *Vedas* and the *Agamas* he passes on to the secret of the Silence [1] and the realization of religion at sight of manifested Deity. This is the principle, apart from the historicity or unhistoricity of such manifestation. Saivism is *Agamic*, and towards Saivism are the poet's leanings. 'The *Vedas* are the road, the *Agamas* the steed,' he says [2] and hastens to add that at the journey's end is the Vision of God. A consistent study of the poet's utterances makes it clear that, while he accepted the traditions of Hindu orthodoxy and conformed to the requirements of institutional religion, he laid the utmost possible stress upon something transcendantly superior to them. The *Vedas* and even the *Agamas* are but stepping-stones to higher things. There is a single psalm in which he makes mention of various religious means intended, he understands, to suit varying capacities for, and stages of, the spiritual life, and makes no secret of what he had been taught is the highest form of religion : [3]

Food for all tastes a feasting-house contains ;
Religion so for every man remains—
Almsgiving, wealth, home-life, then heaven to seek ; [4]
So teach the *Vedas*, *Agamas* so speak,
And of their teaching this the end and 'theme' :
The way of wisdom is the way supreme.
From sight and inference and otherwise
A man may reason [5] till uprooted dies

Yea, powers I may command more marvellous
    Than any I can now desire ;
But oh ! how hard it is to hold my mind
    Unmoved, and in stillness to be,
My God who art the Truth and Wisdom high,
    Who graciously dwellest in me.
O Light beatific, Splendour of Bliss !

In the English, given in the text p. xxiii., of N.M. 425 it is the Tamil முத்தி 'Mukti' that is rendered, 'heaven . . . the home of Good, where never comes an ill.'

[1] On Silence see below, pp. 132, 133, 135. [2] See below, p. 61. [3] N.M., 41.

[4] The *Kural* deals with the first three of these, அறம் (*Aram*) 'Virtue', chiefly almsgiving and other beneficent acts, பொருள் (*Porul*) 'wealth' and இன்பம் (*Inpam*) 'Love', including domestic love.

[5] On reasoning from 'sight', 'inference', etc., see *Siddhiyar*, Book i, in the first verse of which are enumerated the various logical methods.

What crieth ever 'I'; or yearn to know
The four great means; [1] thro' graded stages go
From first to fourth of that good four-fold way [2]
That leads thro' deeds and calm to wisdom's day;
Or tread the path of effort or of grace; [3]
Or test the truth of Maya cult.[4] That phase
Of faith which, tho' all other forms be known,
Thou taughtest me is best and is our own,[5]
Thinks not God and the soul are one or twain,[6]
Stands victor over doubt, wrong thinking slain,
O heavenly Guru granting lore divine [7]
Lord of the Silence,[8] sage of Mūlar's line.[9]

The key to the poet's meaning is the analogy of food for all tastes. The various religious methods are not for every man; it is not improbable, however, there may be men who have tried all. In any case stress is laid on 'the way of wisdom' and the faith and cult common to the poet and his Teacher—'our' faith. The poet, in this psalm at least, is not a Vedantist.

[1] The four great means are the Vedantic *Sādhanas* (சாதனம்) which are விவேகம் (*vivēka*), discrimination between 'eternal' and 'temporal', விராகம் (*Virāgam*) 'indifference', சமாதிசற்சங்கசம்பத்தி (*Samādhi Sadsaga sambatti*) 'quiescence', 'self-suppression', 'concentration', etc., and முமுட்சுத்துவம் (*Mumūttsuttuva*) 'a strong craving for emancipation'.

[2] The stages are *Sariyay*, etc., for which see below, p. 174.

[3] 'Path of effort', அநுபட்சம் (*Anupattcham*) is the method of salvation by individual, unaided effort. It is known in Sanscrit as *Markata Nyaya*, 'the monkey doctrine'—in order to be saved a man must reach out to God and cling to God as a monkey to its mother. The 'Path of Grace' சம்புபட்சம் (*Sambupattcham*) is that wherewith God saves man by His Grace. From the analogy of a cat taking up its kitten, this 'path' is known as *Marjara nyaya*, 'the cat doctrine'. On 'Grace' see below, Introd., part vii.

[4] On *Maya* see below, Introd., part v. The *Māyāvādi* (மாயாவாதி) is a believer in the doctrine that he is himself God and the whole world is an unreality. See *Ṣiddhiyar* 2. 5. 1, and below, Introd. part ii, § 15.

[5] 'Our own', the Tamil is நமது and it implies that the Teacher and the taught hold the faith in common.

[6] See below Introd., part v, on *Advaita*.

[7] 'Lore divine' is the knowledge of the Vedas and the Agamas. The Tamil is மந்திர (*mantra* = Veda) Guru, தந்திர (*tantra* = Āgama) Guru.

[8] 'Silence' see below, pp. 132, 135 and for 'Lord of the Silence' மௌனகுரு (*Mouna Guru*) see Introd., part vii.

[9] 'Mūlar' is Tirumular the author of *Tirumantram*, a Saivite classic to which frequent reference is made in this book. The poet's Guru is in the same succession of teachers as Tirumular. On Tirumular see above, § 8 and below, § 19.

(2) The appeal to the *Vedas* (and sometimes to the *Upanishads*,[1] does make the poet hesitate to assert not so much Agamic superiority as Agamic peculiarity. There is a truth, he says, which is specifically Agamic, and to it he constantly returns. We see this in the following lines[2] out of other hymns of similar tenor of teaching:

The Vedas and the Agamas agree
He only is the Truth who is
Perfection of Eternal Bliss—
O meditate on this and thou wilt see
The Vedas teach God and the soul are kin
And one. 'Till bodied birth 'tis true.[3]
They are not one, they are not two,[4]
When comes Sivagama's saving from sin.[5]

In other places the poet relegates to a background all books when his mind is set on the saving vision of Siva. His attitude towards the Vedas and the Agamas is one of advised consistency · there are loftier things than books however venerable.

The *Rik* and other Vedas
One only end proclaim:
Of Agamas the secret
Unravelled is the same.
Within his heart who ponders
It is the mystic sign
That Siva gave is gladdened
In floods of Bliss divine.[6]

The meaning is unmistakable: the Vedas and the Agamas point to one thing, a saving 'sign.' The sense is clearer in the hymn following:

Vain is all learning, hearing,
Which are but for debate;
'Tis they who see Lord Siva
Who by the banyan sate

---

[1] *Upanishads* are philosophical writings of post-Vedic times and are said to be over 108 in number. See below, § 19, note.

[2] *N. M.*, 470, 475.

[3] Until a soul is given a body (it is taught) it is akin to God, with the great difference that the soul of itself cannot know anything, but, once born, the soul must get rid of all 'taints' before reunion is possible.

[4] Not one, not two.

[5] This knowledge of 'not one, not two' is peculiar to the Saiva Agamic method of salvation from 'sin'. When the Sivagamic light comes, then the *advaita* relationship is perceived.

[6] *N. M.*, 1414.

The sign of sin dispelling
  To seeking ones to give,
And know its mystic meaning,
  Will ever sinless live.[1]

(3) The poet was not a Vedantist. On the contrary he was a very pronounced Saivite with a wide spiritual outlook.

The Saiva Faith of faiths is truest—
  And ye who fain would make your own,
Possess, its precious ancient Treasure,
  Go, guess its meaning where 'tis shown
In Chidambaram's open splendour ;
  Forsake ye faiths where falsehood lies.
O come ye people let us hasten
  To where for gazing of our eyes
The glory of the Presence shineth
  In Chidambaram's sacred Hall,
The glory of the Vision giving
  Deliverance and heaven to all.[2]

The ideals of all religions, says the poet, find their fulfilment in Chidambaram, the common ground of all faiths, and leveller of all creeds.

The meaning of the goodly way of wisdom,
  Or truth its rival creeds maintain,
No single one of all the faiths so many
  Can claim in itself to contain.
But when I gazed into the Hall of Glory,
  Tillai's, whose fame words fail to frame,
I found the feuds of all the faiths forgotten,
  For all men stood with reverend aim,
Adoring, in the openness of splendour
  That sky-wise stretched to seeing eyes,
And even in my heart, its hardness melting,
  I felt divinest raptures rise.[3]

Is the poet sectarian? Does he localize Deity? A negative answer may be confidently given. His catholicity has to make concessions to the needs of the many, and he never despised

[1] *N. M.*, 1415. On the 'sign' and its being given under a banyan shade, see below, pp. 200, 201, 221.

[2] *N. M.*, 554. On Chidambaram see below, p. 174.

[3] *N. M.*, 143. By 'goodly way of wisdom' the poet refers to the Saiva Siddhanta. On Tillai, see below, p. 174.

conformity to institutional religion in the case of those persons to whom, in certain stages of spirituality, it is indispensable. He is to be rightly understood as interpreting the Saiva Siddhanta to be something transcending[1] the traditional requirements of the religion of the many. He is ready reverently to lay aside veneration for holy places.[2] Even Tirutillai, Chidambaram, Ponnambalam the Hall of Gold, is not to bound the horizon of his vision. He sees further. He looks beyond the local and the material. Chidambaram is a magnificent symbol: the reality is beyond it. ***Chidambaram is the mystical presence of God in the human heart which gives Him its full devotion and love.***

We find clear references to this idea in the psalms of the poet:

> The Lord who is One and Many dances in the Hall of my heart.[3]
> Thou dancest in the mind.[4]
> Thou dancest in the Hall of the heart-temple of gladdened saints.[5]
> The hearts of holy men are the House of the red Lotus and the Hall of Gold where Thou dancest.[6]

This spiritual interpretation of Chidambaram is set forth by the poet in the following lines:[7]

> Thou art of three-fold form[8] unfading,
> O Form that form hast none,
> Thou art the splendour of all wisdom,
> And Thou, O wisest One,
> Hast in 'the six great faiths'[9] unfolded
> Thyself its god to each.
> Who has the strength to rend asunder
> Delusion's veil[10] and reach

---

[1] See, for example, his sentiments at pp. 27, 45, 124 below.
[2] See below, p. 21. [3] *N.M.*, 373
[4] *Ibid.*, 378. [5] *Ibid.*, 408. [6] *Ibid.*, 439.
[7] *N.M.*, 182. See Nalla, *Studies*, pp. 19, 20 where the Chidambaram—Heart idea is elaborated.
[8] Siva of the Siddhanta is not Siva of the Hindu Triad—Siva, Brahma, Vishnu—but he manifests himself in the three ways of their activities. On this see *Introduction*, part iv.
[9] On six faiths see below, § 14, where the restricted sense of 'the faiths' is shown.
[10] On 'Delusion,' Māya, see *Introduction*, part v.

Through knowledge unto Thee? Thou makest
The hearts that thirst for Thee
The Hall of Gold [1] where Thou in glory,
O Ruby [2] bright to see,
Dancest in bliss; mine eye, eye's jewel;
Of every bane the balm;
O vastness of the sign [3] unveiling
The secret of the calm
Divine, whose wisdom once Thou taughtest,
High quiet's lofty theme,
To Four [4] beneath the branching banyan–
God over gods, supreme.

No man, the writer says, has the strength to free himself from the mists of Delusion that blind his eyes to the vision of God, but God delights to be the active indweller [5] in the hearts of those who hunger for His presence.

(4) The religion of the poet, while not the Vedanta, is still *Vedic*, through the *Agamas*. It is வைதிக சைவம் (*Vaidika Saivam*).[6] The 'way of silence' is the 'crown of Vaidika Saivam as she sits enthroned'[7] amongst creeds. It is plainly Saivism, and Siva is 'the Bliss inhabiting the praises of Saiva faith'.[8] He is the goal of the Siddhanta [9] which is Saivism.

(5) The Vedanta is not heterodox in its relation to the Siddhanta.[10] The two are related. They have a commonness of origin but the two diverge later in their courses. The difference of outlook is as to the relationship of God and the soul for one thing. This is brought in one of his hymns.[11] ***This view, the poet, as I understand him, considers to be the harmonized association of Vedanta and Siddhanta.*** He adheres to the Siddhanta and finds in it, according to his eclectic predilections, something which can take in the Vedanta. This eclectic harmonizing he calls *Vedanta Siddhanta Samarasa* (சமரச).[12] 'While precious is the *dual* teaching, the *dual* is the

[1] See below, p. 174.
[2] See below, No. 219.
[3] See below, pp. 200, 221.
[4] See below, p. 164.
[5] On Indweller, see below, p. 156.
[6] *N.M.*, 141, 107, 1105.
[7] *N.M.*, 141.
[8] See below, No. 228 and p. 208
[9] See above, § 9 and below, Nos. 36–41.
[10] *N.M.*, 841.
[11] See below, No. 124.
[12] See below, Nos. 8, 11, for example and *N.M.*, 57–66.

fountain-head whence floweth *non-dual* wisdom.'[1] It is the same God 'whose glory burneth bright in Vedanta's goal',[2] and

> In heaven Thy feet, fair lotus,
> Thy saints adoring see:
> To them Thou comest, glory,
> Siddhanta's God to be,
> Lord of all.[3]

It is well to remember, in any study of the religion of our poet, that *samarasam* (சமரசம்) does not denote a doctrine so much as a stage of spirituality. It is even an experience. He says that God, who is the author of the Vedas and all similar writings and the framer of the Saiva and other faiths, has given men the *mōna samarasam*, மௌன சமரசம் which is above all creeds.[4] It is *samarasam*, realizing itself, or realized by silence. He refers to the 'state'[5] of *Vedanta Siddhanta samarasa*, and speaks of the *Vedanta Siddhanta samarasa* knowledge (experience or realization) of Siva.[6] He finds the Vedanta and the Siddhanta agreeing in the understanding that God is the doer of all a man does.[7] That is Vedanta Siddhanta Samarasa Supāvam.[8] It is 'grace' that leads to the conception of Vedanta and Siddhanta in harmony (Samarasa).[9] In the section[10] entitled *Siddhar Kanam* சித்தர் கணம் the adepts, *Siddhar*, are addressed as those who had 'reached the goodly state of Vedanta Siddhanta Samarasa' (வேதாந்த சித்தாந்த சமரச நன்னிலை பெற்ற).

(6) The stress laid on *Samarasam* by the poet should not lead one to the conclusion that the poet was a சமரசி *samarasi*. He was a Saivite of the Siddhanta school of thought, and the state of *samarasam* developing in him an intellectual apprehension was a fact of his experience. There is no such 'religion' as *samarasam*.

[1] Below, at p. 55. On 'dual', 'non-dual', see below, Introd., part v.
[2] Below, No. 59. [3] Below, No. 60. [4] *N.M.*, 29.
[5] *N.M.*, 39, வேதாந்த சித்தாந்த சமரச நிலை.
[6] *N.M.*, 40 வேதாந்த சித்தாந்த சமரச சிவாநுபூதி. In this hymn the poet desires to reach this realization so as to avoid the error of the Lohayats. See below, *Introduction*, § 15 on errors refuted in these psalms.
[7] See below, No. 8 at p 7, and notes at pp. 143–48.
[8] No. 8, *N.M.*, 8, வேதாந்த சித்தாந்த சமரச சுபாவம்.
[9] Below, No. 11 வேதாந்த சித்தாந்த மரபு சமரசமாகவே. [10] *N.M.*, 57–66.

§ 13. What is *samarasam?* The consideration of the poet's religion in the preceding section has prepared us for this inquiry. Samarasam is not a colourless eclecticism, an anaemic acquiescence[1] in the pacific thought that all religions are the same. Tāyumānavar held a very robust faith. He was very pronounced in his adherence to Saivism.[2] On what he considered the highest verity, tested by experience, namely, the relationship of the purified soul to God, he had occasion, as a student of religions, to notice that the Vedanta identified God with the soul in oneness. That tenet was against his Siddhanta upbringing. He would not equate God and the soul: indeed, he protests against such equation.[3] The Siddhanta specifically teaches that the soul is *not* to be identified with God.[4] Therefore, in the postulate that God and the soul 'are not one, *nor yet two*', the two teachings, Vedantic and Siddhantic, are brought into unison, *samarasam*. The poet expressly speaks of 'the godly *samarasa* bliss which consists in an affirmation of neither oneness *nor twoness*'.[5] This, we may take it, is the poet's own definition of *samarasam*. It would be helpful to remember in this connection that the poet's *samarasam* is not an attempt at harmonising *all* creeds but only of the Vedanta and the Siddhanta, and about them also only in respect of the relationship of the soul to God, because in many respects the Vedanta remains different from the Siddhanta.[6] Thus *samarasam* is a not taking in of all religions, nor is the 'God' of Tāyumānavar a composite of the God-idea of all known creeds. We are confirmed in this opinion by the fact that Tāyumānavar in speaking of God speaks of Him as 'the claim and the contest of all creeds.'[7]

There is considerable difference of view among Hindu scholars as to the exact contents of *samarasam*. The

[1] To 'feel very similarly to all sects of religion . . . and be never able to weigh even for a moment seriously the merit of this or that creed on the eternal side of things.' (R. L. Stevenson, *Travels with a Donkey*, p. 96.)

[2] See *N.M.*, 554., translated, above, at p. xxvii.

[3] See No. 43.

[4] *Siddhiyar* 3, 6, 7. See below, p. 186.

[5] *N.M.*, 111. ஒன்றோ டிரண்டெனுஞ் சமரச தெய்வ சுகம்.

[6] See Nalla, *Studies* 358

[7] See below, pp. 1, 129.

observations of Swami Vedachalam[1] in his lucid discourse on *samarasa sanmārkam*, though not of full bearing on the meaning of ***Vedanta Siddhanta Samarasa***, may be reckoned as contributing a vote in favour of interpreting ***samarasam*** as 'a harmonising of all men by pointing to a common truth to which all could subscribe.' A contribution by Mr. Cuppusamy Mudaliyar in ***Sen Tamil***[2] discusses in Tamil the religious views of Tāyumānavar and reaches, in a rather non-committal way, the conclusion that the poet was a Siddhanti. **The learned** writer does not go into the question of ***samarasam***. Two of the most noteworthy contributions to the understanding of ***Vedanta Siddhanta Samarasam*** are enshrined in the pages of ***Siddhantam***, a Tamil magazine at one time edited by Mr. J. M. Nallaswamy Pillai, a great Siddhanta scholar.[3] The first is a methodical statement of the subject of ***samarasam*** by Mr. P. Muttiah Pillai.[4] In his view ***Vedanta Siddhanta Samarasam*** means 'the agreeing in taste of both the Vedanta and the Siddhanta', வேதாந்தமும் சித்தாந்தமும் ஒற்றுமையான சுவை யுடையன, and the 'taste' சுவை, he reasons, consists in the correct valuing of the relations of the three entities ***Pasu*** (பசு), ***Pathi*** (பதி), ***Pāsam*** (பாசம்)—Soul, God, Bond.[5] He quotes the classical definitions given by Tirumūlar[6] of Vedanta and

[1] *Saiva Siddhanta Gnana Bodham* (சைவ சித்தாந்த ஞான போதம்), p. 65.

[2] Vol. iv (1905–06), p. 51.

[3] Mr. J. M. Nallaswamy Pillai, B.A., B.L. (Madras), sometime District Judge of Madura, is the author of many Siddhanta treatises both in Tamil and in English. He was editor of *Siddhanta Deepika* and of *Siddhantam*. His services to Tamil literature and to Saivism are immense. I am deeply indebted to him for elucidation of some difficult Siddhanta subjects. Elsewhere I refer to a letter he had written me.

[4] *Siddhāntam*, vol. i (May–June, 1912), p. 147. [5] See above, § 11.

[6] *Tirumantram*, 2401, 2373, 2372.

2401. [illegible]
[illegible]
[illegible]
[illegible]

2373. [illegible]
[illegible]
[illegible]
[illegible]

2372. [illegible]
[illegible]
[illegible]
[illegible]

The numbering and text are from the Ripon Press 'white' edition of *Tirumantram*.

Siddhanta, and lays stress on Tirumūlar's analogy of நீர் பாலாதல், '.water in combination with milk becoming milk[1]: ' it is the Vedanta understanding. In the Siddhanta idea the soul reaches God: அத்தன் பரன் பாலடைதல் சித்தாந்தம்.[2] The famous passage நானென வேதாந்தந் தானெனுஞ் சித்தாந்தம்[3] he explains to mean, 'In the Vedanta teaching the soul thinks itself God. in the Siddhanta the soul realizes its individuality'. If one teaching be held, he concludes, to be complementary to the other, then there is *samarasam.*[4]

On the other hand the contrary opinion of Mr. J. M. Nallaswamy Pillai, supported by the weight of his great learning, is the second noteworthy contribution[5] to the understanding of the subject of *samarasam*. He gives the word the sense of 'impartiality', an 'indifference to likes and dislikes'. There are six tastes, he argues, and all tastes are not one. With reference to each of the six tastes a *samarasa* attitude would be utter indifference whether the taster finds it sweet or bitter or sour or otherwise. Even so in the six creeds[6] there are irreconcilable differences of outlook, but the *samarasa* mind recognizes the good that is in each and views all with non-contentious, unsectarian 'impartiality'. He expounds the *Tirumantara* line[7] நானென வேதாந்தம் தான் என்னும் சித்தாந்தம் differently from Mr. Muttiah Pillai. 'The Vedanta teaches that the soul does in *soham bhavana*[8] realize itself as Deity: according to the Siddhanta. the soul, in bliss, sees[9] God alone.' The meaning of *samarasam* as 'impartiality' seeks to retain the distinctnesses of each of

[1] *Tirumantram*, 2401, in previous note. The soul is 'water', and God is milk'.

[2] *Tirumantram*, 2373, above, p. xxxii.

[3] *Tirumantram*, 2372, quoted fully above, p. xxxii. See below, *Introd.* part v.

[4] The whole article of ten pages of learning, characterized by very calm reasoning, is well worth perusal.

[5] *Siddhāntam*, vol. i (July-August, 1912), p. 169.

[6] See below, § 14.

[7] *Tirumantram*, 2372.

[8] Explained, below, at p. 184.

[9] 'I saw His beauty, only His' (See p. 104, below)

'And I, not seeing
A second, stand the seer' (See p. 104, below)

It should be noted that in the statement that the soul sees God alone there is postulated the soul's individuality.

the two systems of thought, Vedanta, Siddhanta. Mr. Nallaswami Pillai's idea of *samarasa* is equivalent to all-comprehensiveness, universality within the meaning of the *Siddhiyar*.[1] Referring to the *Siddhiyar* text he writes:

> Who has declared in such unmistakable terms that there is salvation for all, and that there is truth in each and every creed and which is suited to one's needs, and he could progress gradually and ascend in course of time the different steps of the ladder in the spiritual ascent? This *Sōpānamārga* is set out in the Saiva religion alone, and this would account for the greatest toleration displayed by the followers of this ancient faith, and which has degenerated into even indifferentism. We could therefore understand how our books both in Sanscrit and Tamil speak of the religion as *Siddhanta* (the True end), *Sāra* (essence), *Samarasa* (the essence of all or eclectic), and *Sanmārga* (the True Path).[2]

Tāyumānavar, it should be observed, postulates *samarasam* in respect of the Vedanta and the Siddhanta particularly, though it is possible (I venture to doubt this) that he had likewise other schools of religion[3] in his mind. While sincerely deferring to Mr. Nallaswami Pillai's vast erudition I am inclined to let my leanings go in favour of Mr. Muttiah Pillai's exposition of *samarasa*. It is, however, open to the reader to effect a *samarasam* of these conflicting opinions by judiciously combining them!

[1] 3, 8, 13, quoted below at p. 139.

[2] *Siddhiyar* (English Translation), Introd., pp. xxiv, xxv. See also his *Studies in Saiva Siddhanta*, p. 313.

[3] *N.M.*, 39. Mr. R. Shanmuga Mudaliyar (*S. Deepika*, i, p. 57) understands *samarasa* to mean 'unity'. He translates a portion of *N.M.* 39 thus: 'Reverence to you who let all the world know through my initiation the necessity of establishing the six local schools of religion [[illegible]] and the ecstasy of perceiving the supreme stage of unity [[illegible]] between the Vedanta and the Siddhanta.' It seems to me, with all respect to the learned Mudaliyar, that there is some confusion of terms, if not of ideas, in his note (*S. Deepika*, i, p. 57) when he speaks of the poet-saint as 'Vedanta Siddhanti or, still more appropriately Saiva Siddhanti,' and the Saiva Siddhanta as 'True Vedanta'. The Vedanta is rather loosely equated with the Siddhanta.

In a note (*S. Deepika*, i, p. 82) to *N.M.* 49, upon words not actually in the text, the learned writer remarks as the characteristic of real adherents of the Saiva Siddhanta, that they 'perceive no difference between the Veda and the Āgama, and they tolerate all schools, incorporate all schools, assimilate all schools and accommodate all schools in their essence and truth.' This fits in with the 'eclectic' idea of *Samarasa*.

§ 14. In the last stanza but one of a great Siddhanta classic[1] the author tersely reviews his work as an exposition of the truth in regard to God as revealed in the Saiva Siddhanta which is the crown of religions, and those other religions are indicated by him. All religions are thus classified and named by Saivite divines:

Heterodox

1. Externo-External[2] (புறப்புறச் சமயங்கள், *Purap-purach-chamayangal*). These refuse to accept Vedas and Agamas, and are—
   (*a*) Lōkāyta.
   (*b*) Sautrāntīka.
   (*c*) Yōgachāra.
   (*d*) Madhyamīka.
   (*e*) Vaibhāshika.
   [(*b*)–(*e*): Four forms of Buddhism.]
   (*f*) Ārugatha.

2. External (புறச்சமயங்கள், *Purach-chamayangal*). These accept the Vedas only, and are—
   (*a*) Taruka.
   (*b*) Mimämsa.
   (*c*) Ēkānmavāda.
   (*d*) Sāmhya.
   (*e*) Yōga.
   (*f*) Pāncharātra.

Quasi-orthodox

3. Externo-internal (அகப்புறச் சமயங்கள், *Agap-purach-chamayangal*). These accept the Vedas and the Agamas, but hold other revelations as well, and are—
   (*a*) Pāsupata.
   (*b*) Māviratā.
   (*c*) Kāpāla.
   (*d*) Vāma.
   (*e*) Vyrava.
   (*f*) Aikiavāta Saiva.

[1] *Sivapragâsam*, 99. Tiruvilangam's excellent Tamil edition is followed.

[2] The English terms are from Nalla. *Siddhiyar*, p. 184, note. In his *Essentials of Hinduism*, p. 20, Sabaratna Mudaliyar uses the terms 'outermost', 'outer', 'innermost', 'inner', and groups the third six religions with the orthodox last six. The third six I reckon as 'quasi-orthodox' and the last six alone as 'orthodox'. Mr. Nallaswami Pillai (*op. cit.*) calls the first eighteen 'false creeds'. In *Sivapragâsam* stanzas 7 and 99 there is mention of the creeds.

Orthodox

4. Internal (அகச்சமயங்கள், *Agach-Chamayangal*). These accept the Vedas and the Agamas but differ among themselves in the interpretations they put upon the texts, and are—
   (*a*) Pātāna Vāda Saiva.[1]
   (*b*) Bhēda Vāda Saiva.
   (*c*) Siva Sama Vāda Saiva.
   (*d*) Sivasangirānta Vāda Saiva.
   (*e*) Īsuvarava Vikāra Vāda Saiva.
   (*f*) Siva Advaita Saiva.

The attitude of the poet towards the non-orthodox creeds is one of hostility. They are as empty of nourishing contents and unsatisfying as the chaff of paddy.[2] They are to be cast aside.[3] There is falsehood in them.[4] To his own experience he assigns a place of superiority over even the six orthodox creeds, for in it God is 'the Bliss beyond the Six Creeds'.[5] 'Who can claim to know God who manifests Himself differently

[1] A naming of the groups according to Siva Gnāna Munivar is, (1) Saiva, (2) Pāsupata, (3) Mahāvirata, (4) Kālāmuga, (5) Vāma, (6) Vairava. The naming above in the text is that of the *Siva Gnāna Bāshayam*, 5. See Kathiravelpillai's *Tamil Dictionary sub. voc.* அகச்சமயம், அகப்புறச்சமயம். Tiruvilangam in his *Sivapragāsam*, pp. 10, 173, gives the naming I have adopted. Readers of Bhandarkar's *Vaisnavism and Saivism* will find that the Saiva sects named and described by the learned author (pp. 119–140) are in the main according to the naming of Siva Gnāna Munivar (*supra*), and that naming is, according to Tiruvilangam's classification here adopted, of the religions of the 'third' or quasi-orthodox group. Tiruvilangam's groupings and namings agree with those in Kalyāna Sundara Mudaliyar's *Tāyumānavar*, p. 5. Shanmuga Mudaliyar (*S. Deepika*, i, p. 57) speaks of what are grouped above as quasi-orthodox as the six dualistic schools of religion. The same naming of the அகச்சமயங்கள் is found in Singāravelu Mudaliyar's *Pattanattu Pillai*, pp. 260, 261. It should be noted that the 'six true creeds' are 'Saiva creeds' [*Siddhiyar*, 3, 2, 73. See Siva Gnāna Swami and Subramania Dēsikar Swami's *Siddhiyar* (Tamil), pp. 178, 179].

[2] *N.M.*, 303. K. S. Mudaliar's *Tāyumānavar, ad loc.* explains the expression [illegible] as 'perishing creeds'. Our poet undoubtedly borrows the expression from *Tiruvuntiar*, stanza 31 where [illegible] occurs. In the edition of Ēkāmbara Siva Yōgi and Ālālasundaram Pillai of *Tiruvuntiar* (p. 81) the learned commentators say that compared with the Saiva Siddhanta *all other creeds* are as chaff.

[3] See below, No. 230 at p. 84.

[4] *N.M.*, 554, [illegible]. See above, p. xxvii for translation of his verse.

[5] *N.M.*, 392, [illegible].

in the Six Creeds ?', he asks.[1] It is one God the Six Creeds confess.[2] According to the highest aspirations of each of the Six Creeds there is the manifestation of God in each.[3] Although the poet views with favour the orthodox creeds, yet it is possible to think that he concedes a knowledge of God to those religions which are non-orthodox.

> According unto each man's seeking
> That thou becomest unto each

he says.[4] He does not restrict the operations of God to a particular creed, or perhaps even to a special group of creeds.[5] This catholicity of outlook is borne out by the well-known passage in the *Siddhiyar*:[6] 'Whatever God you worship, the Lord of the Lady Uma[7] will appear even as such God.'

The author of the *Siddhiyar*, it has been observed,[8] 'does not condemn the worship of other gods, for the simple reason that all such worship is useful because all such worship, if true, tends to raise the worshipper . . . towards a nearer approach to the Supreme God, and the All-Seer . . . cannot fail to take note of his sincerity and love and to reward him as he deserves. But the worship . . . of the lower gods cannot be the highest object of our aspirations.' In the *Gita* it is similarly laid down :—

> If any worshipper whatsoever seeks with faith to reverence any body whatsoever, that same faith in him I make steadfast.
>
> They also who worship other gods and make offerings to them with faith . . . do verily make offering to me, though according to no ordinance.[9]

§ 15. In the Psalms of Tāyumānavar there are implied or express refutations of certain forms of heterodox teaching

[1] *N.M.*, 69, [illegible] ? cf. *N.M.*, 182, translated at p. xxviii. above.

[2] No. 179 below, at p. 74.

[3] *N.M.*, 1088, 1103.

[4] See below, p. 56.

[5] *N.M.*, 1210 [illegible]
N.M., 1211 [illegible]

[6] *Siddhiyar* 3, 2, 25.
யாதொரு தெய்வங் கொண்டீ ரத்தெய்வ மாகியாங்கே
மாதொரு பாகனார்தாம் வருவர்.

[7] See below, p. 201.

[8] Nallaswami Pillai, *Siddhiyar*, pp. 170, 171

[9] *Gita*, vii. 21, ix. 23. See below, p. 190.

current in his time. A brief notice of these refutations is likely to be helpful in our understanding of what was ***not*** the religion of the poet. This negative approach should lead the careful reader to a confirmation of what has been already indicated to be the poet's religion. Of the refuted heresies we may note the following:

1. The teaching of the Karmavādin who identified karma with Deity.[1]

2. The teaching of the Lōkāyitas (or Chārvākas). Among other things they taught that cowards alone considered vice evil, and that the highest good consisted in the full enjoyment of the pleasures of this life.[2]

3. Māyāvādam is one of the four forms of Ēkānmavādam. The other three are Pārkariavādam, Krīdāpramavādam, and Sabda Brahmavādam. The principal tenet of Māyāvādam consists in the identification of man with Deity.[3]

> (1) The Brāhman is the cause of all worlds and is limitless, pure, formless, without attributes.
> (2) This Brāhman lives in each body, as the sun shining in numerous pots of water leaves its reflection in each.
> (3) God, the Brāhman, is beyond the six kinds of logical proof.
> (4) God is in each body but is untainted by such contact.
> (5) Brahma Jnāna is the knowledge that the Ego is God. 'Thou art God'.
> (6) The phenomenal world is a Delusion. It is like a rope which, in the darkness, one mistakes for a snake.
> (7) By certain purificatory rites man attains to wisdom and realizes 'I am God'.[4]

4. Kālavādimatham teaches that Time is Deity.[5]

[1] No. 7, below = *N.M.*, 7. [illegible].

[2] *N.M.*, 104. [illegible]. The *Siddhiyar*, Book ii, ch. i contains a full statement of Lōkāyita teaching and its refutation.

[3] *N.M.*, 131. [illegible].

[4] *Siddhiyar*, Book ii, ch. v has a statement and refutation of Māyāvādam. See below, pp. 184–190. To our poet the equation 'I am God' is 'the daring of unbridled fancy' (p. 26, below).

[5] No. 279, below at p. 96. That God is the framer of Time corrects the notion that Time is God, although God as the cause of Time may be addressed as Time. See No. 123, p. 54, for the poet's summary of the views of many as to what God is. *Siddhiyar*, 3, 1, 10 refutes the teaching that Time is God, காலமே கடவுள்.

5. Sāruvākan[1] is the believer in Sārvākan and is known also as Niruchravādi. His teaching is the same as that of the Lōkāyita (*supra*).

6. Sabda Brahmavādam[2] considers that *Sabda* (சத்தம்), Sound, is the sole Reality, God.[3]

7. Ēkānmavādam is the general name, as we have seen, (*supra* 3), for a number of heresies. In one form or another it is referred to by Tāyumānavar in many places.[4] Its principal tenet is that 'all is God,' 'I am God'. It is the heresy of stating 'that the ineffable One is I'.[5] 'If I think that I am God will He who is the Expanse of Wisdom come to me ever ?'[6] 'The thought that we are God begets self-assertion'.[7] In some of the Ēkānmavāda passages the references may be more restrictedly considered as applicable to the Bhēda heretics[8] the Pasugnāna heretics,[9] and the Siva Sama Vāda heretics.[10]

It is clear from the refutations in the poet's psalms that his tenets are different from those he expressly or impliedly condemns.

PART III.—TĀYUMĀNAVAR

§ 16. The materials for the life of the poet are scanty. Such details as are usually found in introductions to editions of the psalms are traced to the poet's disciples, particularly Arulayyar, and to the poet's only son Kanagasabāpathy Pillai. It may be possible to gain from the poet's psalms autobiographic

[1] *N.M.*, 173.

[2] No. 123, p. 54.

[3] *Siddhiyar*, Book ii, ch. iv contains a statement and refutation of this heresy.

[4] *N.M.*, 129, 152, 391 (=No. 223, p. 85), 475 (translated, p. xxvi), 484, 622 (=No. 277, p. 96), 1081, 1305, 1415.

[5] *N.M.*, 484 சொல்லுதற்கடங்காச் சப்பொருள் நானேயே.

[6] *N.M.*, 1081 நானே [என்னும் என்றிற] சுபாவம் நிலைப்பட நின்றால் ஞான வாரணமும் வருவாரோ?.

[7] *N.M.*, 1305 நாம்பிரம மென்று வருமே போதந்தடம்.

[8] *N.M.*, 391=No. 233, p. 85.

[9] *N.M.*, 484, 1305. They are ēkānmavādin in that they equate God and the soul.

[10] *N.M.*, 484. See a short notice of heresies in K. S. Mudaliyar's (Tamil) *Tāyumānavar*, pp. 97-101, 208 where there is mention of some heresies not named by me, viz., Arikāravādam, Parināmavādam, Aikiyavādam, Sankiranthavādam.

particulars at any rate for his religious experiences. The traditional facts of his life are accepted here as given in the Tamil introductions to collections of the poet's writings. The Chola prince of Trichinopoly by name Vijayaranga Chokkalinga Naickar, a son of the ruler of Madura, had a steward whose name was Kēdilia Pillai. This steward and manager of the royal estates had a son named Chidambara Pillai whom he gave in adoption to his childless brother. After he had done so, the desire to have a son and heir became strong in Kēdilia Pillai, and he earnestly besought the God Tāyumānēsurar, whose shrine was on the hill of Siragiri, for the blessing of a son. The son of such prayer, was named Tāyumānavar.[1] The birth of the poet took place in the village of Vēdaraniyam near Point Calimere in South India. The Tamil editions of the poet's writings do not give the date of the poet's birth. In the *N.M.*,[2] edition published in 1906 the father of the poet is said, rather vaguely, to have flourished 'about 230 years ago.'[3] In Rama Yogi's edition published in 1912 the floruit of the poet's father is placed 'about 230 years ago.'[4] One of the statements, if not both, cannot be correct. The introduction to Sambanda Mudaliyar's edition published in 1891 says that Kēdilia Pillai lived 'about 200 years ago.'[5] The Rev. G. McKenzie Cobban writing in 1884 says[6] that Kēdilia Pillai 'lived about a hundred and fifty years ago' making the birth of the poet in or after A.D. 1734. The Rev. G. E. Phillips in 1910 wrote[7] that the poet 'was born . . . about 180 years ago,' that is about A.D. 1730. Mr. Arnold in his *Galaxy* published in 1886 states that the poet was born 'about 150 years ago.'[8] According to these statements the birth-year of the poet

[1] See below, No. 114 at p. 48 and see p. 159. In *N.M*, 556, 557 the poet addresses Tāyumānēsurar. The Sanskrit form of the name of the god is Mātribhūtesvara (See Subrahmaṇyam's *S. Tāyumānavar*, p. 2).

[2] See above, p. 1. Note 1.

[3] *N.M. Introduction*, p. 1.

[4] *Introduction*, p. 1. K. S. Mudaliyar's edition (published in the year Keelaga = A.D. 1908) follows the '230 years ago' chronology.

[5] *Introduction*, p. 1.

[6] *Madras Christian College Magazine*, July 1884, p. 2.

[7] *Ibid.*, April 1910, p. 513.

[8] *Galaxy of Tamil Poets*, p. 171

must have been not very far from one of the following years of the Christian era, namely, 1676, 1682, 1691, 1730, 1734, 1736. One only, if any, of these years is entitled to be considered the most probable, and, if Mr. S. Purnalingam Pillai be right (which is doubtful) that the poet died in A.D. 1742,[1] the minimum of probability must be accorded to the years 1730, 1734, 1736.

The floruit of the poet is fixed approximately as 'the latter half of the seventeenth century,'[2] 'the first quarter of the eighteenth century,'[3] 'the beginning of the eighteenth century.'[4] It seems however that we have a statement almost contemporary with the death of the poet as to the date of that event in the *In Memoriam* lines written by Kōdikkarai Gnāni: 'It was on a Monday in January of the Sālivāhana era year 1581 that the saint lost himself in Sivam.'[5] The Hindu year 1581 of the Sālivahana era corresponds to the year 1659 of the Christian era.[6] In the introduction[7] to the N.M. edition this date is, it seems to me rightly, accepted and the learned editor, writing in 1906, observes that the floruit of the poet was 'beyond doubt 248 years ago.' Mr. Kuppusamy Mudaliar, the writer of the introduction to the Rama Yogi edition of the psalms, quotse[8] Sewell[9] in support of the statement that Vijayaranga

[1] *Ten Tamil Saints*, p. 79. This date is accepted by Mr. R. S. Nārāyana Aiyar, B.A., B.L., in *Sen Tamil*, xvii. 254.

[2] Dr. A. K. Cumaraswamy in *Prābuddha Bhāratā*, xxiii. 114.

[3] Purnalingam Pillai, *Primer of Tamil Literature*, p. 172.

[4] Dr. Barnett, *Heart of India*, p. 185.

[5] *N.M., Introduction*, p. 16.

நகாறு சாலி வருடமா யிரத்தைந்
  நூற்றெண்பத் தொன்று தொடரு
மிருகபமிருதாம் வருடத்தை மாதம்
  வெண்மதி வாரநாள்......
தாயுமான வனார்
  சிவத்தினிற் கலந்தநற் றினமே.

[6] In Barnett and Pope's *Catalogue of Tamil Books in the British Museum*, Preface, p. vi, the date ascribed to Tāyumānavar is 'about 1650' of the Christian era. If the year of the poet's death is meant, then it is the nearest European approximation to the statement of Kōdikkarai Gnāni.

[7] p. 24. In Murugadāsa Swamy's *Pulavar Purānam*, part ii, pp. 123-126, there is a short metrical account of Tāyumāna Swami, but no data are afforded for chronological conclusions.

[8] p. 1.

[9] *South Indian Dynasties*, p. 60.

6

Chokkanāta[1] Nayakar flourished A.D. 1704–1731, and is of opinion that Tāyumānavar 'entered into *samādhi*' in the Christian year 1742. If we understand entry into '*Samādhi*' *not to mean death*, and if the statement[2] is correct that Tāyumānavar continued to be *alive* for seventy-three years *after* Chokkanāta Nayakar, then seventy-three years after A.D. 1732 (Sālivāhana, 1654) will end with A.D. 1805. Thus the death-year of the poet was A.D 1659, 1742, or 1805.

§ 17. On the death of Kēdilia Pillai, the poet's father, the poet succeeded him in the service of the King. Tradition states that the poet was then seventeen years of age. This may or may not be so. But the young steward of the King is said to have done his work as well as his father. His duties at court did not prevent Tāyumānavar from continuing and advancing in the studies which before his official days he had begun. The great realities of religion called for his zealous pursuit of them. Above all things he had learnt the need of a 'Guru,'[3] such an one as the books of his faith had taught him to expect. The need grew daily upon him. As if in response to his longings there sojourned in those days in Tarisipuram, worshipping at the shrine of Tāyumānavar,[4] a man of great learning and piety. He was Arul Nandi Sivāchāriar in the line of discipleship tracing succession from the famous Tirumūlar[5] the author of *Tirumantram*, and he, at Chidambaram, had assumed the name 'Mouna Guru,'[6] that is, either 'the silent Teacher', or, better 'the teacher of the Silence.' The young disciple received from the Guru preparatory instruction, and, bidden to do so, continued in his worldly duties. It is said that on the poet's eagerness to follow the Guru he was told the words சும்மாவிரு (*summā iru*), 'Be still'. This saying appears to have made a profound

[1] Some writers have 'Chokkalinga'.

[2] *N.M.*, *Introduction*, p. 24.

[3] See below, *Introduction*, part vii.

[4] See below, p. 159, and above, p. xl.

[5] See above, p. xxv, and below, p. xlvii.

[6] மௌனகுரு. *N.M.*, 37–46 are specially in praise of the Guru, and in 26–36 praise is ascribed *to God as the Divine Guru* See below, *Introduction*, part vii.

impression on the poet by reason, no doubt, of its mystical sententiousness.[1] The mind has to abide unattached, undisturbed, well-balanced, 'like the waveless sea.'[2] Tāyumānavar's continuance in the performance of his secular duties did not appear to have diminished his ardour for spiritual achievements. The case of King Janaka referred to by him [3] in illustration of the possibility of growth in grace in the midst of worldly surroundings, and of work without attachment, is paralleled, on a less royal scale, in the saint's own life, beset though it was with innumerable solicitations to sin.

§ 18. A great temptation came to him on his master's death. It was from the royal widow. Fearing to succumb to her fascinations, he fled the court and retired into a life of brief quietness in the neighbourhood of Ramnad. There, at the temple dedicated to the Goddess of Grace, 'Half of Siva',[4] he sang those verses of exquisite charm, entitled *Malay Valar Kātali*,[5] in the second of which it is possible to detect a haunting consciousness of the fair peril from which he had been delivered. It may be here observed, on a psychological study of his life-details, that the poet would seem, about this time, to have been assailed with repeated solicitations to sensuality, if we may allocate to a particular period those experiences of spiritual infirmity of which he often pathetically complains and which he contritely deplores.[6] It is, on the other hand, no doubt, not difficult to distribute those experiences to various periods of his life, even those of great spiritual strivings.[7] There is also the surmise open, in the regrettable dearth of biographical data, that, soon after his leaving the

[1] The words சும்மாஇரு find mention in numerous passages, e.g. *N.M.*, 39, 40, 100, 116, 118, 162, 353, 416, 436, 464, 510, 511, 537, 538, 631, 685, 705. On சும்மாஇரு சொல்லற என்றலுமே அம்மா பொருள் see *Kantar Anubūti*, stanza 12.

[2] திரையற்ற நீர்போல் சிந்தை தெளிவார்க்கு (*Tirumantram*, stanza 2955).

[3] See below, pp. 106, 226.

[4] On the expression 'Half of Siva' see below, pp. 78, 201, and *Introduction*, part vii.

[5] The expression மலை வளர் காதலி means 'the Maid who had been bred on the mountains.' See below, p. 200.

[6] For some instances see below, Nos. 129, 154, 199, 315, 317.

[7] E.G. such as are indicated in Nos. 103, 148, 221, 258, below.

queen's court, he had betaken himself to mortifying austerities one is familiar with in the lives of all saints. However, his kinsfolk thought their interference with his way of life necessary. He was persuaded to enter upon the duties of the married state so highly commended by Tiru Valluva Nāyanar.[1] His family life was one of happiness, and an only son, Kanagasabāpati Pillai, was the offspring of it. On the death of his wife, some years later, his *Guru* reappeared to him and completed his spiritual instruction.[2] Thereafter the saint broke altogether away from the bonds of kith and kindred and all worldly ties, and lived a life of the joys of which he has left us abundant evidence.[3] The saint 'was lost in Sivam' in the neighbourhood of Ramnad, near the temple of ***Malay Valar Kātali***, in the year 1581 of the Sālivāhana era.[4]

§ 19. There is considerable internal evidence as to the wide range of the poet's learning. We find that he was equally well read in Sanscrit as in Tamil. He could make use of the literature of either language in controversy.[5] There are references to the four Vedas, the Agamas and the Epics.[6] He had read the Upanishads.[7] From Vedic and Upanishadic sources, also from his general store of Sanscrit, the poet introduces into a few of his psalms numerous Sanscrit words.[8] The exceeding great beauty of his Tamil, however, is unaffected by his occasional employment of Sanscrit words. We may note that he speaks with considerable diffidence of his Tamil as compared with that of the famous poet-saints of whom he makes mention, and the language of some of whom he incorporates into his psalms. He thus contrasts himself with 'The Three:'

[1] In his *Kural*, Book iii.

[2] On the state of the 'Grace-matured' see below, pp. 20, 167.

[3] E.G. see below, Nos. 243, 258.

[4] See above, § 16 as to date.

[5] *N.M.*, 66. He modestly refers to his knowledge of Sanscrit in this hymn thus : வடமொழியின் வசனங்கள் சிறிதுபுகல்வேன், 'I can quote a few Sanscrit verses'.

[6] See below, p. 55.

[7] *N.M.*, 136 speaks of 'over 108 Upanishads.' See present writer's *Foregleams of God*, ch. ii, § 8, and ch. viii, § 4, note for a short account of the Upanishads.

[8] *N.M.*, 3, for instance.

The sweet-toned Tamil of the Three
Thine ears delight with psalms sweet-worded ·
My words from theirs how far must be,
Feeble, O three-eyed Lord, soul's Honey ? [1]

He is conscious too that men there may be who speak in public gatherings of his hymns as poor stuff, woven of words as light as unspun cotton.[2] But the world will, he is confident, overlook the faults of his Tamil if the theme of his hymns is the Love of God.[3] The poet's highest satisfaction is that God to whom he sings his psalms would not look at their shortcomings.[4] In this spirit of humility and religious fervour are the psalms sung and presented, and no one can read them without being struck by their exquisite charm.

There are many authors to whom the poet refers. We may notice a few of the principal references.

1. 'The Three'[5] stand out prominently. They are Tirugnāna Sambandar, Tirunāvukkarasu, and Sundaramūrti. It is generally believed that the first two belonged to the sixth or seventh century after Christ, and the third to the eighth or ninth.[6] Sambandar is called by Tāyumānavar 'lord of Shīyāli'.[7] Shīyāli in the Tanjore District in South India was the birth-place of this famous poet-saint whose devotion to Siva and his skill in Saivite dialectics helped in the expulsion of Jainism and Buddhism out of Tamil India. We must assume that Tāyumānavar had good reasons for praising Sambandar as 'the king whose conquest is over births'.[8] It is believed that he was the author of a great deal more than the 384 hymns which have come down to us, and these 384 form the first three collections of the Saivite *Devārams*. I cannot share the opinion recently expressed[9] that 'there is

[1] No. 274, below. See pp. 83, 116, 205.

[2] *N.M.*, 115 பஞ்சுபடு சொல்லர்களைப் [illegible]
பாவிசேரு பாவிசேரு [illegible] சபை கூட்டுவர்.

[3] *N.M.*, 64 என் தமிழ்க் குற்றங்கள் [illegible] மேலிட்டிருந்தாய்.

[4] *N.M.*, 327 தண்டமிழ் மாலைகள்
[illegible].

[5] *N.M.*, 102, 161, 619 (= No. 273, below) speak of மூவர்.

[6] See above, p. v.

[7] *N.M.*, 161, சீகாழித்தலைவனே.

[8] *N.M.*, 1107, [illegible] திருஞானசம்பந்தன்.

[9] Kingsbury and Phillips, *Hymns of the Tamil Saivite Saint*, p. 11.

not very much of heart religion in them.' A juster estimate of a great poet, an earnest and saintly man, is best stated in the words of the late Prof. Sundaram Pillai :

> He is decidedly the greatest and the most popular of the Tamil *rishis*. . . . Even considered as a poet he has more than ordinary claims to be remembered. His hymns . . . are models of pure and elevated diction, generally earnest and touching, but always melodious. . . . A true and great Tamil poet, certainly the greatest in the lyrical department.[1]

Tāyumānavar speaks of Tirunāvukkarasu as 'whom our Lord Siva addressed as Appar'.[2] Tradition has it that Sambandar used to call his elder, Tirunāvukkarasu, *Appar*, 'Father'. Appar had been a Jain once, suffered persecution at Jain hands, and finally relinquished the Jain faith for Saivism. The two poets, Apparswami and Sambandamūrti, are said to have gone from place to place in South India singing the praises of Siva. Tāyumānavar quotes Tirunāvukkarasu twice at least.[3] It is rightly claimed that the hymns of Appar are 'in the purest of Tamil, terse and sweet beyond measure, in every way worthy of the great apostle's mission to the Tamils as "the king of sacred (Tamil) diction" (*Tiru-nāvuk-karasu*). His sayings show how the deepest spiritual truths may be expressed in simple Tamil without the aid of Sanscrit words'.[4] Of Sundarar there is mention made by Tāyumānavar in terms of the highest literary praise :—'one most skilled in Tamil',[5] 'one who knew the rare charm of the ancient Tamil tongue'.[6] He is one of

[1] *Age of Tirugnāna Sambanda*, pp. 4, 5. In Book ii of *Peria Purānam* there are 3,159 four-line stanzas about Sambandar.

[2] *N.M.*, 161, [illegible].

[3] *N.M.*, 1257, '[illegible]'; *N.M.*, 1262, '[illegible]'. He is alluded to in *N.M.*, 1108.

[4] Sir P. Ramanathan's Preface (p. 1) to Mr. Nallaswami Pillai's *S. Appar*. The *Peria Purānam*, Book i, part v, is devoted to Tirunāvukkarasu. A short metrical sketch of each of the three is given in Muruga Dāsa Swamy's *Pulavar Purānam*, part ii, pp. 1-19. A very sympathetic appreciation of the religious experience of S. Appar by the Rev. H. A. Popley appears in *The Young Men of India*, August, 1923, p. 354.

[5] *N.M.*, 1109, [illegible].

[6] *N.M.*, 581, [illegible]. There is a well-annotated (Tamil) edition of Sundarar's *Devāra Patigam*, by Srīmat Ramānatha Yōgi. A useful book *Sundaramūrti*, by S. M. Rama Chandra Chettiar, B.A., B.L., contains much information.

the Tamil poets quoted by Tāyumānavar.[1] Like the others of 'The Three', Sundaramūrti went from place to place in Tamil lands singing the praises of Siva. He is said to have visited Çeylon. Of the religious value of his hymns, their conduciveness to spirituality, opinion has always been uniformly very favourable. The learned authors, however, of ***Hymns of the Tamil Saivite Saints*** speak disparagingly of Sundarar in their twenty-line introduction to fifteen hymns they have selected for translation. They say, 'On the whole his hymns are on a lower spiritual plane than those of the first two writers [Appar and Sambandar], though there are some which bear the marks of real spiritual experience'.[2] But one of the two writers, Sambandar, in the opinion of the same learned authors, writes 'effortless' stuff with very little of 'heart religion' in it:[3] therefore Sundarar's must be very poor stuff indeed, 'on a *lower* spiritual plane'! I cannot find anything in the writings of either poet to justify such a verdict.

2. Tirumūla Nāyanār is the Siddhanta divine most conspicuously mentioned by Tāyumānavar. He is referred to as 'the raja among saints whose fame is in the raja yoga'.[4] He is one of the four deified saints invoked in a hymn.[5] There is a whole section of ten hymns each of which concludes with a reference to Tirumūlar as he to whose line of teachers belonged the Guru of Tāyumānavar himself.[6] According to modern European scholars Tirumūlar lived somewhere about A.D. 800.[7] He is the author of ***Tirumantram***, a very comprehensive metrical treatise on the Siddhanta. It is divided into nine sections and the total number of four-line stanzas as given, for example, in

[1] *N.M.*, 1259, '[illegible]'; *N.M.*, 1260, '[illegible]' See below, pp. 156, 220.

[2] Kingsbury and Phillips, *Hymns of the Tamil Saivite Saints*, p. 71

[3] *Ibid.*, p. 11.

[4] *N.M.*, 113, சக்கரவர்த்தி தவராச யோகியெனு மிக்க திருமூலர்.

[5] *N.M.*, 162.

[6] *N.M.*, 37-46, மூலன் மரபில்வரு மௌனகுருவே. On Guru see below, ***Introduction***, part vii.

[7] Farquhar, *O.R.L.I.*, p. 193. See however, above, p. xvi for present writer's suggestions of an earlier date.

Visuvanāta Pillai's very attractive edition, is 3,047, whereas tradition[1] reckons only 3,000.

3. Mānikkavāchagar ('He whose words are rubies') was the Chrysostom of ninth century Saivism. He is said to have held a high official position in Madura, and to have abandoned it on his 'conversion' upon the appearance to him of his Guru. After his 'conversion' he is believed to have held learned disputations with Buddhists at Chidambaram. His great work is the *Tiruvāchagam*[2] ('Holy Utterance'), a work expressive of almost passionate devotion to Siva. It is one of the classics of Saivite devotional literature. In the psalms of Tāyumānavar we find Mānikkavāchagar referred to[3] as Vātavūr Dēva from his traditional birth place. He is mentioned and quoted in other passages.[4]

4. S. Meykandar, author of *Sivagnāna Bōdham.*[5]

5. Arul Nandi Sivachariyar, author of *Sivagnāna Siddhiyar.*[6]

6. Maraignāna Sambandar, Guru of S. Umāpati.[7]

[1] The tradition is preserved in *Tirumūla Nāyanār Purānam* (*Peria Purānam*, part ii, in Arumuga Nāvalar's edition), stanza 27. In Visuvanāta Pillai's edition, stanza 3045 speaks of the 3,000 stanzas of the book. See a reconciliation attempted by Dr. Rāmanan in his learned foreword to Visuvanāta Pillai's edition, p. 9. Mr. S. Ramasamy Aiyar, B.A., B.L., began in the *Siddhanta Deepika*, vol. i, an annotated English translation of the *Tirumantram*. See *Siddhanta Deepika*, vol. vii.

[2] Dr G. U. Pope's edition contains a full account of the life and times of the poet and an English translation of the entire book of 3,327 lines. The latest Tamil edition of *Tiruvāchagam* is a serial publication with copious notes issued in 1922-1923 by the Saiva Siddhanta Publishing Society, Tinnevelly, as a volume of that Society's Treasury of Tamil Classics.

[3] *N.M.*, 162.

[4] *N.M.*, 102 (reference to *Tiruvāchagam*), 991, 1110 (reference to Manikkavachagar's controversy with Buddhists) 1325. He is quoted in *N.M.* 1263 '[illegible]', 1264 '[illegible]'. (See below, pp. 187, 224 and 1265 '[illegible]'. In Dr. Pope's edition of the *Tiruvāchagam* is given a full account of the life and times of this great Saiva saint.

[5] *N.M.*, 1097, [illegible] 'the seer of advaita truth'. See above, pp. xvii-xx.

[6] *N.M.*, 1098, [illegible] 'he who in half a stanza revealed the whole world of knowledge.' The allusion is to *Siddhiyar* 3.8.30. For the author see above, p. xliii. In *N.M.*, 1258, his words [illegible] are quoted.

[7] *N.M.*, 1099. See above, p. xviii.

7. S. Umāpati, author of eight Siddhanta Sastras.[1]
8. Arunakiri Nathar, author of *Kantār Anupūti*.[2]
9. Pattanattār, author of many hymns.[3]
10. Sivavakkiar, author of many hymns.[4]
11. Uyyavandār, author of *Tiruvuntiār*.[5]

These names are sufficiently indicative of the literary influences to which we may ascribe somewhat of the arresting charm and melody of S. Tāyumānavar's Tamil, and by which we may form an idea of his extensive learning.

§ 20. We have abundant evidence in S. Tāyumānavar's psalms of his progress in religion. The psalms are not in chronological order. This fact, however, does not obscure the conception of right sequences, in our estimate of the poet-saint's religious experience.

1. He had a deep consciousness of sin as a state of wrong relationship to God. This we may gather from his confessions which are as sincere in point of acknowledgment as the less veiled confessions of S. Augustine. The poet shows us the real sinner before he lets us know the change effected by holy influences. There has not been, he tells us anyone known to him among the educated or the uneducated classes of men of his time who had so persistently pursued a life of sensual pleasures.[6] 'I am a slave of my passions,' he owns.[7] He had a vivid remembrance of the enslaving power of a life of sensuality.[8] Often he must

[1] *N.M.*, 1100. See above, p. xviii for the eight works.

[2] *N.M.*, 162, 485. In *N.M.*, 1114 he is praised as ' he who by the inspiration of God spoke the *Kantār Anupūti*, கந்தரநுபூதி பெற்றுக் கந்தரநுபூதிசொன்ன. His words [illegible] are quoted in *N.M.*, 1270.

[3] *N.M.*, 516, 1111. In Dr. Barnett's *Heart of India*, p. 88 there is a short account of this poet. Some of his verses are given in English by the Rev. G. M. Philips, in *Madras Christian College Magazine*, July 1910, pp. 512-13. In *The Young Men of India* of September 1923 at p. 407 there is a fine study of S. Pattanattār by Mr. V. Chakkarai, the able editor of *The Christian Patriot*.

[4] *N.M.*, 162, 142. See below, p. 157, note (2). There is no very convincing reason to justify doubts as to Sivavakkiar having really lived.

[5] Quoted in *N.M.*, 303. The *Tiruvuntiār* and *Tirukkalitupadiar* are companion works, and are two of the fourteen Siddhanta Sāstras. See above, p. xvii.

[6] *N.M.*, 120, 579.

[7] *N.M.*, 583, 433.

[8] *N.M.*, 240 (= No. 199, below), 1448 (= 318, below), 1449 (= No. 319, below).

have succumbed to its solicitations. After his realization of 'wisdom' the vivid recollection of the burning 'flame of lust'[1] and of 'beauty's lure'[2] led him to exhort other men to mortification of fleshly appetites.[3] The sin that most alienates the soul from God is the sin of sensuality. This the poet knew. Hence his renunciation of 'laughter of love-lit eyes,'[4] for fear of consequent perils. All the descriptions he gives of himself cannot be attributed to a sense of modest self-depreciation. Some of the many are: simpleton,[5] dog,[6] wicked man,[7] sinner,[8] deceitful fellow,[9] untruthful person,[10] heinous[11] sinner,[12] hard-hearted man laden with evil karma,[13] insincere in religion.[14] There is quite a black list in many places.[15] We are justified in seeing in the beginning of Tāyumānavar's spiritual experience

(1) A deep, lacerating consciousness of sin.[16]
(2) A realization of sin as a personal matter.
(3) A thought of sin as an element of alienation from God.

2. In the environment of the teaching and traditions of his religious upbringing he does not overlook primal taint,[17] and maya,[18] and the merit and demerit of action.[19] The impact of these forces on his being, he owns, brings about appreciable results. There is no room in Saivite theology for the conception of a Satan, a tempter of souls, an inducer to sinning. His functions are performed by the mind. It is the mind (மனம்) that begets *maya*.[20] In memory and attachment a great deal of the power of sin consists.[21]

3. The soul's struggles with alien influences he finds very hard.[22] In his endeavours after holiness he is confronted with the

[1] *N.M.*, 1445 (= No. 315, below).
[2] *N.M.*, 1446 (= No. 316, below).
[3] *N.M.*, 1447 (= No. 317, below).
[4] *N.M.*, 194 (= No. 153, below). *N.M.*, 453.
[5] *N.M.*, 4, 63, 108.
[6] *N.M.*, 4, 235.
[7] *N.M.*, 26.
[8] *N.M.*, 27, 199, 200, 288, 302, 303.
[9] *N.M.*, 42, 183.
[10] *N.M.*, 51, 180, 201
[11] *N.M.*, 292, 301.
[12] *N.M.*, 52, 58.
[13] *N.M.*, 108.
[14] *N.M.*, 94, 403, 415, 424, 431.
[15] *N.M.*, 74, 75, 83, 434.
[16] On sin see below, part xi.
[17] See § 29.
[18] See below, Part v.
[19] See below, Part vi.
[20] *N.M.*, 349, 397. On mind, see below, Part v.
[21] *N.M.*, 447.
[22] *N.M.*, 45 46. 282 (= No 139, below).

great problems of the spiritual life, problems of practical and not speculative interest:

Why was I born?[1]
Why am I subject to sin?[2]
Why am I compassed about with fate and frailty?[3]
Is it just that I should be left alone?[4]
Is there no means of curbing my mind?[5]
How can I be saved, if desire is strong?[6]

He knows the strength of the lure of the flesh and longs foı freedom.[7] A life of sensuality will, he fears, be a hindrance tc the realization of salvation (from re-birth) in this life.[8] H· battles fiercely with the desires that war in his senses, and crie for succour.[9] He prays to God to call him

From all the ties of life, the bonds
Of births, bewilderments, to Thee,
Me, sinner, moving in their midst.[10]

He lays his spiritual burden upon a Power higher than and is content to ask:

I cast my cares on Thee, and trust
That thou wouldst take corruption's core,
My soul, with all its sins, and melt
Its stoniness, and more and more
By violence of grace, soften
It, and become its Refuge sur‹
Compassionate, till holy hands
Of prayer are mine, and tear-drops pure.[11]

4. A detailed study of all the poet's spiritual longings his psalms will show that they fall into two groups—thc before his one great experience, of which we shall have somethi to say presently, and those after that experience. These lon ings are scattered right through his psalms. We may brie refer to some belonging to the first group. The poet earnest prays for a device whereby the mind may be at rest;[12] for a ste

[1] No. 145, below.
[2] N.M., 67. See below, part v on ev
[3] N.M., 179.
[4] N.M., 305.
[5] No. 12, below.
[6] No. 215, below.
[7] N.M., 80, 112, 301
[8] N.M., 98.
[9] N.M., 306.
[10] No. 144, below.
[11] No. 151, below
[12] No. 12. below.

of mindless sanctity;[1] for God to govern him;[2] for the day when God will call him;[3] for his heart to be made impressionable as wax;[4] for freedom from earthly ties,[5] and for that stage of spiritual initiation in which the feet of God are on the suppliant's head.[6]

5. The one great experience of his spiritual life is that which is very clearly attested by the evidence of his hymns. His Guru's appearance, the communication of a mystic 'word' to him, and his 'surrender' to the Master—these constitute the most conspicuous elements of an experience the reality of which (whatever it was) we may not hastily disregard. Siva had appeared, the poet reminds us, to the Four in some past time and imparted to them the secret of 'Salvation.'[7] His own experience, he would perhaps suggest to the incredulous, is not without precedent. The Four had been told 'one word': the poet's own experience hinges on 'one word' spoken in secret by his Guru. 'He with one word with grace prevenient, made me his, and made me live by love.'[8] 'The one word alone spoken by the Silent One is truth.'[9] 'Hasten ye to the holy experience imparted by the one word.'[10]

One word, a wondrous word, there is
  Which in itself contains
All other words; by it is cleansed
  The soul of all its stains.
It is the word the Guru gave,
  One word, unmoving goal,
Fixed as a mountain-top is firm,
  Towards which moves the soul.
All other words beside it are
  As vain, devoid of aim,
As are the pawns at random moved,
  Moved in an aimless game.[11]

[1] *N.M.*, 13 [illegible] (No. 13, below). *N.M.* 100.

[2] *N.M.*, 42.

[3] *N.M.*, 44, 288.

[4] *N.M.*, 58.

[5] *N.M.*, 313.

[6] *N.M.*, 117, 598. See below, pp. 90, 211.

[7] No. 40, below, and *N.M.*, 120, 131, 132, 174, 182, 310, 420, 509. On the Four see below, p. 164.

[8] *N.M.*, 40 ஒரு [illegible]. On [illegible] at the very significant lines of *N.M.*, 762 (= No. 67 below).

[9] *N.M.*, 460.

[10] *N.M.*, 469.

[11] *N.M.*, 186.

The 'one word' is not a charm, a magical formula mechanically bestowing boons. It is something intelligently to be assimilated and 'lived.'

> The grace to give, the gain of godliness,
> Wisdom of heaven, and power above all speech,
> Nay, heaven itself, the soul's own home of joy,
> Behold, O mind, are all within thy reach
> Thro' that one word the Guru spake to me.
> Be still thereby, O mind of mine be still :
> Upon that word he of the Silence spake
> Rest thou serene, restrain the straying will.[1]

Perseverance in that 'one word' wins deliverance from the bondage of births and re-births.

> My body, being, spirit all I had,
> He asked of me, and I surrendered all
> To him, who made me then his willing slave ;
> By glad submission I became his thrall.
> One word he spoke what time I made to him
> Surrender of my all, and O my mind
> Thou shall not anymore the power have
> Me into bondage of re-births to bind,
> If only day by day upon that word
> I meditate and merge myself therein,
> Forget it never, nay, but persevere
> In it till birthlessness I win.[2]

The surrender spoken of in this hymn is referred to in many places as a definite, determinate act of the will.[3] Associated with 'the surrender' and the 'one word' is the injunction சும்மாவிரு, 'be still,' 'be apart,' 'be detached,' 'be in unruffled quiteness.' Of the acts of the Guru done to the poet one is that he 'bade him be still in a state of self-lessness.'[4] In greater detail the Guru's services are stated, including the imparting of the secret of the silence, in a hymn[5] I render as follows :—

[1] *N.M.*, 529. [2] *N.M.*, 530.

[3] *N.M.*, 117, 149, 195, 201, 362, 491, 530, 536, 588, 601. See below, pp. 38, 178.

[4] *N.M.*, 38 சிந்தையற நில்லென்று 'சும்மாவிருத்தி'.

[5] *N.M.* 116. The terseness of the original has had to be considerably paraphrased.

Refreshing grace is never far from Thee;
O Thou that as a saint [1] camest to me,
And by a mute and mystic sign [2]
Ineffable, unframed in human speech,
Broughtest the truth of heaven within my reach
Bestowing boon of bliss benign ; [3]
As all-where Dancer,[4] Lord, Thou lettest me
The primal sound [5] to hear, the symphony
Eternal that as sense is known,
And hearing have the fulness of the food
Ambrosial [6] of the blessed ones, the good ;
Thou unto me Thyself hast shown
As He that dances in the Hall of Gold ; [7]
So saying Thou hast kept me in Thy hold,
Thereafter bondman unto Thee ;
Thou camest yet again the sign to give
The goal whereunto I should, moving, live,
The mark Thou settest ritefully.[8]
What time Thou wert made manifest to me
Thine was the garb of God's own devotee,
Garb of a Guru of the line
Most noble,[9] when from blessing lips I heard
The blessing of the gift of one great word,
One saving word [10] from lips divine,
When Thou declaredst unto me the way
Of silence and the secret how to stay
In quiet and the calm of mind
In bliss of balanced stillness.[11] I, with these
Thy boons to me, shall I be swayed from peace
And me unto old bondage bind,
With cords of ignorance, unknowing Thee,
And reel in soul-ensnaring vanity ? [12]

Whatever there may be in the above statement of experiences which we are unable to understand, it is beyond all doubt that the poet would have us believe in the reality of one

[1] As a *Siva-Jnani* சிவஞானி.

[2] பேசரிய வாசியாலே, 'Sign ineffable,' etc. See below, pp. 203, 221.

[3] பேரின்ப வுண்மையை யளித்தீர்.

[4] பேரம்பலக் கடவுளாய்.

[5] On நாதம் see below, p. 149.

[6] See below, p. 173.

[7] திருவம்பலமுமாகி. See below, pp. 174, 204.

[8] செறியக் குறித்தளித்தீர். The word குறி is rendered here, 'sign', 'goal', map'.

[9] சன்மார்க்கநெறிசெல் சற்குருக் கோலமாய்.

[10] அசபா நலம்.

[11] மௌனியாய்ச் சும்மாவிருக்க நெறிகாட்டினீர் is freely explained.

[12] எனவிருக்க . . . மயக்கி மிகவறிவின்மை பாசமே is spread out into three lines and a third of the English.

great experience: the appearance of the Guru to the disciple, and the disciple's surrender. The stress seems to be laid on the surrender as the starting-point of new experiences. The surrender marks a new phase of spiritual existence. What followed the act of surrender?

> I gave myself, and lo, on giving.
> The gladness of my soul was great;
> Deep draughts of joy I drank to fulness,
> Deep draughts I drank, insatiate;
> Long years of life were for my gaining;
> And grace divine was ever near;
> Wisdom was mine, and life's renewal;
> From me had fled of births the fear.[1]

The candour, however, of the poet's confessions enables us to see how, after 'surrender'. he often experienced a lapse into a state of spiritual sterility. 'I have not remained firm in the state into which I had been initiated.'[2] 'Why has evil crept into my mind, deluding me, in spite of my surrender?'[3] 'As my Guru Thou hadst taught me the grace of being still,[4] and shown me the mystic sign, but, in spite of all that, I have strayed, following the decrees of my mind.'[5] 'My Guru taught me be still, but I have wandered far into the forest of delusion.'[6] 'My evil deeds assail me who had surrendered my all.'[7] 'The old longings are tormentful, and I am stormed by them.'[8] He complains that the past persists, his pre-surrender past, and he longs for effectual deliverance. It is to this period of strife and struggle that we must assign those many longings (for what he had once tasted) which we find scattered here and there—the burden of all which pathetic cries is, 'Show me the way to win deliverance.'[9] He prays to be made 'heir of Grace'[10] to be restored to 'the bliss of holy silence,'[11] for cessation of sorrow,[12]

[1] *N.M.*, 500. The English considerably amplifies the very terse original.
[2] *N.M.*, 123. [3] *N.M.*, 321. [4] சும்மா.
[5] *N.M.*, 353. [6] *N.M.*, 436. [7] *N.M.*, 440.
[8] No. 154, below. See note at p. 194, on the analogy employed by the Siddhanta theologians to explain the adhesion of some amount of evil to even 'saved' souls.
[9] No. 42, below. [10] No. 43, below
[11] No. 106, below. [12] *N.M.*, 107.

to cross the sea of births,[1] to be freed from darkness,[2] and to be in union with the Divine.[3] The healthy discontent of the poet, coupled with the recollection of God 'at all times,'[4] was an abiding incentive to reach loftier heights of spirituality. God, he believed, had kindled love in him, and he would not be satisfied with anything less than the fulness of the fruition of such love. His yearnings are for the knowing of God by the way of love ·

> O grant me for my inmost gladdening
>   The flood of Love at Love's full-tide,
> Thy Bliss with all my being blending,
>   Bliss-giver! in my soul abide.[5]

This is the mystic's prayer, breathing soul-passion for God.

6. A very remarkable fact in connection with the poet's religious experience is that he would have no postponement of what he considered the highest realization of religion to a future life. '*In the body, in this life,*'[6] here and now, he would know the fulness of God. Did he claim to know it in his lifetime? To his after-years of matured spirituality we must assign that hymn[7] in which he recalls the stress and struggle he had undergone, his lapses, and then gathers strength:

> What time the goodly way of stillness,
>   O Lord, Thou taughtest me,
> I gave[8] my body,[9] goods and being,
>   Surrendering all to Thee,
> What were but Thine.[10] But why thereafter
>   Didst Thou permit[11] the rise,
> Within my senses, of Delusion
>   Which, with assertive cries
> Of lordship, danced in me wild dances
>   Of self-will,[12] till I wailed,

[1] No. 132, below. [2] *N.M.*, 319. [3] *N.M.*, 361.

[4] See below, pp. 145–47. [5] No. 105, below.

[6] See below, *Introduction*, part vi, also p. 115 and *N.M.*, 111, 126, 259, 297.

[7] *N.M.*, 556. [8] In 'surrender' to the Guru.

[9] Literally 'the body which I had assumed,' எடுத்த தேகம்.

[10] [illegible]. The soul has no சுதந்தரம் (inheritance) of its own.

[11] God permits, the Hindu divines say. See below, *Introduction*, part v, and pp. 143–48.

[12] [illegible]

And wept hot tears of supplication,
  The while my spirit failed
With fear ? And how that fear most dreaded
  Thou dravest from my side ?
And how the flood of my attachments
  Didst stay, and stem its tide ?
Say Tāyumānavā whose glories shine,
  O gracious God, on Siragiri's shrine.

These questions addressed to Tāyumānēsurar[1] would seem to suggest that the poet had gained considerable vigour in spirituality, had fallen oft and risen, since his 'surrender', and had reached a stage in which the flood-tide of Desire and attachments had been held back and kept powerless. To the period of such maturity belong those joyous utterances of lofty realization :

What time Thy fulness Lord abounded,
  The bonds I broke of birth and change,
Sense-knowing ceased, and light, and darkness,
  And, beyond all pleasure's range,
And pain's, knew nothing, me not seeing. [2]

And again the triumphant verse :

The seas are troubled in confusion,
  The birth-begetting good and ill ;
The waters roll away affrighted,
  The storms have ceased and all is still.[3]

The *Revel in Bliss*[4] may be placed in the same period of ripe experience. Whatever meaning we may choose to give to the poet's reasoned impressions of the great things of the soul's commerce with God, we notice that it was by the way of 'Grace', and by the path of Love, and not by means of the unsatisfying requirements of institutional religion, that he reached the contentment his writings record. Contentment ? No, he was for ever longing[5] for light, more light ; for union, for peace, and for rest. *He had not found these 'in this life'*.

[1] See above, p. xl.
[2] No. 272, below.
[3] No. 130, below.
[4] See below, p. 100.
[5] See below, pp. 117-21 for some of his longings.

§ 21. Without in any degree derogating from the sincere admiration, hitherto expressed and hereinafter adhered to, for Tāyumānavar's passionate devotion to God, his lofty spiritual excellence, and his sainthood, I desire to record my conviction that, if the poet-saint did not in his day know the Lord Jesus Christ, he fell short of knowing the uttermost reach of the love of God, love that expressed itself in the sacrifice of dying.[1] In this respect he that is least in the Kingdom of Heaven is greater than our poet-saint. This, on the assumption that the poet did not know, or know of, the Lord Jesus Christ. Is it a right assumption? The history of his times affords material for formulating the probability of his having heard of Christianity. While data are not abundant for the formation of a definite opinion as to the extent of Christian missionary enterprise in the places associated with Tāyumānavar, it must be allowed that there was an appreciable amount of Christian propaganda work in Dravidian India in the days of the poet. The period A.D. 1542-1562 covers the activities of S. Francis Xavier in the Malabar coast and the southern district of Madras. In 1606 Jesuits began work in Madura under Robert de Nobili, who died in 1656; and Madura, the very heart of literary Tamilagam, witnessed in 1693 the martyrdom of a Christian missionary, John de Brito. After the establishment in Tranquebar in 1705 of a Lutheran Mission, the religious and literary labours of the great Italian Jesuit and Tamil scholar, Constantine de Beschi, known in Tamil as Viramāmunivar, began. He died in 1742. Forty years before Xavier's time Franciscan missionaries had begun work in Portuguese India.[2] The study of Tamil and of Tamil literature by Christians must have begun very early, earlier than 1661 the year of the publication of a Tamil New Testament, and we may conjecture that there must have been pamphlets and tracts which were precursors of the *Church History* (in Tamil) of 1736.[3] Before 1500 Christianity had

[1] See below, on this subject, *Introduction*, Part vii.

[2] *The Imperial Gazetteer of India*, i, pp. 441, 442. In 1526 Portuguese missionaries were at work in Mangalore (*Imperial Gazetteer*, xiv, 360).

[3] Hough's *Christianity in India*, iii, pp. 87, 175, 247. The writer is not always accurate in his statements, especially as to non-Christian tenets.

been alive in India, for the sixth Christian century saw the Nestorian Missionaries at work in India.[1] We must concede some degree of historicity to the virile tradition, alive to this day in the topography of South Indian Christian Missions, of the preaching of Christianity in India by S. Thomas the Apostle. The tradition is as old at least as the third century.[2] A slab discovered in the eighth century on S. Thomè Mount seems to confirm the traditional belief that S. Thomas was martyred in the neighbourhood in A.D. 68.[3] King Guduphara, to whose court S. Thomas is said to have gone,[4] reigned in India between A.D. 20 and A.D. 46. The other king, with whom tradition associates the Apostle, was Vāsudeva, a contemporary of Guduphara. If the death of S. Thomas falls in the reign of these two kings it was in all probability earlier than A.D. 68.[4] 'There is an actual basis for the tradition in historic reality, and that S. Thomas proceeded to the East and visited the courts of two kings there, of whom one was the Guduphara, Gondophernes of the Takht-i-Bahi inscription and the coins, and the other was very possibly Vāsudeva of Mathura'.[5]

There are thus reasons for asserting the existence of Christianity in India, if not indeed from A.D. 20 (and I see no reason why not) at least from the sixth century. There is, further, a very high degree of probability in favour of the view that Christianity had been known and heard of in the district in which Tāyumānavar lived. If the statement of some writers[6] that the poet died in A.D. 1742, the same year as Beschi,[7] be correct, then, it may be presumed that the poet was not unaware of the Christian activities of the Jesuit Mission in Madura, and

[1] Hough, *op. cit.*, i. 73, 86.

[2] Vincent A. Smith, *The Oxford History of India* (1920), p. 126. *Imperial Gazetteer of India*, ii, p. 288.

[3] *The Imperial Gazetteer of India*, xxi, p. 388.

[4] See *J.R.A.S.*, 1905, p. 234. See *J.R.A.S.*, Oct. 1924, p. 213.

[5] J. Fleet in *J.R.A.S.*, 1905, p. 236. See *J.R.A.S.*, 1905, p. 223; *J.R.A.S.*, 1906, p. 706, and *Imperial Gazetteer*, ii, p. 5, for discussions of the Thomian tradition. For *A Tamil Account of S. Thomas and Kandappa Raja from the Latin* by Father H. Hosten, S.J., see *The Indian Athenæum*, July 1923, p. 8.

[6] See above § 16 and Subrahmanyam's *S. Tāyumānavar*, p. 8.

[7] Dr. Grierson in *Imperial Gazetteer*, ii, p. 436. He refers to Tāyumānavar as the author of 1453 pantheistic stanzas.

probably he had knowledge of some of the fundamentals of the foreign faith. The Madura Mission opened in A.D. 1606 at Madura where, some years before, the Franciscans had worked. The Chief of the Madura Mission was Robert de Nobili, a near relation of Pope Marcellus II., and the nephew of Cardinal Bellarmine, the great Roman theologian. Into the town where Tāyumānavar lived and its neighbourhood rumours, if not more certain knowledge, must have penetrated of the doings and sayings of the members of the Madura Mission, particularly of their 'brahmanizing' themselves in garb, customs, observances and language; of their knowledge of classical Tamil; of their Tamil discourses; of their controversies with the Brahmins; and of the popularity of the *Inyāna Upadēsam* of de Nobili; and, above all, of the astounding 'discovery' of the manuscript of a Fifth Veda![1] For nearly half a century Nobili carried on his work. Knowledge of the literary skill, Tamil scholarship and missionary zeal of Constantine de Beschi, another well-known Jesuit 'Brahmin', author of *Tembāvanai* and other works in scholarly Tamil, must have been widespread in the days of Tāyumānavar.[2] In the history[3] of the Danish Mission at Tranquebar from A.D. 1706 the year A.D. 1708 is one of great importance, for it was in that year that the first attempt to introduce Christianity into Tanjore was made, and we have the memorable fact, most relevant to our inquiry and leading us to very sure ground, that on March 5, 1708, the Danish missionary, Ziegenbalg, had a conference, on matters of religion, *with the Brahmins of 'Dirukuddeur, a town in the kingdom of Tanjore'*.[4] If the town is not the Saiva Tirukkadavūr, it certainly was the Tanjore town of Tirumaraikkādu, more famous

[1] An account of the Madura Mission appears in Hough's *Christianity in India*, ii, Bk. v, c. 3. The pseudo-Veda was known to Voltaire in 1761. He had been led to believe it to be an authentic work, a commentary on the Vedas 'by the Chief Brahmin of the Pagoda of Cherengham'. It was published in 1778 at Paris as *L'ezour-Vêdam*. The forgery was not detected till some years later.

[2] On the assumption that he died in A.D. 1742.

[3] Hough's *Christianity in India*, iii, Bk. vii, c. 3 is devoted to this Mission.

[4] Hough, *op. cit.*, iii, p. 138.

as Vedaranyam, the native place of the poet. In either case a strong presumption in favour of Tāyumānavar's knowledge of Christianity is raised.

§ 22. While it may reasonably be suggested, from the above considerations, that Tāyumānavar had knowledge of Christianity, such knowledge as a man of his wide culture could have had of contemporary religious thought and movements, we are confronted with the problem of the poet's attitude towards the religion of Christ. The poet had no reason to condemn Christianity as an 'alien faith' because it was not one of the eighteen religious systems put on the Siddhanta Index Expurgatorius.[1] If not hostile, was his attitude friendly ? In the eyes of thoes who take his *samarasam* [2] to mean a pose of indifference, framing itself in terms of glib, innocuous, eclectic elasticity one is familiar with in modern times among people who, with the minimum of mental effort, lay claim to the maximum of conclusiveness, Tāyumānavar patted the Nazareth creed patronisingly on the back and let it live—that was the furthest reach of his friendliness to the Gospel of Jesus Christ. I do not see as they. In my view the contact of the robust, unanaemic, Siddhanta faith with the fundamentals of Christianity, in times prior to the poet's, or in his own, would have resulted in the annihilation or assimilation of the latter. Now, *the* outstanding fundamental of the Christian faith is the teaching that God had become incarnate as Jesus Christ, and with it is the teaching of His having become the Guru of souls, of His dying for the salvation of souls, and of His rising from the dead as the great Life-giver of believers. The man-becoming of God as the Guru of souls is a great Siddhanta fundamental. ***Did the Siddhanta theologians before the days of Tāyumānavar assimilate Christian teaching and he, after them, accept it in the matter of the God-Guru idea ?*** An affirmative answer is rendered plausible by reason of the entire absence of any trace of a doctrine of the man-becoming of God in pre-Saivite literature. Such an answer, however, involves the assumption that the God-man idea in the *Gita* is due to

[1] See above, § 14. [2] See above, § 13.

influences purely Saivite.[1] The affirmative answer need not necessarily be weakened into a negative by the fact that the divines of the Siddhanta, if they had been aware of Christian teaching, did not incorporate into their tenets the conception of a dying God or of a God victorious in an act of resurrection from the dead. The explanation of their silence lies in the circumstance that it was hard for them, even with the theological fiction of a 'conditioned Brahma,'[2] to think of subjecting Deity to the limitation of mortality, because of their inherent prepossessions in favour of the obsession of karma-transmigration. The Siddhanta revolt[3] from the doctrine of re-birth under cover of 'the grace of God' did not seem to make the dread of karma-transmigration the less oppressively real. Therefore, a doctrine of expiatory Atonement seemed to them not only irrelevant but unnecessary. The Cross, as ever to others, was to them a stumbling-block. They clung to their prepossessions. Prepossessions die hard, and, Christian prepossessions being no exception, my own leanings are in favour

[1] See present writer's *Foregleams of God*, p. 220. Cf. Max Müller, *S.B.E.*, i, p. 52. The idea of a Teaching God, fully discussed by Robertson in his *Pagan Christs*, part ii, c. 2, does not afford any parallel to the Siddhanta conception of 'God become man to be man's Guru,' and still less is there any similarity between Robertson's 'Teaching God' and the Christian 'God made Flesh.' On the God-man idea of the *Gita* reference may be made to Dr. G. A. Grierson's article on Bakti-Marga in *E.R.E.*, ii, 548, where, in the course of an account of the extent of the probability of Christian influence on the thought of the *Gita*, quoting Hopkins's *India Old and New*, p. 167, the learned writer expresses himself inclined to the belief that some accessories of the Krishna cult had been taken over from the Christ cult. The ascription of Deity to Krishna is traced to the sixth Christian century. At p. 550 it is observed, 'It is possible, and perhaps probable, that the worship of the infant Krishna was a local adaptation of the worship of the infant Christ introduced into India from the north-west. ... *But it was in Southern India that Christianity, as a doctrine, exercised the greatest influence on Hinduism generally.*' Sir G. R. G. Bhandarkar (*Vaisnavism and Saivism*, pp. 36–38) thinks that the Ābhīras brought with them into India in the first Christian century the name 'Christ' and the birth-stories and the story of the massacre of the innocents and identified the cow-herd with Krishna-Vasudeva and Christ-stories became Krishna-stories. The learned orientalist concludes (p. 38), that the identification of Vasudeva-Krishna with Gopala-Krishna cannot be considered to belong to a pre-Christian period.

[2] See *Foregleams of God*, cp. viii. §§ 9–13.

[3] See below, p. 167 and *Introduction*, part vii.

of the obligation of the Siddhanta to Christian teaching; yet, I should be doing the literary sense serious wrong to let my bias sway my judgment. In the absence of decisive evidence a verdict of 'not proven' is the best to be entered. Either answer, affirmative or negative, to the question framed above, has much to be said for it; the negative will develop more doubts than the affirmative could dispel.

PART IV.—GOD

§ 23. The conception of God in many of the psalms of Tāyumānavar is inseparable from associations of Puranic mythology. The environment in which Deity is set in traditional Hindu beliefs is, with reference to the poet's attitude towards it, either fact or fiction. If fiction, then the poet is either employing legendary attributes and descriptions with allegoric meanings or, what is more probable, his acceptance of such mythic details is a mere concession to popular religious fancy. The statement, for instance, that Siva burnt the cities of the enemy,[1] refers to the *Yajur Veda*[2] story of Rudra burning the three fortresses of the Asuras. Long before Tāyumānavar an allegorical meaning had been given this incident by Tirumūlar[3] who says, 'Fools say that the Lord burnt the three cities: the three cities stand for the product of the three mala (மும்மலம்).' Tāyumānavar, being familiar with the ***Tirumantram***, must be presumed to be aware of this interpretation of the three cities story. In so far as this story is concerned, we have Tirumūlar's high authority for its being a fable, literally understood by the ignorant but full of hidden meanings to men of spiritual understanding. Tirumūlar may then be involved in establishing a precedent for disbelief of the historicity of other Siva stories. True he allegorizes,[4] but first he disbelieves and even rebukes belief. Tirumūlar, among the ancients, does not in this manner of thought stand alone. The

[1] *N.M.*, 455 அடையார் புரஞ்செற்றதேவே. [2] c. 2, 3, 12.

[3] *Tirumantram*, Stanza 343. See a full defence of the allegorizing of myths in Nallaswamy Pillai, *Siddhiyar*, pp. 145-54.

[4] On the tendency to allegorize see *Foregleams of God*, p. 359.

learned author of the *Siddhiyar* would not have it taken as a fact that Siva had an eye midway between the eye-brows. The myth of the mid-set eye is an allegory, he teaches.[1] Tāyumānavar, who knew his *Siddhiyar* well, must be presumed to have had the allegorical implications of the fable of the third eye in all the passages in which he addresses Siva as 'the Lord of the mid-set eye.'[2] We may take it to be the tendency of modernists among Hindus to discard as fables all the stories that cluster round Siva and constitute descriptions of him. Such are the following out of those used by Tāyumānavar:

1. Siva killed the God of death and burnt to death the body of the god of love.[3]
2. His throat is dark with poison he had swallowed.[4]
3. He is 'the wearer of white ashes'.[5]
4. He wears the Ganges and the moon in his matted hair,[6] and a snake[7]
5. He is red and eight-armed.[8]
6. He rides a white bull.[9]
7. He is an ascetic with a deer-skin.[10]
8. He is the husband of Uma, the maid of the mountains.[11]

While, by the descriptions of Siva, he is identifiable with Siva of the Puranic Triad, (திருமூர்த்தி *Tirumūrti*), our poet is at considerable pains to make Him, whom he calls Ṣiva, not only superior to Brahma and Vishnu, *but Supreme God.* This is a matter of importance to remember: it reveals the poet's mind in his conception of God. He concedes much to the popular cult in appropriating the attributes of *Siva* for 'God,' but no one can lose sight of his deliberately placing 'God' in a position of

[1] *Siddhiyar*, 3, 1, 52. See below, p. 180.

[2] For instance in Nos. 107, 144, 146, 184, 206–210, 282, below.

[3] *N.M.*, 502. On Yaman see below, pp. 72, 175, 192, and on god of love, see p. 225. In *Tirumantram*, st. 1, the kicking of Yaman is mentioned, and the author who allegorizes the three cities episode cannot be held to accept the Yaman story. See *Siddhanta Deepika*, i, p. 74.

[4] *N.M.*, 578 and below, No. 44 and p. 151.

[5] No. 144, below, and p. 192.

[6] *N.M.*, 168 describes Siva fully. See below, No. 185, and p. 198, *N.M.*, 487.

[7] No. 184, below. *N.M.*, 504.

[8] No. 146, below, and p. 193.

[9] No. 202, below. *N.M.*, 298. This, says Pattanattār, means 'Goodness'.

[10] *N.M.*, 298.

[11] No. 200 and p. 201, below.

utter supremeness over Siva of the Triad. Tayumānavar's Siva is not the Siva of the mythologies. We not only witness the disintegration of the Triad but are led up to the conception of the Sole Supreme who survives all change. In the section entitled ***Tēnmugam*** (தென்முகம்) the poet deals with the subject of supremacy. Of the Triad there is one, he says, who creates, another who preserves, and 'the Lord of the three eyes' who destroys: which of these is the Supreme God?[1] The answer is implied in the question raised in the following verse: Who survives the wreck of the universe and its dissolution?[2] The survivor is described in terms of Puranic fables as the ash-daubed ascetic, wearer of matted locks in which flows the Ganges, he of the mid-set eye, and it is also added that on earth he is openly seen as the Dancer in heart-temples.[3] If Brahma and Vishnu, the poet continues, have to be born often to perform their functions they cannot be God.[4] He elsewhere speaks of the inferiority of Brahma and Vishnu.[5] In all this the poet is following earlier thought.[6] Going a step further with the poet we notice the supremacy asserted of 'The three-eyed one, doer of the three deeds [creation, preservation and destruction], *the first of the Three*.'[7] The functions of the Triad are attributed to 'the three-eyed.' Indeed, he *transcends the Triad*,[8] that is, is *above Brahma*, *Vishnu*, *Siva*, and consequently cannot be Siva of the Triad. Tāyumānavar, in breaking away from the trammels of tradition, is acting according to Siddhanta orthodoxy. Tirumūlar expressly says, 'He is prior to the Three, He is the Highest Being, having none equal to Him . . . He is the golden lotus in the heart'.[9] Again, 'Without Him there can be no devas, . . . and nothing is possible even to the Triad.'[10] The high authority of the ***Siddhiyar*** is equally explicit. 'They call Him one of the devas, but they know that Siva is all the three gods. The gods,

[1] *N.M.*, 166.
[2] *N.M.*, 167.
[3] *N.M.*, 168, 169.
[4] *N.M.*, 170.
[5] No. 225, below, *N.M.* 402 refers to Vishnu's inferiority.
[6] *Tirumantram*, Stanzas 13, 14, 15.
[7] *N.M.*, 490 முக்கண் சுகன் முத்தொழிலர் மும்முதல்வர்.
[8] *N.M.*, 182. translated above at p. xxviii. See No. 44, at p. 27.
[9] *Tirumantram*, st. 7.
[10] *Ibid.*, 6.

Brahma and the rest are manifestations of Hara '.[1] Therefore Tāyumānavar says that One only is supreme, even over destiny,[2] and the grace of One only can give salvation when the very Triad itself has impotently passed into dissolution.[3] Thus in a process of progressive elimination we have the following results presented to us :

1. Siva is invested with Puranic and pre-Puranic attributes
2. Siva is superior to Brahma and Vishnu of the Triad.
3. Siva is greater than Siva, Brahma, Vishnu.
4. Siva is all three and more,
5. Siva, who is not Siva of the Triad, is the supremest One

§ 24. Are there two Sivas? Some scholars suppose that a Siva of the Himalayas and a Siva of South India have been, and are, worshipped, *as one and the same person.*[4] A reader of the passages noted, from Tāyumānavar, in the above section will see that there is room to suppose a fusion of ideas. While the poet expressly distinguishes Siva from the whole Triad, he yet does not divest Siva of the Himalayan attributes and the legendary descriptions. Sir R. G. Bhandarkar[5] traces the conception of Rudra-Siva to the evolution of the idea of a god of wrath appeased into the benignant (*Siva*) one. He finds in the ***Satrudriya*** accounts of Rudra, as the mountain-dweller, ruddy and blue-throated, with matted hair, and wearing a skin, the description of Siva of later times, and the very names Sankara, Sambhu, Siva[6] of Hindu devotional use are first found in that book. 'The terrible and destructive God became', thinks Sir R. G. Bhandarkar, 'when he was propitiated by men in a variety of ways, a benignant God and attained to the whole majesty of the godhead by the time of the ***Yajur Veda*** and the ***Atharva Veda***, and it is on this majestic form of the God that the theosophic speculations of the ***Svetasvatara*** Upanishad are based'.[7] He concludes that *fear* is responsible for Rudra-

[1] *Siddhiyar*, 3. 1, 49, 60. Each God of the Triad has his own *limited* sphere of action.

[2] No. 106, below.

[3] *N.M.*, 59. The One is the *Parabrahmam*, the sole supreme

[4] Dr. Grierson, for instance, in *J.R.A.S.*, 1913, p. 173. See other references in *Foregleams of God*, pp. 110–12.

[5] *V.S.*, pp. 102–10. [6] See below, p 163. [7] *V.S.*, 105.

Siva's exaltation into supremacy. 'In the monotheistic religion of other countries the same God is feared and loved; in India the God that is loved is Viṣṇu-Nārāyana-Vasudeva-Kṛṣṇa, while the God that is feared is Rudra-Siva'.[1] While it is undeniable that, according to Siddhanta scholars,[2] Rudra is equated with Siva and the one identified with the other, I have not been able to see in Tāyumānavar any prayer to Siva as an object of terror which needed appeasing: on the contrary such appellations as 'father', 'mother', 'brother', 'kinsman', 'friend', 'beloved', suggest tenderness and love rather than fear. Dr. Bhandarkar, however, in dealing with the Siva of the *Svetasvatara*, is not oblivious to the gentle side of Saivism, though he writes,[3] perhaps with leanings towards Vaishnavism

> The Svetasvatara-Upaniṣad . . . stands at the door of the Bhakti school, and pours its loving adoration on Rudra-Siva instead of on Vasudeva Kṛṣṇa, as the *Bh. Gita* did in later times when the doctrine was in full swing. Vasudeva-Kṛṣṇa had a historic basis; and the circumstances which led to his being invested with the supreme godhead occurred in later times, while in the age in which the Svetasvatara-Upaniṣad was composed, Rudra-Siva was alone in the field as the supreme god, and the germs of *bhakti*, or love, which manifested themselves at the time, were directed towards him; but when Vasudeva-Kṛṣṇa also came into the field, he appealed more to the hearts of men as the god who had come to dwell[4] amongst them; consequently the germs of *bhakti* speedily developed and he became the object of the heightened feelings in preference to the other.

Instead, perhaps, of postulating two Sivas fused into one, it is preferable to think that 'the attributes of the Dravidian deity Siva were found to be most in conformity with those of the Vedic god Rudra . . . and the conception then grew of a half-Dravidian, half-Aryan deity . . . who became the Supreme Deity, Siva, of the great mass of the Dravidian people'.[5] In the

[1] *V.S.*, 106. But on the terrific aspects of Krishna, see *Gita*, xi. 25–30, 49

[2] Nalla. *Studies*, pp. 88, 133, 178, 285 and his *Siddhiyar*, pp. 143, 144.

[3] *V.S.*, 110, 111.

[4] Was it before or after the time of which it is written: 'The word became flesh and dwelt among us, full of grace and truth' (S. John i. 14) that the germs of *bhakti* speedily developed, and he became the object of the heightened feelings in preference to the other?

[5] R. G. Frazer, in *E.R.E.*, v. 22. See same writer's *Saivism* in *E.R.E.*, xi. 19.

alternative it may be surmised, from the fact of pre-Aryan Dravidian occupation of India[1] that Siva, for whom Vedic attributes were gradually found, had always been a Dravidian deity, one only, without a second, Siva.[2]

§ 25. Tāyumānavar, we have seen, accepts the limitations sought to be imposed upon Deity in the sphere of manifestation, by myths and legends. Manifestation itself is a limitation. He accepts one such limitation, and that is in the sphere of his own experience: the man-becoming of God as Guru.[3] We shall presently see that he breaks away from all other conditioning ideas and argues himself out of the environment of legends into a sober comprehension of the One Reality. We cannot do justice to Tāyumānavar's psalms if we do not see in them a three-fold presenting, not so much of Deity as of ***ideas of Deity***. There is first the conception of God in popular form, that is, God of the myths and fables. Next is the conception of God as manifested especially in the experience of souls. Thirdly, there is room in his hymns for a presenting of ideas of Deity in terms of the Abstruse. The demands of the popular and the philosophical sides of the religion of his day seem to claim the poet's attention.

The transcendence of God is conceded in the hymns. Deity is not to be localised :

> Place has no power to prison His presence ;
> No one can say ' He is here ', ' He is there.'
> Not in this place, nor in that, is the Godhead,
> Unbounded by places bides everywhere.[4]

[1] See above, p. xvi.

[2] In addition to references already given on the subject of this section, and on Siva generally, may be mentioned: Pope's *Tiruvachagam*, p. 152 ; Father Gnānapragāsar's somewhat controversial *Philosophical Saivism*, ch. x ; Kingsbury and Phillips's *Hymns of the Tamil Saints*, pp. 3-8 ; *Siddhanta Deepika*, i. pp. 9, 121, 127 (Ramasamy Iyer's and Shanmuga Mudaliar's comments) ; T. A. Gopinatha Rao's *Hindu Iconography*, vol. ii, part i, pp. 39-43. [The learned author, at p. 41 equates Agni with Rudra and understands *Tryambaka* to mean 'Three-mothered'. For another meaning see my *Foregleams of God*, p. 110 note] ; *J.R.A.S.* [O.S.] v. 81, ix. [N.S.] 211, xiii. [N.S.] 404 xiv. [N.S.] 294 ; and authorities cited in *Foregleams of God*, pp. 111, 112, note. Slater's *Dravidian Element in Indian Culture*, 103.

[3] See below, part vii.

[4] See p. 4, below.

This may not altogether mean transcendence, 'the aloofness of God.'[1] We see it more, however, in another hymn where ideas of transcendence lead the thinker straight on and inevitably to immanence:

> Thy home thou choosest
> Within the hearts of saints on earth.[2]

It is well to remember that Tāyumānavar seldom keeps the thought of immanence apart from transcendence. Immanence is postulated of the transcendent Deity. If we understand the poet to combine in his conception of God immanence with transcendence, then we are certain he has no pantheistic ideas. Since, again, he does not state his belief in a merely transcendent God, he is not a deist.[3] The word *turiya*[4] denotes transcendence, and God, in the Siddhanta, is துரியம் (*turiyam*) and சதுர்த்தம் (*saturtam*) 'the Fourth.'[5] In the following lines our poet speaks of the transcendence of God more than of immanence:—

> O Space unthinkable,
> Say, dost thou know, that all-where outspread art,
> The Vision that is seen
> Beyond thine utmost end, thy furthest part?
>
> O Earth, say, dost thou know,
> What Glory shines where end thy bounds, and where
> The serpent wise thy weight
> Upholds? Can even he the truth declare?
>
> O Word revealed, that art
> To one and all the truth, for unto thee
> Faith turns, O first of books,
> Canst thou thine End and Goal make known to me?
>
> O thou that ragest loud,
> With wave-girt arms outheld, O speechless sea,
> Who let thee circling lie
> Around the earth, thy vastness shoreless be?

[1] See article *Immanence* in *E.R.E.*, v. 167. [2] No. 110, below.

[3] See Illingworth, *Divine Immanence*, ch. iii, 'The logical opposite of pantheism is deism, in the sense of belief in a merely transcendent God.' On pantheism as the opposite of atheism see C. E. Plumptre's *History of Pantheism*, ii, 7.

[4] See below, p. 154.

[5] See this subject treated fully and ably by the late Mr. J. M. Nallad-waray Pillai in his *Studies in the Saiva Siddhanta*, pp. 88-91.

Ye birds that beauteous are
In bosky woodland groves ; ye long-winged bees
That seek the lotus bloom ;
Ye errand-going swans of love and peace ;
Tell me, I ask, have ye at any time had speech
With Him, the great and Perfect One, beyond all reach ? [1]

In the formula எல்லாமாய் அல்லவுமாய், 'as all, yet not all' [2] we have the immanent-transcendent conception of God in the poet's psalms. The intense manner of his statements of immanence has misled many to make him a pantheist. 'So long as transcendence is recognized, the most emphatic assertion of immanence is not pantheism but panentheism—not the doctrine that all is God, but the doctrine that all is *in* God, who is also above all.' [3] In such ideas as 'life of life', 'blending, unblended' and in the analogies of vowels and consonants, oil in seed, butter in cream, fragrance in the flower, [4] we see immanence postulated. The thought of God as indweller [5] diminishes the distance which the idea of transcendence suggests between God and man. The 'Guru' conception of God is the furthest reach of the idea of Divine immanence in any non-Christian faith. The Christian reader, however, misses in Tāyumānavar the thought of 'redemptive immanence' and its allied idea of 'atonement'.

§ 26. Against Siva of the fables and allegories being the poet's real idea of manifested Deity we have the corrective, or perhaps balancing, conception not only of God as Guru but also as ***Sivam***. [6] The equation of Siva and the Guru-sannyasi is

[1] *N.M.*, 158,159. The words in the last English line after 'but' represent the Tamil பெரிய பரிபூரணம் பொருள்.

[2] See below, p. 161.

[3] Nicholson, *The Idea of Personality in Sufism*, p. 27.

[4] See below, p. 155.

[5] See below, p. 156. See No. 45, at p. 27.

[6] On *Sivam* see Nalla. *Studies*, pp. 133, 134, cf. *Māndukya*, 7, 'Sivam, tranquil, the second-less they think is the Fourth' [*Sivam sāntam advāitam chaturtam manyante*]. The word 'Sivam' is also translated as an adjective meaning 'benign'.

brought out in the *Tirumantram*[1] with which no doubt Tāyumānavar was familiar :

> Siva Sivajñāni is,
> Siva yōgi, guru He.
> ' Siva ' whoso calling, seeks
> Siva-guru's feet, will be
> Mighty powers of newness[2] given,
> Fruition and the goal of bliss,[3]
> Grace to break the bonds of births :
> Heaven the land of God is his.

In strictness of thought God has no name, yet fear and devotion have found many names for whatever man tries to know as Deity. God, according to our poet, is ' many-named in the books.'[4] He tells us[5] he remembers ' the three-eyed Guru ' in his prayer and praises by such names, as Sankara, Sambhu, Sadāsiva, Sarvāisa, Sadānanda, Bhagava, Nirguna, Nirāmaya, Nirānyana, Nirālamba, Nishkala, Nirvasana, Nirtonda, Nirvishaya, Kaivalya, Nitya, Sangala-Rahita, Tatpara, Asanya, Visvātīta, Vyōna, Pūrana. Each of these names denotes an attribute and description. Thus the words beginning with *Ni* signify the absence of certain qualities, e.g. *Nirguna* means ' void of *gunas*, properties,' *Nirāmaya* means ' free from infirmities ', and *Nishkala* means ' beyond description ineffable,' and *Nitya* means ' not subject to variation or change, eternally self-existent '. There are positive descriptions in *Sadāsiva*, meaning ' all-beneficent,' *Sadānanda*, meaning ' all-blissful,' and *Pūrana*, meaning ' all-pervader, the perfect,' and similar terms which have no negative prefix.[6] Even the name *Sivam* is an attributive word, meaning ' Love, Beneficence '.

[1] Stanza 1580. In 1581 are the words குருவே சிவம், ' The Guru is *Sivam* ', thus *Siva* being equated with *Sivam*, that is, Deity. On *Sivam* see *Siddhiyar*, 3. 1, 65, and Nalla. *Studies*, pp. 85–88.

[2] நவமான சித்தி.

[3] பர முத்தி.

[4] See below, p. 4. For an account of different names see Gopinatha Rao's *Hindu Iconography*, ii, part i, pp. 1–60.

[5] *N.M.*, 47. In *N.M.*, 3 there is a list of other attributes. In both places most of the words are Sanscrit. The eight principal names of Deity in Hindu thought are Bhava, Sarva, Īsāna, Pasupati, Rudra, Ugra, Bhima, Māhadēva To these should be added Īsa, Īsvara.

[6] On *Sankara*, *Sambhu*, see below, p. 163.

Of the many names, addresses and figures applied to God by Tāyumānavar may be noticed Cloud, Sky, Rain, Honey, Grace, Father, Mother, Light, Beloved, and Satchitānanda. Some of these are specially commented on below,[1] and two call for special note. The term 'Beloved' belongs to the sphere of exalted experience, and is of catholic application. Its use transcends party religion, and oversteps the bounds of sectarianism. When God is realized as the soul's Beloved a very lofty plane of spirituality is reached indeed, and he who so realizes God is indifferent to the cramping limitations of sectarian calls and denominational claims: he has scaled steep heights and reached the summit.[2] The word 'Beloved' is a term in the realm of experience and Divine immanence, and the name *Satchitānanda* places God, not indeed in the inaccessbilities of transcendence, but within reach of the possibility of understanding Him as the lofty One who inhabits eternity and yet is gracious to be manifest in man and indeed to dwell with the humble. It contains elements of immanence and transcendence. The second name is made up of three words *Sat, Chit, Ānanda*. Of these three parts ***Sat*** means 'seen, true, permanent' and hence 'the existent Being.'[3] The ***Upanishads*** use the word to mean 'Being'[4] and also to signify 'the actual, the real, the true'.[5] In ***Chit***, meaning 'Pure Intelligence', we have a strong idea of the transcendence of God. The ***Bodham*** equates ***Chit*** with ***Sivam***.[6] In the ***Upanishads*** we find *citta* in the sense of thought.[7] ***Ānanda*** is 'Bliss,' that is, self-contained Bliss. In the ***Taittiriya Upanishad***, referred to below at p. 224, the second section (valli) ends with the thought of the high spiritual state of him 'who knows the ***Bliss*** of Brahma'. The opening words of the section quote an older verse about the blessedness of him 'who knows Brahma as *satya*, ***jnana*** [=***chit*** or

[1] See below, p. 159 on Motherhood of God.
[2] See below, Introduction, part viii, Mysticism.
[3] See Nalla. *Siddhiyar*, p. 108.
[4] *Chand.* 6.2.1 ; *Mundaka*, 2.2.1 ; *Prasna*, 2.5 ; *Taitt.*, 2.7.
[5] *Taitt.*, 2.6 ; *Prasna*, 4.5 ; *Maitri*, 6.30.
[6] Sutra vi.
[7] *Chand.*, 7.5.1 ; *Kaushitaki*, 3.3 ; *Prasna*, 3.10 ; 4.8.

Intelligence] and [according to the revised text] *ananta* [=Infinite]'. Deussen's emendation of the last word into *Ānanda* gives more sense and fits in with the key-thought of the close of the section. Apart from this particular passage, the idea of God as *Ānanda*, 'Bliss', is well established. This name Sat-Chit-Ānanda, 'Being, Wisdom, Bliss' occurs in the combination சச்சிதானந்த சிவம் *Sat-Chit-Ānanda Sivam* in the concluding address of every hymn of the collection so headed.[1] God is addressed as *Sat-Chit-Ānanda Guru*,[2] the ideas of the unmanifested and manifested aspects of Deity being combined; as *Sat-Chit-Ānanda Vāḻvu*;[3] and simply as *Sat-Chit-Ānanda*.[4] It is God so transcendentally conceived as 'Being-Intelligence-Bliss' that is also thought of in immanent, personal and even intimate relationship. The medium of immanence in the Siddhanta is almost Rabbinic[5] in its exclusion of the idea of God becoming flesh, quite unlike the flesh being, as in Christianity, the vehicle of immanence in the greatest possible closeness of contact of the Divine with the Human in all that is implied in 'God with us,' *Immanuel*.[6]

§ 27. On Tāyumānavar's religious experience, his relationship to God as apprehended by him, see above, §§ 20–22.

PART V.—SOUL

§ 28. There is not in these psalms anything like the inquiries set afoot in the Upanishads[7] as to what the soul is.

[1] *N.M.*, 100–110. [2] *N.M.*, 279.

[3] *N.M.*, 296, வாழ்வு meaning 'being, existence' Same in *N.M.*, 570.

[4] *N.M.*, 415, 1306.

[5] See Abelson's *Immanence of God in Rabbinical Literature*, ch. xiii, and contrast that writer's views on the *Memra* with G. F. Moore's in *The Harvard Theol. Review*, January 1922, p. 41.

[6] S. Matt. i. 27; Isaiah vii. 14; viii. 8,10. 'God dwelling in us . . . one God in us' (Ignatius, *Ad. Ephes.* xv. 3).

[7] The soul is *ḥamsa* (spirit) in the Upanishads, e.g. *Svet.*, 1.6, 3.8, *Brihad.*, 4.3.11. It is *ātman*, ஆன்மா, ஆத்துமா in Tamil, and is immortal, imperishable, infinite, universal (*Svet.*, 1.9, 1.10). It is compared to a wheel, river with five streams, a torrent with five whirlpools (*Svet.*, 1.4, 1.5). In its relation to bodily attachment the soul is called *bhūtātman*, 'elemental soul' (*Maitri*, 3.2).

The soul, பசு (*pasu*) is practically the sum total of human personality, the 'self'. When Tāyumānavar speaks of himself he speaks of his soul, for instance, in the proposition என்று நீ யன்று நான் (literally, 'As long as Thou hast been so long have I also been'), rendered below, with its contextual words,

> Yet this I know
> That ne'er from Thee have I been parted,
> For lo! Thou livest: even so
> My soul lives ever.[1]

In these words the Siddhanta doctrine of the eternity of souls, their co-eval existence with Deity, is stated. In the same way 'we' means 'our *souls*' in என்றுளை நீ யன்றுளம் யாம் freely rendered:

> We live O Lord because Thou livest;
> We live, Thou livest, from of old.[2]

Siddhanta teaching that souls are eternal, co-eternal with God,[3] is accepted by the poet without question. One of the arguments by which the separateness of the soul from the body, and at the same time its identity with 'personality,' is maintained by Siddhanta divines, is that 'it rejects every portion of the body as not being itself; it says "my body"; it is conscious of dreams; it exists in sleep without feeling pleasure or pain or movements; it knows from others.'[4] Any adverse inference possible from the expression 'my *soul*' is provided against: 'He who has really perceived the soul will not say "my soul." It is the ignorant who say so. The phrase "my soul" denotes another, the supreme soul dwelling in your soul.'[5] Tāyumānavar, it need hardly be said, accepts the Siddhanta learning on the subject of the soul. He claims[6] to have been specially instructed to

It is 'person' as will be seen in the answer to the question, 'What is the soul?' in *Brihad.*, 4.3.7. On *manas*, *ātman*, *asu* as Rig Vedic terms for 'soul' and on the later '*ātman*' doctrine, see Dasgupta's *History of Indian Philosophy*, i, pp. 25, 26, and on the general Upanishad ideas of *ātman*, see the summary in P. Deussen's article in *E.R.E.*, ii. 195.

[1] See below, p. 45. [2] See below, p. 96.

[3] *Siddhiyar*, 3.7.3, 3.4.20.

[4] *Bodham*, third Sutra. This is amplified in *Siddhiyar*, 3.3.1.

[5] *Siddhiyar*, 3.4. 27 and 28. The human soul is the clue to the All-Soul (*Brihad.*, 1.4.7).

[6] *N. M.*, 149.

think of the soul in the negative, relative manner of discriminating it from all around it—for instance, the five senses,[1] the five elements, the three *gunas*[2] and the *karanams*.[3] The poet speaks[4] of the soul, of himself, as distinct from, though subject to the influence of the two *karmas*,[5] the three *gunas*, the four *karmams*, the five senses, the six longings,[6] and the eight intoxications.[7] What the soul is not is expressly mentioned by the poet in the lines:

பாரிபூத நீயல்லை—உள்ளறிப்
பாரிந்திரியம் கரண நீயல்லை,
ஆராயுணர்வு நீ . . . . .

rendered below[8] in the syllabic arrangement of the original thus:

Earthly nor elemental art thou, nor yet
Organs nor innermost senses art thou;
Worthier, pondering thought art. Reflect.

The soul which is eternal, and not identifiable with anything in its environment, is unable of itself to know God.[9] 'All the senses can only understand with the aid of the soul, and yet cannot know the soul; so also the soul can only understand with the grace of the Lord, and yet cannot know Him.'[10]

[1] See *Siddhiyar*, 3.3.3. In *Siddhiyar*, 3.3.1-40 the nature of the soul is described principally by negatives. The soul is not, it is taught, the body, or the breath, or the senses, or the sensations, nor is it an atom, nor is it diffused in the body.

[2] See below, p. 149.

[3] The *karanams* are *manas* (the sensorium), *bhuddhi* (intelligence), *ahamkāra* (egoism) and *citta* (thinking). See below note at p. 219. *Manas*, *bhuddhi*, *ahamkāra* are mentioned together in *Maitri*, 6.5 and all three with the fourth, *citta*, in *Prasna*, 4.8, and all are probably referred to in *Svet.*, 1.4. In the *Katha Upanishad* (3.3) the soul (*ātman*) is described as riding in the chariot of the body, with *bhuddhi* as the charioter holding the reins of the *manas*. See below, p. 141, and Nalla. *Bodham*, p. 48.

[4] *N. M.*, 176.

[5] See below, § 36.

[6] The six longings are காமம், *kāmam* (desire generally as in *Aittariya Upanishad*, 5.1), மோகம் *mōkam* (lust), குரோதம் *krōtam* (anger, hate), மாச்சரியம் *māchariam* (envy, impatience), மதம், *matam* (passion, pride, elation), லோபம், *lōpam* (avarice).

[7] The principal of the eight intoxications are pride of birth and intellectual pride.

[8] *N.M.*, 1429, translated below at 109. See notes at p. 219

[9] See below, pp. 6, 140, 143, 150, and *N.M.*, 463.

[10] *Siddhiyar*, 3.5.1, *T. A. P.*, 2.6.

Now, the soul, though eternal as God is, is not, by the circumstances of co-eternity, to be considered God. It is very distinctly taught in the *Siddhanta* that the soul is not God.[1] Whatever affinities the soul may have to God, however God-like it can become, 'the soul cannot become God and God does not become the soul and yet God is one with, and different from, the soul.'[2] Tāyumānaver keeps the distinction between God and the soul intact:

'He who is Bliss, Ineffable,
The Lord, is He :
Whose form words fail to frame.
Then how can we
Babbe the claim,
By day, by night,
Incessant cry, 'Lo! God is I'?
But they,
The godly who have gained the light
Of Sivajnānam, say
I am not He?[3]

In the poet's view it is 'the daring of unbridled fancy'[4] to equate the soul with God. His is the Siddhanta view. It is unaffected by certain other Siddhanta tenets which we shall consider in § 34, namely, the soul's capacity for assimilation, its approach to God-likeness, its union with God, the ascription of Divinity to saints, and the deification of the just.

§ 29. It is taught that the soul, while it is held in the meshes of the senses and subjected to the limitations of sense-environment, flutters about in helpless alienation from God, and 'without the Lord the soul is bound.'[5] The soul, because it is subjected to bonds *pāsa* (பாசம்) from eternity, is called the bound

[1] *Siddhiyar*, 3.1.64, 3.6.9.

[2] *Ibid.*, 3.2.3.

[3] *N. M.*, 484. K. S. Mudaliar (*Tāyumānavar*, p. 501) takes the word [illegible] [illegible] which are rendered here 'They . . . say "I am not He"' to mean, They say, "We are not aliens to God".' The context, it seems to me, however, contrasts [illegible] with [illegible].

[4] See below, p. 26. See *N. M.*, 131, 'The wicked who say "We are God",' யாங்கே கடவுளென்றிடும் பாதகர்கள்.

[5] *Svet.*, 1.4–8. This is the same as saying that the soul has no சுதந்தரம். See *N. M.*, 416, 463.

one, *pasu* (பசு)[1] When Tāyumānavar speaks of கேடில் பசு பாச மெல்லாங் கீழ்ப்பட, 'the deathless *pasu*, *pāsam* to be subdued'[2] he means the state when the soul shall have lost its soul-characteristics of original bondage. It is to the same he alludes where he speaks of கெடுத்தே பசுத்துவத்தை, 'soul-nature being put away,'[3] and it is the much desired condition when 'all the soul's bonds and fetters shall have been broken and flung aside like fine-spun cotton' பாச நிகளங்களெல்லாம் பஞ்சாக.[4] Now the *pāsa* பாச bonds and fetters with which the soul is bound from the beginning form a three-fold cord consisting of the strands of *ānava*, *karma*, *māya*. This triple 'bond' is also spoken of as the 'triple 'impurity' மலம் (*malam*) of the soul.[5] The three constituents of *pāsam* or *malam* are so connected as cause and consequence that they are not three but one in reality. It is important to understand their interrelationship in order to appreciate their oneness. The fact that *ānavam* (darkness, ignorance) is often treated by text-writers as 'the malam' 'pāsam'[6] may serve to give prominence to its value as a causal factor in the career of a soul. Tāyumānavar refers clearly to *ānava* when he speaks of 'souls afflicted by the poison of gripping *malam*' கவ்வு மலமாகின்ற நாக பாசத்தினாற் கட்டுண்ட உயிர்கள்,[7] using the term மலம் to denote particularly *ānava*. This *ānavam* which is 'inherent in the soul',[8] is believed to be an intensely minute[9] defect or taint in the soul, minute but pregnant with immense potentialites. *Ānavam* is

[1] *Siddhiyar*, 3.4.20 பசுத்துவ முடைய துமிப் பசுவெனாநிற்கு மன்றே.

[2] *N. M.*, 1196. [3] *N. M.*, 1248. [4] *N. M.*, 1364.

[5] *Tirumantram*, stanza 2192. ஆணவ மாயையுங் கன்மமு மாமலம். *Siddhiyar*, 3.2.16, மும்மலம்.

[6] E.g. *Tiru Arul Payan*, c. 3 is headed பாசவியல் 'nature of pāsam' and deals only with *ānava*. In *Bodham*, sutra ! *ānava* alone is named, although from the arguments and illustrations to the sutra the other two malams may be inferred.

[7] *N. M.*, 28. *Pōttippahtodai*, line 17 speaks of *ānava* as சகசமலம்.

[8] *Siddhiyar*, 3.2.81.

[9] *Ānava* is usually derived from *anu* (atom) and *anu* is a synonym for soul. The soul is called *anu* (atom) as its real *vibhu* (expansive) state is abridged by the taint *ānava* which is *anu* (atom) (Nalla. *Bodham*, p. 4). Other names for *ānavam* are: *malam*, *ajnāmam*, *avidhyam*, *mūlam*, *pāsam*, *mōkam*, *kēvalam*, *āvasuram*, *tamas*, *sadam* (Tiruvilangam, *Sivapragāsam*, p. 39). Strictly speaking these are synonyms, and some of the terms have other meanings besides what is denoted by *ānavam*

'darkness', 'veiling ignorance', 'veiling itself and all else'[1] deceptively. Therefore the soul is the sightless fœtus, imprisoned unknowing in the womb of the dark *ānavam*, காரிட்ட வாணவக் கருவறையி லறிவற்று கண்ணில்லாக் குழவியைப்போல கட்டுண்டிருந்த.[2] It is the darkness of ignorance, அறியாமை யாகின்ற விருள்.[3] An aspect of *ānavam* is *ahangkāram*,[4] indeed it is, in a way, fiercer than *ānavam* out of which it springs:

Strong is the ancient taint,
  But stronger far
What wrathful from it springs,
  As fierce as are
The huntsmen of the wild,
  The demon pride
Which will not let me know,
  But from me hide,
What I would seek to see,
  And hinder me
From that safe middle way
  Where I would be.
Becoming that to which
  'Tis drawn at will,
High words not to be borne
  It speaks, until
It claims to be a peer
  Of gods the three;
And like the axle-pin,
  While smooth and free
The car-wheels rolling move,
  Unmoving stays
Full-centred in itself,
  And boasting says,
  'There is in all this earth
  No one like me';
Resolves as Ravana
  A king to be;
Reckons the sky-wide space
  Within my heart
The kingdom of the king
  In every part,
Its own wherein to reign,
  While I with it
Unceasing war to wage
  Feel all unfit.[5]

---

[1] *T. A. P.*, 3.3. See below, pp. 141, 150.
[2] *N. M.*, 31.
[3] *N. M.*, 114.
[4] See below, p. lxxix.
[5] *N.M.*, 45 ஆங்காரம் . . . ஆணவத்திலும் வலிது, etc.

The close association of *ahangkāram*, ' self-assertiveness, egoism, self-pride ' with *ānavam* is often stated by the poet.[1]

A favourite Siddhanta analogy for *ānavam* is ' dross '. Our poet employs this figure in speaking of the Siddhanta 'original sin,' *ānavam* :

> My body is the melting pot
>   Wherein, like copper that is stained
> With dross, in darkness and impure
>   Long have I ignorant remained,
> Till Thou enkindledst wisdom's fire,
>   In melting heat refining me;
> Till tempered to be touched by grace,
>   The soul's transforming alchemy,
> And I became God's purest gold . . .[2]

The dross and copper analogy is found in the *Siddhiyar* : ' Pervading through the numberless souls as the dirt in copper, *ānava mala* withholds them from wisdom and effort . . . and is ever the source of ignorance.'[3] The learned English translator of the *Siddhiyar* observes :

> The dirt that is inherent in the copper can be removed once for all only by alchemic processes ; and when it is so removed, the copper no longer remains copper but is transformed into resplendent gold.[4]

It is in terms of dross and copper that the *Sivapragasam* explains *ānavam* :

> செம்பிலுறு களிம்பேபோற் றீதாய்
>   மூலமல மாயறிவு முழுவதையு மறைக்கும்

' Like the inherent taint in copper the eternal, primal, causal impurity obscures the [soul's] intelligence '.[5]

It is, as we have seen, Siddhanta teaching that :

(1) *Ānavam* in an inherent taint of the soul,
(2) It is attached to the soul from eternity,
(3) Out of it springs *ahangkāram*, ' egoism,'
(4) It obscures the soul's intelligence,
(5) It is darkness deceptively unseen,
(6) Its power disappears from souls finally ' saved '.

---

[1] E.g. *N.M.*, 179 ஈஞ்ஞானெனது மானம், ' The pride that cries, " Here, on earth, it is I, it is I " '.

[2] See below, No. 37 at p. 21, and the notes at p. 169.

[3] *Siddhiyar*, 2.2.80.

[4] Nalla. *Siddhiyar*, p. 185.

[5] *Sivapragāsam*, stanza 20.

The Siddhanta teaching as to the soul and *pāsam*, as to its bondage in *ānavam*, whatever interest it may have as an endeavour to formulate a theory of 'original sin,' is best understood as an effort at wishing that the history of the soul should indeed be the history of God, and that the wish is far from fulfilment because of the soul's election to differentiate itself from its Divine affinities, and to travel further and further away from its original kinship with the Divine. Could we so understand the Siddhanta teaching? *Ānavam* is the difficulty in the way: *it has always been with the soul*, and if it is as it must be, in the nature of evil, something not-God, then, the soul, with this inherent and *eternal* taint, could never have co-existed with the taintless, '*nirmala*' Deity. Siddhanta thinkers get over this situation by postulating for God bēthabētham.[1]

Of the three classes into which Siddhanta writers divide souls, *Sakalar* is the class which is subject to all the three *malams*, and souls of the highest order, *Vijnanākalar*, have *ānavam* alone.[2]

§ 30. *Ānava malam*, it is taught, 'affords souls the capacity for experience'.[3] The three *malas* are interrelated.

> *Ānava*, *Māya* and *Karma*, delusive in their character, veil the true nature of souls, and produce in them illusory enjoyments, bondage and capacity for experience, just as the sprout, bran and chaff in paddy.[4]

The paddy illustration is thus explained:

> *Ānava mala*, in conjunction with the efficient cause, provides *jivas* (souls) with the capacity for experience, as the chaff is the efficient cause of sprouting. Māya, being the instrumental cause, makes, with its effects,—bodies and senses,—the bondage of the *jivas*, as the bran favouring the growth co-exists with the other ingredients. *Karma*, being the material cause, affords enjoyments to the *jivas* as the sprout becomes manifest by a process latent in it.[5]

Elsewhere I have expressed some difficulty in understanding Mr. Nallaswamy Pillai's explanation side by side with

[1] 'Co-existence without mutual exclusion or externality as when two different things are connected inseparably like the association of ideas.' (Nalla. *Bōdham*, p. 15.)

[2] See below, p. 167 on the three classes.

[3] *Siddhiyar*, 3.2.80.

[4] *Ibid.*, 3.2.86.

[5] Nalla. *Siddhiyar*, p. 187.

what he says in another place.[1] The learned author himself points out a difference of opinion among commentators.[2] Tirumular refers to the paddy illustration thus:

> *Ānavam*, *māya*, and *karma*, the *pāsam* (*malam*), are to the germinating sprout as bran and chaff to rice, and the soul cleansed of *pāsam* is like the polished rice, but the soul, though so cleansed, is not God.[3]

ஆணவ மாயையுங் கன்மமு மாமலங்
காணு முளைக்குத் தவிடுமி யான்மாவுந்
தாணுவை யொவ்வாமற் றண்டுலமாய் நிற்கும்
பேணுவாய் மற்று நின் பாசம் பிரித்தே

In *Sivapragāsam* the eternity of all three *malas* is expounded by the use of this same 'paddy' analogy:

> It is taught in the Saiva *agamas* that [to the questions whether *ānava* was first and the other *malas* came later] all three *malas* are eternal just as the sprout of paddy, the bran and the chaff.[4]

நெல்லின் முளை தவிடுமிபோ லநாதி யாக
நிறுத்திடுவ ரிது சைவ மிகழ்த்து மாறே

Mr. Tiruvilangam in the Tamil notes in his excellent edition of *Sivapragāsam* comments thus on the above passage:

> The sprout is *karma*, the bran is *māya*, the chaff is *ānava*, and the rice is the *soul*. Just as the capacity for life in the paddy makes it to sprout, so does *karma*, as material cause, [முதற்காரணம்] beget for the soul the soul's enjoyments and sufferings. As the bran facilitates germination, so does *māya*, as instrumental cause, [துணைக்காரணம்] cause body, senses, etc., and fits the soul to its physical environment. As the chaff is the efficient cause [நிமித்தகாரணம்] for the germination of the paddy, so is *ānavam* the cause of all enjoyments and sufferings of the soul in its body and helps the soul taste fully the fruits of life.[5]

It may be useful to tabulate some views of the above paddy illustration:—

Ānavam	*Maya*	*Karma*	
Chaff,	bran,	sprout,	Tiruvilangam.
Chaff,	bran,	sprout	Nalla. *Siddhiyar*.
Bran,	chaff,	sprout,	Nalla. *Bodham*.
Bran,	chaff,	sprout,	Sivāgra Yōgi.[6]

---

[1] See below, pp. 150, 151, and note at foot of p. 151.

[2] Nalla. *Siddhiyar*, p. 188, *note*.

[3] *Tirumantram*, 2192.

[4] *Sivapragāsam*, stanza 25.

[5] Tiruvilangam, *Sivapragāsam* (Tamil), p. 51.

[6] Nalla. *Siddhiyar*, p. 188 agrees with Sivāgra Yogi, and p. 187 follows Sivagnāna Yogi. The latter makes *ānavam* 'chaff'.

Ānavam	*Māya*	*Karma*	
Sprout,	bran,	chaff,	*Siddhiyar.*[1]
Chaff,	bran,	sprout,	*Sivapragāsam.*[2]
Bran,	chaff,	sprout,	*Tirumantram.*[3]

The main point, however, of the analogy admitted by all is that the soul corresponds to rice. In view of the self-assertive, egoistic and differentiating character of *ānavam* it is best considered as the main cause of the soul's experiences, and so 'sprout', the factor of germination. Differentiation, விகாரம் (*vikāram*) is, in Siddhanta theology, the soul's great defect, it is the spirit of strangeness, aloofness, 'going into a far country', the beginning of distance, the forming of non-God and foreign attachments which hold in them the risks of the soul being sundered from its Divine kinship. This is due to *ānavam*.

§ 31. We have seen from the parable of the grain of paddy something of the inter-relationship of *ānavam*, *māya* and *karma*. To get more closely into the subject we have to note that, while *ānavam* is inherent in souls, *māya* is external to souls.[4] By the influence of *māya* there are manifest in a soul, when it is embodied, *icha* (desire), *jnana* (intelligence), *kiriya* (action).[5] What is *māya*?

> Indestructible, formless, one, seed of all the worlds, non-intelligent, all-pervasive, a sakti of the Perfect One, cause of the soul's body and senses, and worlds, cause also of delusion, is *māya*.[6]

Māya is thus the cause of complexity. Through *māya* the *anu*, atom, called 'soul', enters upon a career of almost interminable 'diversity' with the aid of the third *mala*, *karma*.[7] *Māya* is

[1] 3.2. 86, '*ānava*, *māya*, *karma* . . . as sprout, bran, and chaff . . . '

[2] Stanza 20 follows this order: *karma*, *māya*, *ānava* are as sprout, bran, chaff.

[3] Stanza 2192, quoted above, seems to me to indicate that 'as bran and chaff are to the germinating sprout' so are *ānava* and *māya* to *karma*. See *Pōttippahtodai*, line 13 [illegible].

[4] *Siddhiyar*, 3.2.81. See Kaji's *Philosophy of the Bhagavad Gita*, i, p. 5 on Māya.

[5] *Siddhiyar*, 3.2.83.

[6] *Siddhiyar*, 3.2.53. This is what is known as *asutta māya*, அசுத்தமாயை.

[7] Considered below, in Part vi. See *Siddhiyar*, 3.4. 21-22 for a short statement of the soul's pilgrimage from 'the womb of *māya*'.

the material cause of creation.[1] A Siddhanta catechism explains *māya* thus:

> *Q.* Is the world produced from God?
> *A.* It is created from *māya* or non-ego.
> *Q.* What is *māya* ?
> *A.* It is the first cause of the creation of the world.
> *Q.* Is *māya* an inert matter or intelligence ?
> *A.* It is only an inert matter.
> *Q.* Is *māya* eternal ?
> *A.* It is eternal and all-pervading.[2]

It is taught:

> 'The Lord like a potter creates the world out of *māya* as the material cause with the aid of His *sakti* as the instrumental cause. . . . All this universe is spread out and multiplied from the primal, invisible and subtle *māya* into visible and grosser, and still grosser, forms as life and body.[3]

Ānavam occasions *māya*, and *māya* performs its functions by means of *karma*, but the first cause of all, it is taught, is God.[4] Therefore we find Tāyumāṅavar ascribing *māya* to God.[5] *Māya* is of three kinds, *sutta* (pure), *asutta* (impure), *prakrit* (gross). Without going into the bewildering learning on this subject of *māya*, with its related topic, *tatvas*,[6] we may note that *sutta māya* is referred to by Tāyumānavar under the name *Kundalini* or *Kundali.*[7] This *Kundali sutta māya* is a beneficent influence, for with its aid and association are souls prompted into knowledge.[8] It is also called *mahāmāya* and *vindhu*, and is an aspect of the graciousness of Deity manifesting itself in power.[9] Our poet-saint speaks of *sutta māya* as the *good māya* shining in the gloom of *ānava* ignorance.[10] 'When

[1] *Siddhiyar*, 3.1.14 ; 3.1.18. *Sivapragāsam*, stanza 23.

[2] *Siddhanta Gnana Ratnavali*, p. 24. Is 'non-ego' correct ?

[3] *Siddhiyar*, 3.1.18 ; 3.1.27. Causes are said to be three and are thus illustrated : Clay is the material cause, the potter is the efficient cause, and the wheel is the instrumental cause (*Siddhiyar*, 3.1.18).

[4] *Siddhiyar*, Book ii, ch. v. (māyavādi refutation), verse 16.

[5] *N.M.*, 145, 380, 570, 746.

[6] See Nalla. *Studies*, pp. 38-40. See Table of Tatvas in chart facing p. 56 of Tiruvilangam's *Sivapragāsam*.

[7] *N.M.*, 60, 111, 127, 1231.

[8] *Siddhiyar*, 3.1.26.

[9] See an able, but in places obscure, exposition of *māya* by Sriman K. S Sundaramurti Pov·anikar in the 1911 Saiva Conference *Addresses*, p. 146.

[10] *N.M.*, 170.

the dark *ānava* increases, the light of the lamp (*māya*) will remove it a little. . . . Like the lamp . . . *māya* enlightens the soul by its various form of body, senses, etc., as long as the night of *karma* lasts'.[1] An effect of *sutta māya* is called *trodāyi,* a *sakti* (power) which commands the three *malas* to perform their functions,[2] and one of the five acts of God is effected by this *trodāyi sakti,* and that act is *tirobhāvam* which brings about the maturing of *mala* preparatory to complete purification.[3] This maturing grace *tirōbhāva* is what Tāyumānavar alludes to as 'the *sakti* which was manifested to bestow the grace of maturity'.[4] In *Sivapragāsam* is the statement[5] that, while *ānava mala* obscures souls by its power of darkness, it is aided in its work by *trodāyi,* that is, *tirōbhāva sakti,* which acts, in association with *ānavam,* in such a manner as to forward the 'maturing'[6] processes that go to further the soul's redemption. Although this *tirōbhāva sakti* is a beneficent agent, a 'grace of God,' yet, by reason of its co-operation with *ānavam,* it has been itself described as a *malam*.[7] It is *tirōbhāvam* that finally 'leads the soul to the Feet of the Holy One'.[8] The process of the soul's purification is set out in terse detail in *Pōttippahtodai* where it is explained that:

1. God is He who has taken in hand the rescuing of souls from the toils of re-births.[9]
2. God is the permitter of *māya* and births for the getting rid of *ānava*.[10]
3. God's is the great might which causes embodiment.[11]
4. God is the cause of human motherhood and consequent attachments.[12]
5. It is God's mercy which lets human beings go through the processes of actions.[13]
6. It is God's mercy which beholds the sufferings of souls in their bodies and considers them purificatory.[14] '

---

[1] *T. A. P.*, ch. 3, verses 9, 10.
[2] *Siddhiyar*, 3.2.87.
[3] *Siddhiyar*, 3. 1.37.
[4] *N.M.*, 145, பாகமிக வருள வொருசத்தி வந்து.
[5] *Sivapragāsam*, stanza 20.
[6] See below, p. 167 on *mala paripākam.*
[7] *Sivapragāsam*, stanza 20; *Siddhiyar*, 3.2.87; *Tirumantram*, stanzas 431-440.
[8] *Sivapragāsam*, stanza 20.
[9] Lines 7, 8.
[10] Lines 13-26.
[11] Lines 27-37.
[12] Lines 38-45.
[13] Lines 46-67.
[14] Lines 74-103.

7. It is God's *sakti* (*tirōbhava*) which makes souls eat the fruit of both kinds of *karma* and, on their performing good *karma*, makes them enjoy the heavens of good merit in succession, till they join the company of the saints, and makes them 'balance' their deeds and attain the stage of fitness for 'grace'.[1]

In the *Siddhanta* teaching we thus see that, in the language of one of the *Siddhanta* scriptures,[2] it is God who identifies himself with the soul to rid it of its *ānavam* and becomes its conqueror. The purificatory process of the remoral of *ānavam* by *māya* is 'just as the washerman washes all clothes by mixing with them cow-dung and fuller's earth, etc.'[3] The delusive character of *māya* belongs to *asutta māya*, but it does not make *māya* an unreality. An effect of *asutta māya* is *māyeya*,[4] a combination of all the products of *asutta māya*, and these products attaching themselves to the soul create individuality.[5] With *māyeya* and *trodāyi* as distinct malas, although *trodāyi* is in reality a *sakti* of God, it is sometimes said there are *five* malas, not three only.[6] We may conclude this section with a brief statement of some of Tāyumānavar's thoughts on *māya*:

1. There is a good *māyā*, a *sakti*.[7]
2. 'The good *māya* shines in the gloom of *ānava* ignorance.'[8]
3. *Māya* causes bodies.[9]
4. *Māya* originates sinful conduct.[10]
5. *Māya* begets attachments to the world and pleasures.[11]
6. *Māya* finds a way into the intelligence and makes illusory things (which are as unreal as a hare's horn or a lotus in space) seem real and obscures religion.[12]
7. *Māya* makes the fashion of the world and its glamour, however illusory, seem real.[13]

---

[1] Lines 104–115. See below, Part vi for a short notice of *karma* and 'balancing'.

[2] *Tirukkalittuppadiyar*, stanza 4 [illegible] . . . [illegible]

[3] *Siddhiyar*, 3.2.52.

[4] *Siddhiyar*, 3.2.87. *Sivapragāsam*, stanzas, 26, 27.

[5] Nalla. *Siddhiyar*, p. 188.

[6] *Sivapragāsam* stanza, 32; *Siddhiyar*, 3.2.87; *Tiruvachagam*, vi, line 116.

[7] *N.M.*, 60, 111, 127, 1231. [8] *N.M.*, 170. [9] *N.M.*, 300.

[10] *N.M.*, 380. [11] *N.M.*, 103.

[12] *N.M.*, 39. In *N.M.*, 165 to 'the hare's horn and space lotus' is added mirage.' See *N.M.*, 551.

[13] *N.M.*, 165 [illegible]; *N.M.*, 328 [illegible]; *N.M.*, 389 [illegible]; *N.M.*, 401 [illegible]; *N.M.*, 279 [illegible].

8. *Māya* is like a sea,[1] like a forest,[2] like mire,[3] and is the ancient abyss.[4]

9. *Māya* is vanity of vanities.[5]

10. *Māya* is clamant with self-assertion.[6]

11. God causes and permits the activities of *māya*.[7]

12. It is when *māya* shrinks, and the mind shrinks that births cease.[8]

This last leads to a later stage in the soul's ascent where it will be without *mala*, மலமற்று,[9] since God, by His grace, is the soul's mala-destroyer.[10]

§ 32. Any statement of 'the problem of evil', says Dr. Mellone, is defective which does not take into account the unfinished character of creation.

> We have not got the question in the right shape when we ask why God made the world thus and thus. The world is not yet 'made.' It is in the making; and we have a share in the making of it. From this it follows that there never can be a final and complete 'solution' of the problem of evil by thought or reflection alone, without action. The only final solution will be when all evil is overcome by good. And may we not say that the possibility of this is proved whenever, in our actual experiences, some evil thing is overcome by good? [11]

The problem, nevertheless, is with us, perhaps, in a form agreeable to Dr. Mellone's practical outlook: Why does the

[1] *N.M.*, 123, 182. [2] *N.M.*, 436 [3] *N.M.*, 337.

[4] *N.M.*, 275, 559. [5] *N.M.*, 432.

[6] *N.M.*, 556, translated above at p. lvi.

[7] *N.M.*, 448, 570, 746. [8] *N.M.*, 552.

[9] *N.M.*, 33. In *Unmai Vilakkam*, St. 38 'the saints of the silence' are said to 'have overcome the three *malas*', மோனந்த மாமுனிவர் மும்மலத்தை மோசித்து.

[10] *N.M.*, 186, 634.

[11] S. H. Mellone, *God and the World*, p. 133. The ideal of good finally overcoming evil is the teaching of the *Book of Revelation*. In this context of an unperfected world may be quoted the words of Dr. Alfred Garvie (*Expositor*, December, 1923, p. 406) about the soul of man being in the process of maturing: 'We must modify our conception of soul; we must think of it dynamically rather than statically, as a potency to be gradually realized, and not as an entity already complete. . . . We are not so much already souls or persons, as only becoming so.' Dr. F. J. Hall in his *Dogmatic Theology*, vol. v, p. 114 seems to express himself in the same terms as Dr. Mellone in his observation that 'the problem is being practically solved by the general march of events under divine government' In vol. v, chap. iv, §§ 9-11 he outlines what he considers to be the Christian view.

world remain incomplete, unfinished, 'unmade ?' We find Tāyu-mānavar asking himself this question in different words. The question is implied in, and is at the back of, all those longings to which reference has already been made.[1] More specifically he asks :

> Why is all this suffering ?[2]
> Whence comes this human body ?[3]
> Why is man, as if it were, a puppet in God's hands ?[4]
> Whence is evil, and whence is good ?[5]
> Why is there any evil in man ?[6]

The poet himself answers these questions and others involved in the inquiry into the problem of evil in the light of the Siddhanta theology. God is, in a sense not derogatory to the idea of 'His spotless purity, the doer of all things.'[7] 'All-mover, moving all for ill and good.'[8] All things, all befallings to the soul, are 'the sport of God.'[9] From such statements, the poet advances to the somewhat startling, but from the Siddhanta point of view a not irreverent, pronouncement that God is the soul's Evil and its Good.[10] This, to the poet, is the solution of the problem of evil. Once arrived at this stage of thinking he has no more questions to ask : it is a stage above the explanation of life's problems by reference to the soul's three-fold taint, *pāsam*. Were *pāsam* the ultimate answer to all questions as to good and evil in the soul and in the soul's environment it would ignore God, and so the thought is pushed further back, back to God, God who is beyond the workings of *pāsam*. The poet, like others of his school, has chosen wisely between an atheistic fatalism and a theistic arbitrariness.[11]

The somewhat disquieting thought suggested by this

[1] See above, ñ. [2] Below, No. 82. [3] Below, No. 85.
[4] Below, No. 103. [5] Below, No. 122.
[6] *N.M.*, 179, partly translated at p. 144, below.
[7] Below, No. 42, and see below, p. 143, where the subject is discussed at some length.
[8] Below, Nos. 115, 147.
[9] *N.M.*, 178, 521, 1404, and see below, p. 182.
[10] Below, No. 1.2. *N.M.*, 746. See *N.M.*, 67.
[11] See below, p. 181, on the arbitrariness of God.

Siddhanta line of philosophy make the words of a modern theologian relevant here :

> The only point at which a difficulty is created either for Morality or for Religion by the acceptance of Determinism lies in its tendency to make God in a sense the 'author of evil'—a sense which in no way excludes the equally true proposition that man is the author of evil ; for man alone wills the evil otherwise than as a means to the true good. God wills the evil as a means to the good, and to will evil as a means to the good is not *to be* evil, or to will evil as such, or to exhibit any defect of goodness. . . . After all . . . I admit frankly that it would be more satisfactory to be able to say that God was in no sense the cause of evil. That is only to say that I could wish the Universe were better than it is. . . . The desire to avoid the admission that God originates souls with evil potentialities which must necessarily develop into evil actuality is the inspiring motive of those theories of Pre-existence which, from the days of Plato and of Origen to those of modern 'Pluralism', seem always to have sprung up wherever men have grappled in earnest with the problem of evil. According to such theories souls are uncreated ; while the world-process is one by which a good but omnipotent God is getting rid of the evil in those souls, and bringing them to the highest perfection of which they are capable.[1]

The latest exposition of the Zoroastrian Good and Evil Gods,[2] in a study by Professor Raffaele Pettazzoni entitled *La Religione di Zarathustra*,[3] is in favour of doing away with the usually believed 'dualism' of Zoroastrianism.

> In reality dualism is not a negation of monotheism ; therefore it is monotheism itself in two opposed and contrary aspects. It does not precede monotheism ; therefore it is a reflex of it. . . . In dualism all those divine elements are present which monotheism denies and denies again, but they are present in the only form compatible with the concept (also present) of one God. . . . Thus Anrama(i)nya is not essentially another God beside Ahura Mazda ; he is Ahura Mazda himself in the inversion of all his qualities.[4]

Professor Pettazzoni's elimination of an Evil God from the interpretation of the religion of Zoroaster, thus having one God and good and evil together, is almost akin to the Siddhanta view of God, a view which has no place for a Satan.

[1] Rashdall, *The Theory of Good and Evil*, ii, pp. 345, 346.

[2] To whom reference is believed to be intended in *Isaiah* xlv. 7.

[3] Reviewed by Professor Gray in *The Harvard Theological Review*, January, 1922, p. 87.

[4] Translation in *H.T.R.*, January, 1922, p. 88.

Similar also is the reasoning of those thinkers of whom Archdeacon Wilberforce may be taken as typical. He argues that 'the whole mystery of the dark side of life must be within the purpose of the eternal order, and there can be no independent rival to the Author of the Universe.'[1] The Archdeacon, like the Siddhanta divines, has no room for Satan in God's scheme of things. The conception, likewise of Hegel, of a good God as sole Potentate drove that philosopher to find both good and evil in God Himself and to consider evil but a lesser good.[2] In this context and particularly as affording material for comparison or contrast with the Siddhanta *pāsam* (in the two aspects we have so far considered, *māya* and *ānava*) the opinions of Plotinus (*circ.* A.D. 262) may be interesting :

> The soul is neither independent of matter nor by herself perverse. By virtue of her union with the body, which is material, she is mingled with indetermination, and so, to a certain point, deprived of the form which embellishes and which supplies measure. Further, that reason should be hindered in its operation, and cannot see well, must be due to the soul's being hindered by passions, and obscured by the darkness with which matter surrounds her. The soul inclines towards matter. Thus the soul fixes her glances not on what is essence but on what is generation. Now the principle of generation is matter, whose nature is so bad that matter communicates it to the beings which, even without being united thereto, merely look to it. Being the privation of good, matter contains none of it and assimilates itself to all that touches it.[3]

Again, we may compare or contrast with the *ānava* or *māya* teaching these thoughts from Plotinus :

> The soul does not by herself possess privation of good. . . . The soul cannot herself be evil . . . and is not the first evil, nor does she contain evil as an accident, since she is not absolutely deprived of good.[4] . . . Matter is the cause of evil.[5] . . . The bottom of each thing is matter, and every

---

[1] *Mystic Immanence*, p. 54. At p. 23, the same writer says, 'The mythical demonized objectification of what we call evil is greatly in the way of clear thought.' In favour of a *spiritual*, as against a *material*, devil see Maurice's line of reasoning in a letter in the *Life of F. D. Maurice*, ii, 21. 403.

[2] See the discussion of Hegel in his relation to Modernism in Dr. Charles Harris's *Creeds or No Creeds ?* p. 15.

[3] *First Ennead, Eighth Book*, § 4 in the Rev. Dr. K. S. Guthrie's translation, vol. iv, p. 1147.

[4] *Ennead*, 1.8.11.

[5] *Ibid.*, 1.8.8.

matter is dark, because the reason (the form) is the light, and because intelligence is the reason.[1] . . . Matter being that which possesses nothing, that which is in indigence, or rather that which is indigence itself, must necessarily be evil; for it is not indigence of wealth but indigence of wisdom, of virtue, of beauty, of vigour, of shape, of form, of quality.[2] .

It is necessary for the sake of completeness of treatment, rather than for provoking controversy, to state what the Christian may be content with as an explanation, but not an exhaustive solution, of the problem of evil. The problem itself, in its most popular significance, is 'the problem of reconciling the hypothesis of a good and beneficent Deity with the existence of an apparently evil and imperfect world.'[3] The Bible account of sin avoids all the pitfalls into which some human speculation upon the subject has fallen.[4] The problem is essentially a moral one. The Christian sees the hand of God in the march of events towards ultimate good in a world which he believes is working its way along moral lines to reach the goal of final good. Yet to the Christian the problem remains unsolved, only he is aided nearer a solution by the fact of the death of Christ.

The problem becomes less acute in a world in which while sin abounds, grace much more abounds; and no infringement of the attributes of God is necessary when all the facts—free-will, the possibility of sin, actual sin and the provisions for redemption are taken into account. The clearest light upon the problem of evil, both physical and moral, shines from the cross of Christ. We might as well acknowledge first as last that it would be difficult

---

[1] *Ennead*, 2.4.5.

[2] *Ibid.*, 2.4.15. If the reader sees any similarity between *matter* in Plotinus and *māya* in the Siddhanta, between his *darkness* and the Siddhanta *ānava*, the inquiry suggests itself as to whether or no, on the assumption of a contact of Greek with Indian thought, the Siddhanta philosophy is very much earlier than the 12th or 13th Christian century. Dr. J. Estlin Carpenter in his *Theism in Mediæval India*, p. 376, while referring to Plotinus as affording similarity to Hindu thought on the soul's union with God, does not notice other likenesses of Indian thought to the philosophy of Plotinus.

[3] Fuller, *The Problem of Evil in Plotinus*, p. 18 'Since the mere fact of a world at all as separate and individual, as itself and not God is *prima facie* evil, the problem of evil becomes the problem of existence.' (*Ibid.*, p 63.)

[4] Prof. W. H. Johnson in *The Princeton Theological Review*, October 1923, p. 527.

to maintain a full-orbed theism, in view of the mystery of evil, except in the light that is shed upon it by the doctrine of a suffering and sin-bearing Saviour.[1]

From the angle of view of Christian mysticism the problem of evil is approached along lines analogous to the Siddhanta. Tāyumānavar's 'Thou art the doer of all I do'[2] finds a parallel in Mother Julian's 'There is no doer but He.'[3] The context in which Dame Julian makes the statement is so strikingly similar to the Siddhanta setting of Tāyumānavar's theology that I give it here at some length:

> After this I saw God in a Point, that is to say, in mine understanding,—by which sight I saw that He is in all things. I beheld and considered, seeing and knowing in sight, with a soft dread, and thought: *What is sin?* For I thought truly that God doeth all-thing, be it never so little. And I saw truly that nothing is done by hap nor by adventure, but all things by the foreseeing wisdom of God. . . . Wherefore me behoveth needs to grant that all-thing that is done, it is well-done: for our Lord God doeth all. . . . He is the Mid-point of all thing, and all He doeth. And I was certain He doeth no sin. And here I saw verily that sin is no deed: for in all this was not sin shewed. . . . But in another time He gave a Shewing for the beholding of sin nakedly, as I shall tell: When He useth working of mercy and grace. And this vision was shewed to mine understanding, for that our Lord would have the soul turned truly unto the beholding of Him and generally of all His works. . . . A man beholdeth some deeds well done and some deeds evil, but our Lord beholdeth them not so: for as all that hath being in nature is of Godly making, so is all that is done, in property of God's doing. . . . For there is no doer but He.[4]

It is well to note that a passage such as the above is not by itself but belongs to a line of thought and meditation the centre of which is the soul's love of God in Christ Jesus,[5] and

[1] Prof. W. H. Johnson in *The Princeton Theological Review*, October 1923, p. 527. Among modern works on the subject may be named Rashdall's *Theory of Good and Evil*; McTaggart's *Some Dogmas of Religion*; Hall's *Dogmatic Theology*, vol. v, ch. iv; Gore's *Belief in God*, ch. vi; Tennant's *The Origin and Propagation of Sin*; Tennant's *The Concept of Sin*; Hügel's *The Mystical Element in Religion*, vol. ii, the section on 'Mysticism and the Question of Evil'; Illingworth's *Reason and Revelation*, ch. xii; Cobb's *Mysticism and the Creed*, ch. x; Inge's *Personal Idealism and Mysticism*, section xi; Niven's article 'Good and Evil' in *E.R.E.*, vi, 318; Formby's *The Unveiling of the Fall*.

[2] See below, pp. 7. 143.

[3] *Revelations of Divine Love*, ch. xi. (Warrack's edition, p. 28)

[4] *Ibid.* (Warrack's edition, pp. 27, 28).

[5] *Ibid.*, ch. xxvi. (Warrack's edition, p. 54).

the high Christian atmosphere of the mystic is evidenced by an abhorrence of sin:

> Well I wot the soul that truly taketh the teaching of the Holy Ghost, it hateth more sin for vileness and horribleness than it doth all the pain that is in hell. For the soul that beholdeth the fair grace of our Lord Jesus, it hateth no hell but sin. . . . It is the most pain that the soul may have to turn from God any time by sin.[1]

S. Augustine, taking a negative view of evil,[2] cannot even state the problem of evil except in term of Deity. Indeed, he is forced to own that, apart from a deep consciousuess of God, there is no problem at all: likewise apart from God there is no solution of the problem.

> It was manifested to me that those things be good which yet are corrupted; that neither were they sovereignly good nor unless they were good, could be corrupted: for if sovereignly good they were incorruptible, if not good at all, there were nothing in them to be corrupted. For corruption injures, but unless it diminishes goodness, it could not injure. Either, then corruption injures not, which cannot be; or, what is most certain all which is corrupted is deprived of good. But if they be deprived of all good, they shall cease to be. For if they shall be, and can now no longer be corrupted, they shall be better than before, because they shall abide incorruptibly: And what more monstrous, than to affirm things to become better by losing all their good? Therefore, if they shall be deprived of all good, they shall no longer be. So long therefore as they are, they are good: therefore, whatsoever is, is good. That evil then which I sought whence it is, is not any substance: for were it a substance, it should be good. For either it should be an incorruptible substance, and so a chief good; or a corruptible substance; which unless it were good, could not be corrupted. I perceived therefore, and it was manifested to me, that Thou madest all things good, nor is there any substance at all, which Thou madest not; and for that Thou madest not all things equal, therefore are all things; because each is good, and altogether very good, because our God made all things very good.[3]

---

[1] *Revelations of Divine Love*, ch. lxxvi. (Warrack's edition, p. 185).

[2] As Plotinus, *Ennead*, I. 8. 11, 'Evil is privation.' S. Augustine closely follows Plotinus when he says (*De Civit. Dei*, ii, 22) 'The name evil, belongeth only to privation of good.' A positive view is inferred from the stress he lays on the strength of sin, e.g. in *Confessions*, vii, 5, 'Of a froward will was a lust made; and a lust served, became custom; and a custom not resisted became a necessity. By what links . . . a hard bondage held me enthralled.' The great Roman divine, S. Thomas Aquinas, follows S. Augustine and earlier thought: 'The stain of sin is not something positive, existent in the soul. . . . It is like a shadow, which is the privation of light.' (*Summa Theologica*, Book i, part ii, Q. 86).

[3] *Confessions*, vii. 12 (Pusey's translation).

An optimistic outlook on life is sometimes ascribed to the mystics as explanatory of their attitude towards Evil.[1] This optimism of theirs has never made them blind to the banefulness of evil as such. As the late Mrs. E. Herman has rightly remarked, 'Heaven and Hell are born together in the human soul'.[2] Good and evil are principles at war for the mastery within us and no amount of well thinking can succeed in making evil good. The mystics may be presumed not to be courting the Fourth Woe of the Prophet[3] by confounding moral distinctions, in calling evil good, and good evil, when they indulge in extravagant speech seeming to suggest good even in sin and to associate Deity in essence with that which is not of good. It is to optimistic tendencies that we may trace some of the utterances dealt with, at some length, in another place.[4] I do not desire to repeat myself. Without, however, encroaching on what is said below I may refer to the saying of a Roman mystic, the Blessed Angela da Foligno. Mr. Edward Ingram Watkin illustrates the mystic's optimism of faith[5] by quoting Angela da Foligno:

> I understand that He (God) is present in everything that hath being, in the demon, in the good angel, in hell, in Paradise, in adultery, in murder, in every good work.[6]

To make this the norm of mystical opinion is doing scant justice to mysticism generally: it, by itself, does less than justice to

[1] F. Von Hügel, *Myst. Elem. of Religion*, ii, 292.3. See Inge, *Christian Mysticism*, 314.5 on contrast between some mystics' theory of evil and their practical attitude.

[2] *Meaning and value of Mysticism*, 116. [3] *Isaiah*, v, 20.

[4] See below, p. 143. [5] *The Philosophy of Mysticism*, 37.

[6] *Visions and Instructions*, c. xxvii, *apud* Watkin, *op. cit*, 37. Compare in this context the words of William Law: 'When divine love is born in the soul, all childish images of good and evil are done away, and all the sensibility of them is lost, as the stars lose their visibility when the sun is risen.' He follows this up with the paradoxes, 'Nature has all evil, and no evil in it . . . All that is called nature, darkness or self has not only no evil in it but is the only true ground of all possible good' ('The Spirit of Love' in Palmer's *The Liberal and Mystical Writings of William Law*, pp. 37-8). Law has not been approved by many, but not always rightly. Impartial students of Christian mysticism will not agree with everything that is said against Law, by Prof. I. Du Plessis in his excellent *Life of Andrew Murray of South Africa*, pp. 453-6 Andrew Murray (*Life*, 456) himself, while acknowledging his obligations to Law disowned sympathy with some of Law's views.

Angela da Foligno herself. For, as poignant as in Augustine's *Confessions*, is the consciousness of sin, of sin's unmitigated evil, in Angela da Foligno's equivalent to the saint's *Confessions*, namely, her *Book of the Divine Consolation*. We find her penitently candid in her allusions to 'vice re-awakened . . . the work of demons';[1] the state in which she was 'given once to pride and the devil but did feign to have God in the soul, whereas it was the Devil alive in the soul';[2] love as a thing to be feared 'more than all things for herein are all evils committed,'[3] and to 'love without sin'.[4] The memory of sin, she says, made her deem herself 'worthy of hell'.[5] No one can read her meditations on the sufferings of the Lord on the Cross without feeling how enormously real was sin to her as sin, evil as evil and not good, in the severely introspective manner in which she assigns to each member of her body a particular sin.[6] Against Mr. Watkin's '*optimism of faith*' of the Beata Angela we must set, not so much the pessimism of the writer, as the pressing consciousness of evil as a stern reality which no amount of optimism of outlook can make unreal. On the other hand it may be conceded that an intense way of expressing the fact of subordination to the Will of God[7] is possible, and some of the very obtrusively extravagant sayings of some mystics may be so understood. The principle of the explanation of some mystics' extravagance of speech is latent in St. Paul's words, 'Whatsoever ye do, do all to the glory of God'.[8] Apposite to the present context is a passage from S. Ignatius, which brings out clearly the explanation that should be given of the puzzling and hard sayings of some mystics:

> They who are carnal cannot do spiritual things, neither can they who are spiritual do carnal things, just as faith is incapable of the deeds of

---

[1] *Divine Consolation* (The New Medieval Library), pp. 14, 15.
[2] *Ibid.*, p. 19. [3] *Ibid.*, p. 123. [4] *Ibid.*, p. 162.
[5] *Ibid.*, p. 164. [6] *Ibid.*, p. 215. [7] See below, p. 147.
[8] 1 Cor. x. 31. There is a beautiful verse in the *Brihad Aran. Upanishad* (2. 4. 5) which illustrates how *inwardness and intention* of an act or of a relation is to count for everything. A husband, wife, children, wealth, rank, the worlds, the gods, all beings—these are not loved for the love of them but for the love of 'the Soul' (= God). The last sentence of the verse is, 'Lo verily, not for love of all is all dear, but *for love of God all is dear*.'

infidelity, and infidelity of the deeds of faith. But even what you do according to the flesh is spiritual, *for you do all things in Christ Jesus.*[1]

The Christian position is that Evil is Evil and not Good. Out of evil good may come, for God who is able to cause the very rebellion of man to turn to His praise[2] does 'sometimes allow the world . . . and its diverse and various passions' to be one of 'the many ways . . . the many roads . . . to lead men back to grace'.[3]

§ 33. Associated with the problem of evil is the place of 'the mind,' மனம், in Tāyumānavar's psalms. It has already been remarked that there is no provision in the Siddhanta theology for a 'Satan.' His place is in some respects filled by 'the mind.' Hence the merit of a state of 'mindlessness.' A 'mindless state of sanctity' is one of the poet's greatest longings. மனமற்ற பரிசுத்த நிலைமை.[4] The mind is likened to a serpent in its insidiousness,[5] and, for its variety of attachments, to a monkey.[6] It is like a wild elephant in its strength,[7] and is a formidable foe warring with the soul.[8] It is only when the mind is subdued that pure bliss can be born in the soul.[9] The process of getting rid of the mind has to be acquired before peace is possible.[10] To him who possesses control over anger and has the grace of psychic powers his very speech is unprofitable if he has not reached the stage of his mind being dead.[11] All things become clear as daylight

[1] *Ad Ephes.* viii. 2. In the 'longer form' of this passage the last sentence runs thus: 'But ye, being full of the Holy Spirit, *do nothing according to the flesh*, but all things according to the Spirit. Ye are complete in Christ Jesus who is the Saviour of all men, especially of them that believe.' The 'longer' reading amplifies the thought of the 'shorter.'

[2] *Psalm*, lxvi. 10; *Exodus*, ix. 16; *Romans*, ix. 16.

[3] *The Dialogue of S. Catherine of Siena* (Thorold's edition), pp. 34, 35.

[4] *N.M.*, 13, translated at pp. 10, 11, 12, below. On a mindless state see *N.M.*, 33, 118 (translated above, at p. xxiii, note). In *N.M.*, 412 reference is made to the soul being 'cradled in mindlessness.'

[5] *N.M.*, 1380, மனப்பாம்பு

[6] *N.M.*, 449, மர்க்கடமனம்; *N.M.*, 553, மனக்குரங்கு; *N.M.*, 609, 807, பேய்க்குரங்கு.

[7] *N.M.*, 586, மனவேழம் பெரிய மதத்த யானை

[8] *N.M.*, 805, எனக்கு வக்கெதிர்த்த . . . மனம்

[9] *N.M.*, 499, கீழிறந்த வெப்பிலே பரனந்தமே.

[10] *N.M.*, 803, மனதைப்போக்க

[11] *N.M.*, 804, சினமிறக்கக் கற்றலுஞ் சித்தியெல்லாம் பெற்றலும்.
மனமிறக்கக் கல்லார்க்கு வாயேல்,

to him whose depraved mind is dead,[1] and there is no one to whom such a man might be compared.[2] The conquest of the mind is effected by means of 'grace'.[3] 'I shall slay thee and subdue thee with the weapon of Divine grace'.[4] The mind is the source of Delusion, and were 'sins cast behind' the mind might be the soul's own helper.[5] The mind is recognized as indispensable to man and to devas, and it is *sat* and *asat*.[6] It is not the extinction of the mind but its subordination that is meant by its 'death,' and a transformed mind is a help rather than a hindrance to hopes of heaven.[7] When the mind which, in its evil operation, is associated with the 'primal breath,'[8] is brought under control the soul will have gifts as great as those of *raja yoga*.[9] Further realizations follow in this life:

> Birth-bonds that bound me long are broken,
>   Now, in this body, in this state:
> Now springs the Life, the soul's great secret;
>   O mind that changes can create,
> Like thee 's nor cloud nor flowery arbour,
>   And in seven worlds thy fame is great.[10]

The control of the mind, referred to in terms of its death and destruction, is effective on the disappearance of the soul's 'ignorance'.[11] The result of the passing of 'darkness' frees the mind from those attachments which occasion re-births.[12] It is the 'grace' of God that enables the mind to attain this freedom:[13]

> The temple of His glory is His grace
>   Where Bliss beatific, abideth He,
> And I, with Him abiding, could not know
>   Where thou, delusion dead, hadst hidden thee,
> O mind, unreal then to me as hare
>   That hath a horn, or lotus flower in space.
> Or as mirage of desert sands. O where,
>   My darkness gone, hadst thou thy hiding-place?[14]

---

[1] *N.M.*, 997, [illegible] [2] *N.M.*, 998. [3] *N.M.*, 413, 415, 416.

[4] *N.M.*, 450, உன்னைக்கொல்லுவேன் வெல்லுவேனருட் படைகொண்டே.

[5] No. 239, below, p. 87.

[6] No. 240, below, p. 87, and see below, pp. 207, 208.

[7] No. 241, below, p. 87. [8] See below, p. 172.

[9] *N.M.*, 586. [10] No: 242, below, p. 87

[11] *N. M.*, 551, [illegible], 'on the vanishing of darkness wher didst thou disappear?' [12] *N. M.*, 552.

[13] *N. M.*, 361, அருள் வரவேண்டும் 'the gift of grace is neeued.'

[14] *N. M.*, 551.

Where there is no such 'grace,' the mind is a source of continual conformity to the senses and their attachments.[1] The mind begets speech, and speech deeds wherein is delusion.[2] It is 'when the delusion-causing mind is stilled that saving wisdom springs' in the soul.[3] In the *Upanishads* every experience is ascribed to the mind—'desire, imagination, doubt, faith, unbelief, steadfastness, fickleness, shame, meditation, fear, all this is truly mind.'[4] Liberation is reached when the five senses cease, and the mind, and the intellect stir not.[5] Mindlessness is taught to be the 'supreme estate.'[6]

Is the mind, then, to be treated as unreal and neglected as though it were nothing? Our poet answers the question in the clearest negative, 'In the place where truth has been taught the mind has to be reckoned a teacher (*guru*), for there is nothing which is incapable of grace (*arul*).'[7] The importance assigned to the mind lies in the fact of its capacity to be attached to something. A figure, suggestive of the fickleness of the mind's attachments, is that of a monkey leaping from branch to branch or tree to tree, and its attachment to its temporary hold.[8] In the same couplet is the idea of the mind 'going a-whoring after strange lovers.' Its strength and capacity for attachment contain the potentiality of its attachment to God.[9] The mind's attachments, once here, once there, are like 'birth and death, forgetting and remembering.'[10] A state of indecision, a perilous middle way, is sometimes possible to the mind.[11] We thus see the meaning and need of the poet's prayer for mindlessness. The mind's attachments sway the soul's attachments.

§ 34. The teaching that the soul is capable of partaking of the nature of that to which it is attached is the basis of a very great Siddhanta truth. The degree and extent of such

[1] *N. M.*, 305. Cf. *Tirumantram*. 1681, [illegible], 'In the mind there has arisen a mirror reflecting delusion.'

[2] *N. M.*, 349. [3] *N. M.*, 540. [4] *Brihad*, 1.5.3.

[5] *Katha*, 6.10. *Maitri*, 6.30. [6] *Maitri*, 6.34.

[7] *N. M.*, 193. [8] *N. M.*, 1052, [illegible].

[9] *N. M.*, 1406. [10] *N. M.*, 356, 447.

[11] *N. M.*, 429.

participation are measured by the duration and intensity of the attachment. It is Siddhanta teaching that the soul may, even in the human body, realize an affinity to God, a partaking of God-likeness, in the relationship which is known as *Advaita*. The word *Advaita* has not, in the Siddhanta, the same meaning as it has in the Vedanta. From *nadvitīyam*,[1] where *na* is the negative prefix, is *Advaitam*, the *n* dropping out. The word literally means 'not two'. It implies the existence of two things and does not negative the reality or existence of one of the two.[2] It does not mean *ēkam* ஏகம் or monism, 'as without a second, no one can think of himself as one, and as the very thought implies duality. The word simply denies the separate existence or separability of the two. In this sense it is said that the souls exist as one with the Lord.'[3] A unity or identity in duality is intended by the *Siddhiyar* explanation of *Advaita* as being 'one with and different from.'[4] The author of the *Siddhiyar* in another work of his[5] puts the exposition negatively, *Advaitā* 'being neither one nor two nor yet a denial of either.'

> The Siddhanta appeals fully and finally to only One Experience, the Bliss of God and One alone; whereas the Vedanta has reference to the *sōham*[6] paths whereby this experience is gained. Anyone can perceive that the *sōham* is a conscious one and a dual one or *Dvaita*. In this sense the Siddhanta is *Advaita* and the Vedanta is *Dvaita*.[7]

The famous line of Tirumūlar, நானென வேதாந்தம் நான் என்னும் சித்தாந்தம்,[8] is intended to indicate a crucial difference between the Vedanta and the Siddhanta, and that difference lies in the estimate of the soul's relationship to God—is it Dvaita or Advaita, and if Advaita what does it exclude and what does it imply?

[1] As in *Svet. Up.* 3.2.

[2] Nallaswami Pillai, *Studies in Saiva Siddhanta*, p. 65.

[3] *Bodham*, Sutra ii. Nalla. *Bodham*, p. 11.

[4] *Siddhiyar*, 3.2.3. In 3.6.6 we have 'known and knower are one, different, and one and different.'

[5] *Irupā Irupahtu*, stanza 20 ஒன்றாகாமல், இரண்டாகாமல், ஒன்றுமிரண்டு மின்றாகாமல். See Nalla. *Studies*, p. 246.

[6] See below, p. 184.

[7] Nalla. *Studies*, pp. 253, 254

[8] *Tirumantram*, stanza 2372. See above, pp. xxxii, xxxiii, for some comments on this line.

Mr. Ponnambalam-Pillai to whom I have already expressed obligation[1] has these remarks on Advaita :

It may not be out of place to explain the difference between the *Adwitha* [*Advaita*] of the Aryans and our own. The latter is different from the former, which is the *Aduitham* of the Vedantists as taught by the great Sankarāchāriyar, in a very important point. It is also different from the *Dwaitham* of Madawāchāriyar or the *Vishishta Dwaitham* of Ramanujā-chāriyar. The goal of the Vedantists and of the Siddhāntists is one and the same, namely, the Supreme Being. The soul [it is taught] of the Vedantists becomes absorbed in God, the universal soul [Ātman] and loses its individuality. But it is not [taught] so by the Siddhantists. No doubt their [teaching is that the] soul becomes one with God, but at the same time it is distinct from Him that it may express its eternal gratitude for the state of Supreme Bliss in which He is pleased to place it in order that it may adore Him.[2]

The Vedanta doctrine[3] of equating the soul with the All-soul, man with God, is fundamentally distinct from the Siddhanta conservation of individuality at all points of contact of the human with the Divine. Even in the ultimate nearness of the soul to God[4] the soul does not become God, however much it may lose of what it should lose to be worthy of such nearness.

The analogy of a river losing itself in the ocean is employed to illustrate (analogies often take the place of proof)[5] the soul's union with God. The use of this analogy in the *Upanishads* goes the length of implying the soul's loss of individuality:

As these flowing rivers that tend toward the ocean, on reaching the ocean, disappear, their name and form [*nāma-rūpa*[6]] are destroyed and it is

---

[1] Above, p. xix.

[2] *Third Saiva Conference Addresses*, pp. 52, 53.

[3] See below, p. 185.

[4] 'The soul reaches the Feet of its Lord where it sees itself different from the senses, just as a man reaches the ground when the rope of the swing breaks. . . . The soul . . . will not leave the Divine Feet of the Lord . . . after once attaining them, on being freed from the ties of the world like the river which reaches the sea on the embankments being destroyed' (*Bodham*, vii. 4. Nalla. *Bodham*, p. 84). The soul loses its 'soulness,' [illegible], whatever is not conducive to God-likeness, and this is the process of 'wasting away' referred to by S. Mānikkavāchagar in the lines translated below, at pp. 187, 224.

[5] See below, *Introduction*, part ix.

[6] *Nāma-rūpa* is an idiom for identity, individuality. 'What is called space (ākāsa) is the producer of individuality (*nāma-rūpa*)' *Chandog*., 8.14.1.

called simply 'the ocean'—even so of this spectator[1] these sixteen parts that tend toward the Person,[2] on reaching the Person, disappear, their name and form [*nāma-rūpa*] are destroyed, and it is simply called 'the Person'. That one continues without parts, immortal.[3]

Another *Upanishad* saying is of similar tenor:

> As the flowing rivers in the ocean
> Disappear, quitting name and form,
> So the knower, being liberated from name and form,
> Goes unto the heavenly Person higher than the high.[4]

It is added: 'He verily who knows the Supreme Brahma becomes very Brahma'.[5] This probably is 'the selflessness . . . immortality, complete union (*sāyugyatva*), and peace (*nirvṛtatva*)' of another *Upanishad.*[6] The *Chandogya Upanishad* employs the river illustration to teach the origin and, implicitly, the ultimate destiny of souls:

> Look at these rivers, they flow, the eastern ones to the east, and the western ones to the west. From the sea they go to the sea. They become the sea itself.[7]

The idea of such close association of the soul with the All-Soul, as amounts to absence of duality, is insisted upon in more than one Upanishad:

> Thus has it been said: 'Now, where knowledge is of a dual nature [implying both a subject which knows and an object which is known], there, indeed, one hears, sees, smells, tastes, and also touches; the soul knows everything, when knowledge is *not of a dual nature,* being devoid of action, cause, or effect, unspeakable, incomparable, indescribable—what is that?' It is impossible to say.[8]

This apparently is a summary of the earlier and fuller statement which begins, 'For where there is a duality [*dvaita*], as it were, there one sees another . . .',[9] and is an explanation

[1] 'A person consists of sixteen parts' (*Chandog. Upanishad,* 6.7.1). 'The fifteen parts are his possessions, the sixteenth part is his self, *atman*'. (*Brihad,* 1.5.15).

[2] 'This person . . . is just this *Ātman,* this Immortal, this Brahma, this All' (*Brihad,* 2.5.1). 'The Great Primeval Person (Purusha) . . . Soul of all' (*Svet.* 3.19; 3.21).

[3] *Prasna,* 6.5.

[4] *Mundaka,* 3.2.8.

[5] *Mundaka,* 3.2.9.

[6] *Maitri,* 6.22.

[7] *Chandog.,* 6.10.1.

[8] *Maitri,* 6.7., *ad fin.*

[9] *Brihad,* 4.5.15.

of the saying of a sage, 'After death there is no consciousness.'[1] The sage questions :

> Where everything has just become one's own self, then, whereby, and whom . . . would one see ? . . . Then whereby, and on whom, would one think ? . . . Whereby would one understand him by whom one understands this All ? Whereby would one understand the understander ? [2]

The principle of the non-dual relationship between man and God is utter oblivion to external attachments. 'As a man, when in the embrace of a beloved wife, knows nothing within or without, so this person, when in the embrace of the intelligent *Ātman*, knows nothing within or without.'[3] The soul's desire, detached from externals, is towards the supreme *Ātman.*[4] The *Ātman* (it is repeatedly taught) is 'not a second thing, other than the [human] self and separate.'[5] Hence, 'An ocean, a seer alone without duality [*dvaita*], becomes he whose world is Brahma. . . . This is a man's highest path. . . . This is his highest achievement . . . and highest bliss.'[6] The setting of this teaching is implied in such texts as, 'Truly, everything here is Brahma : the self is Brahma,'[7] and 'Without a second [*Advaita*] he is the *Ātman.*'[8] There is Upanishad recognition of 'the state of being one with the *Ātman.*'[9] The teaching of the *Upanishads* on Advaita may or may not be the background of the Siddhanta Advaita doctrine. To concede that it is need not necessarily shut out of notice the Siddhanta divergences from the non-Siddhanta 'state of being one with the *Ātman.*'

> As the soul is attached to its forms and organs [body] and is yet separate from the body, so also is God attached to the souls. Nevertheless, the souls cannot become God, and God cannot become the souls, God is one with, and different from, the souls.[10] . . . The knower will perceive God, by His grace, as *ananya* as the knower and the Known are one and different and one-and-different [11]. . . . If you regard God as not conceivable by the senses.

---

[1] *Brihad.*, 2.4.13. [2] *Brihad.*, 2.4.14. [3] *Brihad.*, 4.3 21.

[4] *Brihad.*, 4.3.21. 'His desire is satisfied, the *Ātman* is his desire, . . he is without desire, and without sorrow'.

[5] *Brihad.*, 4.3. 23–31. [6] *Brihad.*, 4.3.32.

[7] *Māndūkya*, 2. [8] *Māndūkya*, 7.

[9] *Māndūkya*, 7, following the reading (Hume, *Upanishads*, p. 392) *ēkātmya-pratyaga-sāra*.

[10] *Siddhiyar*, 3.2.3. [11] *Siddhiyar*, 3.6.6.

it is of no use. If you contemplate Him as beyond contemplation . . . it is a mere fiction. If you contemplate Him as yourself, it is also a fiction. Giving up these fictitious ideas of God, the only way of knowing Him is by His grace.[1]

Thus Siddhanta theology is different from other teaching on the relationship between God and the soul in some important respects:

1. The soul is not God, however much the soul may approach God-likeness.

2. The soul's individuality is at no stage to be deemed annihilated, however much it may progress in the relationship of being lost in God. 'When "one only without a second" is postulated, the very postulating implies that the thing postulated is different'.[2]

3. God's incessant association with the soul[3] postulates the possibility of the soul being intensely God-like.

4. God and the soul are thus one, and different, and one-and-different.

The union of the soul with God is, in a sense, accompanied by loss of 'individuality,' and that sense is thus stated by Mr. J. M. Nallaswamy Pillai:[4]

When the soul loses its individuality (feeling of 'I'ness, *ahangkāram* or *ānavam*)[5] it becomes merged in God; when it loses its *karma*[6] and when, therefore, it has power to keep in suspension its *mala*[7] with which it has been associated from the beginning. . . . This losing of self is the real sacrifice brought about by love.

What exactly is claimed for Advaita in the Siddhanta is best stated in the words of the same Saivite thinker:[8]

Advaita is defined by St. Meykandan as meaning *ānvō nāsti* or *ananya* or inseparable; his disciple calls the relation 'as neither one nor two.' Advaita, literally meaning not two, simply denies the separability or duality of God and soul and matter, but does not postulate oneness by denying the existence of one or other *pathārta* or by formulating their mutual convertibility as in causation, etc. . . . The illustrations of mind and body, vowels and consonants,[9] are used to denote the Advaita relation of God to the universe of nature and of man. . . . The vowel is not the consonant nor the consonant the vowel. God is not one with the soul and the universe, and yet, without God, where is the universe? . . . The Saiva Advaita Siddhanta postulates

[1] *Siddhiyar*, 3.6.7.
[2] *Siddhiyar*, 3.6.9.
[3] *Siddhiyar*, 3.6.9. See below, pp. 184–190 on the soul's deification.
[4] *Studies*, p. 253.
[5] See above, p. lxxx and below, p. 150.
[6] See below, *Introduction*, part vii.
[7] See above, p. lxxvii.
[8] *Studies*, pp. 310–12.
[9] See below, pp. 18, 161.

that God is neither *abhēda*[1] with the world, nor *bhedā*, nor *bhedābheda* as these terms are ordinarily understood, and yet He is one with the world, and different from the world, *bhedābheda*. . .

Tāyumānavar speaks of *Advaita* as the relationship in which இரண் டொன்றெண் ணுமோர் மானத விகற்பமற வென்று நிற்பது,

That phase
Of faith which . . .
Thinks not God and the soul are one or twain,
Stands victor over doubt, wrong thinking slain.[2]

In his longing:[3]

With God who is true wisdom,
  Nor one nor twain to be,
As I am now with Darkness,
  When dawns the day for me,
When dawns the day?

the poet gives expression to the thought that the 'Advaita' relation is just as possible with good as with evil; with God as with *anava mala*. The soul is capable of being in advaita relationship with any one of contraries, indeed with anything towards which attachment is possible. It is on this capacity of the soul that advaita teaching is based. This characteristic of the soul, capacity for attachment, leads to the soul being ***assimilated*** to that to which it is attached:

This truth is taught in all the Scriptures,
  And has been ever from of old,
That in the end the soul attaineth
  To what its own attachments hold.[4]

---

[1] The soul's relationship to God is thus stated in the *Bodham*, Sutra ii, He is one (*abhēda*) with souls, different from them (*bhēda*), and one-and-different (*bhedābheda*).' The first suggests connection as causation or succession, e.g. gold and ornaments made of gold; the second, co-existence with mutual exclusion, e.g. darkness and light; the third co-existence without mutual exclusion, e.g. word and its meaning. The Siddhanta does not affirm causation nor separable or inseparable co-existence. It does not adopt the first two analogies (See Nalla., *Bodham*, pp. 15-17.)

[2] *N. M.*, 41, translated above, at pp. xxiv, xxv.

[3] *N. M.*, 1298.

[4] *N. M.*, 53, translated below, at p. 28. So in *N. M.*, 149, it is said of the soul பாசென்றது பற்றினத் வியைபாய் நின்று 'assimilated to that to which it is attached.'

The soul's potentialities of attachment and assimilation show themselves in a high degree in worship:

Because by bond and by attachment
That which I worship I would be,
And so by being drawn to Thee ward
Be least of me and most of Thee . . . [1]

And the loftiest form of worship is framed upon the heights of love. It is because of love that the soul puts on one side all that lies between it and its Beloved; then comes that state in which the soul is 'secondless',[2] 'the seer not seeing a second',[3] and 'there is nothing between'.[4] The stage of close affiliation to the Divine is reached by a process of 'wasting' sought to be expressed by St. Mānikkavāchagar:

Yea, closer, until all of me,
Worn to an atom, worn to be
No longer I, was one
With Thee . . . . . . [5]

In this place, as arising out of the subject of the God-becoming of man,[6] the fact may appropriately be noticed that *veneration is given to saints as unto God*, in Tāyumānavar's

[1] *N. M.*, 91, translated below, at p. 56. On non-Hindu analogies see below, pp. 186, 188.

[2] *N. M.*, 1434, below, p. 103.

[3] *N. M.*, 1440, below, p. 111 and p. 222.

[4] *N. M.*, 1422, below, p. 107 and see p. 215.

[5] See below, p. 187. The following passage from the late Sir P. Arunachalam's *A Revel in Bliss*, p. 34 may be quoted here:

The Soul and the Lord apparently distinct, but in fact non-dual, the Soul 'not even for the twinkling of an eye having intelligence of its own' and owing its intelligence wholly to Him, and finally by His Grace merging in Him and standing there non-dual (v. 20), He, all the while remaining unaffected as the magnet is unaffected by the iron which it energizes or as the sun by the flower which opens under the genial influence of its rays,—this is the doctrine of the *Saiva Siddhânta*, that is, the more ancient interpretation of the *Vēdānta* than that which now passes as the *Vēdānta*, the interpretation, in fact by which Masters like Tāyumānavar harmonize and reconcile the seemingly conflicting positions of the Vēdāntic and Saiva Siddhāntic schools (வேதாந்த சித்தாந்த சமரசம்).

[6] I may be permitted to refer the reader to my *Foregleams of God*, ch. viii, § 15 for further observations on 'man-becoming of God' and 'God-becoming of man.'

psalms, and the fact is not foreign to Siddhanta theology generally. Thus அன்பரடி கண்டதே யருளின் வடிவமாம் 'to behold the feet of the saints is to behold the Form of Grace'[1] is one of many Siddhanta statements of the recognition of a very close human approximation to God-likeness. The poet elsewhere is more definite about the deification of the just:

To class or caste he lays no claim,
Or note of character or name:
He knows not any need;
No stir of passions does he feel,
Or of possession's strong appeal,
The lure of gain and greed;
By ties of home he is not bound,
Of child or wife, for he has found
Rest, from all sorrow freed.
So good a man deserves to be
Deemed Siva's self, high Deity,
Whose gift is Heaven indeed.[2]

Equally clear as to seeing in sainthood God is the verse

கண்ணுணின்ற வொளியைக் கருத்தினை
விண்ணுணின்ற விளங்கிய மெய்யினை
யெண்ணி யெண்ணி யிரவும் பகலுமே
நண்ணுகின்றவர் நான்றொழுந் தெய்வமே.[3]

They are God to me who on Him meditate
Day and night drawing nigh unto Him, nigher,
Light of eye-light and innermost sense who is,
Brightly burning Truth in the broad spirit-sky.[4]

To my mind the clearest exposition of this verse and its theme is what the late Mr. J. M. Nallaswamy Pillai very kindly communicated to me in a private letter it was my privilege to receive from him in November 1913:

I am not a great Pundit, but I think the interpretation you give is the correct one. . . . The worship of God's devotees and guru are very efficacious and easy, as they are already filled with the grace of God, and I may

---

[1] *N. M.*, 129.
[2] *N. M.*, 351. The Tamil is as follows:

குலமிலான் குணங்குறியிலான் குறைவிலான் கொடுநாம்
புலமிலான் றனக்கென்னவோர் பற்றிலான் பொருந்து
மிலமிலான் மைந்தர் மனைவியில்லா னெவனவன்சஞ்
சலமிலான் முத்திதரும் பரசிவனெனத் தகுமே.

[3] *N. M.*, 268.
[4] Below, p. 84, and the comments on this text at p. 207, below,

refer to verse 23 in எனக்கெனச்செயல்.[1] You are also right in referring to the *Siddhiyar* verses.[2] God's devotees being filled with God's light and grace are indistinguishable from God Himself. Though the sun's light shines everywhere it is easily focussed in certain lenses and is reflected and deflected. So too are God's devotees who are able to transfer to us God's light and grace. As a Christian you will be able to appreciate the point, since in Christianity salvation is deemed possible through Christ only, which will be more intelligent[3] from the standpoint of the Siddhanta. As Dr. Drummond puts it—through love of Christ we reflect Christ in ourselves, we become Christlike, Godlike, and Godly, we become Christ or God. I dare say you have already become familiar with some of my views on these topics. I may refer you to my notes under Sutra iii in *Siddhiyar*.[4]

Mudaliyar R. C. Kailasa Pillai who was a Tamil scholar of repute in Ceylon favoured me with his comments in 1913 on the verse in question:

> There is no man-worship in the Saiva Siddhanta; the saints are only the media through whom or in whom Divinity manifests Itself and is worshipped.

His rendering of the verse is as follows:

> He is the light within their eye; He is the object of their thought.
> He is the absolute truth or reality resplendent from within the etheric space (of omniscience).
> Those (saints) who meditate on Him night and day, and realize, attain, approach Him are the divinities I worship.

---

[1] Heading of a section of S. Tāyumāuavar psalms. The verse is *N. M.*, 384, where occur the words

> கண்மணிக்குள் மணியேபோலே தொழுமன்பர் கருத்துள்
> அணுகின்ற நின்னருள் . . . .

'Thy grace which draws nigh and abides as the apple of the eye in the consciousness of Thy loved ones who adore Thee.'

It may be noted that in *N. M.*, 268 the அணுகின்ற 'drawing nigh' is the act of the devotees and in *N. M.*, 384 of God.

[2] *Siddhiyar*. 3.12.3, quoted below, at p. 207.

[3] Henry Drummond, *The Changed Life*. 'I have never come upon a more remarkable book than the pamphlet by Prof. Henry Drummond called *The Changed Life*.' (J. M. Nallaswami Pillai in his English edition of *Siddhiyar*, p. 195). In the same devout Hindu scholar's *Studies in the Ṣaiva Siddhanta*, pp. 308-9 reference is made to *The Changed Life*. A prominent place is found for Andrew Murray's great classic of soul-culture, *Abide in Christ*, in the same Siddhanta scholar's English edition of *Siddhiyar*, pp. 252-57. Mr. Nallaswami Pillai's death is a distinct loss to the cause of literature and religion in Tamilagam.

[4] Eng. Edition of *Siddhiyar*, pp. 193-96.

It seems to me that a sympathetic appreciation of the Siddhanta doctrine of seeing God in sainthood—that God can and does so fill men with godliness and grace that they deserve reverence because of God in them, that men can become (in Christian language) 'temples of God'—is a great approach to the Christian teaching of the man-becoming of God: the possibility is suggested of there being in one Man 'the fulness of the Godhead bodily.'[1]

PART VI. SIN, KARMA, BODY

§ 35. A keen sense of the significance of sin is characteristic of the psalms of our poet.[2] Sin is disharmony. Sin is whatever estranges man from God and keeps him so alienated. Hence the numberless longings[3] in all these psalms for nearness to, and union with, God. The poet lays stress on the fact that the closer the soul is to God the more immune it is from sin. Whatever may be said as to the rightness or wrongness of the poet's acceptance of the Siddhanta theology of sin, we can find no trace in his writings of any tendency found elsewhere[4] towards minimising the reality of sin as evil. We have already seen in studying the Siddhanta theory of evil[5] that evil is ascribed to ***malam*** in its three-fold aspect of ***ānavam, māya***; and ***karma***, three principles to which, singly or jointly, sin and suffering are attributed. The third of these remains for consideration.

§ 36. 'Karma' means 'action' and includes good and evil actions. The soul is spoken of in an *Upanishad* as 'being overcome by the bright or the dark fruits of action (***karman***) and entering a good or an evil womb.'[6] Karma is the fruit of action and is productive of results after death.[7] One result is embodiment 'according to action' (***karman***).[8] The soul, in the ***Upanishads***, is 'like a lame man, bound with the fetters made of the fruit of good and evil.'[9] The wandering, in births and re-births, of the soul thus handicapped is known as ***samsāra***.[10]

1 Col. ii. 9.

2 See above, § 20.

3 See above, § 20 (4).

4 See below, p. 185, for Swami Vivekananda's views on 'sin'.

5 See above, §§ 2[illegible]-31.

6 *Maitri*, 3.1.

7 ***Brihad.***, 3.2.13.

8 *Katha.*, 5.7.

9 *Maitri*, 3.2.

10 *Katha.*, 3.7; *Maitri.*, 1.4.

Again, the beginnings of *samsāra* are taught to be 'just one's own thought . . . what is one's thought, that he becomes.'[1] Thus we see that the earliest Hindu use of the term ***karma*** applied it to deeds good and deeds evil, although in later and more popular and less accurate, thinking, ***karma*** is restricted to '***evil*** deeds.'[2] Early Upanishadic speculations as to the destiny of souls seem to indicate that in Hindu philosophic thinking ***karma*** was associated with a soul from the moment of death. In other words, it is not definitely discussed whether or no ***karma*** is co-eval with the soul in any pre-bodily state. Thus, in the *Brihad-Aranyaka Upanishad*[3] to Yājgnavalkya's inquiry, 'What becomes of this person, *purusha*, on death[4] and dissolution?' Arttabhaga's answer is, 'We two only will know of this, which is not for us to speak in public', and it is added:

> The two went away and deliberated. What they said was *karma*, what they praised was *karma*, verily one becomes good by good action, bad by bad action. Thereupon Arttabhaga held his peace.

We read elsewhere[5] that the *karma* theory was at first a non-Brahmanic, Kshattriya secret. In the early stages of the history of this theory speculation does not appear to have been directed towards formulating a doctrine of the co-evality of ***karma*** with the soul. I am not certain that even in the more advanced and less ancient portions of the ***Upanishads*** one really does find a definite postulation of the ***eternity*** of ***karma***. It was reserved for the Siddhanta divines, whether or no upon

[1] *Maitri*. 6.34.

[2] The Tamil word கருமம் is an instance of the lax, unphilosophic employment of *karma*, கன்மம், கர்மம். Tamil words for *karma* as வினை, ஊழ், தொல்வினை lay stress, in common usage, upon *evil* deeds.

[3] *Brihad*., 3.2.13.

[4] Death is described as leading to the dissolution of 'the voice into fire, breath into air, sight into the sun . . . and *the soul* (*atman*) *into space*.' The inquirer's question is as to what becomes of 'personality'. See as to *atman* in this passage a view of more than one *aspect* of *atman* in *Maitri*, 3. 1–3, where mention is made of 'the elemental soul' and a higher. For a learned account of the teaching of Yajgnavalkya see Dr. B. Barua's *History of Pre-Buddhistic Indian Philosophy*, ch. xi.

[5] *Chandog. Upanishad*, 5.3.7. For treatment fuller than is possible here of the origins and history of karma and transmigration the present writer would refer the reader to his *Foregleams of God*, ch. x.

Upanishad intimations, to build the doctrine of *karma* being co-eternal with the soul, undismayed by the fact that, logically pursued, this doctrine of co-eternity would suggest the possibility of the problem, 'If *karma* is action how could a soul have karma *before ever it had its first body or did its first deed?*'[1] The *Upanishads* and Buddhism deal with karma as from a man's death and dissolution in time: the Siddhanta deals with it as from times before birth, from eternity.

§ 37. 'Karma', meaning 'action', and, by extension of thought, the accumulated effect and energy of deeds, may be considered under the following heads of inquiry:

1. The nature of karma
2. The kinds of karma.
3. Karma and the soul.
4. Karma and God.
5. The dissolving of karma.

1. As to the nature of karma, it is taught in the *shastras*:

> Gain and loss, pleasure and pain, honour and dishonour, all these six, become attached to a man in the womb. They manifest themselves as the result of one's endeavour. They are the result of the endeavour made in a previous birth. Result of present endeavour will be manifest in a future birth.[2]
>
> As the fruits of husbandry yield us food for present enjoyment and seed for to-morrow, so also our acts account for our present enjoyment, and form the seed, the fruit springing from which will be enjoyed in a future birth. This is the eternal order of *karma*.[3]
>
> *Karma* comprises virtuous and vicious acts and their results, becoming loss and gain, and pleasure and pain.[4]

2. Deeds are good and bad. The main division of *karma* is into good and evil, or merit and demerit. Perhaps the classification into merit and demerit is not accurate, since it is *action* (whatever its aim) that really counts in determining destiny.[5]

Tāyumānavar speaks of இருவினை, 'two-fold karma' in

[1] Buddhism, by its relentlessness of reasoning, posited *karma* apart from 'soul', it denied 'souls'.

[2] *Siddhiyar*, 3.2.9. [3] *Siddhiyar*, 3.2.12. [4] *Siddhiyar*, 3.2.39.

[5] The *Bodham*, ii. 2, speaks of 'good and bad karma'. *Siddhiyar*, 3.2.6, also mentions 'two kinds of karma'.

many places.[1] Karma is further divided into three kinds.[2] They are

(1) *Sanchitam*, சஞ்சிதம்—store of deeds 'accumulated' (*sanchitam*) though a whole succession of infinite births. This follows the soul from birth to birth.

(2) *Prārattam*, பிராரத்தம்—fruit ripe out of the *sanchitam* store and inducing fresh births.

(3) *Āgāmyam*, ஆகாமியம்—deeds done in a given birth, and they are good (புண்ணியம், *punniyam*) and bad (பாவம், *pāvam*).[3]

What is *āgāmyam* in one birth is *sanchitam* for the next. There is a cyclic connection between these three kinds. It is to *prārattam* and *āgāmyam* that our poet-saint refers when he speaks of முன்னே செய்வினை . . . பின்னே வந்து மூளும்வினை 'the deeds, misdeeds . . . as fruitage past . . . said to follow',[4]—the past becoming the present. The 'fruit of former deeds' is the fear that is taught in some very striking verses in *Nāladiyar*.[5]

3. The bond between the soul and *karma* is from eternity.[6] The soul is said 'to eat the fruits of karma'.[7] The past karma is eaten in this birth and 'the karma of the last body causes a new body'.[8] The operations of karma lead the soul, and limit it, to சாதி (genus) ஆயுள், (length of life), போகம் (experience).[9] When souls, as the result of deeds, assume any body, that body must be of some genus, have some limit of life, and experience some joys and sorrows. 'Death gives a prolonged rest to the human monad to enable it to eat its karma in the next birth. Why should it have a next birth? Because it must eat the fruits of previous karma, and unless it does so, its *ānava mala* cannot be removed. This latter then is the reason for reproduction.'[10]

[1] E. G., *N. M.*, 45, 112, 176, 179. In the last verse he speaks of நல்வினை தீவினை 'good and bad karma'.

[2] *N. M.*, 1162, சஞ்சிதமோதி . . . மூன்றே 'The three taints called *sanchitam*, etc., *Sivapragasam*, stanzas 28, 29, 30.

[3] *Sivapragasam*, stanza 28.

[4] *N. M.*, 632, translated below at p. 98. 'Old karma' is mentioned in *N. M.*, 489, 546.

[5] Ch. xi, verses 101, 104, 105, 108, where we have the expressions பழவினை (old karma), முன்னைவினை (former karma), செய்தவினை (deeds already done).

[6] *Siddhiyar*, 3.2.40. *Sivapragasam*, stanza 28.

[7] *Siddhiyar*, 3.2.4. [8] *Siddhiyar*, 3.2.10. [9] *Sivapra ̣āsam*, stanza 29.

[10] Nallaswami Pillai, Eng. Edition of *Bōdham*, p. 7.

The rules regulating births and re-births belong to the subject of the doctrine of the transmigration of souls.

4. If the soul is projected into embodiments by the sheer force of ***karma***, what is God's position with reference to both the soul and the soul's ***karma*** ? It is taught :

> The soul enjoys the fruits of *karma* through the *sakti* [Power] of God, in the same way as a king metes out rewards and punishments . . . or a physician applies remedies. The fruits cannot attach to a future birth . . . of their own force [1]. . . . The Supreme Lord understands your deserts and makes you suffer pleasure or pain accordingly[2] . . . . God in union with His Gnana Ṡakti causes souls to undergo the processes of births and re-births by inducing their good and bad *karma*.[3] Siva makes souls eat *karma* and obtain liberation [4]. . . . The Lord cures the ills of *karma* by subjecting mankind to pain and pleasure.[5]

It is ***karma*** that determines the number of births, but it is God who 'adjusts the birth according to karma and makes the souls eat the fruit thereof. Without His Divine Presence and Energy the soul cannot take for itself its own material body, and it can have no progress except when it is in conjunction with its material body'.[6]

God's share in human destiny is recognized by Tāyumānavar. 'It is Thy grace that has bidden us to be bound by births because of our bondage to ***karma***'.[7] He asks, 'Why hast thou implanted in me good and bad ***karma*** and laid on me the load of this body'?[8] He complains that God had made him and 'fettered him with the bonds of karma'.[9] Again :

> Laying on me load of my self,
>   Burden of births and deeds on me,
> A puppet in Thy hands, for good
>   And ill, thou madest me to be.[10]

The poet is constrained to confess that it is God 'who doeth as He pleaseth . . . moves all for ill and good.'[11] Man is

[1] *Siddhiyar*, 3.2.4.
[2] *Siddhiyar*, 3.2.13.
[3] *Bodham*, sutra 2, *T.A.P.*, iv. 2.
[4] *Siddhiyar*, 3.2.34. *Siddhiyar*, 3.2.35.
[5] Nallaswami Pillai, Eng. Edition of *Bodham*, p. 7.
[6] *Ibid*, p. 7.
[7] *N. M.*, 107, [illegible]
[8] *N. M.*, 179, [illegible]
[9] *N. M.*, 455, [illegible]
[10] *N. M.*, 291, below at p. 66.
[11] *N. M.*, 324, below at p. 48.

God's prisoner in the prison-house of the senses, God's puppet.[1] So convinced is the poet of God's close association with man's destiny that he does not hesitate to say of God, 'Thou art my evil and my good'.[2]

5. Karma, linked, as we have seen, to the soul from birth to birth, and its operativeness overseen and directed by God, is like a running account. There are items of the account settled in one birth and some carried forward to another birth and then they are augmented by fresh liabilities. Is a balance never to be struck? Is the debt never to be cancelled? If so

> The moving Finger writes; and having writ
> Moves on: nor all thy Piety nor Wit
> Shall lure it back to cancel half a line
> Nor all thy tears wash out a word of it.[3]

In India the law of karma is sometimes taught to mean a principle in respect of the workings of which God remains an unconcerned spectator, and whose terrible processes, which perchance He may have instituted, He is powerless to prevent.[4] *In the Siddhanta theology the dissipation of karma is contemplated:*

(1) The effect of a deed may be annulled by another deed; or by the hired expiatory services of other people and observance of certain rules the greater portion of the debt may be cancelled, and the residue carried forward into a future birth.[5]

(2) At the end of an aeon there takes place a dissolution of the universe, but *karma* [apparently if it remained attached to a soul at the time of that event] is kept alive and enters into activities in the new aeon.[6]

(3) 'The Grace of God as the sun appears and sheds everywhere great light for *karma* and its consequences'.[7] 'Old karma [*prārattam*] disappears with the body, and karma accumulating in the meanwhile [*āgamyām*] is burnt up by Grace'.[8]

---

[1] *N. M.*, 1023, below at p. 41.

[2] *N. M.*, 286, below at p. 65. See above, § 32.

[3] *Rubaiyat* of Omar Khayyam, verse 51.

[4] See Haigh's *Leading Ideas of Hinduism*, pp. 128–30 for a discussion of this aspect of karma.

[5] *Sivapragāsam*, stanza 31.

[6] *Siddhiyar*, 3.2.40; *Sivapragāsam*, stanza 28, where the 'dissolution' is called புடைகலம், known also as ஒடுக்ககாலம் ('time of shrinking'). Tāyumānavar refers to this dissolution in *N. M.* 273 (at p. 61, below) and *N. M.* 622 (at p. 96, below).

[7] *T.A.P.*, iv. 2,

[8] *T.A.P.*, vi. 8,

But Grace does not work till the soul has been made fit for it, in its fulness of time. There is a stage of maturity.[1] It is the time when karma 'is balanced,' the time of இருவினை யொப்பு (*Iru vinay oppu*) 'the adjustment of both kinds of karma.' This is மலபரிபாகம் (*mala pari pākam*) to which Tāyumānavar refers.[2] Tirumūlar speaks of this 'balancing' time as that when by God's Grace the soul becomes 'indifferent to deeds, has the triple *mala* [karma included] destroyed, and reaches God'.[3] It is this indifference to deeds, action without attachment that is known as balancing.[4] Because of the realized efficacy of Grace, Tāyumānavar declares victory over karma.

> My deeds, the demons of my making
> Shall never trouble me again.[5]

He rejoices that every approach of *karma* to the soul has been cut off.[6] The means is Grace, for Grace puts karma to fight.[7] It is as if 'a single stone scatters in hasty flight a crowd of crows'.[8] The part played by Grace in the liberation of the soul from *karma* is ascribed in non-theistic philosophies to effort.[9] The truer perspective takes in Grace and effort, the former conducing to, and co-operating with, the latter.

§ 38. The doctrine of *karma* is linked to the doctrine of the transmigration of souls. The Siddhanta divines seem to have accepted without question the theory of soul-transmigration as propounded in the *Upanishads*, at any rate, they have not expressly or impliedly repudiated the elaborate system of metempsychosis as set forth in *Manu* and earlier authorities. We are, however, on surer ground in stating that the Siddhanta theologians have not given the world anything in lieu of what is enunciated in the *Upanishads* and the *Brahmanas*. It is outside

[1] See below, pp. 20, 21 and 167.
[2] *N.M.*, 454, 583.
[3] See below, p. 168.
[4] See below, p. 168.
[5] *N.M.*, 54, translated below, p. 28.
[6] *N.M.*, 76, [illegible].
[7] *N.M.*, 1160, 1161.
[8] *N.M.*, 94, translated below, p. 57.
[9] In the articles by Dr. L. De La Vallée Poussin and Mr. R. L. Turner in *E.R.E.*, vii, pp 673 and 676 respectively there is no reference to the Siddhanta doctrine of emancipation by Grace.

the scope of this Introduction to discuss[1] the origins or even details of the theory of transmigration as held by almost all theistic Hindu religious sects. Tāyumānavar, writing in an environment of Siddhanta theology, recognizes the fact of numerous births, even numerous human births.[2] He refers thus to his own past births:

> Tale and total of all it is hard to tell,
> Male and female, my numberless births on earth.[3]

He laments the heat of birth-bonds[4] and dreads 'the dark sea of sorrow.'[5] When we find him referring to his past births we are not necessarily to infer remembrance on his part of his previous births. In the absence of his testimony to any such recollection it is safer to believe that the poet *accepts without controversy the theological implications of the Siddhanta hypothesis of karma-transmigration* rather than that he gives any hint of any *experience of prior existences.* However it be, one is sure that a genuine fear of the risk of rebirths is a factor in the poet's reasons for redemption. Rightly or wrongly, the terror of *samsāra* is something to reckon with. He prays to be delivered from that dread. He knows that by அருள், 'Grace,' a man is secure against the obsession of transmigration.

> A single stone is strong to scatter
> In hasty flight a crowd of crows.
> So all past deeds, the sum of karma,
> Cause never hurt or harm to those
> Who, for Thy grace love-thirsty, longing,
> Its fruition and its fulness find.
> That I so thirst not, is no secret;
> All my misdeeds, before, behind,
> Oppressively beset my body.[6]

Towards the body our poet, in common with many Siddh antawriters, with one brilliant but anonymous exception,

[1] The present writer has done this to some extent in his *Foregleams of God*, ch. x. §§ 3-6 (details) §§ 7-9 (origins).
[2] *N.M.*, 2, translated at p. 3, below.
[3] *N.M.*, 249, translated at p. 80, below.
[4] *N.M.*, 1189, translated at p. 119, below.
[5] *N.M.*, 1190, translated at p. 119, below.
[6] *N.M.*, 94, translated at p. 59, below.

takes an attitude of disparagement. He is not so forbiddingly realistic in his loathing of the body as is Pattanattu Pillayar,[1] but most of his references to the body are not overflattering. It may be stated as correct that all the poet's references to a body are to the human body and that he is not concerned with the births of the human soul in non-human bodies. He accepts the theory of re-births as a fact and restricts his comments to the human body. The human body, says the poet, is

> A filthy hovel built of bone, flesh, sinew, skin and hair.[2]
> The hut of the five senses.[3]
> The house of nine doors.[4]
> The muscle-drawn chariot in which the god of lust rides in state.[5]
> A leathern bottle for holding tears and all excretions.[6]
> A vessel whence oozes *karma*.[7]
> Cremation ground where grows Desire which, however much pruned and trimmed ceases not to flourish.[8]
> Rice-bag on which the crow, vulture, dog and fox have their eyes.[9]
> Two-posted nine-windowed dancing hall of lust.[10]
> Tank of overflowing *malam*.[11]
> The three-*mala* hell.[12]
> Pit of worms.[13]
> Land of karma-begetting forces.[14]
> A pit where *kundala sakti* is made to dance.[15]
> A food-bag.[16]
> A stinking object made of rice-paste.[17]
> A thing rotten from inside as a pot holding salt.[18]
> A fleeting thing.[19]
> A burden.[20]
> An earthen pitcher smashed by Death.[21]
> A worthless drug in the market.[22]

---

[1] See for example *Mum-Mani Kōvai*, iii. 13, and *Kachitiru Akaval*.

[2] *N.M.*, 80 (at p. 44, below) 206 (below at p. 203), *N.M.*, 1443 (below, at p. 104) 348, 418. See *Maitri Upanishad*, 3. 4.

[3] *N.M.*, 101. [4] *N.M.*, 101, 587. [5] *N.M.*, 101.

[6] *N.M.*, 101, 1116. [7] *N.M.*, 101, 584, 587. [8] *N.M.*, 101.

[9] *N.M.*, 122, 1118, cf. Pattanattar, *Mathurai*, St. 26. [10] *N.M.*, 122.

[11] *N.M.*, 122, 418. [12] *N.M.*, 1124. [13] *N.M.*; 122, 418, 1126.

[14] *N.M.*, 1120. [15] *N.M.*, 1231.

[16] *N.M.*, 1125. [17] *N.M.*, 418. [18] *N.M.*, 581.

[19] *N.M.*, 280, 460, 493, 626 (below, at p. 97).

[20] *N.M.*, 493, 609. [21] *N.M.*, 122.

[22] *N.M.*, 122. The section. *N.M.*, 1116-1126 is headed, 'The mockery and despising of the body.'

A shore ever tumbling down.[1]
A water bubble.[2]
A load of limbs skin-covered.[3]
Prison of luring senses.[4]

The Siddhanta poets no doubt speak of God dwelling in man,[5] and of the temple of the heart.[6] They even approach the Pauline saying, 'The body is the temple of God.'[7] The reasons that impelled the Siddhanta saints to loathe and despise the body are not unlike those which drove many of the early Christians into the deserts of Egypt where they practised excesses of physical mortification. There is one Siddhanta writer, unfortunately anonymous, who seems to be Pauline in his conception of the body as a temple. He is the author of *Gnānakkummi* ஞானக்கும்மி a very readable poem in 740 lines, divided into 185 four-line verses of arresting simplicity and charm.[8] The lines relevant to the present context open the thirty-eighth verse beginning thus:

There is a temple of Siva
Known as the body of man,

and are continued in other verses locating tower and turret, flag-staff, altars, lamps, doors, windows and other temple parts and accessories with reverent ingenuity. I write, subject to correction from those better informed, that there is not, in the writings of any Siddhanta poet of any note, anything analogous to the body-temple description in *Gnānakkummi*. The lines of Tāyumānavar descriptive of spiritual worship[9] are so detached

[1] *N.M.*, 17, below at p. 24. [2] *N.M.*, 815, below at p. 37.
[3] *N.M.*, 818, below at p. 38. [4] *N.M.*, 1023, below at p. 41.
[5] See below, pp. 156, 157. [6] See above, p. xxvii. [7] 1 Cor. vi. 19.

[8] The *Gnānakkummi* begins at p. 423 of Mr. Saravana Muttu Pillai's *Patinen Sittarkal Periya Gnānakkōvay* (Treasury of Mystical Poems of Eighteen Mystics).

[9] *N.M.*, 54, translated below, at pp. 47, 48. In *N.M.*, 496 S. Tāyumānavar refers to the habit, a useless one, of speaking of the body as a mere burden and thinks it juster to the body to speak well of it, since in it the soul has the experience of the bliss of God, [illegible]. The words of S. Appar (Nallaswamy Pillai, *S. Appar*, 45) காயமே கோயிலாக . . . பூசனை ஈசனுக்குப் போற்றவிக்காட்டினோமே, 'with the body as the temple . . . we have shown the way to worship God,' are far from the descriptive beauty of the *Gnānakkummi*

from physical figures as not to afford any parallel to the *Gnānakkummi* passage.

§ 39. While Tāyumānaswāmy, in common with many Siddhanta poets, sets a low value on the human body by reason of the fleshly instincts, appetites and susceptibilities which war against the spirit, he prays and hopes for the realization of high religious experiences '*in this life, in this body.*' The birth of a soul in a human body, he says, is the best of births and it were wise to use the best of births for the highest use and not take risks :

> Of births and bodies without number
>   This present, human is the best.
> This missed, who knows what I may suffer
>   In births to be, and go unblest :
> While in this birth and in this body,
>   My spirit's shelter, halting place,
> 'Tis best that I in joy be blended
>   With bliss that from the sky of Grace,
> A cloud with bounty laden, raineth
>   Beatitude [1]. . . .

If, says he, there is the probability of other births for him, then, his prayer is for the boon to be given him, *in this life*, of birthlessness.[2] It is only where there is no attachment, and the mind is in peace and advaita is realized that the human body is no longer needed, but till then there remains a desire for embodiments.[3] Since he is in the body, says the poet, what is necessary for 'salvation'' could be known 'in this the best of many births'.[4] He is convinced that all the travail and trouble of re-births could cease *in this life.*[5] This body is the best of many.[6] Therefore is the poet's prayer that, before the dissolution

---

passage. The principle that the body is not to be despised since it is the temple of God is enjoined by S. Tirumūlar in *Tirumantram*, stanza 725.

> உடம்பினை முன்னம் இழுக்கென் றிருந்தேன்
> உடம்பினுக் குள்ளே உறுபொருள் கண்டேன்
> உடம்புளே உத்தமன் கோயில்கொண் டானென்
> றுடம்பினை யானிருந் தோம்புகின் றேனே.

[1] *N.M.*, 60, below at p. 115. [2] *N.M.*, 108.
[3] *N.M.*, 492. [4] *N.M.*, 126. [5] *N.M.*, 400.
[6] *N.M.*, 812, below at p. 37 ; *N.M.*, 60, below at p. 115.

of this body, before he 'takes off this coat',[1] grace might be given him to find joy and peace with realization of God.[2]

> The seas are many, and the mountains many :
>   So many are deeds done and deeds to be,
> For deeds so many many are the bodies,
>   As multitudinous as sand of sea.
> Would'st Thou not drive afar, O God All-Filling,
>   The gathering clouds of ignorance from me
> That I, before I leave this present body,
>   May draw near Thee and, Lord, abide in Thee ? [3]

No perusal of the poet-saint's psalms does his estimate of the human body, in its setting of karma as a curse and transmigration as a consequence, adequate justice which lays not proper stress upon his emphasis on the present, human birth, in this present, human body, as the highest probationary opportunity.[4]

PART VII.—DELIVERANCE, GRACE, GURU

§ 40. Karma is one of the contrivances of a merciful providence for the purifying of souls.[5] Karma is based upon a law as rigid as relentless, and if God is behind the workings of this law as Grace, then it is still His Grace that sustains the law in its operations, watches its retributive processes, and, at the same time, has *power to snap the cycle of samsāra and effect the freedom of the fettered soul.* If this were not so, then karma in Siddhanta would be the same as in non-theistic philosophies. *There can be no manner of doubt as to Tāyumānavar's belief in the liberating efficacy of Grace.*[6] What is Grace ? The Tamil word in Tāyumānavar is அருள், *arul.*[7] In

[1] *N.M.*, 1346, சட்டைபோற்ற இவ்வுடம்பத் தருமுன்னே.

[2] *N.M.*, 259 (below p. 82), 297. 555, 930, 1341.

[3] *N.M.*, 438.

[4] Thus the *Siddhiyar*, 3.2.89.92 : 'When we consider the case of a soul which, after passing though eighty-four hundred thousand wombs. . . . born in a human body, we can but compare its case to that of a man who, with his own hands, has swam the white ocean. . . . Was it not the purpose, when souls are endowed with human birth, that they should with mind, speech and body serve God ?' See *Siddhiyar*, 3. 8. 16, 'In one birth.'

[5] *Siddhiyar*, 3.2.35, 3.2.51, 3.5.8, 3.7.4, 3.8.17.

[6] See above, § 39 *ad. fin.*

[7] Equivalents are கருணை, தயவு, இரக்கம்.

அரு + உள் or அர் + உள = அருள the உள் or உள is the noun-forming suffix added to the root அரு or அர், the principle of formation being the same as in the words கடவுள், இருள், மருள், பொருள்.

The part அர் or அரு has the meaning 'rare, precious, hard, difficult,' and by அருள், *arul*, is generally understood 'benevolence, favour, grace, mercy, compassion.' Thus *arutporul*, அருட்பொருள் (*arul*+ *porul*) is 'the riches of grace.'[1] To be 'possessed, of benevolence, grace' is enjoined on men, அருளுடையீர் ஆகுமின்.[2] The classical χάρις, the New Testament χάρις, 'grace' has, it may be confidently stated, the same meaning as the Tamil அருள்,—this, apart from the theological colouring the words have in any particular creed. As mere words, χάρις and அருள் and 'grace' are interchangeable identities, and in theological thought they are *not to be deprived of this commonness of signification:* it is in the special doctrinal setting of each of the three words that something is found added to the normal contents of each. To the Christian, for instance, 'grace', χάρις அருள் cannot be thought of *apart from Christ*, and so it is right to say that the contents of the Christian 'grace' are not quite the same as the contents of the Siddhanta அருள், 'grace.'[4] It is the setting that makes the difference. The same may be said of the Sanscrit *prasāda*,[3] 'grace' both as to its being equivalent, as a word, to χάρις, அருள், 'grace,' and yet *not having the full contents of the Christian 'grace.'* The one great point of commonness between *prasāda* அருள், χάρις, 'grace'—the obtaining of something unearned, unmerited[4] and undemandable—should not be obscured in any appraisement of the significance of 'grace', அருள், in Christianity and in the Siddhanta. To my mind the reason why I may not equate the Christian 'By grace ye were saved'[5] with any analogous

[1] *Kural*, ch. xcii, § 914, where the 'riches of wealth' are contrasted with the 'riches of grace.'

[2] *Nāladiyar*, ch. i, § 7.

[3] *Katha Upanishad*, 2. 20, 'Through the grace [*prasāda*] of the creator.' In *Svet*. 3. 20 the same expression occurs, 'through the grace [*prasāda*] of the creator.' In the *Gita*, xviii, 56, xviii. 58, xviii. 62, xviii. 73, we have 'the Grace' of Krishna. See present writer's *Foregleams of God*, p. 221.

[4] See Romans iv. 4 : xi. 6.

[5] Ephes. ii. 8.

statement in the Siddhanta is simply Jesus Christ, for 'grace and truth came through Jesus Christ'[1]:—

> The grace of God hath appeared, bringing salvation to all men, instructing us to the intent that, denying ungodliness and worldly lusts, we should live soberly and righteously and in godliness in this present world, looking for the blessed hope and appearing of the glory our great God and Saviour Jesus Christ, who gave Himself for us, that He might redeem us from all sin and purify unto Himself a people for His own possession, zealous of good work.[2]

No one nurtured on the New Testament can think of 'grace' அருள், *in its fulness*,[3] apart from Christ. Accordingly a full equation between the Siddhanta and the Christian 'grace' ideas is not possible. It follows that Mr. Nallaswami Pillai's statement, I have quoted elsewhere,[4] to the effect that grace in the New Testament is the same as 'grace' in the Siddhanta, can but apply, therefore, *to something less than the fulness of grace in Christ*. This, it seems to me, is juster to the Siddhanta than the view[5] which has the same conclusion in sight but declines to see in the Siddhanta a sense of personal responsibility for sin or a doctrine of redemption from the bondage of sin. A seeming qualification of the free character of 'grace' is inferable from a *Siddhiyar* passage in which works are commended as conducive to future rewards, and it is added of the doers of such meritorious deeds, 'If, at the end of time they do not yet *deserve* God's grace, they will be re-born. If they *deserve God's grace*, they will at once reach the Feet of the Lord'.[6] The rendering 'deserve' is somewhat infelicitous. The original expressions are *அரன் முன் நிலாது ஒழியன்*, 'if the

[1] S. John i. 19.

[2] Titus ii. 11–14; cf. 1 Cor. i. 4 for 'the grace of God in Christ Jesus'.

[3] S. John i. 14. 'We have no exactly equivalent word in modern English to express the many-faceted jewel of the Greek.' (Dr. C. Anderson Scott, *Dominus Noster*, p. 21.)

[4] *Foregleams of God*, p. 363.

[5] *E.g.*, in Dr. Sydney Cave's *Redemption: Hindu and Christian*, p. 136. See also Sir Charles Eliot's *Hinduism and Buddhism*, ii, p. 217 where the author sets a low value on grace-evoked emotional religion in Siddhanta because the emotion has a strain which jars on Europeans—hardly a good reason.

[6] *Siddhiyar*, 3.8.25. (Nallaswami Pillai's translation).

Lord does not show Himself', and நாதனே முன்னின்றிடினே, 'if God shows Himself'.[1] On this rendering the passage leaves 'grace' unaffected by merit. There must be receptivity in the soul to make grace operative.[2] The true character of 'grace' as something unearned, unmerited is shown in many Siddhanta sayings, one of which is from S. Appar :—

உன்பாலன்பர்

பிழை பொறுத்தி என்பதுவும் பெரியோய் நின்றன்
கடனன்றே பேரருளுன் பாலதன்றே.

And when Thy lovers cry
'Forgive our sin', great One forgiveness is Thy duty meet ;
For with Thee is great grace.[3]

§ 41. Grace, in its operative aspect, as the energy of divine benevolence, is personified in Siddhanta theology, under the name '*Sakti*'.

அருளது சத்தியாகும் அரன்றனக் கருளையின்றி
தெருள்சிவ மில்லை யந்தச் சிவமின்றிச் சத்தியில்லை.

'God has Grace as His *Sakti*. Apart from this Grace there is no manifested Sivam, and apart from Sivam there is no *Sakti*.'[4] Grace, known thus as *Sakti*, is Uma, 'the Half of Him', and 'she who abides in Siva's left side'.[5] She is every form of divine activity.[6] The Sakti is not many but only one.[7] It is however differently manifested according to its divine functions. In the sphere of Life it is called *Para Sakti*, that is God as manifested existence, and as Divine Life is manifested in

[1] The Tamil may more literally be rendered, 'if the Lord does not stand in front', 'if God Himself stands in front' (compare the *Prayer Book* word 'prevent'). See the Tamil notes in Sivagnana Swami and Subramania Desika Swami's *Siddhiyar*, p. 308.

[2] See this point well explained in Sharvananda's *Sayings of Sri Ramakrishna*, ch. xxvi.

[3] Kingsbury and Phillips, *Hymns of the Tamil Saiva Saints*, p. 65. How the doctrine of 'grace' has modified the doctrine of karma and for other modifications of karma see the article of Prof. E. W. Hopkins in *J.R.A.S.*, 1906, p. 581.

[4] *Siddhiyar*, 3.5.9.

[5] *Ibid.*, 3.1.49. See below, p. 201.

[6] *Ibid.*, Prologue, 3.

[7] *Ibid.*, 3.1.61.

creation, in providence, and in love, the *Para Sakti* is known in its operations as

> *Kriya Sakti*, the instrument of creation,
> *Jnana Sakti*, the all-knowing, all-providing agency,
> *Ichchā Sakti*, the desire for the welfare of all creatures.[1]

An action of benign, purposeful concealment and obscuring is ascribed to Grace which, under that aspect, is known as *Tirobhava Sakti*.[2] It is named and described by Tāyumānavar:

> எம்மை யிறையை யிறைமை யெம்பாற் கட்டறத்
> அம்மை திரோதை யகலுநா ளெந்நாளோ ?

> The time when Mother Trodai
> Who now obscureth here
> The Lord, the soul, soul's bondage
> Shall truly disappear,
> When dawns the day ?[3]

It is by 'grace' that the following, among other acts are done:

1. The five-fold functioning[4]
   (*a*) Of dissolution of the universe to give rest to souls.
   (*b*) Of creation to enable souls to wear out karma.
   (*c*) Of making souls eat the fruits of karma.[5]
   (*d*) Of maturing of deeds.[6]
   (*e*) Of finally freeing from 'bonds.'[7]
2. Giving out the shastras.[8]
3. Revealing the sense of the shastras.[9]
4. Granting psychic powers.[10]
5. God's manifesting of Himself in forms.[11]
6. God's accepting every act of faithful worship.[12]
7. Granting knowledge to the soul.[13]

---

[1] *Siddhiyar*, 3.1.63 ; *Sivapragasam*, stanzas 2, 14, 15.
[2] *Ibid.*, 3.2.87 ; *Ibid.*, stanza 20. See above, p. lxxxiv.
[3] *N.M.*, 1165. In *N.M.*, 582 பூரணி புராதனி சுமங்கலை சுதந்தரி are some names of *Sakti*.
[4] *Siddhiyar*, 3.1.37.
[5] See *Siddhiyar*, 3.1.36, 3.2.4, 3.2.13, 3.2.34, 3.2.51, 38. 17.
[6] See above, p. cxi.
[7] See *Siddhiyar*, 3.7.4, 3.8.35.
[8] *Siddhiyar*, 3.2.33.
[9] *Ibid.*, 2.6.6. (Statement).
[10] *Ibid.*, 3.1.40.
[11] *Ibid.*, 3.1.45, 3.1.46, 3.1.68
[12] *Ibid.*, 3.2.25, 3.9.12.
[13] *Ibid.*, 3.1.64, 3.5.1, 3.11.7

8. Enabling God to be known.[1]
9. Special manifesting of God as *guru*.[2]
10. Leading the soul into union with God.[3]
11. Destruction of karma and all other *mala*.[4]

In the psalms of Tāyumānavar the reader will find reference to most of these operations of 'grace'.

§ 42. According to the Siddhanta, of the grace-aspects of the benevolence of Deity in action the most noteworthy is ***Ichchā Sakti.*** It is by *Ichchā*, 'desire, longing, love', that God is closely associated with the career of the soul in every endeavour to save it for Himself. Our poet's psalms open with a clear reference to the 'love' aspect of Divine energy. When we read in the very first hymn

அருளொடு நிறைந்ததெது தன்னருள் வெளிக்குளே
யகிலாண்ட கோடியெல்லாம்
தங்கும்படிக் கிச்சைவைத் துயிர்க்குயிராய்த் தழைத்ததெது

That, in its infinite fulness of loving grace,
  Foldeth the worlds that are, all things;
Grace that in graciousness willeth all life to lie
  In Him the Life of life's essence.[5]

The *Ichchā Sakti* of God is co-extensive with the full diffusiveness of Love in prolific expression. Its aim is to draw men into God-likeness, தன்னிலைமை மன்னுயிர்கள் சார, 'that human beings may attain unto Divinity.'[6] This is God's endeavour and is effected by close association with the soul in its vicissitudes. God becomes, in identification, 'the life of life', 'the soul of soul.'[7] It is of God thus close in manifestation of grace to man that Tāyumānavar says:

தண்ணரு டந்தெனைக் காக்குஞ் சாக்ஷிப்பேறே
இமையளவு முபகார மல்லால் வேறொன்றறியகா. . .

The witness true gives loving grace
  The guardian of my soul to be,
And every moment does He spend
  In doing only good to me.[8]

---

[1] *Siddhiyar*, 3.6.7, 3.11.11.
[2] *Ibid.*, 3.8.1. See below, § 43.
[3] *Ibid.*, 3.8.30, 3.8.37, 3.9.4. [4] *Ibid.*, 3.8.10, 3.10.4.
[5] Below, p. 3. *N.M.*, 1. See reference to *Sakti* in *N.M.*, 127, 145, 473 582, 1089.
[6] *T.A.P.*, i. 2. [7] See below, pp. 124, 125. [8] *N.M.*, 136.

By His grace God makes Himself known to the soul in loving nearness of kinship.

Be gracious, O Thou honey-sweet,
Sweetness in which, divine, delicious,
The many sweetnesses all meet,
And mix, O bliss of bliss uncloying,
That seekest with my sense to blend
By little and by little, openly
At last as this poor sinner's friend
In closeness of good-granting kinship.[1]

A sense of personal nearness and love to God thus brought close to the soul by 'grace' is expressed in numerous passages. The following hymn[2] is typical:

Thou art my life and Thou my inward knowing
Who by the way of my own love hast found
A way whereby, with my own being blended,
Sweetness in whom all sweetnesses abound,[3]
Thou hast become nearest of mine, close kinsman.[4]
That I be never parted, Lord, from Thee
Bestow on me the boon of grace to conquer
My wayward mind that it may subdued be.

The workings of 'grace', of *Ichchā Sakti*, are represented as God's incessant striving and seeking to save souls. ***God's*** quest of man is a Siddhanta belief far removed from the Upanishad speculations which are mainly along lines of ***man's*** quest of God. Tāyumānavar speaks of the Divine seeking under the figure of a cow in search of her calf, and draws out the sense of the tender, solicitous motherliness of God.[5] It is true his psalms show that man continually has to strive, but it is also true they show that all the while God keeps seeking the soul.[6] Man's helplessness and God's solicitude for him are very distinctly taught in the Siddhanta. Tāyumānavar's psalms abundantly illustrate this. His appeals for 'deliverance' can otherwise have no meaning. Now, this seeking of the soul by God is a truth recognized in non-Hindu religious thought. God, says the author of that grand Hebrew meditation on the

[1] *N.M.*, 54, below at p. 29.
[2] *N.M.*, 361, more freely rendered at p. 49, below.
[3] See below, pp. 16, 159. [4] See below, p. 183. [5] *N.M.*, 494.
[6] See below, pp. 6. 16, 17, 18, 39, 68.

transcendent-immanent Deity, the One-Hundred and Thirty-Ninth Psalm, 'besettingly besieges'[1] the soul. This is one of the most striking aspects of the immanence of God. On this Hebrew song of the Divine immanence, with its thought of a loving God in pursuit of a soul He is eager to win, may be quoted here Mr. Edward Shillito's Christian interpretation of the human flight and the Divine chase:

> He is the Pursuer, or rather the inevitable Presence from which there is no escape ; but it is the Lord of Mercy who holds and leads the pitiful soul ; it is not a doom but a bright destiny that man should be shut into His presence. It is not in vengeance but in mercy that the fugitive Jonah is intercepted as he flees unto Tarshish. But all such thought of a merciful Pursuer were fulfilled by the Christian revelation of One who came to seek and to save the lost. There is still a Huntsman after the souls of men ; they are still ready to take refuge from Him. There is still the wrath which is the reaction of love ; but He is known beneath all disguises to be the Holy Love that will not rest till the Lover and the beloved are reconciled. . . . In this manner Christ takes over the old language, and claims it for Himself ; so He completes and crowns all the partial truths which men had learned concerning that Someone who was after the souls of men. Man is still the fugitive, God still the Pursuer ; but the children of men can understand now what their flight means ; if they are trying to escape it is from One whose character and purpose they can discover.[2]

In Francis Thompson's *The Hound of Heaven*[3] we have the same thought, clothed in the language of poetry, 'of the deliberate speed, majestic instancy' of the Pursuer, and, when 'comes on at hand the bruit of that long pursuit' of the pursued finding realization of Love in what he had so long sought to avoid :

> Halt's by me that footfall :
> Is my gloom, after all,
> Shade of His hand outstretched caressingly ?

The symbol of the Love-chase is in Rysbroeck's saying, 'The Spirit of God gives chase to our spirit', and has affinities

[1] Ps. cxxxix. 5. The R.V. rendering is borne out by the use of the verb (occurring here) similarly in Deut. xx. 12, 19 ; 1 Kings xx. 1 ; Isa. xxix. 3. See Abelson's *The Immanence of God in Rabbinical Literature*, p. 36.

[2] *The Pilgrim*, July, 1922, p. 451. The article is entitled, 'The Long Pursuit', and aims at xpressing the writer's 'thought upon a metaphor of the mystics'.

[3] 'Modern Library' edition of Thompson's Poems, p 88.

to Eckhart's 'He who will escape Him runs only to His bosom, for all corners are open to Him '.[1] 'Flight and pursuit', writes Dr. Geraldine E. Hodgson, 'fill the earlier pages of *Grace Abounding*', and formed the story of Bunyan's spiritual life 'long after he had come to man's estate'.[2] It is flight and pursuit that is the theme of S. Augustine's *Confessions*.[3] God ever pursues, and in none but Christ is love's tender pursuit of straying souls so perfectly exemplified:

> I am true love that false was never;
>   Mine own—man's soul—I loved her thus,
> Because we would nowise dissever,
>   I left my Kingdom glorious,
> I purveyed her a palace full precious;
>   She fled, I followed, I loved her so,
> That I suffered this pain piteous,
>   *Quia amore langueo.*[4]

§ 45. The idea of a seeking God finds in the Siddhanta (and we have numerous illustrative passages in our poet's psalms) its highest expression in the conception of the *Guru*, the spiritual instructor. In over three hundred different references to the *Guru* the poet's identifying of the *Guru* with Siva is very distinctly maintained:

> The Guru who three-eyed sat in the banyan shade.[5]
> The three-eyed Lord, the heavenly Guru who teaches.[6]

---

[1] See E. Maynell's *Life of Francis Thompson*, p. 165.

[2] *English Mystics*, p. 260.

[3] 'Where then wert Thou then to me and how far from me? Far verily was I straying from Thee. But Thou wert more inward to me than my inward part' (*Conf.* 3.6.11). 'Thy faithful mercy hovered over me from afar' (3.3.1). 'I was becoming more miserable, and Thou nearer. Thy right hand was continually ready to pluck me out of the mire and to wash me thoroughly, and I knew it not' (6.16.26). 'Dare I say that Thou heldest Thy peace, O my God, while I wandered further from Thee?' (2.3.7).

[4] Anonymous fifteenth century lines quoted in Percy H. Osmond's *The Mystical Poets of the English Church*, p. 16. The refrain of each of the three verses quoted is adapted from the vulgate of Canticles ii. 5, 'I faint with love'.

[5] *N.M.*, 47, [illegible]. On 'three-eyed' see below, p. 180 and on 'banyan' see below, p. 169.

[6] *N.M.*, 85, [illegible].

God who is ever the inward Guru in the mind became the *mouna* Guru.[1]

As the decoy deer is employed to capture other deer, God, when he became the gracious *mouna* Guru, assumed human form and subjected Himself to hunger, sleep, pain, pleasure, name, and place and other incidents.[2]

ஊணுறக்க மின்பதுன்பம் பேராதி
பொருந்திடவு மெனைப்போல வுருவங்காட்டிச்
சேனைநெறித் மான்காட்டி மானைப்பிடிக்கும்
செய்கைபோ லருள்மௌன குருவாய் வந்து

Uma's Beloved is God and Guru.[3]

Let worship be given the gold-red feet of God the Silent One.[4]

The *mouna* Siva taught all truth.[5]

The Lord of all coming as the Silent One and Mother granted Grace.[6]

The Light of heaven, Lord of all, took on Him the form of a Guru, and the form is not soon forgotten.[7]

The Perfect One, All-Fulness, became the Guru.[8]

In the section entitled *Sinmayāṉanda Guru*[9] each psalm is addressed to God as the 'Teacher of wisdom's bliss.' The Guru is Siva, Brahma, Vishnu, 'in all the creeds, to calling voices, the gracious Guru.'[10] It is in terms of Deity that the poet speaks of the Guru, his Guru, who is also unmistakably identified as the Guru of others.[11] The speaker of the 'one mystic word'[12] is the God-Guru.[13] The God-Guru is the giver of 'the sign.'[14] Siva is to the poet 'the Teacher of Wisdom,'[15] 'the Silent

[1] *N.M.*, 128, எக்காலுமே அறிவினின்று குருவாயுணர்த்தியதுமன்றி மோனகுருவாகி.

[2] *N.M.*, 148.

[3] *N.M.*, 286, translated below at p. 65.

[4] N.*M.*, 336, தேவெனு மோனி செம்பொற் சேவடி சிந்தைசெய்வாம்.

[5] *N.M.*, 509, உண்மையெல்லாம் போதித்தான் . . . . மோனசிவன்.

[6] *N.M.*, 761, மௌனத்தாயாக வந்தருளைத் தந்தாய் பராபரமே.

[7] பரஞ்சோதி நீ குருவாய் வந்தவடிவை மறவேன் பராபரமே.

[8] *Ahaval*, குருவடிவான குறைவிலா நிறைவே.

[9] See below, p. 20.

[10] *N.M.*, 51, translated below at pp. 26, 27.

[11] *N.M.*, 26, below, pp. 20, 164, and *N.M.*, 182 translated above, p. xxviii. See *N.M.*, 310, 345, 419, 420, 520, 965.

[12] See above, p. lii and below, p. 164.

[13] See below, pp. 20, 25; *N.M.*, 40, 48, 464, 529, 916.

[14] See below, pp. 200, 203 [illegible] and *N.M.*, 239, 281, 310, 353, 520, 621

[15] *N.M.*, 16, 39 ஞானகுரு.

Teacher,'[1] 'the expounder of *samarasam*,'[2] 'the ascetic with the matted hair,'[3] 'the Father bestowing the Wisdom of Silence,'[4] 'the perfect Teacher,'[5] 'the Satchitananda perfect Teacher,'[6] and 'the Mother imparting Silence.'[7] This God become Guru is, by the poet, placed in human environment just as explicitly as his identification with Deity is stated. Reference need be made to but one group of verses in proof of this proposition. Each verse of the section headed மௌனகுருவணக்கம் *Mouna Guru Vanakkam*,[8] 'adoration of the Mouna Guru,' ends with the address.

> O heavenly Guru granting lore Divine.
> Lord of the Silence, sage of Mular's Line.

The Guruis here idefinitely identified, and a place assigned him, in the sphere of earthly, human associations.[10] The poet says of his Guru, so clearly conceived as God-man and described in terms of Deity and in terms of humanity, that He is the seeker of souls and is continuously solicitous for the soul's welfare, keeping Himself in close well-willing contact with souls. God as God, the poet suggests, is the soul's eternal seeker,[11]

[1] *N.M.*, 19, குருமௌனி.

[2] *N.M.*, 29, 'He who uttered the Vedas and framed the creeds is the Guru who taught the சமயங்கடந்த மோன சமரசம், the *samarasam* which is above all the creeds.' On *samarasam* see above, § 13 and to the authorities noted and discussed there may be profitably added a careful Tamil exposition of *samarasam* in *Sen Tamil Selvie*, June 1924, p. 177.

[3] *N.M.*, 82, சடைமௌனி.

[4] *N.M.*, 108, மௌன ஞானதாதா.

[5] *N.M.*, 218, சற்குரு, *N.M.*, 277, மௌன சற்குரு, *N.M.*, 791.

[6] *N.M.*, 279 சச்சிதானந்த சற்குரு. On 'satchitananda' meaning Deity see above, p lxxii.

[7] *N.M.*, 761, மோனத்தாய்.

[8] *N.M.*, 37–46.

[9] மந்த்ர குருவே யோக தந்த்ர குருவே மூலன் மரபில்வரு மௌனகுருவே. See above, p. xxv. and notes (7) (9).

[10] Tamil writers somewhat vaguely suggest that this Guru was Arul Nanti Sivachariyar, author of the *Siddhiyar*. See above, § 16, and K. S. Mudaliyar's *Tāyumānavar*, p. 3, and *N.M.* Edition, p. 4. This is probably due to an early tradition that the Guru referred Tāyumānavar to the *Siddhiyar* for spiritual guidance, and the author of the book was consequently identified with the Guru. Tāyumānavar praises the author of the *Siddhiyar* in *N.M.*, 1098, quoted above at p. xlviii.

[11] See above, § 42.

well-willing in *Ichchā Sakti*, and God manifested as Guru cannot but be exactly so. It may be supposed that the Guru instructed the poet in whatever was essential to spiritual advancement, particularly laying stress on the sublimity of holy silence. The Guru came to be called *mouna Guru*, 'Lord of the Silence', meaning either the 'Teacher of the secret of being still' or else the 'Teacher who practised speechlessness.' A combination of both meanings seems better suited to the contexts in which the Guru is mentioned by the poet. Silence is, in the Siddhanta as in other systems of thought, associated with Deity.[1] In names the Guru bears[2] according to his functions 'silence' forms a part: *siddha mownie*, சித்த மௌனி, 'Lord of the Silence' in his aspect of seeking souls and compassing them with prevenient grace; *vada pāl mownie*, வடபால் மௌனி, 'Lord of the Silence' in his aspect of session; and *suddha mownie*, சுத்த மௌனி, 'Lord of the Silence', in his aspect of imparting instruction, தீட்சை '*deeksha*'.[3] To aid one to think that 'silence' is not simply 'speechlessness', but it and more, it should be remembered that the *suddha mownam* சுத்த மௌனம் imparted and practised by the Guru as *suddha mownie* சுத்த மௌனி, is 'silence in thought, word and deed',[4] suggesting the three-fold 'mortification' of the *Gita*.[5] The understanding of 'silence' as something much more than 'muteness' gives a practical meaning to the idea. Action, strenuous action, is implied in 'silence'. And so 'the Lord of the Silence' is not merely the possessor or imparter to the elect of a secret of stillness and confident quietude but also the inculcator of self-denying principles which issue in ethical activities. 'The Lord of the Silence' is a worker: the disciple of silence is not inactive. The doctrine of the 'Lord of the Silence' is a doctrine of the lordliness of restraint.

§ 44. The God-Guru idea is foreign to the Upanishads. It is possible, however, to trace in the Upanishads the suggestion

[1] See below, pp. 131, 135. [2] *N.M.*, 426.

[3] See below, p. 167, and *Siddhiyar*, 3.8.1 on *deeksha*.

[4] *N.M.*, 911, சுத்த மௌனஞ் செயல் வாக்கெல்ல மௌனம் . . .

[5] *Gita*, xvii. 14.15.16.

of material out of which has been evolved the God-Guru conception of Siddhanta theology. The evolution is purely conjectural. It is necessary, says an Upanishad,[1] for the seeker of knowledge to become the disciple of 'a *guru* who is learned in the scriptures'. A *guru* is necessary since 'knowledge learned from a *guru* best helps one to attain his end'.[2] These references are obviously to human instructors. It may appear a step in advance, from the human to close proximity to the Divine, when we come across the injunction, 'Be one to whom a *guru* is as a God,'[3] but it has to be borne in mind that God-reverence is to be accorded likewise to father, mother, guest.[4] We approach something more than an apparent advance in thought in the *Svetasvatara* reference 'to him who has the highest *bhakti* for God and for his *guru* even as for God'.[5] The guru's indispensableness prompts his being reverenced, and the reverence is to be as for *a god*, and lastly *bhakti* (love) for a guru should be equal to love for God Himself—the Upanishads do not go further than this. It must be confessed that in the Upanishads we do not discover the full-fledged God-Guru idea which meets us in the Siddhanta writings, however suggestive of such an idea we may consider the Upanishad passages we have noticed.

The Siddhanta divines expressly teach that God manifests Himself as the Guru,[6] grants His grace,[7] and liberates the mature soul from future births and *anava* mala.[8]

As a type of the uniform teaching of the Siddhanta doctors, that Siva becomes Guru, may be mentioned the clear and

[1] *Mundaka*, 1.2.12. *Maitri*, 6 28.

[2] *Chandogya*, 4.9.3.

[3] *Taittiriya*, 1.11.2.

[4] *Ibid*, 1.11.2.3.

[5] *Svet.*, 6.23. See Dr. L. D. Barnett's remarks at p. 48 of vol. ii. of *Third International Congress for the History of Religions* on this text. On the God-Guru idea in the *Gita* see present writer's *Foregleams of God*, ch. ix, § 10 *ad fin*.

[6] *Siddhiyar*, 3.8.1; *Bodham*, viii; *T.A.P.*, v. 1; *Tirumantram*, 1527; *Sivapragasam*, 8.

[7] *Siddhiyar*, 3.12.6.

[8] *Ibid.*, 3.8,10.

unambiguous teaching of Tirumūla Nayanār in his *Tirumantram* :

> இறையே சிவகுருவாமே, 'God Himself is the Saiva Guru '[1]
>
> குற்றற்றகுரு அம்பலவனே, 'It is God the Omnipresent who is the taintless Guru '[2]
>
> எல்லாவுலகிற்கு மப்பாலோளிப் பாலாம் . . . .
>
> சொல்லார்ந்த நற்குரு சுத்த சிவமே, 'He who is above all worlds, the holy Siva, is in this world the praiseworthy holy Guru '[3]
>
> சுத்த சிவன் குருவாய் வந்து, 'The holy Siva becoming the Guru. . . .'[4]
>
> சிவனே சிவஞானி, 'It is Siva who is the Sivagnani.'[5]
>
> குருவே சிவமுமாய்க் கோனுமாய், 'The Guru, as Siva and King.'[6]

S. Tāyumānavar, as we have already seen, equates God and his Guru, and in so doing he states nothing new to the Siddhanta. He closely and clearly follows the '*Mular*'[7] of whose line was the Mouna Guru, the poet's own Guru.

Tāyumānavar's God-Guru conception, like that of other Siddhanta saints,[8] has, in recent times, been sought to be explained away as a mistake. The Rev. F. Kingsbury, a Tamil versed in Tamil as his scholarly father, Rao Bahadur C. W. Kingsbury Tāmothirampillai, in his anxiety to avoid the possibility of an argument for the Deity[9] of Christ being evolved out of the Guru analogy of Tāyumānavar, aims a blow at the Siddhanta poet himself: 'When Tāyumānavar *identifies* his guru with God Himself, we are not bound to accept his statement.'[10] This is hardly fair to the poet, even if this statement, so summarily refused a hearing, were an original and isolated pronouncement peculiar to the poet. With all deference to Mr. Kingsbury's scholarship, I venture to think that he is declining a hearing not only to Tāyumānavar but (it must

[1] *Tirumantram*, 1573.

[2] *Ibid.*, 1574, cf. *N.M.*, 116, சிவஞானி . . . போற்பவன் கடவுள.

[3] *Ibid.*, 1576.

[4] *Ibid.*, 1578.

[5] *Ibid.*, 1580, cf. *N. M.*, 116, பிறிவறத் தன்னைக்குட் சிவஞானியப்பனத.

[6] *Ibid.*, 1581.

[7] See above, p. xxv and notes (7), (9).

[8] Above, p. cxxx, note (6).

[9] The Deity of Christ is briefly dealt with by the present writer in Appendix, note F, of his *Foregleams of God*.

[10] In *The Christian Patriot*, August 12, 1922, p. 5.

appear from what we have given above) also to Tirumūlar and to the authors of the *Siddhiyar*, the *Bodham* and the *Tiru Arul Payan*. Mr. Kingsbury is no doubt free to say that *all* the Siddhanta theologians were as wrong, as mistaken, as self-deceiving, as Tāyumānavar himself, but such sweeping condemnation of a body of competent, sane thinkers should surely be based on something more reasoned and reasonable than, 'Oh! I don't believe you!'

Mr. V. Chakkarai, a learned and devout Indian thinker, and editor of *The Christian Patriot*, has been contributing to his paper a series of thoughtful articles headed, '*Is Jesus the Avatar of God?*'. They have been occasioned, probably, by Mr. Kingsbury's endeavour in print to disprove the belief of Christians in the Deity of Christ. Incidentally, or perhaps as supplementary to some of his thoughts on *Jesus as the Avatar of God*, Mr. Chakkarai criticizes[1] Mr. Kingsbury's views on Tāyumānavar's God-Guru. The able critic understands Mr. Kingsbury's line of reasoning to be, 'Jesus is a teacher like this Mouna Guru, but we have no more right to regard Him as God than Tāyumānavar has to conceive his Guru as God.' Mr. Chakkarai rightly observes that the poet's God-Guru idea is in accordance with Saiva theology and that 'there is no process of first meeting a man, a guru, and then making him Siva or God.'[2] He however explains Tāyumānavar's God-Guru thus:

> The poet saw him in vision and wrote of him sometimes as having been externally present to him, and sometimes as the object of his fervent aspiration. . . . The poet saw him only in vision as Isaiah saw Jehovah in the temple and took Him for the guru. That is, the guru was the internal teacher whose figure is described as that of a man.[3]

This 'vision' hypothesis, applicable to the Siddhanta God-Guru idea, may borrow strength from the Theophanies of the Old Testament, those God-appearances which have points of contact, but not full correspondence, with some Hindu God-manifestations. At the same time, it seems to me, Tāyumānavar's God-Guru conception is fundamentally different from the notion

[1] *The Christian Patriot*, August 12, 1922, p. 4.
[2] *Ibid.*, August 19, 1922, p. 4.
[3] *Ibid.*, August 12, 1922, p. 5.

suggested by Isaiah's vision where *the Manifested is in no sense a Teacher.*[1] There are further these facts about Tāyumāṉavar's God-Guru,[2] and they militate against the 'vision' theory:

1. The Guru, admittedly Deity, is in frequent communication with the poet, appearing to him as the same man.
2. The Guru is definitely stated to be a man, a sage in Tirumalar's line of teachers.
3. The God-Guru, sage in Tirumalar's line, has subjected himself to the human limitations of name, rank, hunger, sleep, etc.

The 'vision' explanation has thus its difficulties. One cannot resist the conclusion that Tāyumānavar's Guru is contemplated by him as God-Man, a contemplation distinct from, and not evolved out of, the Siddhanta thought that 'the form of God's devotee is His Form'.[3]

§ 45. The conception of a 'conditioned Brahma' is the Hindu philosophic explanation of what we may call the idea of 'limitation' of Deity. That Deity is transcendent, '*Sat*, pure Being who as such can never reach us' is half the truth. That Deity is immanent is half the truth.[4] The full truth is God is transcendent-immanent.[5] God manifests Himself. The medium of manifestation is Love. 'Chit or Arul or Love denotes God's aspect in which He can reach us, and we can know Him.'[6]

[1] In *Isaiah*, vi, the prophet has a vision of the Lord in the beauty of Holiness; is conscious of his own unworthiness in such presence; and, cleansed from sin, receives a call and commission. The prophet did *not* take the Lord God for his Guru. In a general way of speaking *all* Israel had the promise made to them of becoming לִמּוּדֵי יְהוָֹה 'the learned of Jehovah', 'disciples of the Lord' (Isa. liv. 13). The LXX version renders the Hebrew by διδακτοὶ Θεοῦ, and the Isaiah phrase occurs in S. John vi. 45 as διδακτοὶ Θεοῦ. In Isaiah the idea is *not* of a guru-disciple relationship but illumination by the Spirit of God, as will be seen from Numb. xi. 29, Isa. xliv. 3, Jer. xxxi. 34, and Joel ii. 2. In my opinion it is only in 1 Thess. iv. 9, 'taught of God' θεοδίδακτοί, that a guru-disciple relationship, at any rate, something as nearly *personal*, is intended.

[2] *N.M.*, 148, the verse beginning [illegible] See p. cxxxv for an English rendering of the verse.

[3] *Siddhiyar*, 3.1[illegible]. See below, p. 207.

[4] Nalla. *Studies*, 227; *Siddhiyar*, 3.6.1.

[5] See above, p. lxviii and *Siddhiyar*, 3.2.1. On Immanence, see p. lxx.

[6] Nalla. *Studies*, 227.

This cannot be questioned. It is along lines of Grace, Ichcha Sakti, Love, that the theologians of the Siddhanta develop the idea of manifested Deity. Hence it is taught:

> If God did not assume form out of Love and give out the Vedas and Agamas[1] none could be saved . . . and the message of the Guru could not reach men or devas.[2]

When form is postulated of Deity in the Siddhanta, it would seem, according to the text-writers, that the form (confining ourselves to the human form) is not a *material* limitation of Deity. It is explained that souls, by reason of their eternal attachment to *anava mala*,[3] have the substance of the bodies for them evolved out of *māya*,[4] but that, God being not subjected to *anava mala*, the 'substance' for His body, in human form-assuming, is evolved out of His own *sakti* and not out of *maya*.[5] It is expressly stated so as to warn one off 'material' ways of thinking:

> *Arul* (Grace, Love அருள்) is the form of God; the attributes and sense appertaining to such form are *arul*; the acts associated with such form are all *arul*; the limbs and lineaments of the bodily form are *arul*; feelings and enjoyments are all *arul*. Not for His sake but for the benefit of souls does God assume this *arul* form.[6]

According, then, to the Siddhanta, the form assumed by God is a non-material, spiritual one, somewhat akin to the

[1] See below, p. 139.

[2] *Siddhiyar*, 3.1.46. The Tamil உய்ப்பவரில்லை literally means 'none shall live'.

[3] See above, p. lxviii.

[4] See above, p. lxxxii.

[5] *Siddhiyar*, 3.1.41. காயமோ மாயை யன்று காண்பது சத்தி தன்னால்.

[6] *Ibid.*, 3.1.47. Mr. Nallaswami Pillai (English edition of *Siddhiyar*, p. 139), renders அருள் in this verse throughout by 'Love', and quotes *Taittiriya Upanishad*, ii. 5, rendering the Sanscrit thus, 'His head is surely Love; Joy, His right wing, Delight His left; Bliss is His self. Brahman whereon He rests.' A slightly different rendering is given by Hume (*Upanishads*, p. 286), 'Pleasure, *piriya*, is its head; delight, *moda*, is its right side; great delight, *pra-moda*, the left side; bliss, *ānanda*, the body, *atman*; Brahma, the lower part, the foundation'. This Upanishad description is of 'one with the form of a person'. I am not sure that *piriya* of the Sanscrit is the அருள் of the Tamil, for அருள் has the Sanscrit representative in *prasāda*. On *prasada* see p. cxix and present writer's *Foregleams of God*, pp. 214, 221.

docetic[1] body ascribed to Christ in early Christian heresy. It is hard to think, with one's Christian prepossessions, that it is of such a semblance of a human body, of an unsubstantial thing, of a shadow and no 'thing' at all, that Tāyumānavar writes :

Unnumbered though the ills of karma
  In great abundance grow,
Gracious the Guru of the Silence
  Has come to make me know
Wisdom whereby these ills unrooted,
  Unharvested, shall die—
Wondrous as when a camphor mountain
  Ablaze burns flaming high,
And burning goes into non-being :
  This truly has He done,
The Guru, who, man's form assuming,
  Became as I, yea one
With name and native-place and parents,
  One needing sleep and food,
And knowing pain and knowing pleasure,
  With His form of manhood
Beguiling me to Him, and breaking
  The twist of sin, ill's taint,
Just as a deer a deer decoyeth
  With stratagem and feint.[2]

In this the poet thinks consonantly to earlier thought ; there is a long passage for example in Umā Pati Sivāchāriyar's

[1] See Ignatius, *ad Trall*, ix. 1. 2 ; *ad Smyrn*. i. 1. 2.

[2] *N.M.*, 148. காணரிய வல்லவெல்லாந் தாவோங்கிக்
  கட்டாக விளைவு மறைக்கட்டோடேபோதான்
விண்ணிலிற் கர்ப்பூரமலை பற்றிப்பட்ட
  விக்கைதயெனக் காணவொரு விவேகங்காட்ட
ஊணுறக்க மின்பதுன்பம் பேரூரிதி
  யொக்கவிடவு மென்னைப்போல வுருவங்காட்டிக்
கோணற வோர்மான்காட்டி மானைப்பிக்குங்
  கொள்கைபென வருண்மவுனகுருவாய் வந்து

Karma.—The residue of karma (see above. p. cxii) is burnt up by the Grace of Siva, even as fire burns away, and dissipates into air, a whole mountain of camphor, and the camphor ceases to be, with no ashes being left behind.

Deer.—In *T.A.P.*, v. 5 it is taught that the human form is assumed by Siva to ensnare men.

Pōttippahtodai, portions of which are here given in English, and which our poet may have had in mind :

> To Him be praise
> Who nor beginning has nor birth,
> But, deigning to bestow on us the boon
> Of birthlessness, became a man on earth
> Was born and bore a name,
> Who name has none,
> And felt in human form and frame
> Hunger and thirst, felt joy and fear,
> Cravings for restful sleep,
> And, tasting all, rejoiced,
> Because he held all souls to Him so dear
> And wished their weal,
> And, for their saving, Guru He became—
> To Him be praise.[1]

In the statement that 'He who has no birth . . . was born and bore a name, who name has none' *பிறவா முதல்வன் பிறந்து . . . பேரிலாதவொரு பேர்புனைந்து*, we have, it seems to me, something a great deal more than the projection of an apparition into a devotee's sphere of vision—we have in the whole passage an express statement, as of a very substantial fact, of ***birth, name, parts, passions and all human incidents*** predicated of Deity on the plane of Time. Add to this the fact that, in a line and a half[2] not translated above, S. Umā Pati gives the name borne by the God-Guru as ***Sampandha Nātan,*** which name the Tamil commentator[3] explains is in full *மறைஞான சம்பந்தர்*, Marai Gnāna Sampandhar, who is, in Siddhanta literature, an historical personage,[4] and you have an authoritative[5] doubt, if not an utter dissipation, of the theory that the God-Guru manifestation is a mere form, a gracious apparition, at best a theophany. Umā Pati Sivāchāriyar is understood by his Tamil commentator to be stating a very marvellous happening in *பிறவா*

[1] *Pōttipahtodai*, parts of lines 131-189, and 42-45.

[2] Lines 135 (*b*). 136, [illegible] சம்பந்தநாதனென்று.

[3] In K. S. Mudāliyar's edition of *Pōttipahtodai*, p. 17.

[4] See above, p. xviii.

[5] The author of *Pōttipahtodai* is the author of eight out of the fourteen Siddhanta shastras. See above, pp. xvii, xviii.

முதல்வன் பிறந்து . . . , for he interprets the text of S. Umā Pati thus·

> For our salvation God manifested Himself. He assumed a holy body திருமேனிகொண்டு and, although by His own nature He has no name, He yet took on the name Marai Gnāna Sambandha Nāthan மறைஞான சம்பந்த நாதனென்றொரு பெயர் தரித்துக்கொண்டு and, like men on earth, He experienced hunger and sleep, and fear, pleasure and pain, and was glad withal. In consequence it must be said, 'It is marvellous that the birthless God has come to be born [a man]' பிறவா முதல்வன் பிறந்து வந்தானென் றதிசயமாய்ச் சொல்லும்படி.

The marvel, means the commentator, lies not in the fact of a theophany, but in the stupendous happening of *பிறவா முதல்வன் பிறந்த* 'the birthless Deity being born a man', and subjecting Himself willingly and gladly to the limitations and experiences of humanity. It would be nothing less than intellectual perversity to refuse to see in S. Umā Pati's account of the God-Guru the fact of God *born* a Man. Both Umā Pati Sivāchariyar and Tāyumānaswāmy in giving historical associations to the God-Guru, in investing Him with human parts and attributes and in generally contemplating Him under flesh and blood aspects, seem to me to be having in mind no form, phantom or even theophany. It is contended that S. Umā Pati is consistent with himself and with the *Siddhiyar* when he states elsewhere[1] that apart from Grace the world cannot know the God-Guru, it needs spiritual intuition to discern, recognize and reverence Deity in the human form. The *Siddhiyar* view[2] that the body of the God-Guru is not evolved out of *maya* but of Deity's own *sakti*, and is all 'grace',[3] is not in conflict with S. Umā Pati's description of the Guru on the plane of the physical. The *Siddhiyar*[4] cannot be understood to suggest that the tangible, visible, passible, concrete 'body' of the God-Guru *is* 'grace', as if 'grace' were some seeable, touchable stuff; it rather means no more than that it is by Grace the God-Guru manifests Himself, assuming, according to the resources of Grace, human form. The *Siddhiyar* cannot for one moment be considered as claiming to give in Book iii, Sutra i, Stanza 47 an analysis of

[1] *T.A.P.*, v. 3.4.5. [2] *Siddhiyar*, 3.1.47.

[3] *Siddhiyar*, 3.1.47; cf. Umā Pati's *Sangalpa Nirā Karanam*, § 16. அருளே வடிவான மேனித்து, 'form of Grace.'

[4] *Ibid.*

18

the God-Guru's body.[1] *What the Siddhanta divines carefully guard against is any suggestion that the body of the God-Guru, though of a born being* பிறவா இறைவன் பிறந்து, *is susceptible of death or corruption.* Thus Umā Pati Sivāchariyar expressly teaches :

தெரிய

அருவா யுருவா யருவுருவு மில்லா

மரியான்

The formless One, assuming form, and yet is One who has neither form nor formlessness, dies not.[2]

He adheres to his identification of his God-Guru with Sambandhar :

சம்பந்தநாதக் குருவென் நம்பிரான்

Sambandha Nāta Guru is my Lord.[3]

And this Guru is He whose splendour fills all space :

குருவேடமாகிக் குணக்குறியொன்று மில்லாப்

பெருவேடமாய் நிறைந்த பெம்மான்

The Lord whose glory fills all space and who has neither passion nor parts became the Guru.[4]

God so highly conceived, the doctors of Siddhanta theology declare, may be born, may graciously assume a body, may take on human name, and even live within the limitations of human history, *but He does not see death,* மரியான். So S. Umā Pati in the refutation[5] of teaching not acceptable to him reasons :

. . . . . தேசிக

னருளுரு வென்ற பொருளிதனாலின்

மரணமுறுவன் மாயவுருவில்லை

சேரான்

The meaning of the statement that the form of the Guru is the form of Grace is that *the deathless One does not assume a body liable to death.*

---

[1] The mystery of the Body of the risen Christ in S. Luke xxiii. 39-43 cannot furnish any analogy to the body of the Guru in the Siddhanta writers.

[2] *Nenju Vitu Tūdhu,* lines 10-12.

[3] *Ibid.,* line 165. See the same author's *Vinā Venba* where 12 stanzas out of 13 are devoted to the praise of Sambandha Nātan.

[4] *Nenju Vitu Tūdhu,* lines 170, 171.

[5] *Sangatpa Nirākaranam,* § *18 Saiva Vāti Sangatpa Nirākaranam.*

Every intellectual endeavour is made by the Siddhanta thinkers to avoid entertaining, even in the very least possible degree, the conception of a dying God. They concede, S. Umā Pati does, that the birthless One may be born a man, பிறவா இறைவன் பிறந்து, but they decline to carry the incident of human birth and human existence to the point of death, மரியான்.

We have seen[1] that Tāyumānaswāmy brings the God-Guru into the sphere of human history, all but naming him; and Umā Pati Sivāchariyar, we have noticed, likewise finds room in history for the God-Guru, as Marai Gnāna Sambandhar. A third instance of similar treatment (as authoritative as Umā Pati Sivāchariyar's) of the God-Guru is furnished by Arul Nanti Ṣivāçhaṛiyar author of the *Siddhiyar.*[2] He clearly states that Deity became Guru, was native of Nellore, manifested there, being known by the name Meykanda Devar. Now, S. Meykanda Devar is a great person in Siddhanta history and hagiology and author of one of the fourteen Sastras.[3] In Arul Nanti Sivāchariyar's mind the Guru is Ṣiva Himself:

> மதிநுதல் பாகனுமிக் கதிதர
> வெண்ணெயந் தோன்றி.

> He who holds in His side the Lady[4] whose fair brow is as the moon has, for men's salvation, manifested Himself in the town of Tiruvennai Nellore.[5]

Again, he says[6] with equal explicitness:

> தருமா தருமத் தலைநின்றும் வேண்டா
> கருமா கடல்வீழ்ந்தன் கண்டப்—பெருமான்
> திருவெண்ணெய் நல்லூர்ச் சுவேத வனத்தா
> னுருவெண்ணா வந்தெடுத்தா னுற்று.

[1] Above, p. cxxxv.

[2] It is well to bear in mind that these three instances of identification of God with the Guru are not cases of seeing the form of God in the devotee (see above, pp. cv, cvi) for these three Siddhanta writers do *not say, or suggest, that beholding a devout man they had deified him:* they clearly state Deity manifested itself as Guru in each case. It is quite another matter whether in fact they did, or did not, *deify three devout and learned men.*

[3] See above, p. xlviii.

[4] See below, p. 201.

[5] *Irupā Irupahtu,* Stanza 5. See p. cxl for reference to Nellore.

[6] *Ibid.*, Stanza 19.

> To save me from the toils of my good and bad karma, there appeared, taking a form human like mine, in Tiruvennai Nellore, and known as he of Swēta Vanam,[1] the Lord Himself who once changed the poison[2] of the black sea into nectar.

All this teaching of the manifestation of the God-Guru on the physical plane is quite consistent with the Siddhanta insistence on the fact that the Guru is, however, to be discerned by the spiritually-minded, by Grace, and is not to be seen as such except with Grace-lit eyes, அருளே கண்ணாகக் காணினல்லால்.[3] Analogous to the non-discernment of the Siddhanta God-Guru by the worldly-minded men may be noted (without conceding identity or comparison) that the Lord Jesus Christ was in the world and the world knew Him not.[4]

§ 46. Starting with the postulate that Deity, out of love for mankind and seeking man's 'salvation,' assumes human form, one may ask why a *human* form is necessary. A Tamil commentator of the *Irupā Irupahtu* lines quoted above interprets உருவென வந்தெடுத்து thus: 'He assumed a body like mine in which I was suffering ills,' or 'He assumed a bodily form and became even as I who was suffering ills of the flesh,' சரீர தொந்தனைப்பட்டு நிற்கிற வென்னைப்போலே யுருப்பட்டு வந்து.[5] The reason for God's *man*-becoming or for assuming *human* form is suggested to be to bring Deity into close touch with *human* suffering. Indeed, for this reduction of the Divine to the human denominator we have words more authoritative than a commentator's opinion, and they are in Umā Pati Sivāchariyar's *Tiru Arul Payan*:

> அகத்துறு நோய்க்குளினியர் அன்றி யதனைச்
> சகத்தவருங் காண்பரோ தான்.
> பார்வையென மக்களைப் பற்றிப் பிடித்தற்காம்
> போர்வையெனக் காணுய் புவி.

[1] Meykanda Devar is known by this title also. Sweta Vanam is south of Sidambaram. [2] See below, p. 151.

[3] S. Appar (Nallaswamy Pillai's edition of *Select Psalms*), p. 48. In this hymn Apparswamy says that He who is to be seen with the eyes of Grace is not the native of any town, ஒரூரனல்லன், that is to say, the poet-saint speaking of Siva, lays stress on the Deity of Siva, and in saying ஒரூரனல்லன் he emphasizes the fact that Siva, although as Guru he was associated with places on earth, was not a mere man. [4] S. John i. 10.

[5] K. S. Mudaliyar's edition of *Irupā Irupahtu*, p. 62.

A man's secret disease is known only to persons intimately associated with him, and not to the world at large. . . . The world does not know that the Guru's human form is a cloak worn for the luring of souls.[1]

The Guru, is thus, in the language of a great Siddhanta divine, one with the soul's disease, the secret gnawing disease which eats into the very being of the soul. The Guru is the physician of the soul. Is the Guru, however, represented as having the opportunities of knowing the uttermost bitterness of the disease? Let me here quote the words of a Christian writer who lived very close to the age of the Apostles and most probably much earlier than the earliest Siddhanta philosopher. He speaks of:

One Physician who is both flesh and spirit, born and yet not born (*σαρκικός τε καὶ πνευματικός γεννητὸς καὶ ἀγέννητος*), who is God in man, true life in death, who is born of Mary and of God, first passible, then impassible, Jesus Christ our Lord.[2]

Death is the acutest form of the disease of sin, and a fatal symptom of it is the fear of death. That physician of souls can best know the secret ills of the soul who claims to have tasted their bitterness. Let us hear another Christian writer,[3] a thinker who lived before S. Ignatius:

Since then children have in common blood and flesh, He also hath in like manner assumed the same, that through death He might annihilate him that holdeth the power of death, that is, the Devil, and deliver those who through fear of death had been then life-long held in bondage. For not indeed of angels[4] does He take hold, but taketh hold of the seed of Abraham, whence He needed in every respect to become like unto His brethren, that He might become a merciful and faithful high priest as towards God, to make atonement for the sins of the people. . . . For we have not

---

[1] *T.A.P.*, v. 2, 5. On the luring of souls, see above, p. cxxxv.

[2] Ignatius, *Ad Ephes.* vii. 2. He wrote probably between A.D. 98-117. The words rendered 'flesh and spirit' are adjectives in Greek. For 'God in man' *ἐν ἀνθρώπῳ Θεός* some manuscripts read *ἐν σαρκὶ γενόμενος Θεός*, 'God become incarnate'. The longer version has these, among other, additional words, 'Being life, He became mortal that He might free our souls from death and corruption, and heal them, and might restore them to health'.

[3] Author of *Hebrews*. Heb. ii. 14-17.

[4] The A.V. has, 'He took not on Him the nature of angels . . .'

an high priest unable to sympathize [1] with us in our infirmities, but who has in all points been tempted in like manner, yet without sin.[2]

Here we have a statement about a pre-Siddhanta Guru, which has in it a fundamental mark of difference from all we know of what is said of the Siddhanta Guru—*the pre-Siddhanta Guru identified Himself to the uttermost with ill-ridden, diseased humanity even unto death :* here is achieved the *ultimate* reduction of Deity to the human denominator. Now, the Siddhanta does not deny to Deity the capacity for complete man-becoming, since it teaches, 'It cannot be postulated that He is this *and that He cannot become this and that* '.[3] In other words '*with God nothing is impossible*'.[4] The Siddhanta theologians lived in the Christian era, long after the Christian teaching of a dying God, dying to rise again from the dead, had found its way into Tamil India,[5] and it is possible that because of knowledge of such teaching, they, while conceding to their God-Guru some degree of humanity, recoiled from postulating of him death. If, however, we do not refuse to the words already quoted of Uma Pati Sivachāriyar and Tāyumānaswāmy their logical and legitimate implications, we must recognize in the Siddhanta a likeness to the Christian conception of the God-Guru. On the other hand, the insistence of Siddhanta scholars[6] upon the man-becoming of God as something phantasmic, makes the cleavage between the two conceptions, the Christian and the Siddhanta, very wide indeed. Into the mouth of the God-Guru according to Christianity the words could truly be put, 'A body hast thou prepared for Me',[7] a body, as distinguished from a docetic semblance of a body. In

[1] The word συμπαθειν places the sympathizer in the position of the sufferer.

[2] Heb. iv. 15. The translation is from F. Deteitzsch's *Hebrews*, vol. i, p. 220.

[3] *Siddhiyar*, 3.1.44.

[4] S. Luke i. 36.

[5] See above, § 21.

[6] E.g. Nalla, *Studies*, p. 242. In the *Christian Patriot* of June 7, 1924, Dr. A. J. Appasamy of Madras is represented as stating, on the authority of his father, that the 'form' of God in the Bible corresponds to the *sukshma* body of the Siddhanta. See *Siddhiyar*, 3.2.36. 40.47.48.

[7] *Hebrews* x. 5.

addition to two points of difference between the God-Guru conceptions,

(1) the God-Guru's body, in Christian thought, is a real, human body, and not a ' form ',

(2) the God-Guru, in Christian thought, is one tasting the uttermost bitterness of the ills of human life, *death*,

we have, on this matter of a dying God-Guru, a further and striking mark of difference,

(3) the God-Guru's dying is the furthest humanly conceivable reach of the Love of Deity, for ' greater love hath no man than that he should lay down his life for his friend '.[1]

The idea of a dying Christ is not the idea of a *man* dying for his friends : it is the sign of the uttermost stretch of God's love for souls. ' God so loved the world . . . .'[2] The Cross is an offence[3] to the Siddhanta. The Siddhanta has no Cross—it is lacking in the highest possible proof of Love that will go the length of sacrificing itself for the sake of sin-sick souls. The Cross is in the very heart of God. It is in the fibre and essence of Love, God is Love. Love can never love fully, if it cannot sacrifice freely. Tāyumānavar says தன்னைத்தந்து[4]—does he mean that ' God *so* loved . . . that He *gave* His only Son '?[5] Are the contents of தன்னைத்தந்து the same as the implications in, ' I lay down my life for the sheep ' ?[6]

Can Almightly God suffer ? Is not God impassible ? If God is passible, if He can suffer, does not this bring Him down from His supreme pedestal of omnipotence, of unchangeableness, of eternal bliss ? The answer is short : God is Love, we must take God off any pedestal on which love cannot stand. Such pedestals are of our own making. That God is a God of power and order and knowledge—this is true. But in relation to His spiritually-conscious creatures all this is of minor importance ; to us the crucial point is that He is love. Now love is passible ; and if God is love, God is passible. A person who can love, and yet cannot suffer is unthinkable ; and if God is such, He is unthinkable ; for we cannot think of a love that is out of range of suffering. . . . If the love be great, great also is the power of suffering ; and if God's love be infinite, then He can suffer infinitely too. . . .[7]

---

[1] S. John xv. 13. [2] S. John iii. 16. See below, p. 160.

[3] ' A crucified Christ is to the Jews a stumbling-block, and to the Greeks foolishness ' (1 Cor. i. 23).

[4] See below, p .34. [5] S. John iii. 16. [6] S. John x. 17.

[7] Dr. Douglas White, *Forgiveness and Suffering*, pp. 83, 84.

The Siddhanta conception of the God-Guru, in spite of its sublimity, and its uniqueness in Indian religious thought,[1] and, indeed, in spite of the grand inspiration it has given the Siddhanta saints for a passionate, personal love for God, however named, lags considerably behind the Christian idea. The most vital difference is the Cross which is to the Christian the high-water mark of the Love of God. Love that, remaining sinless, dares 'becoming sin'[2] for sinners and tastes death for them has reached the uttermost limit of sacrifice.[3]

PART VIII. MYSTICISM

§ 47. Between God and the soul there is 'a great, though secret affinity, an affinity that each knows, and that so few understand, an affinity that cannot be denied, but that cannot be fathomed.'[4] On this kinship is based religion, and mysticism in its sane, sober, well-balanced aspects, is one of the fruits of religion. The whole of religion is not mysticism. A man may profess and practise religion without being a mystic. Mysticism is the practice of the presence of God. A sure means of practising such presence is prayer. Prayer, when it passes beyond the stage of mere petitioning and becomes communion with God, takes one well into the experience called mysticism.

Of what do we discourse in prayer? . . . In it we speak of God

---

[1] See present writer's *Foregleams of God*, pp. 182-85, and 220.

[2] 2 Cor. v. 21.

[3] Attention should be drawn to Prof. Radhakrishnan's *Hindu Thought and Christian Doctrine* contributed to *The Christian Patriot*, February 22, 1924 and March 8, 1924, and to the editorial utterance in the *Patriot* of February 22, 1924. A discussion of the limits of redemptive immanence is raised by Prof. Radhakrishnan's learned articles. A striking passage in the professor's contribution seems to go counter to what I have stated above is the Siddhanta view. He says, '*The Cross is not an offence or a stumbling-block to the Hindu but is a great symbol of the redemptive reality of God. It shows how love is rooted in sacrifice*'. I am not sure if Siddhantists will subscribe to this Christian manner of thinking. Both to Christians and to Hindus much interest and stirring up of thought will be found in the series of articles on the Jagad-Guru contributed by Mr. J. C. Winslow to *The Guardian* (Calcutta) of April, May, June, 1924.

[4] S. Francis De Sales, *On The Love of God*, i. ch. xv. (Knox Little's Edition, p. 21.)

> only; for of what can love discourse and talk save of the well-beloved? *And therefore prayer and mystical theology are one and the same thing.*
>
> Now, it is called mystical because its conversation is altogether secret, and there is nothing said in it between God and the soul, save only from heart to heart by a communication, incommunicable to all but those who make it. Finally, prayer or mystical theology is nothing else but a conversation in which the soul amorously entertains herself with God, concerning His most amiable goodness to unite and join herself thereto.[1]

In prayer, and there is a prayer without words,[2] a prayer not bounded by place or time, 'we retire to God, because we aspire to Him, and we aspire to Him that we may retire to Him,' and 'when our spirit devotes itself to the company, the privacy, and the familiarity of its God, it will be perfumed with His perfection.'[3] Is this mysticism possible to all? King Henry IV of France desired S. Francis De Sales

> to write a book concerning true religion, such as should set it forth in its rightful beauty, and show the world that holiness of life was not incompatible with a busy, active career, whether at court or in the provinces, amid the whirl of affairs or the claims of society, holiness alike free from repulsive severity and treacherous laxity.[4]

The book written in response to the royal request was *L'Introduction à la Vie Dévote*, 'Introduction to the Devout Life.' There is no monopoly in mysticism. Man is capable of religion. Man is capable of prayer. Man is capable of mysticism. The experience called mysticism is not for an esoteric few, for spiritual aristocrats.[5] It is for democratic, universal benefit that 'the most

[1] S. Francis De Sales, *On The Love Of God*, vi, ch. vii. (Knox Little's Edition, pp. 167, 168).

[2] No single book deals with the subject so clearly and in so simple a manner as does *The Practice of Mental Prayer and of Perfection* by the Rev. Father Alphonsus, translated from the French into English, in six readable volumes, by the Rev. Father Jerome O'Connell. The work is based upon the writings of S. Teresa and S. John of the Cross. The present writer is not a member of the Roman Communion, but he has no hesitation in humbly recommending *The Practice of Mental Prayer and of Perfection* to all who would reach the mystical heights of religion.

[3] S. Francis De Sales, *Introduction to the Devout Life*, Part ii, ch. xiii, pp. 118, 119, in the translation of the Rev. Thomas Barns.

[4] English Edition by the Rev. Thomas Barns of *Introduction to the Devout Life*, p. xix.

[5] On 'aristocrat'cism' among mystics see the Rev. O. C. Quick's article in *The Journal of Theological Studies*, January 1912, pp. 182, 183, October

general, necessary function of mysticism is to keep the eternal before us in our earthly and temporal life.'[1] Mysticism is not made exclusive by its claims, and 'the claim to inward experience of God is the essence of mystical religion.'[2] If eternal life, begun in this temporal life and realized as a present possession,[3] is to be acquired by ***all men***, then, the inward experience of God, which is part of the ***present*** possession of eternal life, is essential to ***all mankind***. Mysticism, far from being a close preserve, is the open right of all. At the same time the fact is undeniable that mysticism is liable to abuses, like most good things.

(1) There are professing mystics who claim to be experts and the elect.[4]
(2) The occult is associated, and confused, with mysticism.[5]
(3) Visions, trances, ecstasies are claimed to be essentials.
(4) The *sense* of God's presence is identified with the presence itself.
(5) Mysticism is confused with asceticism.[6]
(6) Self-deification is mistaken for the Divine Presence.[7]
(7) Encouragement is given to the belittlers of institutional religion and the duties of life.

There are other dangers to which mysticism is exposed: the abuse need not necessarily make the use immoral.

When we come to consider Tāyumānaswamy as a mystic we are in contact with questions which cannot be answered satisfactorily, especially on the comparative side of any such consideration. Concede to Tāyumānavar's mysticism ***the*** element of true mysticism, namely, the practice of the presence of God, raised to a degree of intense awareness, then, ***what is the place sought to be found for Christ and His Cross in the scheme of***

1912, p. 8, and the Rev. Father Kelly's contribution in the same journal for July 1912, p. 487.

[1] The Rev. O. C. Quick in *J. T. S.*, January 1912, p. 188.

[2] *Ibid.*, October 1912, p. 4.

[3] S. John v. 24, '*has* eternal life.'

[4] This weakness is not peculiar to mystics. There are whole bodies of Christians who claim to be the elect of God.

[5] *Der Mystik* is the sane variety, and *Mysticismus* is the counterfeit, in German.

[6] See the Rev. Father Pourrat's ***Christian Spirituality***, p. v.

[7] It is the danger feared by Mr. G. K. Chesterton of 'Jones worshipping Jones.' (*The Biblical Review*, April 1917, p. 188.)

salvation by mysticism? It is in this form that the opposition to mysticism generally, and to Christian mysticism in particular, is usually framed.[1] The basic fallacy of the problem so formulated is the *assumption* that mysticism is a medium of salvation. Mysticism is *not* a means, most decidedly not *the* means, of salvation. Mysticism is a name for the experience, of which there are degrees, of conscious, rational, personal relationship to God on the part of men and women who have been, or who honestly think they have been, redeemed from sin. In a Christian setting, this experience is that of persons who have 'passed from death into life',[2] and this passage from death into life is effected by the redeeming love of the Lord Jesus Christ. Mystical experience, the Christian can say, is the life, in close communion with God of one to whom Christ, and the Cross and Calvary, and the empty tomb and the ascension heights of the glory of Olivet are intense realities. The Christian

[1] Prof. Warfield of Princeton Theological Seminary writing in *The Biblical Review* for April 1917, on mysticism and Christianity, gravely concludes (p. 190) 'The question is whether we need, whether we have, a provision in the blood of Christ for our sins; or whether we, each of us, possess within ourselves all that can be required for time and for eternity. Both of these things cannot be true, and obviously *tertium non datur*. We may be mystics, or we may be Christians. We cannot be both.' The foundation fallacy of this attack on Christian mysticism lurks in the statement: 'This Christian mysticism [ascribing the movements of one's religious feelings to the Holy Spirit or "the Christ within us"] now, *obviously differs in no essential respect from the parallel phenomena which are observable in other religions.* It is only general mysticism manifesting itself on Christian ground and interpreting itself accordingly in the form of Christian thought. It is mysticism which has learned to speak in Christian language'. One of the essential phenomena in the passage I have italicised above, is 'listening to the inner voice' and to which is added 'the common element' of seeking 'the knowledge of God in human feelings.' (*Ibid.*, pp. 173, 174, 175). The fact of essential phenomena being common, for instance, to all human foods should not obscure the distinction of a particular food. The commonness of essential factors in all religions is not a reason against *the* outstanding feature of any one faith. Mysticism amongst Hindus may have analogies to mysticism amongst Christians, but the points of similarity need not, of necessity, simplify the conspicuous dissimilarities. Intolerance of similarities should not blind the inquirer to the differentiating unlikenesses. Further, 'listening to the inner voice' and finding the knowledge of God in human feelings are, in mysticism, aberrations from the normal.

[2] S. John v. 24; 1 John iii. 14.

advancing in spiritual experience, stumbling often, can lay claim to know, as a fact, fellowship and communion with God,[1] and to have foretasted of that fulness of joy which awaits all who shall be bidden to the marriage supper of the Lamb.[2] It is true that there is danger where 'the inner certainty of a specific experience is made the one authoritative channel of religious truth' and 'the external evidence of historic fact becomes secondary and even logically superfluous '[3]—no doubt there is grave danger. Christian mysticism truly so called, however, does *not* make any experience the authoritative channel of religious truth and does not go counter to historic Christianity.[4] If love, *bhakti* in the language of Hindu devotees, is, as it indeed is, a conspicuous element in mysticism, then the highest point of God's love to man, and man's reciprocating love to God, is in the Cross. Christian mysticism cannot keep away from the Cross, for Calvary is the very essence of that attraction which draws all men to Christ and of that *bhakti* which frames itself in a burning desire to be closest to God.

It is only tenacity to the commercial instinct of securing a 'corner' in religious experience that will deny to Tāyumānavar a mysticism as high as a Cross-less mysticism could be. How high his mysticism is may be gauged by the fact of his loftiest religious experiences being associated with the revelation and teaching vouchsafed to him by his *Guru* whom he identified with God. The God-Guru idea saves the mysticism of Tāyumānavar

[1] The *ἡ κοινωνία* of 1 John i. 3 means more than the 'fellowship' of the A. V. It is not Christian, New Testament, teaching which Dr. Hermann lays down, 'There can be no such thing as communion with the exalted Christ'. *Communion with God*, p. 193.

[2] Rev. xix. 9. See *The Eucharistic Life*, p. 28.

[3] The Rev. O. C. Quick, *J.T.S.*, October 1912, p. 7.

[4] *Ibid.*, p. 9 startles one by his unqualified pronouncement, 'It is very hard to find traces of mysticism in the New Testament, except perhaps in S. Paul in whom it is abundantly corrected by other influences'. For the overwhelmingly proved, more than merely asserted, contrary the reader is referred to the Rev. W. K. Fleming's *Mysticism in Christianity*, ch. ii; the Rev. W. F. Cobb's *Mysticism and the Creed*, pp. 39, 40; Dean Inge's *Christian Mysticism*, Lecture ii; Bishop Hall's *Christ Mystical*; and Miss Evelyn Underhill's *The Mystic Way*, chs. ii., iii, iv.

from the reproach of substituting for revealed authority the sanctions of mere emotions. His psalms show him passing from a severe analysis of feelings into that healthy discontent out of which comes a strong God-ward craving which will not be denied its goal.[1] His regard for the duties of institutional religion does not stand in the way of his testing its efficacy in so far as the ultimate end of all religion is concerned—union with God. Tāyumānavar was a man of prayer, prayer punctuated with the pangs of the mystic's purgative way. Along lines of intense strenuousness we see him struggling, his soul illuminated by 'Grace' and sustained by strength which was not his, and striving to reach the end of all quests—the Feet of God.[2] Joy alternates with sorrow, hope with despair, assurance with derilection, in his experience of the Divine, and one cannot hesitate to trace in his practice of the presence of God the evident signs of the scaling of lofty heights in his seeking to climb the steep ascent that leads upwards unto God.

§ 48. When we introduce the element of comparison into our estimate of the mysticism of Tāyumānavar the judgment must be that the poet-saint has striking points of commonness with Christian mystics, and that, at the same time, Christian mysticism has distinctions which we fail to discover in the Siddhanta.

1. The God-Guru idea is indispensable to Siddhanta mysticism. The appearance of the Guru at a certain stage of spirituality[3] marks an advance in the mystical standing of the disciple. Christian mysticism is similarly unthinkable apart from Christ. The once physically manifested God-Guru, the historical Jesus Christ, is the ever present Christ of the believer. It is the distinction of Christian mysticism that the God-Guru is the soul's Redeemer. The Cross,[4] the rubric of the soul's exalted ritual, is the dividing mark between the mysticism of

[1] See above, § 20 on the poet's religious experience.
[2] See below, pp. 211, 226.
[3] See below, p. 167.
[4] See above, p. cxliii.

Tāyumānavar and Christian mysticism. The impression is erroneous that Christian mysticism relegates to a background of obsolete conventions the Cross and the Christ of Calvary. The *Via Dolorosa* has to be trodden by every Christian mystic, indeed, the Cross is ever in sight throughout his spiritual pilgrimage and, without doubt, when the goal of Love is reached, the Cross, as the sign and symbol of God's infinite Love, will not pass out of the mystic's vision. 'The first token of Love is that Jesus has given us His flesh to eat and His blood to drink'.[1] In the words of the late Mrs. Herman, '*What we contend for, and can never afford to lose sight of, is that the heart of mysticism—that which makes it a genuine spiritual movement and experience, and not a mere theosophy—is its passionate, personal apprehension of Jesus Christ the Redeemer*'.[2] While aberrations from the sane, mystical norm of the Christian saint are possible, it is hardly fair to Christian mysticism as a whole to state[3] that Christ is 'not confessed in any true sense as a redeemer'. We have seen[4] that in the Siddhanta conception of the God-Guru there is the element of 'kinship' with the human soul and the kinship is one of the Guru's qualifications for his office, and we have also seen how the conception of the Divine Kinsman-Guru is best realized in the Lord Jesus

[1] Ruysbroeck, *Flowers of a Mystic Garden*, p. 69.

[2] *The Meaning and Value of Mysticism*, p. 300.

[3] As the Rev. D. M. McIntyre does, for instance, in *The Expositor* for April 1918, p. 243. As typical of the mystic's estimate of the place of the Cross in Christian spirituality may be cited that of Richard Rolle of Hampole. He speaks with unmistakable stress of 'Christ's gainbuying [redeeming] . . .' 'the blood by which we are gainbought [redeemed]', in his *Fire of Love*, ch. xviii. So too in the very first chapter of *The Cloud of Unknowing* the unnamed author says, 'Thou wottest well that . . . the everlasting love of His Godhead . . . bought thee with the price of His precious blood wher thou wert lost in Adam'. Of exactly similar import are the words of S. John of the Cross in *A Spiritual Canticle*, St. xxiii, 'As it was by the forbidden tree . . . that our nature was corrupted in Adam and lost, so it was by the tree of the Cross that it was redeemed and restored. The Bridegroom there stretched forth the hand of His grace and mercy in His death and passion. . . .' The thoughts of Bishop Hall in his *Christ Mystical* (ch. v, § 1), one of the three favourite books of General Gordon, do not overlook the Cross: 'Christ is made unto us . . . our full redemption'.

[4] Above, pp. cxl, cxli.

Christ. We may now go further and find in the very term 'Redeemer' the sense of kinship. In *Isaiah*[1] 'the Lord God is the Redeemer', and the Hebrew word for 'Redeemer' גֹּאֵל *goel*, means '*blood-relation*' whose duty is to redeem and avenge his kinsman.[2] God becomes man's 'blood-relation'—in Christ Jesus is God most nearly man's Redeemer, his 'blood-relation'.[3] The *Redeemer* God-Guru idea of Christian mysticism is one of its great distinctions.

2. I am not sure if Dr. Macnicol had Tāyumānavar in mind in the somewhat general judgment that in the 'devotional mysticism' of India there is not that sense of sin which one finds in Christian and Hebrew saints.[4] When we see Tāyumānavar and other Siddhanta *bhaktas* laying stress on their sense of separation from God we shall not be far wrong in ascribing that sense to a deep consciousness of sin.[5] To such consciousness must be attributed all those strivings after, and longings for, a state of 'mindlessness.'[6] No one can read Tāyumānavar's psalms without being struck by the reality of the saint's conflicts with 'a sin-burdened "I",' a selfhood as rebellious as you see in the hymns of Kabir or Tukaram.[7] All this being conceded it must yet be added that it is in the light of the Cross of Christ that a severe, searching analysis of sin is possible, for the conception of Love must be at its highest before the enormity of the pain of sin to the soul's Beloved could be adequately understood. The Cross represents Love at its highest.

3. The wholesome idea of the mystic as a man of duty is illustrated in Tāyumānavar's case. He himself holds up the

[1] xli. 14 and in eight other passages in Deutero-Isaiah.

[2] Lev. xxv. 25; Ruth iii. 12.

[3] In Isa. liv. 5 God is spoken of as 'Redeemer and Husband'.
In Titus ii. 13, 14 we have mention of 'Our great God and Saviour, Christ Jesus who gave Himself for us that He might redeem us . . .'

[4] Dr. Macnicol in *The Expositor*, August 1918, p. 145.

[5] See above, § 20 on Tāyumānavar's sense of sin, and present writer's *Foregleams of God*, pp. 72-4 on consciousness of sin in Vedic religion.

[6] See above, § 33.

[7] This is not the view of Dr. Macnicol (*Expositor*, August 1918, p. 148).

example of King Janaka.[1] He, like the author of the *Gita*, believed in the doing of duty without distraction.[2] When the poet shows a preference for serving the saints,[3] the devotees of Siva, he sets to himself a standard slightly lower, and scope of ministration more restricted, than service in Christian mysticism. The ideal is framed in the lines of Christina Rossetti.[4]

> '*In Me thou lovest Me : I call,*
> *Thee to love Me in all.*'—
> Brimful my heart, dear Lord, that so
> My love may overflow.
>
> '*Love Me in sinners and in saints,*
> *In each who needs or faints.*'—
> Lord, I will love Thee as I can
> In every brother man.
>
> '*All sore, all crippled, all who ache,*
> *Tend all for My dear sake.*'—
> All for Thy sake, Lord : I will see
> In every sufferer Thee.
>
> '*So I at last, upon My Throne*
> *Of glory, Judge alone,*
> *So I, at last will say to Thee :*
> *Thou diddest it to Me.*'

It is well to note further that Tāyumānavar's sense of service is coloured by an expectation of merit. Not for others does the saint in the Siddhanta live. ***All his actions are for the saving of his own soul.*** Herein lies one of the most striking differences between the mysticism of Tāyumānavar and the mysticism of the Christian. The isolation of the Siddhanta mystic is impossible to one to whom Christ is the ideal and the rule. The Christian mystic dare not seek great things for

[1] Below, p. 226. [2] Below, p. 57. [3] Below, pp. 58, 72.

[4] W. M. Rossetti's edition of Christina G. Rossetti's *Poetical Works*, p. 257. The article by Dr. Gillies in *The Biblical Review*, October 1922, p. 555 on 'the mystic in a social age' is an interesting study of the practical possibility of mysticism co-existing with supreme human activity. Among examples cited of the fact are S. Teresa, S. John of the Cross, S. Catherine of Genoa, S. Catherine of Sienna, Ignatius Loyola, and Elizabeth of Schoenau—all mystics, but persons interesting themselves in the affairs of life. Dr. R. F. Horton's *The Mystical Quest of Christ* (see specially, chs. vi-viii), is a book of mysticism in practical life.

himself. He lives for others. It is what he has striven to achieve for the saving and well-being of others that becomes the standard by which he will be judged at the last—'Ye have done . . . not done . . . unto these . . . ye have done . . . not done . . . unto Me.'[1] The self-saving aloofness of holy men, even of the type of Tāyumānavar, is very poor quality in comparison with the impelling, compelling, constraining spirit of self-sacrifice so sublimely characteristic of Paul of Tarsus, Catherine of Genoa, Francis of Assisi, Francis de Sales, David Brainered, Henry Martyn, William Law and a host of others whose mysticism made them heroic adventurers for the Cross. Love seeks not its own, but, like light, like life, is self-diffusive.

4. A striking feature in the mysticism of S. Tāyumānavar is his silence as to visions associated with specific revelations. Herein his mysticism seems to conform to S. Teresa's counsel that the desire for visions is a soliciting of danger, since one is often deluded and deceived by seeming visions, and there are visions *not* vouchsafed by God. 'Any one who longs for these graces cannot really be humble. . . . Such a one is certain to be deceived, or at least in great danger of delusion, for an entrance is thus left open to the devil, who only needs to see the door left ajar to slip in at once to play us a thousand tricks.'[2] Tāyumānavar speaks indeed of visions of God's beauty and glory, but, like S. Paul,[3] he is silent as to the contents and details of what he had been permitted to see. Many mystics are credited with visions and the ecstatic state both in the East and in the West. The latest claimant for the experience of visions is Sundar Singh of the company of 'Sadhus' of India. He is a Christian convert from Hinduism, an earnest and zealous follower of the Lord Jesus Christ. He has been preaching Christ in Tibet, Ceylon, the Straits Settlements,[4] the Malay

[1] S. Matthew xxv. 44-6.

[2] *The Interior Castle*, Sixth Mansion, ch. ix, §§ 13-19.

[3] 'It is not lawful for man to utter.' 2 Cor. xii. 4.

[4] Sadhu Sundar Singh was the honoured and revered guest of the present writer in Penang on two occasions. On the second occasion, in 1920, the Sadhu did the writer the honour of borrowing his copy of Underhill's *Mysticism* for reading in India. The copy, when returned, was found well

20

States, and latterly in England and America. During his English tour it was that, for the first time since his conversion in 1904, the Sadhu laid bare to public gaze the secrets of his inner sight.[1] It is to Sadhu Sundar Singh's credit that he is the first Indian Christian, probably the first among all Indians, to whom a revelation of holy things which I should not presume even to repeat had been vouchsafed. His praise, however, is not in his visions but in the Gospel, to the transforming power of which the life of this man of God bears abundant testimony.

5. It is, perhaps, of the intellectual mysticism of India that Dr. Macnicol asks the question,[2] 'Is the goal of silence, of "emptiness and nothingness," the true mystic goal?' In the case of mysticism strictly so called, the *bhakti* mysticism of Tamil India, the mystic's goal is *not* silence in nothingness. Silence[3] does play a very important part in the mysticism of Tāyumānavar, but is God silence?

> Silence is not God; nor speaking is not God; fasting is not God, nor eating is not God; onliness is not God, nor company is not God; nor yet any of all the other such two contraries. He is hid between them, and may not be found by any wish of thy soul but all only by love of thy heart. . . . Choose thee Him, and thou art silently speaking and speakingly silent, fastingly eating and eatingly fasting. . . .[4]

Thus an early English mystic on the safe middle of thought for the contemplative. In Tāyumānavar the mystic's goal is foreshadowed by his present realization of nearing 'Siva-land's sweep of bliss.'

> Where in pure infinite whiteness stretches
>   Siva-land's sweep of bliss boundless I drew nigh;
> Tares of my darkness uprooted I saw;
>   Naught but the Lord I saw high in His splendour.[5]

---

marked on almost every page. I believe Underhill's *Mysticism* is a book whose thoughts and terms had been found to be of considerable suggestive value to the Sadhu.

[1] Drs. Streeter and Appasamy, *The Sadhu: A Study in Mysticism and Practical Religion*, pp. 109–56. See the Rev. C. W. Emmett's sympathetic but critical appreciation in *The Hibbert Journal*, January 1921, p. 308, of some of the miracles recorded about Sadhu Sundar Singh.

[2] *The Expositor*, August 1918, p. 143.

[3] See below, p. 133.

[4] *The Cell of Self-Knowledge* (Epistle of Discretion), pp. 107–8.

[5] Below, p. 110. The rendering is in the syllabic arrangement of the original.

The poet-saint's seeing the beauty of God proves that what he saw was not a blank.[1] The goal the saint longs to reach is hinted at in his words[2]:

'A place of mystic secrets',
  The books bewildered cry:
I long to climb that holy
  Mountain of God most high—
    When will it be?

Nor sun, nor moon, there shineth,
  Nor star where God is Light;
I long to reach that City
  Of glory, heavenly bright—
    When will it be?

The pure in heart have vision
  Of Bliss the boundless sea:
I long for its sweet waters
  And therein merged to be—
    Oh for that day!

The last of the three verses indicates experience of the present and expectation for the future. The vision of Bliss in this life leads on to the union, here or hereafter, of the soul and its Lord in that Bliss.

6. An unjust and distorted picture of the soul's relation to the indwelling God is often painted[3] by those who would disparage mysticism. The relationship is looked at from a wrong angle. The no doubt possible aberrations from the thoroughly sane conception of indwelling Deity are made much of by the non-mystical, and even material, detractors of the good that is in mysticism. Exaggeration in the spirit of ridicule can reduce one of the fundamentals of Christian certitude to absurdity—God in us. It is New Testament teaching that not only is the Holy Spirit the soul's Indweller, but God the Son, and God the Father are where the soul is made fit for such indwelling.[4] The believer's union with Christ does not make

[1] On this see below, p. 223.
[2] Below, pp. 118, 119.
[3] See Prof. Warfield's criticism of mysticism referred to above, at p. cxlvii.
[4] S. John xiv. 20, 23; Rev. iii. 20; 1 Cor. iii. 16, and other passages.

the believer worship himself, 'Jones worshipping Jones'.[1] The union however is real.

> Know that this is a true, real, essential, substantial union whereby the person of the believer is indissolubly united to the glorious person of the Son of God. Know that this union is not more mystical than certain: that in natural union there may be more evidence, there cannot be more truth. As the head and members are but one body, as the husband and wife are but one flesh, as our meat and drink are part of ourselves, as the tree and branches but one plant, as the foundation and the walls are but one fabric, so Christ and the believing soul are indivisibly one with each other.[2]

The non-acceptance by S. Tāyumānavar and other Siddhanta saints of the doctrine of the complete man-becoming of God as in Jesus Christ, and of the doctrine of God's love manifested to the uttermost in the idea of a dying God—the silence of this great mystic on the Incarnation and the Cross—must exclude from their conception of the indwelling God the fulness and perfection implied in the Christian idea of the indwelling God. I am reluctant to deny to the Siddhanta saint not only a deep longing for, but, even in this life, a realization of, fellowship and communion with God. At the same time I am impelled by a reasoned conviction, an inexplicable inness of certitude, and not by any habit or convention or prepossession, to think that fellowship and communion with God have their fulness and fruition in 'the love of God which is in Christ Jesus our Lord . . . Christ Jesus who died, yea, rather who rose again, and is at the right hand of God, and maketh intercession for us.'[3] Again, whatever theophagous ideas may be proved lurking in non-Christian faiths and pre-Christian customs[4]—what if they were foreshadowings finding fulfilment where all types ceased?—there is nothing in the institutional religion associated with the mysticism of the Siddhanta that bears comparison with the Christian conception of 'eating the flesh of the Son of Man and drinking His blood . . . true food . . . true drink,'[5] and

[1] Above, p. cxlvi.

[2] Hall's *Christ Mystical*, pp. 36, 61.

[3] *Rom.* viii. 34, 39.

[4] See Dr. Preserved Smith's *A Short History of Christian Theophagy*, chs. i and ii.

[5] S. John, vi. 53-63. See Dr. H. A. Watson's *Mysticism of S. John*, Lecture iii. Those interested in a study of the significance of the Lord's supper in the

in that conception is such close communion of the human with the Divine, such ineffable fellowship, as they only know who 'taste and see how good the Lord is.'[1] The Eucharist is to the Christian mystic more than a mere commemoration and is not magic: it is a manner of the practice of the Incarnation. Christian mystics have spoken in very unmistakable terms of the association of the Holy Eucharist with mystical union.

> This I pray, this I long for, that I may be wholly united to Thee, and withdraw my heart from all created things: and by means of sacred communion and frequent celebration may learn more and more to taste things heavenly and eternal. . . . Be thou favourable unto me O Jesus, good, sweet and benign: and grant unto me Thy poor beadsman sometimes at least in Holy Communion to feel if it be but a touch of Thy hearty, affectionate love; that my faith may grow stronger, my hope in Thy goodness fuller, and that charity once perfectly kindled after tasting this heavenly manna may never decay.[2]

How ill-founded the charge is that Christian mysticism takes note of the Passion of the Lord Jesus Christ, not as a matter vital to spirituality, but as a concession to the claims and conventions of institutional religion, is seen by what Tauler (among many other mystics) says of the Passion and of Holy Communion:

> All our blessedness and salvation are contained in Christ and His Passion. For whoso seeketh his salvation outside the Passion of Christ, loseth much more than he seeketh. The wounds of our Lord are alone the fountains from which all salvation floweth; whosoever seeketh salvation let him seek it in the Passion of our Lord; there he findeth it surely, and nowhere else. . . On the field of the Passion of Christ grow wine and corn, in order to have meat and drink at the same time. They who come to this field and eat and drink here are full of divine graces.[3]

---

early Church, will find the Rev. Darwell Stone's *A History of the Doctrine of the Holy Eucharist*, 2 vols., by far the best book of its kind. A very stimulative recent study, on original lines, of the meaning of 'This is My Body', 'This is My Blood' is furnished by Dr. R. H. Kennett's *The Last Supper*. Rule's *Doctrine of the Holy Eucharist* and Dyson Heglis *Holy Communion in the Church of England* are more recent contributions to the subject.

[1] *Ps*. xxxiv. 8.

[2] Thomas à Kempis, *Imitation of Christ*, Bk. iii, chs. xiii and xiv (Dr. C. Bigg's translation).

[3] Tauler, *The Following of Christ*, Part ii, § 48

More explicitly does Tauler speak:

> The sacrament of the Body of our Lord is the fruit of the Holy Cross . . . He who willeth to consider the Passion of our Lord in all earnestness, let him go joyfully to the Table of our Lord, for it is useful to him, and he will become rich in graces.[1]

There is a mystic, real power in thus contemplating the Passion:

> In the contemplation of the Passion of our Lord, God poureth a power unto him [the believer] whereby He draweth man unto Himself. This is the great fruit produced by the Passion of our Lord.[2]

The Holy Communion is not only a great factor in the practice of the Incarnation, within which is included the practice of the Passion, it is also much of the practice of the real presence of God. The mystic thereby 'in a special manner stands before the Lord whole and entire.'[3] He possesses God in great tranquillity.[4] He realizes how God 'suffers unto sacrifice that He may save us.'[5] The mystic, the true believer, feels a transport of love and unitive joy in the Holy Communion.[6] As 'the property of love is to be always giving and always receiving, the love of Jesus is generous and hungry, and all that He has, all that He is, He gives: all that we are, all that we have, He takes.'[7] The unitive contemplation of the Love of God in Christ evokes responsive love in the soul and fills it with a thirst insatiable in time. Because of the love kindled by the Holy Communion, and not merely because the Sacrament is 'a perennial fountain of sanctification and perfection',[8] the God-longing souls 'always hungering . . . run with great desire to the sacrament, and their hunger is great that God could not satisfy them with all that He hath created but only with Himself: nor can they ever be satisfied so long as they

[1] *The Following of Christ*, Part ii, § 11.
[2] *Ibid.*, Part i, § 124.
[3] Gerlac Petersen, *The Fiery Soliloquy with God*, ch. xviii.
[4] Brother Lawrence, *The Practice of the Presence of God*, p. 26.
[5] A. M. Faribairn, *Christ in Modern Theology*, p. 487.
[6] *The Spiritual Journal of Lucie Christine*, pp. 16, 31.
[7] Rysbroeck, *Flowers of a Mystic Garden*, p. 69.
[8] Sacramelli, *Directorium Asceticum*, vol. i, Article x, ch. i, § 390.

live in time, for they desire always more.'[1] Christian mysticism, far from forgetting the Cross of Christ, maintains a perpetual remembrance of His death and Passion: Christian mysticism, unlike any non-Christian mysticism, is in touch and tune with the infinite by the means and mediation of a once dead, but risen and evermore living Person.

§ 49. In common with many Christian and Sufi mystics Tāyumānavar employs love-imagery to express the soul's relationship to God. It is by the way of love that the soul has the beginnings of God-knowledge, and love comes not to the immature:

Till knowledge comes of man to maiden
  She has no thought of happiness:
When love possesses all her passions,
  She smiles she thought of love so less.[2]

The Lover of the soul pursues the soul and kindles love in her:

When I the way of love not knowing
  Was moved and stirred to love by Thee,
My spirit with love-languor fainted,
  Love for Love's fulness came on me.[3]

The love-filled soul has the likeness of the lover engraved in her innermost consciousness.[4] The soul's beloved is God, and God's beloved is the soul:

If Thou to me, Beloved,
  Art dearest, I should be
To Thee Thine own beloved,
  As dear as Thou to me.[5]

At a stage of the soul's career she is the beloved in the Divine Lover's embrace:

The arms of love around me are,
  'Tis God embraceth me,
And in His bliss unspeakable
  He holds me His to be,
Enfolded in His boundlessness,
  Engulfed in ecstasy.

[1] Tauler, *The Following of Christ*, Part ii, § 10. On the witness of the Holy Communion to Christian mysticism see Underhill's *The Mystic Way*, ch. vi.

[2] Below, p. 42. So in *N.M.* 192, [illegible].

[3] Below, p. 42. So *N.M.* 1064, [illegible].

[4] *N.M.* 1035 [illegible]. . .

[5] Below, p. 40.

No tongue of man the joy can tell
  The bliss beyond word's reach,
And humble I with mortal lips
  Its meaning cannot teach——
Sooner the dumb their dream declare
  In joyousness of speech.[1]

An analogous imagery is the Rabbinic more intensely described kissing with the kisses of love,[2] the kiss signifying, in Rabbinic theology, 'the union of the soul with its root' (*Zohar*, i. 168).[3] The inherent longing of the soul for union with the beloved leads her on, says Rabbi Bachye Ibu Bakudah, till 'she drinks of the cup of love to God'.[4]

In Tāyumānavar we have the love-imagery freely employed in *Ānandak kalippu*, ஆனந்தக்களிப்பு.[5] It is a ballad of high spiritual bliss in the soul's recognition of the non-dual relation[6] between it and God. The joy of union is celebrated in the ***kalippu***. The soul is represented as a young woman telling her friend, in the language of maidenly confidence, and yet of reserve, of the joy of her lover's visit to her, of his guile, of whispered secrets, of love's surrender, and oneness. Much is left unsaid. The soul tells her sister-soul with charming casualness[7] of her state before her lover's visit, and how overjoyed she is because she had been wooed and won by the sweet stratagem of her Lover. The erotic character of the poem is not allowed to obscure the high spiritual meaning veiled by the imagery. The poet clearly states that God is the Lover of the soul,[8] and the

[1] Below, p. 84.

[2] See below, p. 214, for the passage from *The Zohar*, ii. 97.

[3] Dr. Abelson, *Jewish Mysticism*, pp. 168, 169.

[4] *Duties of the Heart*, quoted by Dr. S. Schechter in *Some Aspects of Rabbinic Theology*, p. 73. In *Isaiah* xli. 8 'Abraham my friend' is more correctly 'Abraham my beloved.' So Moses is called by Philo (see Ryle, *Philo and Holy Scripture*, p. xix) 'the friend of God, the best beloved of God.' Moses, according to the Rabbis, died being kissed by the word of God. (See Palestine *Targum* on Deut. xxxiv. 5.)

[5] The late Sir P. Arunachalam's rendering of the verses he called *A Revel in Bliss*. See below, pp. 100 and 106 for renderings in two different styles.

[6] *Advaita*. See above, § 34.

[7] Below, p. 100.

[8] Below, p. 101, No. 296.

Christian is reminded of what had been said two thousand years before Tāyumānavar, 'Behold thy Maker is thy Husband'.[1]

Objection has been taken[2] to the use of erotic language by mystics, by the Sufis particularly and by oriental mystics generally by implication. The expression of great spiritual truths in terms of the closest of human relationships is justified by the early Jewish interpretation of the *Song of Songs*, as seen in *The Targum to the Song of Songs* in which the Targumist handles the 'Song of Songs' as an allegorical outline of Jewish history from the Exodus to the coming of the Messiah and the expected building of the third temple.[3] The Christian makers of the *Authorized Version* of the Bible framed a reason for the retention of the *Song* in the Canon by their page-headings and chapter-summaries, interpreting the chief speakers in the *Song* to be Christ and the Church, and thus merely Christianized the Targumist's method. The translators in their 'argument' at the head of the *Song* said:[4]

In this Song, Solomon, by most sweet and comfortable allegories and parables, describeth the perfect love of Jesus Christ the true Solomon and

---

[1] Isaiah liv. 5.

[2] By Dean Inge for instance. See his *Christian Mysticism*, p. 371. At p. 43, the Dean says, 'As to the Song of Solomon its influence upon Christian mysticism has been simply deplorable.'

[3] Dr. Hermann Gollancz, *The Targum to the Song of Songs*, p. 5. The Targumist makes the Lord and Israel speakers in the Song. In ch. ii. i, 'I am the narcissus of Sharon, the rose of the valleys' (in the more familiar *A. V.* 'I am the rose of Sharon, the lily of the valleys') the Targumist (in the translation of Dr. Gollancz, p. 21) says, 'The Assembly of Israel speaketh As long as the Sovereign of the universe suffers His Divine Presence to dwel in my midst, I am like the narcissus fresh from the Garden of Eden, my action are comely as the rose in the plain of the flower-garden of Eden.' An interesting old book on the *Song* is, 'A discovery of the neere and deere Love, union and communion between Christ and the Church, and consequently between Him and every believing soul,' by the Rev. Dr. Sibs of Cambridge, of date 1639. Among modern protests against anything but literal understanding of the *Song* prominence must be given to the edition of the *Song* by Dr. Morris Jastrow, jnr. His translation, introduction and note are attractively secular.

[4] The 'argument' which has disappeared from modern editions of the *A. V.* with almost all the marginal comments and other 'most profitab

king of peace, and the faithful soul or His Church, which He hath sanctified and appointed to be His spouse, holy, chaste and without reprehension. So that here is declared the singular love of the bridegroom toward the bride, and His great and excellent benefits, wherewith He doth enrich her of His pure bounty and grace without any of her deservings. Also the earnest affection of the Church which is inflamed with the love of Christ, desiring to be more and more joined to Him in love, and not to be forsaken for any spot or blemish that is in her.

It will be noticed that 'the faithful soul' is alternated with the Church, thus making a *personal* application of the *Song* possible side by side with the corporate. The translators, as their preface[1] suggests, were undoubtedly familiar with the writings of some of the Greek Fathers, and the Latin, who apply the symbolism of the *Song* to 'the faithful soul' and Christ.[2] Nearly a century before the 1672 Bible, and nearly thirty years before the first edition of the *A.V.*, a great Spanish mystic, S. John of the Cross, had composed *The Spiritual Canticle*, 'an abridged paraphrase of the Song of Solomon, wherein under the image of passionate love are described the mystical sufferings and longings of a soul enamoured with God'.[3] It is not implied that the *A.V.* translators had read S. John of the Cross. He was following the Greek Fathers in his interpretation of the *Song*. The erotic symbolism of the *Song* (its sole defence for its place in the Canon) is not the only incentive of Holy Scripture to the use of love-imagery by Christian mystics. The prophecy of Hosea contains a picture of the Divine Husband's remonstrance with His faithless wife, His love-laden pleadings with her, and the surpassing tenderness of His re-espousing her.[4] The book of Hosea is indeed the Book of the Beloved. The symbolism of love is found in

annotations' appears in the edition of the year 1672. The present writer is happy to possess a copy of the 1672 Bible.

[1] Retained in the 1672 edition.

[2] See Keble's Tract 'On the Mysticism attributed to the Early Fathers of the Church', for a statement of general principles as to the 'mystical' and allegorical use of Holy Scripture by the Early Fathers. S. Cyprian's spiritual exposition of the *Song of Songs* is typical of that of other early Fathers. See his *Epistles*, lxxiv, § 15; lxxv, § 2; *Treatises*, iii § 4; iv, § 31.

[3] The Rev B. Zimmerman's edition, Introduction, p. xii.

[4] Hosea ii. 19, 20.

Isaiah,[1] *Jeremiah*,[2] in S. Paul,[3] and in the apocalyptic call to the love-feast at the marriage of the Lamb and the bride of the Lamb,[4] and the echoes of that call linger in the last voices of the New Testament in the longing cry of the Spirit and the Bride.[5] The assembly of Israel or the Church is a body of individuals, and what can be said of a body can be said of the individual. These Scriptural representations of the love of God for Israel, love of Christ for the Church, yielded to the devout imagination of the mystics a symbolism of intense erotic application. Spiritual espousals and spiritual nuptials have since become commonplace of Christian mysticism.

> On this happy day the soul not only ceases from its anxieties and loving complaints, but is, moreover, adorned with all grace, entering into a state of peace and delight, and of the sweetness of love . . . in which it does nothing else but recount and praise the magnificence of the Beloved, what it recognizes in Him, and enjoys in the union of the betrothal.[6]

In defence of the love-language of mysticism, Christian and non-Christian, may be urged the circumstance that even the most realistic, erotic phraseology barely expresses the truth of the soul's union with God. 'You have now heard', says S. Teresa, 'that God spiritually espouses souls. . . . Though but a homely comparison, yet I can find nothing better to express my meaning than the sacrament of matrimony, although the two things are very different'.[7]

[1] *Isaiah*, liv. 4.

[2] *Jeremiah*, ii. 2, iii. 8, 14, 20. In *Psalm*, xlv. 10–16 much erotic freedom of speech is seen.

[3] *Rom*. vii. 1–4 ; 1 *Cor*. xi. 3 ; *Eph*. v. 23–33.

[4] *Rev*. xix. 7.

[5] *Rev*. xxii. 17.

[6] S. John of the Cross, *The Spiritual Canticle*, xiv. 1.

[7] *The Interior Castle*, Mansion, v, Ch. iv, § 1. Coventry Patmore (*Angel in the House*, Canto viii, Prelude iii) says :

Female and male God made the man ;
His image is the whole, not half ;
And in our love we dimly scan
The love which is between Himself.

And he complains (Canto vi, Prelude iv), that there are those who,

Cannot see the robe of white,
In which I sing of love.

What has been said of erotic symbolism in Christian mysticism applies to the mysticism of Tāyumānavar, especially to his *Anandak Kalippu* in which the poet-saint very thinly veils, in sensuous phrasings, the burning purity of a soul's passion for its God.

The principal details in which the mysticism of the *Anandak Kalippu* has similarities to thoughts in non-Saivite mysticism may be here very briefly noticed.

1. The individual and *personal* character of some great experience is an unrevealable 'whispered secret'.[1] 'The soul of the lover shall not wax cold but shall remain in comfortable heat and the heart shall not be bruised [disturbed] by continual thought of the Beloved. Soothly in this steadfastness the excellence of love happens to a true lover, so that he shall be raised up to a fiery heaven and there shall be stirred to love more than may be spoken, and shall be more burned within himself than can be shown. . . .'[2] This hearing of ineffable secrets suited to the needs and necessities of each individual soul is when the soul is exalted to the heights, and 'heaven being opened to the eye of the mind it offers privy things to be beheld'.[3] The state of 'secret' communication between God and the soul is the beginning of the stage of spirituality in which God and the soul are one 'not by fusion of nature but by identity of will, that is, of love'.[4] What Tāyumānavar felt is paralleled in the experience of many Catholic mystics of whom S. Catherine of Genoa may be taken as typical. She said, 'O would that I could tell what my heart feels. . . . I cannot find words appropriate to so great a love.'[5] Similarly confessed S. Angela da Foligno, 'If thou seekest to know what I beheld, I can tell thee nothing . . . I cannot describe it.'[6]

2. The soul has to be made ready for the beginnings of the relationship that results in ultimate union. 'Cut thyself off

[1] Below, p. 100 and p. 213.
[2] Rolle of Hampole, *The Fire of Love*, Bk. ii, ch. iii.
[3] *The Fire of Love*, Bk. ii, ch. ii.
[4] The Rev. A. Devine, *Manual of Mystical Theology*, p. 488.
[5] F. Von Hügel, *The Mystical Element in Religion*, i. 179.
[6] *The Book of Divine Consolation*.

from all attachments and cling to me'.[1] This is the casting aside of distractions, and is, in Catholic theology, facilitated when the process of vocal prayer passes into the mental. 'This attention comes not till a soul be arrived at *perfect contemplation by means of which the spirit is so habitually united to God*, and, besides, the imagination so subdued to the spirit that it cannot rest upon anything that will distract it'.[2]

3. The soul has self-knowledge when in the relationship that results in ultimate union.

> Upon my head His feet He rested—
> Self-knowledge came: I died to me.[3]

In that state of prayer in which, according to Catholi theology, the soul is vouchsafed a vision 'not intellectual bu imaginary',[4] one of the graces granted to the soul is that c 'self-knowledge'.[5] A right and humble knowledge of one own self, what it is in God and what apart from Him, is th foundation of all spiritual growth.[6] The correct Christia attitude towards what may seem to be the attainment of sel knowledge is to test impressions by Scriptural principles. Th is well put by an English mystic, Richard of St. Victor:

> If the mind would fain ascend to the height of knowledge, let its fi and principal study be to know itself. Full knowledge of the rational spi is a great and high mountain. . . . Even if you think that you have be taken up into that high mountain apart, even if you think that you see Chri transfigured, do not be too ready to believe anything you see in Him or he from Him, unless Moses and Elias run to meet Him. I hold all truth i suspicion what the authority of the Scripture does not confirm, nor do I receiv Christ in His clarification unless Moses and Elias are talking with Him.[7]

4. The soul not only sees itself, but sees the Beauty o God in that state of contemplation which prepares it for wha results in ultimate union.

> 'See with the eye of grace,' tho' bidden,
> I strove with other eyes to see;
> Darkness was all I saw, thick darkness;
> Nor saw the seeing one, e'en me.

---

[1] Below, p. 100, and pp. 215, 216, 218.

[2] Father Baker, *Holy Wisdom*, Book i, ch. ii, § 14.

[3] Below, p. 102.

[4] *The Interior Castle*, 6, 5, 9.

[5] *Ibid.*, 6, 5, 12.

[6] *Holy Wisdom* Book ii, Part i, ch. i, § 3.

[7] *Benjamin Minor*, §§ 75, 81. See below, pp. 209, 210, 220.

> I neared the grace of God, its vastness,
> Its stretches of unending bliss,
> And lo! my darkness far was driven—
> I saw His beauty, only His.[1]

In this condition, according to Plotinus, 'he who sees does not, in the strict sense of the word, see; nor does he imagine two things. He becomes other, he ceases to be himself, he retains nothing of himself . . . yet the soul is other than the Divinity. . . . This manner of vision is very difficult to describe.'[2] The soul's endeavour and yearning to be wholly in touch with Deity, 'to embrace Divinity by our whole being' makes the soul a shining light.[3] This 'seeing Him Who is invisible'[4] is something much higher and more spiritual than abnormal visual impressions.[5] The way of God-seeing is a way of love, and the sight is not the result of any manner of sense-training or physical process. 'The mind's sight is truly taken up to behold heavenly things, yet by shadowy sight. . . . As we, standing in darkness, see nothing, so in contemplation that unseemly [invisibly] lightens the soul, no seen light we see . . . what is felt is full delectable. . . . Holiness consists in the sweetness of perfect charity and heavenly contemplation . . . . Contemplative sweetness is not of man's merit but God's gift. . . A man ought to be used in healthful meditation and devout prayer before he comes truly to the contemplation of heavenly joys. Contemplation is the joyful song of God's love taken into the mind.'[6]

5. There is a relationship between God and the soul, and it, for want of more expressive language, is usually known as union, and this union is possible while the soul is in the body. Tāyumānavar, under the term *Advaitam*,[7] refers to the possibility

[1] Below, pp. 102, 103, and notes at pp. 222, 223.

[2] *Enneads*, 6, 9, 10.

[3] *Ibid.*, 6, 9, 9. Tāyumānavar speaks of 'Seer, the seeing, and the sight' [illegible]. (*N.M.* 309, 1290, and below, p. 92).

[4] Hebrews, xi. 27.

[5] Archdeacon Wilberforce, *Inward Vision*, p. 13.

[6] Richard Rolle, *The Mending of Life*, ch. xii.

[7] Above, § 34.

of this great relationship. He speaks of the 'blending' of the soul with Deity.[1] It is the rare experience of the saints.[2]

> As I from self detached was growing,
>   My love for Him began to grow;
> And He, one day, in joyous silence,
>   Made me with Him oneness to know.
>
> 'What in thy thought seems truth or fancy'
>   He said, 'be cast away from thee.'
> So saying, forthwith worked a marvel—
>   His very self He made me be.[3]

Clement of Alexandria, referring to the Christian as the true 'gnostic,' lays stress on the necessity of being 'allied to God by divine love, so that by like we may see like.'[4] 'The knowledge of ignorance is the first lesson in walking according to the word. An ignorant man has sought, and having sought, he finds the Teacher; and finding has believed; and believing, has hoped; and henceforward having loved, is assimilated to what was loved,—endeavouring to be what he first loved'.[5]

The mystical life is a continual endeavour of the soul to conform to the image of the soul's Beloved,—of being progressively transformed from glory to glory.[6] The perfection of the prayer which is rapture in God ραπ γὴ πρὸς Κυριον in the thought of S. John Climacus in his famous and much criticized *Ladder of Paradise,* consists in the perpetual union of the soul with God.[7] It is not a fitful feeling or occasional emotion but a *life,* a sustained, continuous relationship progressing towards the fruition of final oneness. The Gospel way of putting it is 'abiding in God,'[8] and such abiding is *not* an inert quiescence but active, fruitful living. '*I am the vine, ye are the branches; he who abideth in Me, I also abiding in him, bringeth forth much*

[1] Below, pp. 29, 49, and *N. M.*175, 245, 246, 309, 314, 361, 367, 370.

[2] Below, p. 43.

[3] Below, p. 101, and notes at pp. 184, 218.

[4] *Stromata*, Book v, ch. 1.

[5] *Ibid.*, ch. 3.

[6] Galatians iv. 19; Ephesians iv. 13.

[7] Pourrat, *Christian Spirituality*, p. 292.

[8] S. John xv. 3, . . . 1 John ii. 28, iii. 24. Andrew Murray's *Abide in Christ* is the best single exposition of the Johannine theme. With it may also be read Hall's *Christ Mystical*, one of the three great books of General Gordon.

fruit.'[1] The analogy of the vine and the branches is more consistent with practical mysticism than are the analogies of salt in water,[2] flame on camphor,[3] and iron in fire,[4] which do not convey the conception of life while they lay stress on the *intensity* of the union. The life of union is that of one seeking for the source of the fountain of grace 'till he cometh to the first original source which is in the heart of God, and there he drinketh the hidden wisdom of God, which no one knoweth save he who hath received it.'[5] The life of union is a life of active, diffusive love, for 'the more anyone is in union with God, the more is he filled with love.'[6] In spiritual union there is between God and the soul much giving of Himself by God, 'with such romantic exclusiveness, that we feel He belonged to us alone, and that all of Him was ours.'[7] The expression called 'union,' it is attested by Christian and non-Christian mysticism, begins as a realization in this present life.[8] Let us have done, says Dr. Rendal Harris, with postponed heavens.[9] 'The reunion of man with God and the will of God is what constitutes heaven in this life and heaven in the next.'[10] The attainment of the knowledge which leads to union is not a matter of formulas. Each soul's experience, and experience is highest when it is in Christ Jesus, is its best proof. There is always a residuum of the ineffable in mystical experience. The things of the spirit have to be discerned spiritually. 'I abhor

[1] S. John xv. 5. See the Rev. Hugh Macmillan's *The True Vine*, ch. vi, 'Abiding in the vine.'

[2] Below, p. 35, and *N. M.* 160, 1276.

[3] Below, p. 121, and see below, *Introd.*, Part ix.

[4] *N. M.* 123, 1277. S. John of the Cross, *The Living Flame of Love*, Prologue, § 3, employs the analogy of a log of wood set on a fire and 'transformed into fire and united with it' to explain the state of the soul 'transformed and glowing intensly in the fire of love united with the divine fire, and become a living flame.'

[5] Tauler, *The Following of Christ*, Part ii, § 47.

[6] S. Bernard of Clairraux in Grimley's *Selections*, p. 97.

[7] F. W. Faber, *Creator and Creature*, Book ii, ch. iii.

[8] See above, for Tāyumānavar's testimony, p. lvi.

[9] *Union with God*, p. 20.

[10] Rendal Harris, *Union with God*, p. 23.

to see man's salvation thrown into a demonstrative syllogism, or the things of God weighed by the short measure of man; and not by the measures of the sanctuary. I wish to see a mind bowed down before the seven-branched candlestick of the spirit, deeply influenced by the air of the temple, the fumes of the frankincense, and unearthly light of the glorious pillar of the presence. I like to see it just glancing with half-averted eye to a deep, mysterious subject, scarcely daring to rest there because it feels the ground so holy. All things around him are full of God, and God visible is before him, so that, as Solomon says, his words are not only wary, but FEW'.[1]

PART IX. ANALOGIES, ILLUSTRATIONS, FIGURES

§ 50. It is characteristic of the reasoning in the *Upanishads* that analogies are employed with the force of argument. 'As water adheres not to the lotus leaf, so evil adheres not to him who knows that the self is Brahma.'[2] The illustration does not *prove* either why water does not adhere to the lotus leaf or why action does not adhere to the knower. Botn statements are *assumed* to be true, and one is *paralleled* with the other. This is the case with almost all the analogies in the *Upanishads*, but they are undoubtedly used there, as in Hindu reasoning generally, as proofs instead of suppositions. 'As a snake sheds its skin, so the knower is freed from sin',[3]—two assumptions, two facts, but one does *not* prove or explain the other. 'As birds and deer do not resort to a mountain on fire, so faults reach not the knower of Brahma'[4] —one does not *prove* the other. A few of the *Upanishad* analogies which are intended to be suggestive of proof may be mentioned here:

1. As water rained upon rough ground runs to waste among the hills, so he who sees qualities as different runs to waste after them.[5]

---

[1] Letter xxix, in the Rev. J. E. Bowden's, *The Life and Letters of the Rev. Dr. F. W. Faber*, p. 87.

[2] *Chandog*. 4. 14. 3. *Maitri*, 3. 2, *Prasna*, 5. 5.

[3] *Prasna*, 5. 5.

[4] *Maitri*, 6. 18.

[5] *Katha*, 4. 14.

22

2. As pure water poured forth into pure becomes the very same, so becomes the soul of the seer.[1]

3. As the one fire entering the world becomes correspondent in form to every form, so the Inner Soul of all things corresponds in form to every form.[2]

4. As the sun is not sullied by the faults of the eye so the Inner Soul is not sullied by the evil in the world.[3]

5. As an overlord sets his overseers over villages, so this life-breath controls the other breaths.[4]

6. As birds resort to a tree for rest, so everything resorts to the All-soul.[5]

7. As rivers flowing into the ocean disappear, their name and form destroyed, and the whole is ocean, even so this one's parts on reaching the Person disappear, name and form destroyed, and the whole is simply the Person.[6]

8. As a mirror stained with dust shines brilliantly when cleansed, so the embodied one, on seeing the nature of the *Atman*, becomes unitary.[7]

9. As a lump of iron, overcome by fire and beaten by workers, passes into a different form, so the elemental soul, overcome by the Inner Person and beaten by qualities, gets a different form.[8]

10. As there is no one to touch harlots in an unoccupied house, so he who does not touch objects of sense is an ascetic.[9]

11. As the huntsman draws in fish with his net and sacrifices them in the fire of his stomach, thus does one draw in these breaths with *Om* and sacrifice them in the fire that is free from ill.[10]

12. As ghee in a heated cauldron lights up by contact with [*lighted*] grass. . . . So does he also who is called non-breath light up by contact with the breaths.[11]

13. As a lamp exists because of wick, support and oil, so the self and the sun exist because of the combination of the Inner Self and the world-egg.[12]

14. As a lump of salt cast in water would dissolve right into the water. . . . and whenever one takes it, the water is salty, so this great, infinite, limitless Being is a mass of knowledge.[13]

15. As all the spokes are held together in the hub and felly of a wheel, so in this All-soul all things . . . all selves are.[14]

16. As a falcon . . . having flown around here in space, becomes weary, folds its wings, and is borne to its nest, so this person goes to that state where, asleep, he desires no desires, and dreams no dreams.[15]

17. As herbs arise on the earth, as the hairs of the head and body from a living person, so from the Imperishable arises everything.[16]

---

[1] *Katha*, 4. 15. [2] *Ibid.*, 5. 9. [3] *Ibid.*, 5. 11. [4] *Prasna*, 3. 4.
[5] *Ibid.*, 4. 7. [6] *Ibid.*, 6. 5. See above, p. xcix.
[7] *Svet*, 2. 14. [8] *Maitri*, 3. 3. [9] *Ibid.*, 6. 9.
[10] *Ibid.*, 6. 26. [11] *Ibid.*, 6. 26. [12] *Ibid.*, 6. 36.
[13] *Brihad*, 2. 4. 12. That everything here is what the All-soul is argued from sixteen analogies in *Brihad*, 2. 4. 7-12
[14] *Brihad*, 2. 5. 15. [15] *Ibid.*, 4. 3. 19. [16] *Mundaka*, 1. 1. 7.

18. As from a blazing fire sparks, so from the Imperishable are produced manifold beings.[1]

The reasoning in most of the *Upanishad* analogies is in the unsatisfactory form, 'A is B, therefore C is D.'' There is a seeming comparison, a suggested connection, a surreptitious conclusion.

§ 51. In Tāyumānavar all figures are not analogies, nor all analogies intended to be arguments. Most of his illustrations are comparisons. At the same time it may be observed that some of them, if cast into the *Upanishad* mould, may have the mischievous effect of seeming to have the force of argument, if not of proof. Seven of his illustrations are capable of such misapplication.

1. The soul may remain related to God as the eye is to the sun.[2] This means, as the first line of the stanza shows,[3] that if God, who is all expanse, were to be in contact with the smaller expanse of the human mind, then, the soul would be so related to God as the eye, deriving its light from the sun, is to the sun. The eye and sun analogy is obviously illustrative. As the light in the eye is related to the light of the sun, so is the soul in union with God—in this *Upanishad* form the statement may be construed to suggest that *union is proved* by what is admittedly true of the eye and the sun. The poet does not intend this.

2. 'As light of lamp by sunlight '[4] is an analogy of great significance. The poet does not contemplate the extinguishing of the light of the lamp, but the sustained existence of the lesser light in the sphere of the greater. The lamplight retains its character: the soul in union with God retains its individuality. The analogy of lamplight in sunlight does not *prove* the survival of all individuality in union with God. It illustrates a teaching.[5]

[1] *Mundaka*, 2. 1. 1. [2] *N.M.* 406, ஒளியாகுங் கண்ணு மிரவியும்போல்.

[3] வெளியான நீயென் மன வெளியூடு விரவின்.

[4] *N.M.* 1280, below p. 121. In *N.M.* 1274 the same idea is expressed by the analogy of moonlight in sunlight.

[5] See below, p. 219 for the Christian analogy of two lighted tapers; and that of the stream of water losing itself in the ocean. See above, p. c.

3. The nature[1] of the soul is to be attached to good or bad. In its condition of association with its original taint[2] the soul is like a piece of iron in fire, the iron remaining iron and not becoming fire.[3] The soul retains its individuality as the iron its iron character. The union of the soul with God, in a state of love, is as iron in fire.[4] The poet implies that in sin or in salvation the soul retains its personality, however corrupt or however cleansed. The analogy of iron in fire is employed by S. Bernard of Clairvaux.[5]

4. Resembling the iron and fire analogy is that of camphor on fire. It is used to illustrate three different thoughts: (1) When the saint approaches God-likeness in its nearest manner his physical side disappears as camphor encased in fire.[6] Such a saint's appearance shines as does camphor in a flame of fire.[7] (2) God is the heavenly lamp in whose light the mind, its carnality, of the saint melts as a ball of camphor in fire.[8] (3) In union with God the humanity of the soul is swallowed up by the Divinity of God's grace.[9] On the appearance of the *Guru* the soul is as a camphor mountain on fire, the grace of God so operating on it that it is all fire, and the sins are burnt.[10] It is with reference to spiritual union that God is likened to the light of a camphor-flame unassailed by any evil.[11]

5. 'As salt in water,' so is the soul merged in the Divinity

[1] Above, § 34. [2] Above, § 29.

[3] *N.M.* 123, அனலொழுக நின்றிடு மிரும்பனல் உடலின்றிடு. See above, § 50 analogy

[4] *N.M.* 1277, தயமதியான கருகுபசேரி தன்பாற்
றிமிலிகும்பெண்ணாற் றிருவாசகனே.

[5] S. Bernard, while not ignoring the soul's individuality, lays stress on its partaking of the Divine likeness. 'The iron becometh very like fire itself.' So when S. John of the Cross (see above, p. clxviii) speaks of a log of wood set on fire and 'transformed into fire' he does not ignore individuality.

[6] *N.M.* 153. கப்பூரதீபம்போலப் பொலிவொளிப்ப நல்லதை புலம்பேசுகின்றும்.

[7] *N.M.* 880. நித்த திருவிசையுஞ் சேர்த்தருடத்தும்
வித்த கப்பூரம்போல வயக்கும்.

[8] *N.M.* 894. உள்ளு மனக் கப்பூர வுண்டைபோலே கரைய
மின்று மாணிக்க விளக்கே.

[9] *N.M.* 160.

[10] *N.M.* 148, translated above, at p. cxxxv.

[11] *N.M.* 1278, below, p. 121.

of God's grace.[1] The converse of the saints with God blends souls with Deity as salt in water.[2] The poet longs for the day when he will be in oneness, as salt in water, with God who is the perfection of wisdom and bliss and ineffable grace most refreshing.[3]

6. The analogy of milk in water[4] conveys the same idea as that in the salt and water illustration. The milk analogy occurs in the famous *Tirumantram* lines quoted in a different context elsewhere.[5]

7. The idea of union is illustrated by the analogy of the air in the expanse of the sky.[6]

Each of the above seven illustrations is capable of being transformed into the *Upanishad* implication, 'A is B, therefore C is D.' As illustrations calcula ted to be helpful in explaining, not proving, a fact of spiritual experience, they are of value.

The *Upanishad* figure of the river losing itself in the ocean[7] is not directly employed by Tāyumānavar. We have it, however, suggested, though not with the *Upanishad* implications, in the idea of all religions being merged in Siva. As the sea receives unto it all rivers, even so Siva is the receiver of all religions.[8] Siva's Sakti is she who has swallowed up all creeds as the sea the rivers.[9]

§ 52. An alphabetical view of some of the other illustrations in the psalms of Tāyumānavar may be of interest.

Axle-pin—

Whatever may be happening to the soul, its original taint of sin remains as unmoving as the axle-pin of a temple car.[10]

Bee—

1. God as the soul's lover approaches the grace-matured soul in the same way as a bee goes to the open flower and not to the bud.[11]

---

[1] *N.M.* 160. உப்போடப்பை மருவிட்டு.

[2] *N.M.* 782, below, p. 35

[3] *N.M.* 1276. செப்பரிய நல்லருளைச் சிறக்குஞ் பூரணத்தி
லுப்பினிடை யப்பா யிணையுவதெந்நாளோ.

[4] Below, p. 121. [5] Above, p. xxxii.

[6] *N.M.* 1275. வானூடடக்கும் வளிபோல. [7] Above, p.xcix.

[8] *N.M.* 134. ஆறனைத்தும் புகுங்கடல்போற் சமயகோடியத்தனையுந்தொடரத்துப்புகும். So *N.M.* 411.

[9] *N.M.* 578. நதியுண்ட கடலெனச் சமயத்தையுண்ட. See *N.M.* 630.

[10] *N.M.* 45, translated above, p. lxxviii. [11] *N.M.* 78, below, p. 43.

2. The joy of experienced religion makes the devotee as inebriate with peace and happiness as 'a drunken bee.'[1]

Beetle—

1. God is active in man's spirit as the beetle in the lotus bud.[2]

2. It is to those who, like the beetle in a bud, find themselves attracted to the fragrance of the flower of *mownam* that God grants blessing.[3]

Child—

1. The soul in its original condition is startled into remembrance and sense-impressions as a child in the cradle when pinched on its thighs feels pain.[4]

2. Apart from God, the soul is as a motherless child.[5]

3. The soul feels God's protection as a child is aware of its mother's.[6]

4. The devotee in times of depression feels lonely as a child whose mother is far from it.[7]

5. The saint remains in peace as a child slumbering in its cradle.[8]

Cloud—

1. God is a cloud grace-laden and descending on the devout in abundance of blessing.[9]

2. God is the cloud watering the true religions.[10]

Cotton—

1. The poet fears that his critics may look upon his verses as light as cotton.[11]

2. The mind is moved about as a piece of cotton in the wind.[12]

Cow—

1. The soul, like a calf whose bleatings attract the cow, calls to God.[13]

2. As the cow will seek out her lost calf, so God cares for souls.[14]

3. As the cow is tender towards the calf, so God feels for souls.[15]

Crow—

1. As crows are put to flight by a stone thrown at them, so grace dispels Karma.[16]

2. Crows feed together with other crows. So let all men come together to feed on the abundance of grace.[17]

3. The saints flee from the very words of worldliness as a crow at sight of a stone.[18]

Deer—

God assumes human shape to win men just as a tame deer is employed to decoy other deer.[19]

---

[1] *N.M.* 154, 360. [2] *N.M.* 563. [3] *N.M.* 745.
[4] *N.M.* 92, below, p. 55. [5] *N.M.* 100, 306. [6] *N.M.* 421.
[7] *N.M.* 984. [8] *N.M.* 713.
[9] *N.M.* 84. See below, p. 115 and *N.M.* 319, 335, 405. [10] *N.M.* 585.
[11] *N.M.* 115. [12] *N.M.* 1335, and below, p. 48. [13] *N.M.* 137.
[14] *N.M.* 494. See above, § 42.
[15] *N.M.* 669.
[16] *N.M.* 94, below, p. 57 [17] *N.M.* 555.
[18] *N.M.* 1249. [19] *N.M.* 148. See above, p. cxxvii.

Eggs—

The worlds are held up in space as marvellously as a magician balances on his hand eggs piled one on top of the other.[1]

Elephant—

1. When closest to God and not to know Him to be so near is like the trainer looking inside an earthen pot for the elephant which is already in his keeping.[2]

2. The uncontrolled mind is like a wild elephant.[3]

3. By association with God man will be able to use divine wisdom as a man directs a once wild elephant.[4]

Forest—

Desire is a forest in which one is likely to lose his way.[5]

Fragrance—

1. As the pent-up fragrance in the flower diffuses itself under a full moon when its time for doing so has come, so does joy possess the spirit of the grace-matured.[6]

2. God is in the soul as fragrance in the flower.[7]

3. God is in all life and matter as fragrance in the flower.[8]

Fair—

Earthly ties are like acquaintances at a fair, meetings in the market-place.[9]

Gold—

1. As gold refined in the fire are those who daily disciplines their mind.[10]

2. Grace transmutes the soul into the gold of Deity.[11]

Hare—

Unrealities are likened to 'the horn of a hare, lotus in mid-air and a mirage.'[12]

Hunters—

The senses are to the soul as those who with bow and arrows seek game.[13]

This figure of the soul being beset by the senses as an animal by hunters is used in the *Bodham*.[14]

Iron—

1. In fire (See above, p. clxxii.)

2. The soul is drawn to God as iron is by a magnet.[15]

---

[1] *N.M.* 390, below, p. 85. [2] *N.M.* 160 [3] *N.M.* 586. [4] *N.M.* 1284.
[5] *N.M.* 284, and below, p., 137. [6] *N.M.* 62. [7] Below, p. 15.
[8] Below p. 155. [9] *N.M.* 113. [10] *N.M.* 989. [11] Below, p. 21.
[12] *N M.* 39, 189, 419, 551, 1225, 1228.
[13] *N.M.* 125, 306, 900, 1147.
[14] *Sutra*, 3.
[15] *N.M.* 55, 217, 342, 1041. See below, pp 73, 196. The figures of magnet and iron, iron and fire, fire and wood, salt and water are used in *Siddhiyar*, 3, 11, 12.

Ladder—

To lay foundations of grammar and other learning whereon to build a knowledge for obtaining heaven is like planting cotton trees in the hope of getting cotton for the making of a ladder of thread to reach the skies.[1]

Lotus—

As the lotus in sunlight so rejoices the soul in God.[2]

Maiden—

See above, p. clx and below, pp. 42, 43.

Mirror—

The soul has a capacity for attachment to good or bad as a mirror reflects colours and receives impressions.[3] In the *Tiru Arul Payan*[4] is this comparison, 'As the crystal, (mirror) reflects itself and several colours in the light of the sun, so the world is related to the Light of the Lord.' In the *Gita*[5] another Hindu thought is expressed by the figure of the mirror, 'As the mirror is covered by rust so is this (soul) covered by it (taint).' The Siddhanta view of soul, it is explained,[6] is different from the Vedanta, in their context of the mirror analogy, in that the Vedanta in this respect takes no account of God.

'*Nelly*' *Fruit*—

To the saint divine knowledge is clear and transparent and he possesses God as clearly as the hand holds in its hollow the 'nelly' fruit.[7]

This is a common Siddhanta figure expressing assurance of relationship to God.[8]

Nightingale—

As the nightingale longs for moonlight so the soul longs for God.[9]

Oil—

As oil in seed so is God's indwelling in the soul and in immanence.[10]

Peacock—

The joy of the soul at sight of God is as that of the peacock at sight of the sun.[11]

---

[1] *N.M.* 821 [2] Below, p. 119. [3] *N.M.* 149. [4] vi. 5. [5] iii. 38.

[6] Nalla, *T. A. P.*, pp. 28, 29 and *Studies*, pp. 44, 68, 328, 335. For a use of the mirror analogy in Catholic mysticism see below, p. 210. With the thought in *N.M.* 1035 (see above, p. clxvii) of the image of the Beloved in the soul may be compared the words of Rumi the Persian 'Like a mirror the soul has received Thine image in its heart' (Davis, *The Persian Mystics*, i. 52).

[7] *N.M.* 105, 106, 138, 139, 643, and below, pp. 197, 198.

[8] *Tiruvāchagam*, iii. Line 112, xxvii. Line 15. Sundaramūrti, *Tēvāram*, *Tiruvanyaykkalam*, section i, stanza 2. In *Gnanakkummie*, stanza 134 are the lines,

நெல்லியிருக்குது காட்டுக்குள்ளே கரு
நெல்லியிருக்குது வீட்டுக்குள்ளே. . . i.e. the 'nelly' fruit in the jungle is the 'nelly' fruit in the house, the figure of the other, and the house is the heart. Those who seek it afar know not it is in the house.

[9] Below, p. 120.

[10] *N.M.* 21, (below, pp. 15 and 155) and *N.M.* 1203.

[11] Below, p. 120.

Pearl—

The mystic speaks of God as a pearl, an unpierced pearl.[1]

Rain—

God in His graciousness is as the abundant rain.[2]

Sand—

It is easier to count the sand of the sea than to describe Deity.[3]

Sea—

1. God is the vast sea of souls and creeds.[4]

2. The poet speaks in numerous places of the sea of bliss,[5] of silence,[6] of grace,[7] of pain,[8] of desire,[9] of darkness,[10] of self-seeking love.[11]

Ship—

1. God's grace is the ship which carries the soul over the sea of births.[12]

2. The soul is a frail ship to be piloted by God through life's tempestuous seas.[13]

3. God is the cargo of the ship of *mownam* (silence).[14]

Sky—

1. God's grace is as the sky.[15]

2. There is sky-space within the heart.[16]

3. To endeavour to see God by devices of religion is like climbing a hill for the purpose of seeing the sky which could be seen everywhere.[17]

Tiger—

As a deer in sight of a tiger is the soul in the environment of worldliness.[18]

Tilling—

The process of attaining spiritual perfection according to the Siddhanta is described in two beautiful psalms undert he analogies of tilling the earth, and of other agricultural acts.[19]

Top—

1. The mind is as a top moving under the will of God.[20]

2. The soul in the sphere of attachments is like a top whirling after the string had been withdrawn.[21]

3. The mind when free from distractions is like a top that had ceased to whirl.[22]

Toy-house—

To be contended with the lesser things of life without knowing 'the way of stillness' is like being as children happy in their 'toy sand-houses'.[23]

---

[1] Below, pp. 71, 196. [2] Below, pp. 29, 31, 43, 44. [3] *N.M.* 339.
[4] Above, p. clxxiii. [5] Below, p. 64. *N.M.* 393, 641. [6] *N.M.* 424, etc.
[7] *N.M.* 452 and below, p. 61. [8] *N.M.* 497. [9] *N.M.* 942.
[10] *N.M.* 1194. [11] Below, p. 30. [12] Below, pp. 30, 88.
[13] Below, p. 47. [14] *N.M.* 750. [15] Below, pp. 30, 62.
[16] Below, p. 17. [17] *N.M.* 735. [18] *N.M.* 401.
[19] *N.M.* 72 (Below, p. 51), and *N.M.* 587.
[20] *N.M.* 324 (Below, p. 48).
[21] *N.M.* 1326. [22] *N.M.* 114. [23] Below, p. 26 and *N.M.* 822.

Water—

As water runs down a slope and meets a stream so is the soul's joy when it meets the joy of God.[1]

2. A stone thrown into a pool clears the film off the face of the water, so are the words of the wise to a man.[2]

Wax—

1. The soul in ecstasy is as wax in fire.[3]
2. In yearning for God the soul is as wax in fire [4]
3. The mind is capable of receiving spiritual impressions as heated wax to receive material impressions.[5]

These few are intended to be representative of the many illustrations with which the poet makes beautiful his utterances, and deepens the meaning of his thoughts, about (among other subjects) sin, deliverance, the sorrows of the soul, the mind of man, the blessedness of abiding in God, and the joy of the soul's union with God.

PART X. THE TEXT AND TRANSLATIONS

§ 53. The Tamil original of the printed text was at first in books made of palmyrah leaves strung together. The Tamil word for the leaf when so used is ஓலை (*ōlay*) and the book of such leaves is ஏடு (*ēhdhu*). From time to time the poet would write down for the benefit of his disciples or friends his experiences in verse, or sing to them some of his compositions. His cousin Arulayyā Pillai was among those who were constantly with the poet, particularly when he had finally renounced the world and betaken himself to the devout life. Arulayyā Pillai is described by a Tamil editor of the Psalms [6] as the chief of 'those disciples who followed the poet from place to place as his very shadow.' The poet's only son Kanagasabāpathi Pillai received spiritual instruction from Arulayyā Pillai. To Arulayyā Pillai's zealous interest in his Master, and to Kanagasabāpathi Pillai's filial enthusiasm in his sainted father's spiritual enterprise, must be ascribed the preservation of the poet's utterances. In a

[1] *N.M.* 440. [2] *N.M.* 849. [3] Below, pp. 44, 47.
[4] *N.M.* 88, 577, 1329. [5] *N.M.* 421.
[6] The editor of *N.M.* edition, at p. 16.

place called Annappan Pēttai, south of Tanjore, is a *mutt* where Ambalavāna Swamy, one in the line of discipleship from Tāyumāna Swamy, had gathered round him a number of devout students of religion. Among those students was Arunāsala Swamy, latterly head of the *mutt*, and he is believed to have had in his possession the original ஏடு books from which the Psalms came to be first printed.[1] It is conceivable that more than one ஏடு copy of the poems had been made, and probably by more than one disciple either of the poet or of Arulayyā Pillai, and that such copies are extant in Tanjore. The printed text, however, has become so standardized that there is in no Tamil edition any variant reading occasioning an appeal to the original manuscripts. There is one point however to which attention should be drawn. The psalms of Tāyumānavar are given in all Tamil editions as 1452 in number, while Arnold,[2] referring to an edition of 1836 as apparently the first printed, gives the number as 1453. If the 1836 edition contained 1453 hymns, then it is very early testimony to the 1453rd psalm being the one of 32 lines which, in *N.M.* and some later editions, is headed *Kochchagam* and printed, unnumbered in *N.M.* after the regular 'finis,' முற்றியது, 'here endeth.' The *N.M.* editor says of this extra psalm, 'This is found in an edition lately come into our hands.' The extra-canonical position allotted to this psalm in the *N.M.* edition would seem to show that the learned editor had doubts as to the paternity of the foundling. If the 1836 edition, however, had this as its 1453rd psalm, then the reasons for withholding recognition of its right to a place with its fellows are considerably weakened. On the other hand—assuming, a right assumption it seems to me, that Tāyumānavar addressed in the *Kochchagam* is the poet's name for God[3] and not the poet himself—internal evidence is unfavourable to the *Kochchagam* being attributed to Tāyumānavar. The

[1] Sambandha Mudaliyar's edition, p. iii.

[2] J. R. Arnold, *Galaxy of Tamil Poets*, p. 171. Dr. Grierson in *The Imperial Gazetteer of India*, ii. 436 describe Tāyumānavar as the author of 1453 pantheistic hymns.

[3] See above, p. xl.

disparity between it and the poet's admitted work, in thought and diction, is sufficient at least to suggest a doubt and to put the critical reader upon inquiry.

§ 54. It is difficult to say whether the recension of Saravana Perumāl Aiyar, or any earlier one, was available to the editor of what, according to Mr. J. R. Arnold,[1] was the first printed edition of Tāyumānavar's Psalms, the edition of 1836. There is apparently no copy of the 1836 edition in the British Museum.[2] The recension of Saravana Perumāl Aiyar is the basis of Karunānanda Swamy's edition published in Madras in 1851, and of Ādimūla Mudaliyar's edition published in 1885 at Trichinopoli. The present writer regrets he does not possess copies of the editions of 1836, 1851 or 1885. Among other principal Tamil editions of the psalms may be noted the following:

1. T. Sambandha Mudaliyar's edition, published with a short biographical note and a commentary, as a volume of the Vidhya Vinōdhini Series, in 1891 at the American Mission Press, Madras. This edition contains 1,452 hymns, and has like all other editions the memorial 232 lines composed by Tāyumānavar's disciple Arulayyā Pillai.

2. K. Kuppusami Mudaliyar's edition published in Madras in 1905.

3. The 1905 Madras edition was re-issued in 1912 revised and enlarged, by Kuppusami Mudaliyar, B.A. The edition contains a life of Tāyumānavar by the editor, full notes on the first three Psalms taken from the Ms. notes left by Kuppusami Mudaliyar, the editor of the 1905 edition, and Rama Yogi's short notes on the rest of the psalms. The 1453rd psalm is accorded a doubtful position.

4. The *N.M.* edition, the text of which is the basis of my translation, was published in Madras in 1906 edited by K. Nagalinga Mudaliyar who is responsible for the glossary and biography in the book. There are no notes. This is the only edition in which the hymns are throughout continuously numbered. The last number is 1452. The *Kochchagam* is printed after the 'finis.' This is the best edition so far as the bare text is concerned.

5. Pārthasārati Naidu's edition issued in 1910 from the Sri Patmanāvilāsa Press, Madras, has only the first 271 hymns continuously numbered. The commentary has much in common with that in T. Sambandha Mudaliyar's edition.

6. The edition published in Madras in 1909 by K. M. Swamy and Co. (referred to in the body of the present work as K. S. Mudaliyar's edition) has

---

[1] *Galaxy of Tamil Poets* (Tamil), p. 171.

[2] Barnett and Pope's *Catalogue*, column 371, makes no mention of an 1836 edition.

notes written by Kalyānasundara Mudaliyar. The notes are the fullest of any edition of the psalms and are illustrated by Sanscrit and Tamil quotations from text-writers. The learned commentator differs in places from others. This is the best edition from the point of view of exposition of the text.

§ 55. A short survey of English renderings of selections from the psalms of Tāyumānavar before the present writer's undertaking may be of interest. The survey does not claim to be exhaustive, but it is very nearly so. I am indebted to Mr. O. S. Mahendram, Barrister-at-law, Federated Malay States, for a copy of perhaps the earliest English version of any portion of the psalms. The translation is by Dr. Graul.[1] It was made in the year 1876. The hymns translated are selections from *Pārāparakkanni.*[2] The following may be taken as typical of Dr. Graul's work :—

Thou nectar never cloying, Thou stream of heavenly bliss,
O Thou the good that dwells in perfect loveliness,
O Supremest Being.[3]

My coral Thou, my pearl, my mine of purest gold,
My beam of brightness, spirit, light, my priceless wealth untold,
O Supremest Being.[4]

My eye, my thought, my tree, my heavenly stream,
Thou art my ether-ray, my joy, and wonder-dream,
O Supremest Being.[5]

The object Thou of love, of every heartfelt pleasure,
Of souls that prize alike the potsherd and the treasure,
O Supremest Being.[6]

Who'd gaze at heaven first climbs the mountain-height :
Self-contemplation's wings towards Thee aim their flight,
O Supremest Being.[7]

The pages of back volumes of *The Madras Christian College Magazine* have enshrined in them many valuable contributions on Tamil religious literature. In 1884 the Rev. G. McKenzie Cobban contributed to that magazine an article entitled

[1] *The Indian Antiquary*, Volume for 1876. [2] See below, p. 31.
[3] *N.M.* 639.
[4] *N.M.* 644.
[5] *N.M.* 645.
[6] *N.M.* 651.
[7] *N.M.* 735. The opposite of this translation is the sense of the lines. See above, p. clxxvii.

Tāyumānavar and his Poetry,[1] giving English renderings of *N.M.* 1–13. The first Psalm[2] is thus translated :

What is that which full of joy, shineth ever everywhere,
So that men henceforth may never speak of Him as ' here ' or ' there,'
In whose grace ensphered, abiding, all the worlds unnumbered roll,
He hath willed it so who giveth life to every living soul,
What alone hath passed unhindered [3] into mind and speech of man,
Theme of endless disputation 'mong the sects since time began ?
Clamoured over, grasped as treasure, ' our's,' ' our's,' ignorant they cry,
The All-powerful, All-knowing, joyous through eternity ?
What is that, unchanging ever knowing neither night nor day ?
That indeed my mind desireth,[4] that can give me joy alway.
Think on Him who great and silent, as the heaven us bendeth o'er,
Him the soul of all we gaze on—let us worship and adore.

Mr. Cobban gives this version of *N.M.* 10[5] :

Who built this house of darkness for my home,
Where only lightning gleams of truth may come,
And make my knowledge but a little sum ?

Who wrote upon my head that I should keep
With care this knowledge, and should hide it deep
As treasure in my heart ? Anon, to sleep

Who lulled me, and, as if 'twould last for aye,
Caused me to feed this body day by day,
Careless of soul-bliss which knows no decay ?

By my desire did worldly goods invest
Me ? Father, Mother, whence are they possessed
By me ? On others must the burden rest

Of blame for all ? The fruit of lives long gone ?
The fault of circumstances or my own ?
What is it ? The great reason lies unknown

Beyond my ken. O Perfect Joy that fills
All places, even the least, with silent thrills
Of bliss ! To Thee are known my varied ills.

Reading the six pages of translation and the prose appreciation of the poet one regrets that a Christian scholar like

[1] July, 1884, vol. ii, No. 1, p. 1. [2] See below, pp. 3, 4.

[3] The original மன வாக்கினில் தட்டாம லின்றதெது means ' what is that which is not within reach of mind or speech.'

[4] The Tamil கருத்துக் கிசைந்தது' suggests the idea that the transcendent may yet be comprehended.

[5] See below, p. 8.

Mr. Cobban, gifted with a fine literary sense and sympathetic insight, did not translate more than what he has contributed to the pages of a college magazine.

The Rev. G. E. Phillips in an article on *Hindu Devotional Literature in Tamil*[1] has three pages for a few remarks on Tāyumānavar. He translates the six couplets[2] which form the section *Illayō*, 'Is there not'? thus:

> Naught know I, in deep dark of error shrouded;
> But Lord, hast Thou no wisdom lamp for me?
>
> Light of my eyes, is there no flood of glory
> For me, when, never moved, I cease from deeds?
>
> My knowledge ended, hast Thou no contrivance
> That with Thee only I should rest in peace?
>
> Lord, worse than dog am I, is there no magic
> That will bestow on me Thy form of bliss?
>
> I think this flesh is I. Is there no secret
> For me to change to Thee and so abide?
>
> O Form unseen, is there for me no teaching
> That day and night I may be joined to Thee?

The year 1897 saw the beginnings of a great revival of Tamil literary enterprise in South India. The first number of a monthly journal, *The Siddhanta Deepika*,[3] was issued in that year under the editorship of that great Siddhanta Scholar Mr. J. M. Nallaswamy Pillai. Among translations of Tamil religious classics contributed to the first volume was an English rendering[4] of a selection from Tāyumānavar's psalms by Mr. R. Shanmuga Mudaliyar, a lawyer of Salem. He had the translation later issued as a book with the title, '*The Philosophical Poem of the Saint Thāyumānavar* (A great Tamil Vedanta Siddhanti), translated by R. Shanmuga Mudaliyar, Pleader, Salem'.[5] Except in the case of a few verses[6] the translation is all in prose. The

[1] *The Madras Christian College Magazine*, April, 1910, p. 505
[2] *N.M.* 1373–78.
[3] The Journal failed with its thirteenth volume.
[4] *S. D.* vol. i, No. 1, p. 2. The translation ran into the third volume.
[5] C. N. Press, Madras, 1897.
[6] *The Philos. Poem*, pp. 8–12 (of Part ii of the 5 parts of the book).

following is an example of the learned Mudaliyar's verse-rendering :—

> Though letters, consonants, if joined to '*a*'
> Can only sound and otherwise are mute,
> Yet they are not by nature, birth, the same;
> So Pasupathi th' Beneficent Lord
> Is the guide of all things and yet not all :
> With no likes nor dislikes He does His act ;
> The *Maha Chaitanyam* in form He is ;
> By Himself He stands *not* describable ;
> Lo ! Then on Him with love I meditate.[1]

It will be noticed by the reader familiar with the original that the translator had to introduce explanatory words like ***maha chaitanyam*** to make the original better understood. This is a necessary expedient to save a translation from inelegant literalness and at the same time to keep the poet's meaning unimpaired. The use of explanatory expedients may not, however, always prove happy.

The late Sir P. Arunachalam contributed to the *Siddhanta Deepika* translations of two of Tāyumānavar's Psalms. The poet's ***Akaval***[2] அகவல் 'A supplication' is one of them. From the English rendering[3] the following is taken :—

> O perfect fulness that in the shape of Teacher, beauteous with holy grace and knowledge, showerest grace,
> Thou that ever stoodst as One, O Pure Form, never-waning Substance, great Ocean of Goodness,
> O splendour that art the beginning and the end and every bliss, O Truth, wealth imperishable,
> Thou didst of Thy great and divine grace set the earth and all the spheres of this wide universe. . . . .
> And in order that helpless souls may prosper which not even for the twinkling of an eye have intelligence of their own,
> Thou didst according to their deeds of old cause bodies, from atom to mighty mountain, to be, and time from an instant to measureless æons.

To Sir P. Arunachalam's *A Revel in Bliss*,[4] his other contribution towards the understanding of Tāyumānavar by

[1] *N.M.* 25, below, p. 18. [2] *N.M.* 1451.

[3] *S. D.*, vol. i, p. 173.

[4] Later issued in book form from his *Studies and Translations from the Tamil*, Madras, 1898.

English-reading people, I have made grateful references elsewhere.[1] The death of this distinguished countryman of mine in 1924 removes from the ranks of Tamil scholars one in whom the graces of the cultures of the East and the West were happily blended. Dr. L. D. Barnett in *The Heart of India*, ch. xviii, writing on 'Two Tamil Votaries of Siva,' gives[2] a prose English rendering of Tāyumānavar's *Ānandak kalippu*, A Revel in Bliss.[3] He does not translate ten verses. I quote the translation of two verses:

'By grace behold everything!,' he said. I had beheld with my understanding in conceptions without understanding; I saw naught but darkness, saw not even myself the seer. What is this sister?

'Think not in thy heart of Me, as other than thee; be thou without a second.' When he uttered this one word, how can I tell the bliss that grew from that word?[4]

In the pages of *Prabuddha Bharata* for 1913 appeared[5] a series of translations from the psalms of Tāyumāna Swami by 'A. K.' The initials represent most probably Dr. Ananda K. Coomara Swamy who has written a great deal on Hindu and Buddhist religion and art. I very heartily agree with and appropriate to my own effort, his observation, 'Though the Psalms of Tāyumāna Swamy are, truly speaking, untranslatable, yet I hope the following translation of his verses will give a faint idea of the spirit of the original'.[6] Dr. Coomaraswamy's translation covers *N.M.* 1— 45 and ran in the *Bharata* issues of three years.[7] As a specimen of his translation I give the following:

Reason Thou art and blind delusion too!
Thou art the whirling wind, the souls as well,
That linked to mind, evolve, and yet besides
The All-embracing Light of Love Supreme!
Diverse yet constant, Thou hast still become
The manifold of sense, the organs five,
The senses five and yet the el'ments five!

---

[1] Below pp. 217, 218, 219. [2] *The Heart of India*, pp. 85, 86.

[3] *N.M.* 1421-1450, translated below, p. 100.

[4] *N.M.* 1433, 1434, translated below, pp. 102, 103.

[5] Commencing with the issue of June 1913, p. 114.

[6] *Prabuddha Bharata*, June, p. 1913, 114.

[7] *Prabuddha Bharata*, June, December, 1913, September, October, November, 1914 and July 1915.

Without and yet within, remote, yet near,
Thou dost still come and go. Thou art withal
Darkness and light and good and evil too!
Thou art the present, Thou the time to be,
Eternity art Thou! Thou art the One,
Thou art the many and all and yet beyond!
They only know on whom Thy grace descends!
O! How can any else know Thee with ease.[1]
O Bliss Supreme that fills embracing all
The globes near us and systems far away?

In 1919 the publication, in a small volume, of *Ponnai Mātharai* and *Ānandak kalippu*, translated by me into English, was projected. The English publisher, a somewhat autocratic and otherwise unamiable person, declined to send proofs, and had decided to put on the market the collection under the title, *A Tamil Mystic* with his own introduction (as if he knew anything of Tāyumānavar) and with numerous errors (of which even he knew nothing) when the intervention of the Society of Authors frustrated the publisher's non-literary designs. A few copies, I fear, of the publication thus withdrawn from circulation have found their way into New York. The publisher sent me six copies, one of which I had occasion to present, with an explanatory and apologetic letter, to the Royal Society of Literature. If I am not too severely criticizing *A Tamil Mystic*, the best part of the book that is to the credit of the troublesome publisher is the cover. The contents, duly corrected and revised, are embodied in the present work.[2]

§ 56. Translation, the greatest and most prolific translators in the world, namely, the British and Foreign Bible Society, recently declared, is not transverberation. The three—transliteration, transverberation, translation—are very distinct processes. To expect a translation to be transverberative is to look for confusion. It is claimed for the translation of the psalms of Tāyumānavar in this book that it is an endeavour to present as faithfully as possible the sense of the original, and at the same time to conserve in English somewhat of the combined beauty

[1] *N.M.* 68, translated below at p. 161.
[2] Below, pp. 69–84 and pp. 100–113.

of alliteration, lilt, cadence and assonance of the original. This has been no easy task, I own. That the results of my seeking to impress upon an English mould the image of the Tamil have not been the success I wished they should be I hasten to confess. As Mrs. Rhys Davids has said, 'The verses have been translated as faithfully as lay in my power consistently with the attempt to convey something of the poetic and religious feelings of the metrical original. To do this for a foreign idiom and an alien and ancient tradition, it was often necessary to expand each head in some rosary of terms into a phrase.'[1] Paraphrases by way of explanation had to be freely employed, at the same time there has been kept in view the mean between a terse literalness and a wordy diffusiveness. 'Let it be readily admitted,' to quote and apply the words of Mrs. Rhys Davids again, 'that the renderings are so far free as to disqualify the book from serving as a "crib" to the student'.[2] There are words and expressions in Tāyumānavar which, as Mr. Cobban had noticed before me,[3] are better rendered by euphemisms. As an example of expansive translation may be mentioned the latter part of No. 46 at p. 28, below, where many a 'bead in the rosary of terms' has been beaten out into a phrase.

How far the English in the following pages has succeeded in reproducing and retaining the alliterative charm of the original is not for me to maintain. The reader familiar with the Tamil is better able to judge than one unused to Tamil poetry. In regard to the varieties of metre employed in the translation I do not at all feel urged to offer any 'apology for my poesie.' He who thinks that all verse must march to the melody of Mary and her little lamb; or that all metric compositions ring false if they sound not in time with the curfew that tolls the knell of parting day—he who insists on verse being not verse if it is not trochaic or iambic is welcome to hug that delusion.[4]

[1] *Psalms of the Sisters*, p. xxxix.

[2] *Ibid.*, p. xli.

[3] *The Madras Christian College Magazine*, July 1884, p. 5.

[4] In the course of a very instructive discourse on the art of narrative-peotry (Royal Society of Literature *Essays by Divers Hands*, iv, [1924], p. 55).

The experiment of initial rhymes[1] need not jar upon ears used to terminal rhymes—they have only to treat the stanzas as written in blank verse. Varieties of syllabic arrangements have been attempted, but not one of them is constructed on any basis of defiance of rule.

§ 57. I wonder if any one reading this Introduction will construe my sympathetic understanding, or at least an endeavour at such understanding, of the theology of S. Tāyumānavar into a non-recognition of the differences, in fundamentals, between it and Christianity. If, further, the Christian reader finds that the translation recalls Christian thought, let him remember not only that the original so recalls, but also that a Christian translator cannot easily resist the temptation to use Christian phraseology. The translator, Hindu or Christian, would be false to his obligations were he to tone down the original into innocuous neutralities or to colourless abstractions just to suit a possible reader's prepossessions. Some of the great questions raised by the psalms are treated in this book, with all possible impartiality, from the point of view of the poet. The translator's assent to the poet's beliefs is not at all thereby, or otherwise, suggested, nor is the Christian reader's agreement with them solicited. Stress has been laid, without making towards polemics, in express statements in this Introduction and in the notes, on points of difference in a manner sufficient to safeguard positions and conclusions of the translator against any probable charge of confusion of *Siddhanta* with Christian essentials. We must not, on the other hand, seek to thin the poet's greatness into the commonplace, for he was, in a sense, in advance of his age.

Professor R. Warwick Bond observes about the Pegasus of poetry: 'Burdened with the load of critical formulae he essays his former flight, only to find it much harder. His wings grow sooner weary, his mouth continually pulled and wrenched; and ere long he is seen dragging along the crowded streets some heavy lorry of an "Essay on Criticism" with a rather abusive driver; or he trots quietly in the Park harnassed to the smartest little *balade* or *villanelle*. . . Is there no *via media* between the neglect of form and the idolatry of it. . . ? Must our force be a mere flare or a floundering, our skill an eternal strait-waistcoat, and its result only a delicate trifle for the watch-chain?'

[1] As below, at pp. 1-10.

In respect of caste, for instance, he was a liberal, knowing only one caste, the caste of the godly. Note, again, the emphasis he lays upon inwardness in religion in contrast to the many ritual exercises to which he sometimes conformed but with no spiritual profit. The Christian declines to follow the poet into the maze of Puranic mythology, even if a courteous, withal a decidedly unconvinced, hearing be accorded to the allegorizations of Indian commentators and apologists. The doctrine, again, of Karma-Transmigration cannot hold any appeal to the Christian. To the Hindu, the wages of sin is life: to us the wages of sin is death. There is a great gulf fixed between the two conceptions, unbridgeable by any compromise. Again, however fine the Christian's sympathy of treatment may be of a non-Christian faith, it is impossible, even with all the refinements of a Catholicity of appreciation, to parallel the nature of human salvation in and by Christ Jesus with the scheme these *Psalms of a Saiva Saint* represent. As in the gladness of recognizing that God had never left Himself without a witness among the nations of the world, so in the unflinching conviction that the Incarnation of our Lord, His atoning Death, and His glorious Resurrection and Ascension are essentials to salvation, I claim to stand second to none.

ABBREVIATIONS AND REFERENCES

I. Abbreviations

A.V. ...	... The Authorized Version of the English Bible.
Ad. Ephes. ...	... Epistle of S. Ignatius to the Ephesians.
Ad. Smyrn. ...	... Epistle of S. Ignatius to the Smyrneans.
Ad. Trall. ...	... Epistle of S. Ignatius to the Trallians.
Adv. Haer. ...	... Four Books of S. Irenæus Against Heresies.
Apoc. ...	... Apocalypse.
Apoc. Mos. ...	... *The Apocalypse of Moses.*
Apud. ...	... In the writings of . . .
Aran. ...	... *Āranyaka.*
Arun. ...	... Arunāchalam.
Bodham ...	... *Siva Gnāna Bōdham.*
Brihad ... Brih. Ar. ... Brih. Aran. Up.	... *Brihad Āranyaka Upanishad.*
C. H. Ind. Camb. Hist. of India	... *Cambridge History of India.*
Chand. Chandog.	... *Chandōgya Upanishad.*
Chron. ...	... The Books of Chronicles.
Col. ...	... S. Paul's Epistle to the Colossians.
Conf. ...	... The Confessions of S. Augustine.
Contra. Ad. ...	... S. Augustine's Treatise against Adimantus.
Contra. Ar. ...	... S. Athanasius against the Arians.
Cor. ...	... S. Paul's Epistles to the Corinthians.
De Civit. Dei	... S. Augustine's work on the City of God.
De Doct. Christ.	... S. Augustine's work on the Christian Doctrine.
De Ord. ...	... S. Augustine on Order.
De Trin. ...	... S. Augustine's work on the Holy Trinity.
Deut. ...	... The Book *Deuteronomy.*
Devout Life ...	... *Introduction to the Devout Life* by S. Françis de Sales.

Dir. Ascet. ...	... Scaramelli's *Directorium Asceticum.*
Eccl. ...	... *Ecclesiastes.*
E. G. ...	... For example.
E.R.E. ...	... *Encyclopædia of Religion and Ethics.*
Eng. ...	... English.
Enoch ...	... *Book of the Similitudes of Enoch.*
Eph. ... / Ephes. ...	... S. Paul's Epistle to the Ephesians.
Essentials ...	... Sabaratnam's *Essentials of Hinduism.*
Ex. ... / Exod. ...	... The Book *Exodus.*
Gen. ...	... The Book *Genesis.*
Gita ...	... *The Bhaghavad Gita.*
H.D.B. ...	... Hastings' *Dictionary of the Bible.*
H.T.R. ..	... *Harvard Theological Review.*
Heb. ..	... *Hebrews.*
Hind. Icon. ..	... Rao's *Elements of Hindu Iconography.*
Ibid. ...	... The same work.
Ind. and the W.W.	... Rawlinson's *Intercourse between India and the Western World.*
Ind. Hist. ...	... Indian Historical.
Int. Castle ...	... S. Teresa's *Interior Castle.*
Introd. ...	... Introduction.
Is. ...	... Isaiah.
J.R.A.S. ...	... *The Journal of the Royal Asiatic Society.*
J.T.S. ...	... *The Journal of Theological Studies.*
Kaush. ...	... *Kaushittaki Upanishad.*
Levit. ...	... The Book *Leviticus.*
LXX. ...	... *The Septuagint Version of the Bible.*
Madras C. C. Mag.	... *The Madras Christian College Magazine.*
Maitri. ...	... *Maitriyani Upanishad.*
Matt. ... / Mt. ...	... *Gospel according to S. Matthew.*
Myst. El. ... / Myst. Elem. / Myst. Element. / Myst. Elem. of Rel.	... Hügel's *The Mystical Element of Religion.*
Myst. of S. John's Gospel.	Watson's *The Mysticism of S. John's Gospel.*
N.M. ...	... Nagalinga Mudaliar's Edition of Ṭāyumānavar's *Psalms.*

N.S. ...	... New series.
N. Hist. ...	... Pliny's *Natural History.*
Nalla. ...	... J. M. Nallaswamy Pillai.
No. ... Nos. ...	} ... Number, Numbers.
Numb. ...	... The Book *Numbers.*
Op. cit. ...	... Work already cited.
O.R.L.I. ...	... Farquhar's *Outline of the Religious Literature of India.*
O.S. ...	... Old series.
O.T. ...	... *The Old Testament.*
Pet. ...	... Epistles of S. Peter.
Phil. ...	... S. Paul's Epistle to the Philippians.
Phil. of Plotinus Philos. of Plotinus	} ... Inge's *The Philosophy of Plotinus.*
Philos. Poem	... Shanmuga Mudaliyar's *The Philosophical Poem of S. Tāyumānavar.*
Prab. Bharata	... *The Prābuddha Bhārata.*
Ps. ...	... *The Book of Psalms.*
Q.V. ...	... See which.
R.V. ...	... The Revised Version of the Bible.
R.V. ...	... *The Rig Veda.*
Rev. ...	... *The Book of Revelation.*
Revel ...	... Arunachalam's *A Revel in Bliss.*
Rom. ...	... S. Paul's Epistle to the Romans
Sanskrit Texts	... Mūir's *Original Sanskrit Texts.*
S.D. ... S. Deepika ... Sidd. Deepika	} ... *The Siddhanta Deepika.*
S. Ind. ...	... South Indian.
Siddhiyar ...	... *The Siva Gnāna Siddhiyar.*
Song ...	... *The Song of Songs.*
Studies ...	... Nallaswamy Pillai's *Studies in the Saiva Siddhanta.*
Sub. voc. ...	... Under the word in a dictionary.
Svet. ... Svet. Upan. ...	} ... *The Svetasvatara Upanishad.*
T.A. ... T. Antiq. ...	} ... *The Tamilian Antiquary.*
T.A.P. ...	... *Tiru Arul Payan.*
Taitt. ...	... *Taittiriya.*

25

Thess.	...	... S. Paul's Epistles to the Thessalonians.
Tiru.	...	... *Tiruvāchagam.*
Tirukalit.	...	... *Tirukalittuppadiar.*
Tr.	...	... Translated by.
Up. / Upan.	...	... *Upanishad.*
V.S.	...	... Bhandarkar's *Vaisnavism and Saivism.*
V.V.	...	... *Vidhya Vinodhini.*

II. Reference

N.B.—(1) Works marked with an asterisk are in Tamil. (2) Books about which no particulars are given are quoted here from other books. (3) Where date of publication does not appear in the book itself no date is here given.

Abide in Christ. By the Rev. Andrew Murray, M.A., London (first published 1881).

* *Abidhāna Kōsam.* By A. Moothutamby Pillai, Jaffna, 1902.

Ad. Ephesios. Epistle of S. Ignatius, in Prof. Kirsopp Lake's Edition of *Apostolic Fathers*, 2 vols., London, 1914.

Also in Ante-Nicene Christian Library, Edinburgh, 1887.

Also in Bishop Lightfoot's *Apostolic Fathers*, London, 1889.

Ad. Magnes. Bishop Lightfoot's *Apostolic Fathers*, London, 1889.

Ad. Trall. Bishop Lightfoot's *Apostolic Fathers*, London, 1889.

Ad. Smyrneos. Bishop Lightfoot's *Apostolic Fathers*, London, 1889.

Adv. Haer. Treatise of S. Irenæus *Against Heresies*, in the Library of the Fathers, Oxford, 1872.

Also in Ante-Nicene Christian Library (*supra.*)

Age of Tiru Gnāna Sambandhar. By Prof. P. Sundaram Pillai, M.A., Madras, 1894.

Ancient Indian Historical Tradition. By Judge F. E. Pargiter, I.C.S., London, 1922.

* *Ancient Tamilian and Aryan.* By Pundit Vedāsalam, Madras, 1923.

Andrew Murray of South Africa. By Prof. J. Du Plessis, London, 1920.

Antiquary, The Indian, Madras, 1876.—(Monthly Magazine).

Apocalypse, The. Edited by the Rev. Prof. H. B. Swete, D.D., D.LITT., London, 1911.

Apocrypha and Pseudepigrapha, The, of the Old Testament. Translated and edited by the Rev. R. H. Charles, D.D., D.LITT., 2 vols., London, 1913.

Apology, The, by Plato. Edited by J. Adam, B.A., Cambridge, 1887.

Appar, St.: His Life and Philosophy. By J. M. Nallaswamy Pillai, B.A., B.L., Palamcottah, 1910.

* *Arya Mitran*. Monthly Magazine, Madras, 1923.—

Ascent through Christ, The. By the Rev. E. Griffith-Jones, B.A., London, 1901.

Atonement and Personality. By the Rev. Prof. R. C. Moberly, D.D., London, 1901.

Augustan Age of Tamil Literature, The. By S. Krishnaswamy Iyengar in *The Tamilian Antiquary, 1910*.

Benjamin Minor. By Richard of St. Victor, in E. G. Gardner's, *Cell of Self-Knowledge*, London, 1910.

Belief in God. By the Rt. Rev. C. Gore, M.A., D.D., D.C.L., London, 1922.

Bernard, Selections from the Writings of St. By Horatio Grimley, M.A., Cambridge, 1910.

Biblical Review, The. Quarterly Magazine, New York, 1915.—

Buddhism. By Prof. T. W. Rhys Davids, LL.D., PH.D., D.SC., London, 1890.

Buddhism, A Manual of. By the Rev. Spence Hardy, London, 1853.

Cambridge History of India, The. Cambridge, 1922.—

Canticle, A Spiritual. By S. John of the Cross, translated and edited by D. Lewis, London, 1909.

Castes and Tribes of Southern India, The. By E. Thurston, 7 vols., Madras, 1909.

Catalogue of Tamil Books in the Library of the British Museum. By the Rev. G. U. Pope, M.A., D.D., and Prof. L. D. Barnett, M.A., LITT.D., London, 1909.

Cell of Self-Knowledge. Edited by Edmund G. Gardner, London, 1910.

Ceylon, History of. By Sir J. E. Tennent, K.C.S.I., LL.D., 2 vols., London, 1850.

Changed Life, The. By Prof. H. Drummond.

Christ in Modern Theology, The Place of. By Prof. A. M. Fairbairn, D.D., London, 1905.

Christ Mystical. By the Rt. Rev. Joseph Hall, D.D., London, 1906.

Christian Mysticism. By the Very Rev. R. W. Inge, M.A., D.D., D.LITT., London, 1913.

Christian Patriot, The. Weekly Magazine, Madras, 1890.

Christian Spirituality. By the Rev. P. Pourrat, London, 1922.

Christian Theophagy, A Short History of. By Prof. H. Preserved Smith, LL.D., Chicago, 1922.

Christianity in India, History of. By the Rev. J. Hough, 4 vols., London, 1839.

Chronology of Ancient India. By N. Gopala Aiyer, Madras, 1901.

Cloud of Unknowing, The. By Richard Rolle, edited by E. Underhill, London, 1912.

Communion of the Christian with God, The. By Prof. W. Hermann. D. Theol. 3rd edition. Tr. the Rev. J. S. Stanyon and the Rev. R. W. Stewart, London, 1913.

Confessions, The, of S. Augustine. Translated by Dr. E. B. Pusey, Library of the Fathers, Oxford, 1838. [*See* below, p. 123.]

Consolations, Book of the Divine. By Blessed Angela of Foligno, translated by Mary G. Steegmann, London, 1909.

Crashaw, Richard, *Poems of*, ed. A. R. Waller, London, 1904.

Creator and Creature. By the Rev. F. W. Faber, D.D., London.

Creeds or No Creeds. By the Rev. C. Harris, D.D., London, 1922.

Cynewulf's *Christ.* Translated by Prof. I. Gollancz, M.A., London, 1892.

Cyprian's (ST.) *Epistles and Treatises*, translated in Library of the Fathers, 3 vols., Oxford, 1844, and in Ante-Nicene Christian Library, 2 vols., Edinburgh, 1868.

Dark Night of the Soul, The. By S. John of the Cross. Translated by D. Lewis, London, 1906.

De Civitate Dei. By S. Augustine, edited by Bishop Weldon, 2 vols., London, 1925.

De Vera Contemplatione. By Ruysbroeck.

De Justorum Deificatione per Jesum Christum. By the Rt. Rev. L. Laneau, Hongkong, 1887.

De Verbi Dei Incarnatione. By S. Athanasius. Edited and translated by the Rev. A. Robertson, M.A., London (Text), 1882 (Translation), 1891.

Devout Life, Introduction to the. By S. Francis de Sales. Translated by the Rev. Thomas Barns, M.A., London, 1906.

Dialogue of the Seraphic Virgin, S. Catherine of Siena. Translated by Algar Thorold, London, 1907.

Dictionary of the Bible. Edited by the Rev. James Hastings, M.A., D.D., 5 vols., Edinburgh, 1898–1904.

Directorium Asceticum. By the Rev. Father J. B. Scaramelli, 4 vols., London, 1917.

Discovery of the Neere and Deere Love, Union and Communion between Christ and the Church. By the Rev. Dr. Sibs, London, 1639.

Divine Immanence. By the Rev. J. R. Illingworth, D.D., London, 1903.

Divine Wisdom of the Dravida Saints, The. By A. Govindāchārya, Madras, 1902.

Dogmatic Theology. By the Rev. Prof. F. G. Hall, D.D., 10 vols. London, 1918–1922.

Dominus Noster. By the Rev. C. Anderson Scott, M.A., D.D. Cambridge, 1918.

Dravidian Architecture. By the Rev. Fr. G. Joveau-Dubreuil Madras, 1917.

Dravidian Element in Indian Culture, The. By G. Slater, D.Sc London, 1924.

Dravidian Grammar, A Comprehensive Grammar of the Dravidian or South Indian Family of Languages. By the Rt. Rev. R Caldwell, D.D., LL.D., London (first published 1856), (third edition), 1913.

Ecclesiastical Polity, The Laws of. By the Rev. Richard Hooker M.A. Edited by the Rev. Ronald Bayne, M.A., in Everyman's Library, London, 1907, and English Theological Library London, 1902.

Encyclopædia Britannica, The. London, 11th edition.

Encyclopædia of Religion and Ethics. Edited by the Rev. J Hastings, M.A., D.D., 12 vols., Edinburgh, 1908–1921.

Ennaratio in Psalmos. By S. Augustine, 6 vols., translated in the Library of the Fathers, Oxford, 1849.

Enneads, of Plotinus, in *The Complete Work of Plotinus*, 4 vols. translated Rev. Prof. K. S. Guthrie, M.A., M.D., PH.D., New Jersey, 1918.

Essays by Divers Hands. Edited for the Royal Society of Literature by Sir Edmund Gosse, LL.D., London, 1924.

Essentials of Hinduism, The. By Mudaliyar P. Sabaratnam, Madras, 1913.

Eternal Life. By Baron F. von Hügel, D.D., London, 1913.

Eucharist, The Doctrine of the Holy. By the Rev. U. Z. Rule, London, 1923.

Eucharist, A History of the Doctrine of the Holy. By the Rev. Darwell Stone, M.A., 2 vols., London, 1909.

Eucharistic Life, The. By members of the Oxford Brotherhood of the Epiphany, London, 1918.

Expositor, The. Monthly Magazine, London, 1874.—

Expository Times, The. Monthly Magazine, Edinburgh, 1890.—

Faber, Life and Letters of Father F. William. By the Rev. Fr. J. E. Bowden, London, 1869.

Faith and Knowledge. By Dean Inge, Edinburgh, 1905.

Families of Speech. By Dean Farrar, D.D., F.R.S., London.

Fellowship of Silence. Edited by the Rev. Cyril Hepher, London, 1918.

Fiery Soliloquy with God, The. By the Rev. Gerlac Peterson, London, 1921.

Fire of Love, The. By Richard Rolle. Edited by Frances M. M. Cowper, London, 1924.

Flowers of a Mystic Garden. By John Ruysbroeck, London, 1912.

Folk-Songs of Southern India. By R. Gover, London, 1872.

Following of Christ, The. By the Rev. Dr. John Tauler. Tr. by J. R. Morell, London.

Foregleams of God. By T. Isaac Tambyah, London, 1925.

Forerunners and Rivals of Christianity. By Prof. F. Legge, F.S.A., 2 vols., London, 1915.

Forgiveness and Suffering. By Douglas White, M.D., Cambridge, 1915.

Fourth Gospel, The, Its Purpose and Theology. By the Rev. E. F. Scott, London, 1909.

Freedom of the Soul. By Swami Vivekananda, Madras.

Fruits of Silence, The. Edited by the Rev. C. Hepher, London, 1918.

* *Galaxy of Tamil Poets, The.* By J. R. Arnold, Jaffna, 1886.

* *Gnānakkummie.* Anonymous. [In *Patinen Sittarkal Peria Gnānakkōvai*, Madras, 1907.]

God and the World. By the Rev. Prof. S. H. Mellone, M.A., D.SC., London, 1919.

Good and Evil, The Theory of. By the Very Rev. H. Rashdall, M.A., D.LITT., D.C.L., 2 vols., London, 1907.

Guyon, Poem of Madame. Translated by W. Cowper, London, 1904.

Harvard Theological Review, The. Quarterly, Harvard, 1908.—

Hastings' *Dictionary of the Bible.* [*See* Dictionary].

Heart of India, The. By Prof. L. D. Barnett, London, 1908.

Hebrews, Commentary on. By Prof. F. Delitzsch, D.D. Translated by T. L. Kingsbury, M.A., 2 vols., Edinburgh, 1872.

Hibbert Journal, The. Quarterly Magazine. London, 1902.—

Hidden Life, The. By J. N. Grou. Translated by the Rev. W. H. Hutchings, M.A., London, 1917.

Hindu Devotional Literature in Tamil. By the Rev. G. E. Phillips, B.A., in *The Madras Christian College Magazine*, April, 1910.

Hindu Thought and Christian Doctrine. By Prof. Radhakrishnan in *The Christian Patriot*, February, 1924.

Hinduism and Buddhism. By Sir Charles Elliot, 3 vols., London, 1921.

Hindu Iconography, Elements of. By T. A. Gopinatha Rao, M.A., 4 vols., Madras, 1914-1916.

Hinduism, Some Leading Ideas of. By the Rev. H. Haigh, London, 1904.

History of Indian Philosophy. By Prof. S. Dasgupta, M.A., PH.D., D.LITT., Cambridge, 1922.

History of Pre-Buddhistic Indian Philosophy. By Prof. B. Barua, M.A., D.LITT., Calcutta, 1921.

Holiness of Pascal, The. By the Rev. H. F. Stewart, B.D., Cambridge, 1915.

Holy Communions in the Church of England, The. By the Rev. D. Hague, M.A., London, 1924.

Holy Spirit, The Book of S. Basil on the. Edited by the Rev. C. F. H. Johnston, Oxford, 1892.

Holy Wisdom. By the Ven. Fr. A. Baker, London, 1876.

Hymns of the Tamil Saiva Saints. By the Revs. F. Kingsbury, B.A., and G. E. Phillips, B.A., Calcutta, 1920.

Idea of Personality in Sufism, The. By Prof. R. A. Nicholson, M.A., LITT.D., LL.D., Cambridge, 1923.

Imitation of Christ, The. By Thomas à Kempis, translated by the Rev. C. Bigg, D.D., London, 1913.

Immanence of God in Rabbinical Literature, The. By the Rev. J. Abelson, M.A., D.LITT., London, 1912.

Imperial Gazetteer of India, The. Oxford, 1919.

India Old and New. By Prof. G. W. Hopkins, New York, 1901.

India and the Western World, Intercourse between. By Prof. H. G. Rawlinson, M.A., I.E.S., Cambridge, 1916.

India through the Ages. By F. A. Steel, London.

Indian Athenaeum, The. Monthly Magazine, Calcutta, 1923.—

Indian Culture, Some Contributions of South India to. By Prof. S. Krishnaswamy Aiyengar, M.A., PH.D., Calcutta, 1923.

Indian History and Polity. By K. N. Krishnaswamy Aiyengar, Madras, 1916.

Interior Castle, The. By S. Teresa, tr. D. Lewis, London, 1917.

Interior Peace. By L. Scupoli, tr. the Rev. W. H. Hutchings, London, 1917.

Inward Vision. By Archdeacon Witberforce, London, 1914.

* *Irupa Irupaktu.* By S. Arul Nandi Sivāchāriyar, edited by K. S. Mudaliyar, Madras, 1892.

Islam, Mystics of. (See *Mystics of Islam.*)

Islamic Mysticism. (See *Mysticism, Islamic.*)

Journal of the Royal Asiatic Society, The. Monthly Magazine, London.

Jewish Mysticism. By the Rev. J. Abelson, M.A., D.LITT., London, 1913.

John, Epistles of Saint. Ed. by the Rt. Rev. B. F. Westcott, M.A., D.D., D.C.L., London, 1883.

* *Kāchitiru Akaval.* By Pattanattu Pillayar, edited by A. Singaravelu Mudaliar, Madras, 1911.

* *Kailāyam.* By Pattanattu Pillayar, edited by A. Singaravelu Mudaliyar, Madras, 1911.

* *Kaivalya Navaneetam.* Edited by Srimat Ponnambala Swami, Madras, 1913.

* *Kamba Ramayanam.*

* *Kantar Alangaram.* By Arunagiri Nāthar, edited by M. Tiruvilangam, Jaffna, 1920.

* *Kantar Anubuti.* By Arunagiri Nātar, edited by Shunmugam Pillai and Rāmānanda Yōgi, Madras, 1909.

* *Kānchi Purānam.*

Kashmir Saivism. By J. C. Chatterji, London, 1914.

Koran. (*See Qur'an.*)

* *Kural.* By Tiruvalluva Nāyanār, edited and translated by the Rev. Dr. G. U. Pope, London, 1886.

Also edited by Arumuga Nāvalar, Madras (fifth edition).

La Religione di Zarathustra. By Prof. R. Pettazzoni, Bologna, 1920.

Ladder of Paradise. By S. John Climacus.

Lalita Vistara. Tr. R. Mitra, LL.D., Calcutta, 1886.

Last Supper, The. By Prof. R. H. Kennett, D.D., Cambridge, 1921.

Liberal and Mystical Writings of William Law, The. Edited by W. Scott Palmer, London, 1908.

Also in *The Works of the Rev. William Law*, 9 vols., London, 1762.

Literary History of India, A. By R. W. Frazer, LL.B., I.C.S., London.

Lives of the Fathers, The. By the Very Rev. F. W. Farrar, D.D., F.R.S., 2 vols., London, 1907.

Lives of the Saints. By Butler.

Living Flame of Love, The, by S. John of the Cross, translated by D. Lewis, London, 1919.

Love of God, On the, by S. Francis de Sales, translated by the Rev. W. J. Knox Little, M.A., London, 1902.

Luma. Translated by Dr. R. A. Nicholson in *J. R. A. S.*, 1913.

Madras Christian College Magazine, The. Monthly Magazine, Madras, 1883—

Mahavansa, The. Translated by George Turnour, London, 1837.

Manimēkalai. Translated by Dr. G. U. Pope, Madras, 1911.

Manual of Mystical Theology, A. By the Rev. Fr. A. Devine, London, 1903.

* *Mātcya Puranam.*

* *Mathurai*, by Pattanattu Pillayar, edited by A. Singāravelu Mudaliyar, Madras, 1911.

Maurice, Life of F. Denison, by his son, 2 vols., London, 1884.

Maya and Freedom. By Swami Vivekananda, Madras.

Mending of Life, The. By Richard Rolle, edited by F. M. M. Cowper, London, 1920.

Mental Prayer and Perfection, The Practice of, by the Rev. Fr. Alphonsus, 6 vols., translated by the Rev. Fr. J. O'Connell, Bruges, 1910.

Mile Stones in the History of Tamil Literature. By Prof. Sundaram Pillai, M.A., Madras, 1895. (Same as *Age of Tiru Gnana Sambandhar*, q. v.).

Mind of the Master, The. By the Rev. J. Watson, D.D., London, 1896.

Mirror of Simple Souls.

* *Mummanik Kōvai*, by Pattanattu Pillayar, edited by A. Singāravelu Mudaliar, Madras, 1911.

Mystery of Godliness, The. By Sir P. Ramanathan, Colombo, 1895.

Mystic Bride, The. By Mrs. A. Richardson, London.

Mystic Immanence. By Ven. Basil Wilberforce, D.D., London,

Mystic Way, The. By E. Underhill, London, 1913.

Mystical Element of Religion, The. By Baron F. Von Hügel, 2 vols., London, 1909 (new edition, 1923).

Mystical Poets of the English Church, The. By P. H. Osmond. London, 1919.

Mystical Quest of Christ, The. By R. F. H. Horton, M.A., D.D., London, 1923.

Mystical Religion, Studies in. By Rufus M. Jones, M.A., D.LITT., London, 1909.

Mysticism. By E. Underhill, London, 1916.

Mysticism and The Creed. By the Rev. W. F. Cobb, D.D., London, 1914.

Mysticism Attributed to Early Fathers of the Church, On the. By the Rev. John Keble, M.A., Oxford, 1868.

Mysticism, Christian. (See *Christian Mysticism*).

Mysticism in Christianity. By the Rev. W. K. Fleming, M.A., London, 1913.

Mysticism, Studies in Islamic. By R. A. Nicholson, M.A., D.LITT., Cambridge, 1921.

Mysticism, Jewish. By J. Abelson, D.LITT., London, 1913.

Mysticism, Meaning and Value of. By E. Hermann, London, 1916.

Mysticism of S. John's Gospel. By the Rev. H. A. Watson, D.D., London, 1916.

Mysticism, The Philosophy of. By E. I. Watkin, London, 1920.

Mystics of Islam, The. By R. A. Nicholson, M.A., LITT.D., LL.D., London, 1914.

* *Naladiar.* Edited and translated by the Rev. Dr. G. U. Pope, London, 1893.

Natural History. By Pliny.

* *Nenju Vidhu Tūtu*, by Umāpati Sivāchāriyar, edited by K. S. Mudaliyar, Madras, 1892.

* *Nenjari Vilakkam*, in *Patinen Sittarkal Peria Gnānakkōvai*, p. 401.

* *Nigandu.* Edited by Ārumuga Nāvalar, Jaffna, 1904.

* *Oliviḷodukkam.* Edited by S. Anavaratha Nāyagam Pillai, M.A., L.T., Madras, 1906.

Oraons of Chota Nagpur, The. By S. C. Roy, M.A., Ranchi, 1915.

Outline of the Religious Literature of India. By the Rev. Prof. J. N. Farquhar, M.A., D.LITT., London, 1920.

Oxford History of India, The. By Vincent A. Smith, LL.D., Oxford, 1919.

Pagan Christs. By J. M. Robertson, London, 1911.

* *Pāmbātti Sittar Pādal* in *Patinenn Sittarkal Peria Gnānakkōvai*, q. v.

Pantheism, General Sketch of the History of. By C. E. Plumptre, 2 vols., London, 1878.

* *Patinenn Sittarkal Peria Gnānakkōvai*, 2 parts, edited by V. Saravanamuthu Pillai, Madras, 1907.

Patmore, Coventry K. Deighton, Memoirs and Correspondence of. By Basil Champneys, 2 vols., London, 1900.

* *Pattanattu Pillayar Pādal.* Edited by A. Singāravelu Mudaliyar, Madras, 1911.

* *Peria Purānam.* Edited by Arumuga Navalar, Madras, fourth edition, in the Hindu year Sāthārana.

Periplus Maris Erythrae. Translated by J. W. McCrindle, London, 1879.

Persian Mystics, The. By F. H. Davis, 2 vols., London, 1912.

Personal Idealism and Mysticism. By Dean Inge, London, 1907.

Philo and Holy Scripture. By the Rt. Rev. H. E. Ryle, D.D., London, 1895.

* *Philosophical Poem of S. Tāyumānavar, The.* Edited and translated by R. Shunmuga Mudaliyar, Salem, 1897.

Philosophic Saivism. By the Rev. Fr. S. Gnāna Pragāsar, Jaffna, 1917.

Philosophy of the Bhaghavad Gita. By C. G. Kaji, 2 vols., London, 1909.

Philosophy of Mysticism, The. (See *Mysticism*)

Pilgrim, The. Quarterly, London, 1920—

Plotinus, The Philosophy of. By Dean Inge, 2 vols., London, 1918.

Plotinus, The Problem of Evil in. By B. A. G. Fuller, Cambridge, 1912.

Plotinus, Select Works of. Tr. T. Taylor, London, 1912.

* *Pottippahtodai*, by Umāpati Sivāchāriyar, edited by K. S. Mudaliar, Madras, 1892.

Prabuddha Bharata. Monthly Magazine, Almora, 1895—

Practical Vedānta. By Swami Vivekananda, Madras.

Practice of the Presence of God, The, being Conversation and Letters of Nicholas Herman of Lorraine ('Brother Lawrence'), translated and edited by Mrs. Pearsall Smith, London, 1897.

Prayer Book, The. i.e. *The Book of Common Prayer* of the Church of England.

Princeton Theological Review, The. Quarterly Magazine, Princeton, 1902—

Proverbs, The Book of, Commentary on. By the Rev. R. F. Horton, M.A., D.D., London.

Psalms of the Sisters, The. Translated and edited by Mrs. Rhys-Davids, London, 1909.

Psalms of Solomom in *Apocrypha and Pseudepigrapha* (q.v.)

Quest, The. Quarterly Magazine, London, 1909—

Qur'ān, The. Sale's translation.

Rabbinic Theology, Some Aspects of. By S. Schechter, M.A., LITT.D., London, 1909.

Rāma Krishna, Sayings of Sri. Edited by Swamy Sharvānanda, Madras, 1920.

Reason and Revelation. By the Rev. J. R. Illingworth, M.A., D.D., London, 1908.

Redemption, Hindu and Christian. By the Rev. Prof. Sydney Cave, D.D., London, 1919.

Religions of India, The. By Prof. E. W. Hopkins, PH.D., LL.D., Boston, 1895.

Religions, Transactions of the Third International Congress for the History of, 2 vols., edited by P. S. Allen, M.A., Oxford, 1908.

Revel in Bliss, A. By Sir P. Arunachalam, Madras, 1895.

Revelation, The, of S. John the Divine, translated and edited by the Ven. R. H. Charles, D.D., D.LITT., 2 vols., Edinburgh, 1920.

Revelations of Divine Love. Recorded by Mother Julian of Norwich, edited by Grace Warrack, London, 1901.

Rig Veda, The. Translated by T. H. Griffith, M.A., C.I.E., 2 vols., Benares, 1896.

Rosetti, Poetical Works of Christina. Edited by W. M. Rosetti, London, 1906.

Rubaiyat of Omar Khayyam, The. Collins' Edition, London.

Ruysbroeck. By E. Underhill, London.

Sadhu, The. By the Rev. Prof. H. B. Streeter, D.D., and J. Appasamy, M.A., B.D., PHIL.D., London, 1921.

Saiva Conference Addresses. Madras, 1911, Palamcottah, 1914.

Saiva Siddhānta Gnāna Bōdham. By Swami Vedāsalam, Madras, 1915.

Saiva Siddhānta, Studies in the, by J. M. Nallaswamy Pillai, B.A., B.L., Madras, 1911.

Sangatpa Nirakaranam, by Umāpati Sivāchāriyar, edited by K. S. Mudaliyar, Madras, 1892.

Scale of Perfection, by the Rev. Walter Hilton, M.A., edited by the Rev. Fr. Dalgairns, London, 1908. Also edited by E. Underhill, London, 1923.

Secret of the Presence, The. By the Rt. Rev. H. C. G. Moule, M.A., D.D., London, 1901.

* *Sen Tamil.* Monthly Magazine, Madras, 1901—

* *Sen Tamil Chelvie.* Monthly Magazine, Madras, 1923—

Siddhanta Deepika, The. Monthly Magazine, Madras, 1897–1913.

* *Siddhānta Gnāna Ratnāvali.* Madras, 1909.

* *Siddhantam.* Monthly Magazine, Madras, 1912—

* *Silappatikāram*, edited by V. Sāminatha Aiyer, B.A., Madras, 1892.

Sin, The Concept of. By Prof. F. R. Tennant, D.D., D.SC., Cambridge, 1912.

Sin, The Origin and Propagation of. By Prof. F. R. Tennant, D.D., D.SC., Cambridge, 1902.

* *Siva Gnāna Bōdham.* By Meykand Devar, edited by P. Muthiah Pillai, Madras, 1918.

Siva Gnāna Bōdham. Translated by the Rev. H. R. Hoisington, Madras, 1854.

Siva Gnāna Bōdham. Translated by J. M. Nallaswamy Pillai, B.A., B.L., Madras, 1895.

Siva Gnāna Siddhiyar. Translated by J. M. Nallaswamy Pillai, Madras, 1913.

* *Siva Gnāna Siddhiyar.* Edited by Siva Gnāna Swamy and Subramanya Dēsiga Swamy, Tinnevelly, 1923.

* *Siva Pragāsam.* Edited by M. Tiruvilangam, Jaffna, 1919.

* *Sivatarumōtram.* Edited by S. Subramaniya Pillai, Madras, 1888.

* *Skanda Purānam.* Edited by Srimat Arumuga Nāvalar, Madras, Sittärti year.

Song of Songs, The. Translated by M. Jastrow (jnr.), PH.D., LL.D., Philadelphia, 1921.

Some Dogmas of Religion. By Prof. J. E. McTaggart, LITT.D., LL.D., London, 1906.

South Indian Dynasties, i.e., *A Sketch of the Dynasties of Southern India*, by Robert Sewell, Madras, 1883.

South Indian History, The Beginnings of. By Prof. S. Krishnasamy Aiyengar, Madras, 1918.

South Indian Paleography, Elements of, by A. C. Burnell, PH.D., London, 1878.

Spinoza and Time. By Prof. S. Alexander, M.A., LL.D., F.B.A., London, 1921.

Spiritual Combat, by L. Scupoli, translated by the Rev. W. Hutchings, M.A., London, 1917.

Spiritual Journal of 'Lucie Christine', The. Edited by the Rev. Fr. A. Poulain, S.J., London, 1920.

Spiritual Marriage. By J. Ruysbroeck, translated into French by Maurice Maeterlinck, Brussels, 1900.

Stromata of S. Clement of Alexandria, in Ante-Nicene Christian Library, Edinburgh, 1868.

Summa Theologica, The, of S. Thomas Aquinas, translated by the Fathers of the Dominican Province, London, 1913.

* *Sundara Murti's Devara Patigam.* Edited by Rama Yogi, Madras, 1913.

* *Sundara Murti's Devarams.* Edited by K. Nagalinga Mudaliar, Madras, 1908.

Sundara Murti: His Life and Times. By S. M. R. Chandra Chettiar, B.A., B.L., Madras, 1923.

Tamil Books in the Library of the British Museum. (*See* Catalogue).

* *Tamil Dictionary* (*Sol Akarathi*). By W. Katiravelu Pillai, 3 vols., edited by Hon'ble Mr. K. Balasingam, Madras, 1910.

* *Tamil-English Dictionary.* By the Rev. W. Winslow, PH.D., Madras, 1862.

* *Tamil-English Dictionary.* By the Rev. J. P. Rottler, D.PH., Madras, 1838, 1841.

Tamil Literature. By Prof. M. S. Purnalingam Pillai, B.A., Madras, 1904.

* *Tamil Literature.* By Pandit G. S. Duraisamy Pillai, Calcutta, 1923.

Tamil Literature, Essay on, by M. Shesigiri Sastri, Madras, 1897.

Tamil Plutarch, The. By Simon Casie Chitty, C.C.S., Jaffna, 1859.

Tamil Prose Literature. By V. S. Chengalvaraya Pillai, B.A., Madras, 1904.

Tamil Studies. By M. Srinivasa Aiyengar, M.A., Madras, 1914.

Tamil, Studies and Translations from the. By Sir P. Arunachalam, M.A., Madras, 1898.

Tamilian Antiquary, The. Trichinopoly, 1909-1911.

Tamils Eighteen Hundred Years Ago, The. By V. Kanagasabhai Pillai, Madras, 1904.

Targums on the Pentateuch, The. Translated by the Rev. J. W. Etheridge, M.A., 2 vols., London, 1862.

Targum to the Song of Songs, The. Translated by Prof. H. Gollancz, D.LITT., London, 1909.

* *Tāyumānavar's Psalms.* Edited by Kalyana Sundara Mudaliyar, Madras, 1899.

* *Tāyumānavar's Psalms.* Edited by K. Nagalinga Mudaliyar, Madras, 1906.

* *Tāyumānavar's Psalms.* (Other editions, see above, *Introduction*, p. clxxx.)

* *Tāyumānavar's Psalms.* Edited and translated by R. Shunmuga Mudaliar, B.A., B.L., Salem, 1897.

Tāyumānavar: His Life and Teaching and Mission. By R. S. Subrahmanyan, Madras, 1912.

Tāyumānavar and His Poetry. By the Rev. G. McKenzie Cobban, M.A., in *Madras Christian College Magazine*, July, 1884.

Ten Tamil Saints. By M. S. Puranalingam Pillai, B.A., Madras.

Tēvāram of S. Sundaramurti. (*See* Sundaramurti).

Theism in Mediæval India. By the Rev. J. Estlin Carpenter, M.A., D.D., D.LITT., London, 1921.

Theologia Germanica. Translated by Suṣanna Winkworth, London, 1913.

Thomas, A Tamil Account of Saint. By the Rev. Fr. Hosten, S.J., in *The Indian Athenaeum*, Calcutta, 1923—

Thompson, Life of Francis. By E. Meynell.

Thompson, Complete Poetical Works of. (Modern Library Edition), New York, 1913.

Three-Fold Life of Man, The. By Jacob Boehone, translated by the Rev. E. W. Allen, London, 1909.

* *Tiru Arul Payan.* Edited by K. S. Mudaliyar, Madras, 1892.

* *Tiru Arul Payan.* Translated and edited by J. M. Nallaswamy Pillai, B.A., B.L., Trichinopoly, 1896.

* *Tirukkalittuppadiyar.* Edited by Ekāmbara Siva Yogi and Āḷāla Sundaram Pillai, Madras, 1922.

* *Tirukkalittuppadiyar.* Edited by K. S. Mudaliyar, Madras, 1892.

* *Tirukkalittuppadiyar.* Edited by K. S. Nagalinga Mudaliyar, Madras, 1920.

* *Tirukkaruvai.* Edited by N. S. Thandapāni Pillai, Tinnevelly.

* *Tirukkōvayar.* Edited by Senthi Velu Mudaliyar, Madras, Turmuki Year.

* *Tirumantram,* by Tirumūla Nāyanār, edited by V. Visvanāta Pillai, Madras, 1912.

* *Tirumantram.* Edited and translated by S. Ramasamy Aiyar, B.A., B.L., in *Siddhanta Deepika*, Madras, 1897.

* *Tiru Untiār.* Edited by Ekambara Siva Yogi and K. Ālāla Sundaram Pillai, Madras, 1922.

* *Tiru Untiār.* Edited by K. S. Mudaliyar, Madras, 1892.

* *Tiru Vāchagam.* Edited and translated by the Rev. G. U. Pope, M.A., D.D., Oxford, 1900.

* *Tiruvatikay Veerattānam.* Section of Sundaramurti's *Tevaram* (q.v.)

* *Tolkāppiam.* Saiva Siddhanta Publishing Society's Edition, Tinnevelly, 1923.

* *Tolkāppiam.* Edited by Arumuga Nāvalar, Madras,

Tract in 1 Ep. S. Joann, by S. Augustine, translated in the Library of the Fathers, Oxford, 1849.

Travels with a Donkey. By R. L. Stevenson, London, 1906.

True Vine, The. By the Rev. Hugh McMillan, D.D., LL.D., London, 1890.

Union with God. By Prof. J. Rendel Harris, D.D., D.LITT., London, 1896.

* *Unmai Vilakkam.* Edited by K. S. Mudaliyar, Madras, 1892.

Unveiling of the Fall. By the Rev. W. Formby, M.A., London, 1923.

Upanishads, The Thirteen Principal. Translated by Prof. R. E. Hume, M.A., PH.D., London, 1921.

Upanishads. Translated G. R. A. Mead, B.A., 2 vols., London.

Upanishads. (Natesan's), Edited by V. C. Seshachari, B.A., B.L., Madras, 1899.

Upanishads. Translated by Prof. F. MaxMuller, PH.D., D.C.L., S. B. E. Series, 2 vols., Oxford, 1879, 1884.

Vaisnavism and Saivism. By Sir R.G. Bandharkar, Strassburg, 1913.

Vedic India. By Madame Z. A. Ragozin, London, 1915.

Victoria Institute, Journal of the Transaction of the, London, 1865—

* *Vina Venba*, by Umāpati Sivāchāriyar, edited by K. S. Mudaliyar, Madras, 1892.

Vishnu Purānam. Translated by Prof. H. Wilson.

Vishnu Purānam. Translated by S. Subba Ram Aiyar, Madras, 1904.

Yajur Veda. Translated and edited by Prof. A. B. Keith, D.C.L., D.LITT., 2 vols., Cambridge (U.S.A.), 1914.

* *Yāpparungalam.* By Amrita Sākaianār, edited by Rao Bahadur S. Bavānandam Pillai, Bombay, 1917.

Young Men of India, The. Monthly Magazine, Calcutta, 1889—

Zohar, The.

Psalms of a Saiva Saint

SELECTIONS

From the Psalms of S. Tāyumānavar

Note :—1. The Tamil text followed is that in the edition of Nagalinga Mudaliyar, Madras, 1906. In it, referred to in this book as N.M., the stanzas are continuously numbered. The N.M. numbering is here given in brackets on the right hand side of the page, and in the Notes the reference is to N.M. Edition.

2. The left side continuous numbering is that of the English rendering.

3. The hymns are grouped in sections in Roman numbering, and the grouping, except in the case of Section XXI, is as in the Tamil. The section-headings are in most cases as in the original. Sub-divisions and sub-headings are not in the Tamil. The N.M. figure will show where the section order of the same is not followed.

4. The English rendering is in many places a paraphrase translation. The result has been that in some sections, e.g., IV, V, the number of lines of a hymn in English does not correspond to the number of lines of its original.

5. Initial rhymes and the line arrangement of the Tamil are attempted in parts of Sections I, II, III, IV, and in XIV, XX.

6. The verses in Sections XIV and XX are chantable to the tune of the Tamil.

7. Short introductory notes are given at the head of each section. Explanatory notes on the hymns are at the end of the book.

Of flowers many, flowers rare,
Are garlands woven, garlands fair,
But these, Thy holy ones declare,
Delight not Thee.

Delight Thee more the garlands strung
Of syllables of praises sung
By those who sing with heart and tongue
Of piety.

Self-knowers they who so can sing.
Unlearned I weave many a string
Of pearls of tears, and Lord I bring,
Love melting me.

Word-garlands woven for Thy praise,
Call, me, Need-Knower, by Thy grace,
That, praising Thee, I, all my days,
May with Thee be.

TAYUMANAVAR.

I.—PRAISE THE ALL-PERVADING GOD

In all editions the section entitled *Para Siva Vanakkam*, பரசிவவணக்கம், consisting of three psalms begins the entire collection. The title includes the meaning, 'Praise the All-Pervading God,' praise not excluding worship. Two of the Psalms are translated here. They retain the initial rhyme and line arrangement of the original, and a different pres[illegible] of the first of the two concludes this section.

1. THE ALL-FILLING GOD (1)

Place has no power His presence can imprison,
Boundless Bliss, all-filling Splendour,
That, in its infinite fulness of loving grace,
Foldeth the worlds that are, all things ;
Grace that in graciousness willeth all life to lie
In Him the Life of life's essence ;
Measureless by the mind, by speech unsearchable ;
Claim and the contest of all creeds ;
Ways which bewilder the warring religions He
Taketh, none guessing His greatness.
He is the only Almighty, Eternal One,
Being beatific, Bliss He
Praise Him on whom never night or forgetting falls,
Dawneth no day of remembering ;
Who is yet knowable, imaged in all we see,
In the still sweep of His Silence.

---

2. SEEK HIM (2)

By many names to be in many lands begot ;
Kindred to many men counted ;
In many bodiments to be born, and to be
Cause and the consequence of deeds,
My many doings from my many thinkings sprung,
Fame to earn, name to make often ;
Hells many to be feared ; and the good gods many ;
Many the heavens for our hoping ;

Lie in bewilderment creeds many : weariness !
Therefore thro' wisdom of His grace
Seek Him who on His saints raineth soul-gladdening bliss
Cloud as from clouds heavy-laden,
High who transcendent in Turiya liveth, God,
Of the great Silence the Treasure,
Many-named in the books, Being ineffable,
Endless Bliss, wisdom : Him worship !

---

3. SAME AS No. 1 (1)

(1)

Place has no power to prison His presence ;
No one can say, ' He is here ', ' He is there.'
Not in this place, not in that, is the Godhead,
Unbounded by places, bides everywhere.

(2)

He is the infinite, all-filling splendour,
He is the bountiful fulness of grace
That, in its allness, the worlds that are foldeth,
And in it encompassed creation stays.

(3)

His is the grace that in graciousness willeth
In Him the Life of life all life to be ;
He is the life of all lives, and life's essence,
But for Him nothing lives, life's fulness He.

(4)

Mind of no mortal God's greatness can measure ;
He is the claim and the contest of all creeds ;
Ways which bewilder the warring religions
Are His, unsearchable are all His deeds.

(5)

Who can His greatness guess ? Who claims to know Him ?
Mind cannot measure, nor speech reach the heights
Where the Eternal One, Almighty Lord, is,
Being beatific, Bliss, Light of lights.

(6)

Praise Him to whom is no night of forgetting,
Nor of remembering dawneth the day ;
Praise Him to know whom who has to all made known,
In the still sweep of His silence, the way.

II.—ALL-EMBRACING BLISS

The following are Nos. 4–13 in N.M. edition and from the second section in that edition and in the other editions of the Tamil. The English 6 to 13 follow the initial rhyme and line arrangement of the Tamil as far as possible. Different metrical presentings of the verses are also given. The title of this section is in Tamil *Paripūrana Ānandam*, பரிபூரணானந்தம், meaning 'Perfect Joy', and is from the last address in each Psalm. The English heading combines the thoughts of two addresses given in the closing portion of each Psalm.

4. SHOW ME THE WAY (4)

Be it to stay my breath or to abate my thoughts,
Practiceless, inadept am I ;
Wordily worship I, weaving of syllables
Garlands of praise of lip-service.
Seen with the saintly, I feign to be following
Ways of unworldliness with them.
Then I, forgetting this, fall into slumber ;
Sleep, till by fear of death startled.
Me, the unknowing one, oh ! what great distance gulfs
Far from the bliss of the Silence.
Evil and low am I. All-knower, point me
Path unto ecstatic stillness,
Tree of Grace, Thou, whose fruit ripens for those whose feet
Thread not the tanglements of sin,
Oh, Thou Whose presence pervadeth without a void
All things, Thou, Bliss, All-embracing.

---

5. THE TRANSCENDENT TEACHER (5)

Beings all life-possessed, crawling or walking ones,
Flying, or feetless or fixed,
All bodied existence, forms and phenomena,
Pass into non-being from birth ;
Even the elements shrink into inaction.
Only Thou, Spirit, transcendent,
Always abidest, the Vastness, all-absolute,
Wisdom of Vedas, Vedanta.

Free, unsupported ; Peace ; Boast of the grace-gifted ;
Grace eternal, Light glorious,
God, in my fulness of time to me manifest,
Teacher that soughtest me loving,
Teaching the Bliss of the Silence beatific,
Birthless and deathless for ever,
O Thou, whose presence pervadeth without a void
All things, Thou, Bliss all-embracing.

---

6. THINE IS ALL DOING (6)

Deeply considering all things, I gather, Lord,
No one, none even of devas,
Anything doeth of himself ; the moon-perfect,
Famed to be men of the Silence,
Keep not their balance, but break into anger oft ;
Groan, unadvisedly speaking.
Those who are skilled in the language of reasoning
Let their words waywardly, sometimes,
Leap into alien by-ways, beyond the line,
Leaving the argument unlinked ;
Holy men, vowing to keep Siva's night-vigil,
Heavy-eyed often sit ; sitting,
Sleep, in the semblance of wakefulness slumbering.
Thine are all doings, Thine, ever,
O Thou, Whose presence pervadeth without a void
All things, Thou, Bliss all-embracing.

---

7. THE SEEN ARE TEMPORAL (7)

Systems of worlds anigh, worlds afar, are the forms
Framed of the manifold maya ;
Maya as unreal is perceived, and, beyond
Knowing the sense that so knoweth,
Is the calm consciousness that the sole real is
Grace of God girdling with glory
Uttermost ends of creation, and *there* is love
Longing to find in all fulness

Bliss in the standing self-sundered. So are the seen
Temporal. Fain would I prove this,
Closing my eyes in the quietness, sense-stilling,
But for the warrings of Karma—
This will not lead me to deem the soul's primal load
Mighty to be the soul's master,
O Thou Whose presence pervadeth without a void
All things, Thou, Bliss all-embracing.

---

8. GUARD AGAINST RE-BIRTHS (8)

Thou art the Doer of all I do. I am I
Only when not in Thee biding,
Non-being. This is the harmony balancing
Vedanta Siddhanta wisdom.
How I had striven and struggled to reach that goal,
Gracious One, surely Thou knowest.
Fain would I bide there, but selfhood in subtleness
Cometh in, coming me conquers.
Doubting I dread should there follow me as of old
First taint, and falseness, and fruitage
Of doings leading to bodiments. Gird thou me,
That I be guarded from re-births,
Now with the weapon of wisdom, sword of Thy word,
Boldly my bondage to sunder,
O Thou Whose presence pervadeth without a void
All things, Thou, Bliss all-embracing.

---

9. OH! FOR PEACE (9)

Cause of all say some is where the five elements
Melt into maya; and others
That the First is where all faculties, functions, fail;
Or it is where the soul suffers
Loss of the senses internal; nay, It is
Where the three principles perish;
Form of the sound It is; seed of the universe;
Form It is; formlessness; the soul;

Draws the soul itself there far from all sense-touches,
Standing non-different from God ;
Grace, say some ; some 'tis the nothingness unbegun
Unended ; otherwise others.
Pause I bewildered, mind restless as mercury—
Where is the rapture reposeful,
O Thou Whose presence pervadeth without a void
All things, Thou, Bliss all-embracing ?

---

10. THE PUZZLES OF LIFE **(10)**

Who made the darkness the dwelling-place of the soul ?
Who has placed sense in it spark-small ?
Whose is the skill that has charactered on my skull
Fate to hold fast to what I grasp ?
Who tells me heedless of heavenly bliss to slumber
Deeming this food-bag, my body,
Permanent ? Parents and kinsfolk with world-fetters
Has my desire to me fastened ?
Rue I my lot thus, bewailing, and blaming me—
Nay, others should for this answer ?
Is the time present accountable for my fate ?
Or the past source of the evil
Cruel in fruitage of re-births ? Bewildered, I
Miss the high mystical meaning,
O Thou Whose presence pervadeth without a void
All things, Thou, Bliss all-embracing.

---

11. FOLD THOU ME IN THY GRACE **(11)**

Boldly to bear what befalleth, and not to fear
Fate unbefalling, 'tis Thy Grace
Giveth strength ; diligence too to seek, seeking find
Vedanta Siddhanta systems
Holden in harmony. Wisdom is of thy Grace,
Showing my body unlasting.
Thrilled into love by grace longeth my soul for home,
Life everlasting, its haven.

Fold Thou me close in that grace incomparable,
Helping me, but for Thee helpless,
That my faith falter not but be incessantly
Stayed in the peace of the Silence,
Told not in height or depth, known not or otherwhere,
In the whole range of creation,
O Thou Whose presence pervadeth without a void
All things, Thou, Bliss all-embracing.

---

12. GIVE GRACE TO STAY THE UNSTABLE MIND (12)

Lie not the deeps undammed keeping appointed bounds,
Wall-less the great ocean waters?
Did not the bane become balmy ambrosia?
Bideth not in the sea burning
Dry the deep ocean-fire? Fixed in the firmament
Roll not orbs numberless mid-aired?
Own not the clouds the seven sway of the Thunder-armed?
Bent not as bow-stick Mount Meru?
Nigh on the treading of Rama's feet, breath-given
Stood not the slab of stone, woman?
Gain not by magic men boons for the life that is,
Blessings by pills and by potions?
Why not the means devise whereby, Lord I may be
Mindlessly safe and holy
O Thou Whose presence pervadeth without a void
All things, Thou, Bliss all-embracing?

---

13. KEEP ME FROM DESIRE (13)

Knoweth no limits Desire nor hath bounds any:
Kings who are conquerors of lands
Numberless seek the sea also to subjugate;
Gold-ful as god of wealth rich men
Grow discontented and seek methods alchemic
Gross things and base to turn to gold;
Long-living ones gather lust for a longer life;
Longing, disquieted are they,

Probing all nature for secrets of deathlessness,
This is the sum of needs human—
Hunger appeased with bread, slumber to soothe the limbs;
These I have. Dead to mind keep me,
Holy, lest, flitting from this to that, self-driven,
Into Desire's sea I sink,
O Thou Whose presence pervadeth without a void
All things, Thou, Bliss all-embracing.

---

14. SAME AS No. 6 (6)

(1)

Deeply considering all things, I gather
No one of himself doeth any deed,
Even the devas too, Brahma and others
Lack not impulses, direction and lead.

(2)

Famed as the moon-perfect, men of the silence,
Lapse into anger erringly often,
And, with their lips unadvisedly speaking,
Lay bare their thoughts their speech does not soften.

(3)

Reasoning men let their language run, sometimes,
Into thought's bye-ways, from the theme astray,
Leaving the line of the argument unlinked,
And the main discourse dragging its lone way.

(4)

Holy men, vowing to keep Siva's vigil,
Holy of all nights Siva's own to keep,
Often, in semblance of wakefulness, sit they,
Sitting so, slumber, heavy-eyed with sleep.

(5)

Thine are the doings of mortals, immortals,
Thine only real all else effacing,
O God Whose presence pervadeth without void
All things, Thou, Bliss, in bliss all embracing.

15. SAME AS No. 12 (12)

(1)

Lie not the deeps undammed,
Unwalled the waters stand,
Within their boundaries
Between the sea and land ?
Did not dread poison turn
Into the nectar sweet,
Into ambrosia bane,
Which it were death to eat ?

(2)

Bides not the burning fire
Dry on the ocean bed ?
Far in the firmament
Mid-aired and over-head
Roll not unnumbered orbs
In glory night and day ?
Own not the clouds the seven
The Thunder-Indra's sway ?

(3)

Was not Mount Meru bent
To be the archer's bow ?
Did not the slab of stone,
That once was woman, know
The tread of Rama's feet,
And woman move again
With life, who erst, in death,
A slab of stone had lain ?

(4)

Gain not my magic men,
By potions and by pills,
Blessings and boons of life,
Freedom from fleshly ills ?

(5)

Why not the means devise
For safely keeping me
In holy mindlessness
Right-centred Lord in Thee.

O God, without a void
  Whose presence all-where is,
All things pervading fills,
  O all-embracing Bliss ?

---

16. SAME AS No. 13 (13)

None can the limits set
  To longings of the mind,
Ways of Desire are wide,
  Their windings none can find.

(1)

Kings whose possessions are numberless,
  Conquerors of many lands,
Seek the sea also to subjugate,
  Gain for the greed of their hands.

(2)

Rich men unsatisfied, tho' they own
  Riches, as Kwera's untold,
Fain would learn alchemic means to turn
  Gross things and base into gold.

(3)

Long-living men, full of longings are
  Longer and longer to live,
Seek in all secrets that nature hides
  One that might deathlessness give.

Considering all things, this I know
  The body needs but bread
Appeasing hunger, soothing sleep,
  . Somewhere to rest the head.
These I have, and for this pray—
  Pure unattached keep me,

Lest I, by longings driven, rush
    Into Desire's deep sea,
O God, without a void
    Whose presence all-where is,
All things pervading fills,
    O all-embracing Bliss.

---

17. SAME AS No. 13 (13)

Bounds there are none to desire ;
    Much are we greedy of gain ;
Longings high lead but to higher
    Satisfied ne'er we remain !
Sceptred and crowned tho' we be
    Kings of all kingdoms word-wide,
Yet for the sway of the sea
    Sighing in unrest we bide.
What in our hands if we hold
    Plutus's wealth ? Yet, to turn
Base things and grossest to gold
    Fain would the knowledge we learn.
What if the blessing be ours
    Longest to live ? Yet what pain
All that is sweet in life sours,
    Soul-sick we seeking in vain,
Seeking though struggle and strife,
Secret of unending life.

Hunger appeased with bread,
    Slumber to soothe me to sleep—
All my need. Lest I be led
    Lust-driven down to the deep
Of my desires, the vast sea
    Ruinous, O Lord, I pray
Unspotted that I may be,
    Mindlessly in Thee may stay,
O Thou Whose presence all-where is
Voidless, O, all-embracing Bliss.

III.—ADORATION

In the Tamil this section of twelve hymns, all of which are given here in English, is headed *Porul Vanakkam*, பொருள் வணக்கம், meaning 'The Adoration of Being.' In N.M. the Psalms are 14 to 25. The first four in English are slightly shortened forms of N.M. 20, 18, 15 and 21 respectively, and their fuller English equivalents are respectively Nos. 28, 26, 23, 29 in this section. The English 22 to 33, representing N. M. 14 to 25, follow the initial rhyme and line arrangement of the original. Different presentings of some of them are the English 18, 19, 20, 21, 34, 35. The English 32 and 33 show, which is the case with their Tamil originals, a syllabic and line arrangement different from that of the other hymns.

18. THE SOUL'S SPLENDOUR (20)

He is the cause of creation
And of all causes the First.
He is the Honey that healeth
Heart-hunger of saints and thirst.
He is the joy of the saintly.
Darkness shall near them no more,
All gloom by grace He dispelleth—
Him, the soul's Splendour let us adore.

---

19. THE SAINTS' SOLACE (18)

Unto no tribe He belongeth,
Him for it claimeth no caste.
Form He has none; nor is formless,
Nameless His splendour so vast.
Doing, or deedless, unfettered,
Life of life lives He e'ermore
Non-dual in Turiya fulness—
Him the saints' Solace, let us adore.

---

20. LIGHT OF SIDDHAN (15)

He is the thought of all thinking,
Immanent, undifferent,
Being, with all being blended,
He is the self-existent.

He is the bliss of His seekers,
Sea of love that has no shore,
Spring of the nectar of heaven—
Light of Siddhanta, let us adore.

---

21. THE GREAT FULNESS (21)

Close as in flower is fragrance,
Oil within the seed lies,
And in the flesh is the spirit
So is He unseen of eyes.
Glory of Agamas, Vedas,
Unfound of learning and lore,
Life of all life He abideth—
Him, the great Fulness, let us adore.

---

22. THE IMMANENT TRANSCENDENT (14)

Him, the eternal One ;. taintless, the holiest ;
Who has no fashion nor form,
Limb nor yet lineament ; ill-less sustaining all ;
Perfect, the far and the near ;
Limitless ; flame in the fulness of Turiya,—
Spirit transcending sense, speech ;
Immanent ; made manifest in bliss ; peerless One ;
Boundless Beatitude let us adore.

---

23. SAME AS No. 20 (15)

He is the thought of all thinking within the mind ;
Immanent ; undifferent ;
Being with all living blended, the life of life ;
Passion nor parts possessing ;
Seen of love ; Bliss to beloved ones imparted ; pure
Spring of the nectar of Heaven ;
Evil-less, over all, sole the Supremest One ;
Light of Siddhanta : Him let us adore.

24. THE INDWELLER (16)

Vastness evolving the elements ; boundlessness,
Bourne of the Silence of saints ;
Past all the reach of or speech or of thinking, Bliss ;
Grace by the guru revealed ;
Fast who the faithful in fellowship enfoldeth
Linking them to Him in love,
Casting the dross of their self out, Who indwelleth
In them, unknowable : let us adore.

---

25. LIFE OF LIFE (17)

He is all life in heaven, life of all life on earth,
Friend of forsakers of self,
Bliss ever boundless, supportless, the Absolute,
Homed in the Turiya heights ;
Is honey of the heart, flavour three-fruited sweet,
Nectar. So draw nigh to Him ;
Crystalline let the tears overflow, pearls of love :
Palm to palm pressing, Him let us adore.

---

26. SAME AS No. 19 (18)

Caste cannot claim Him, to no tribe belongeth He,
Being unbounded by birth,
Past bonds of dying and deed-fetters and freeing,
Name, form, and formlessness, aught ;
Lasting non-dual the life in all, Turiya
Fulness, the solace of saints,
Vastness and splendour ; the ill-less Supremest One—
Him, by His grace guided, let us adore.

---

27. THE COUNSELLOR (19)

Show and illusion, a dream, a mirage to deem
World-life ; by wisdom the way
Know of communion with Him the self-existent,
Deathless ; and, flooded with love,
Glow with ingladdening of incessant joyousness,
Ever He counselleth me,
Lo ! He, the Lord of the Silences, seeking me,—
Daily His lotus-feet let us adore.

28. SAME AS No. 18 (20)

First, and the cause of phenomena ; luminant
Wisdom, the honey that heals
Thirst and heart-hunger of all His love-longing ones,
Blessing them bounteously full ;
Bursts He all barriers of in-being, out-going,
Bliss of the grace-gifted saints ;
Erst-while was darkness, now He hath dispelled the gloom.
Light of light's splendour : Him let us adore.

---

29. SAME AS No. 21 (21)

Glory and crown of the Vedas and Agamas ;
Greatness unguessed by the gods,
Known not to sages or saints ; cause and creation
Bound not Him ; bountiful riches ;
Close as in flower the fragrance, in the grain oil,
In the flesh spirit is,
So, in all, blending unblended abideth He ;
Thuriya fulness, Him, let us adore.

---

30. THE REVEALED COMFORTER (22)

Sky and all elements in Thee enfoldest Thou
All-filling vastness. By faith
Eye that beholdeth Thee finds Thee a sea of bliss ;
And Thy belovéd are kept
By Thy grace firm in their love for Thee, O, First One,
Lovingly coming to them
Thyself in meekness manifesting, Comforter.
Raising obeissant hands Thee I adore.

---

31. MELTING LOVE (23)

Space of the open sky fillest Thou. So fillest
Soul-space within me ; and all
Place in the sweep of my senses pervadest Thou,
Nectar refreshing. Thine is

Grace ever blissful, O, Great, One : and love for Thee
    Melts my heart, words fail framing
Praises, as, joy-flooded tears shedding, with palms joined,
    Ecstatic, in me Thy Grace I adore.

---

32. MOTHER, MY SOUL'S GUARDIAN (24)

He who is First, the Beginningless, unending, seeking us
    Motherlike, has unto Love's bondage brought us.
Teacher the Righteous; the Truth above thought and speech; Holi-
    Unattached unto ill ; Luminant beyond [ness
Reach and the range of the warring religions ; Light manifest
    Unto the men of the way of the Silence,—
Thee, my soul's Guardian, drawing nigh with my eyes love-flooded,
    Palm to palm pressing, obeissantly, I adore.

---

33. ALL AND ABOVE ALL (25)

" A ", of all vowels, is life of all consonants, vocally
    Blending unblended with each of them.
Way of the Lord in the universe is so : He is all,
    Universe and all perceivable is He ;
Nay, he is yet not all, all He transcendeth, ineffable,
    Untouched by likes or by dislikes, true Wisdom,
Taintless, All-Pure, incomparable, Lord of the herd of souls—
    Singing, I draw near Him, love-longing I adore.

---

34. SAME AS No. 33 (25)

(1)

" A," of all vowels, is the life
    Of all the consonants, with each
Unblended, blending vocally,
    In assonance of speech.

(2)

So in the universe is God,
    In all the universe is He,
The world and all perceivables
    Are God in unity.

(3)

Yea. He is all, and yet not all
For everything transcendeth He,
By likes untouched and by dislikes,
Taintless, in majesty.

(4)

True wisdom He, ineffable,
There's none like Him, pure evermore,
Him, the Lord of the herd of souls,
All-loving, I adore.

---

35. SAME AS No. 27 (19)

(1)

The God of grace my comfort;
His counsels are which ever
In ways of wisdom keep me,
And I shall wander never.

(2)

With him I hold communion
Who liveth always, deathless,
He teacheth me this world-life
Is vain, a show, all worthless.

(3)

My Counsellor, He, counsels
The seen the fleeting things are
A dream. mirage, illusion
From Life and Lastingness far.

(4)

My soul with love is flooded,
And lo! in fulness floweth
The joy of God, ingladdening,
The joy that no end knoweth.

(5)

Lord of the lofty silence
In love, for Him, He sought me.
His Lotus feet I worship
Who way of Truth has taught me.

IV.—TEACHER OF WISDOM'S BLISS.

Four out of eleven psalms headed in the Tamil *Sinmayananda Guru*, சின்மயானந்த குரு, are presented here in English. The four are 26, 27, 32, 36 in N.M. The English 36, 39. 40 are three different presentings of the Tamil N.M. 26. The English 40 and 41 follow the rhyme and line arrangement of the original.

36. UNLIKE THE SAINTS (26)

The hands are fair that offer Thee
    Of flowers fair the sacrifice.
The bodies with delight are thrilled
    While tears run down from love-filled eyes.
Deep in uncloying joy divine
    In bliss submerged as in a sea,
Bless Thee Thy saints in broken words
    Of adoration, hailing Thee,
" Sankara, Suyambu, Sambu "
    And glad and willing worship give.
But I am not as these Thy saints,
    In ignorance and ill I live.
When wilt Thou grant to such as I
    The guidance of refreshing grace,
Who gavest to the grace-matured
    The Four, the faultless in their ways,
Thy saving truth ineffable,
    In one brief word of blessing said,
What time Thou satest lotus-red
    Beneath the stone-grown banyan's shade,
The Guru in the form of grace
    Arisen for th' obeissant Four
Who stood around adoring Thee,
    Siddhanta's Goal, First evermore,
O God whose glories high on Siragiri shine,
Teacher of wisdom's bliss, Lord of the Southern Shrine ?

37. THE DROSS TO GOLD (32)

My body is the smelting pot
　　Wherein, like copper that is stained
With dross, in darkness and impure
　　Long have I ignorant remained,
Till Thou enkindledst wisdom's fire,
　　In fusing heat refining me,
Till tempered to be touched by grace,
　　The soul's transforming alchemy,
And I became God's purest gold
　　Thine own thy willing slave to be.
O Lord, for such transfiguring love
　　What shall I render unto Thee
Who art beyond the six Great Ends,
　　Above them all transcendent far,
Of which the rarest in renown
　　Vedanta and Siddhanta are,
O Glory risen 'neath the shade
　　Of one fair holy banyan tree,
Indweller in the hearts of saints
　　Who give glad service unto Thee,
And in advaita keepest me
　　Thine own, O Victor of the soul,
O Thou who art the only First
　　For evermore Siddhanta's Goal,
O God whose glories high on Siragiri shine,
Teacher of wisdom's bliss, Lord of the Southern Shrine!

---

38. OF WHAT AVAIL? (36)

The way of faith some follow well
　　And firm they are in piety:
Of continents nine circuit make;
　　In rivers bathe and in the sea;
While in the seven-forked fire they stand
　　They eat dry leaves of forest trees,
Drink water or the mountain air,
　　And pangs of thirst and hunger ease:
Within some lofty mountain's cave
　　In silence sit, dead unto speech

And there the veins they purify;
Force upwards to the moon's high reach
The spark that's in the primal breath;
The food ineffable they eat,
The moon-drawn Soma of the gods
To mortals given, ambrosia sweet,
And gain thereby the mystic means
Of keeping their frail bodies whole
Undying unto length of days
While ages over ages roll.
Can all this liberation bring,
Achieve salvation of the soul,
Except by knowing Thee, O Lord,
The Ever-First, Siddhanta's Goal,
O God whose glories high on Siragiri shine,
Teacher of wisdom's bliss, Lord of the Southern Shrine?

---

39. SAME AS No. 36 **(26)**

(1)

Fair flowers from fair fingers fall,
Rare offerings at Thy shrine,
Rare flowers culled with love and care
Fair flowers for Thy shrine.

(2)

Thrilled with delight their bodies are
Whose tears love-melted run.
Unpalling joy of Heaven is theirs
When tears love-melted run.

(3)

They call on Thee, Thy worshippers,
Blessings in broken words,
Suyambu, Sambu, Sankara,
Blessings in broken words.

(4)

Lord I am evil, unlike these;
I worship not as they.
Is there not grace to govern me
Who worship not as they?

(5)

Thou satest Saint among the saints
Once 'neath a banyan shade,
Red was the seat Thou satest on
Beneath that banyan shade.

(6)

The Four of faultless sanctity
There stood adoring Thee ;
Thine was the Form of grace they knew
Who stood adoring Thee.

(7)

It was the fulness of the time
For them the faultless Four
When Thou showedst Thyself in grace
To them the faultless Four.

(8)

Their eyes were gladdened, seeing God
Risen within she soul ;
One saving word Thou spakest thu
God risen in the soul,
The First, Siddhanta's Goal,
O God whose glories high on Siragiri shine,
Teacher of wisdom's bliss, Lord of the Southern Shrine.

---

40. SAME AS No. 36 (26)

Fall from fair fingers the flowers of offering ;
Thrilled with delight is the body ;
Love-melted tears run in rivers ; plunged in the deep,
Joyous of Heaven's bliss unpalling,
Call to Thee worshippers, blessings in broken words,
" Saukara, Suyambu, Sambu."
Me who am evil and not thus will grace govern ?
Thou to the Four, in their fulness,
Faultless, of sanctity, closest adoring Thee,
Showedst, by one word, Salvation,
When 'neath the banyan shade Thou, in Thy form of grace,
Saint on a seat of red satest,

All-bright their eyes to see God risen in the soul,
First and the Goal of Siddhanta,
Glorious on Sira's hill, Lord of the Southern Shrine,
Guru of bliss of true knowing.

---

41. WHEN WILL THOU COME TO ME? (27)

Frame of my frailty, a shore ever tumbling down,
Sinner, I, holding all real,
Likest the lame man that longeth for tree-honey,
Long to be drawn up to Godward.
Aiming at Bliss which absorbeth all thought-making,
Sariya, Kiriya, Yoga,
Discipline have I served until now. Passing these,
Oh! for a way to Thee, Wisdom,
Claim of all ways who excelling art far above
Word or thought, Perfection! To drink
Deep at the ocean of bliss the beatific
Draughts of deliciousness, cloyless
Same ever! When wilt Thou come to me, granting this,
First and the goal of Siddhanta,
Glorious on Sira's hill, Lord of the Southern Shrine,
Guru of bliss of true knowing?

V.—THE LORD, THE SOURCE OF GRACE

This section of ten verses is headed in the Tamil கருணாகரக்கடவுள், 'The Lord, the Source of Grace' or 'The Lord the Grace-Giver,' a title taken from the last words of each stanza. Eight of the ten are given here in **English.** In **N.M.** edition they are Nos. 49 to 56 inclusive.

42. SHOW ME THE WAY **(49)**

For Thee are all, all in Thy service,
　　All are Thine own that doest all,
And all-where Thou, O Lord, art present—
　　Thus unto us the voices call
Of Vedas and of saints and sages,
　　And of all creeds is this the cry.
None other there is for our hearing,
　　And this alone is truth know I.
Yet I not staying in this knowledge
　　Have missed the healing of the soul
And to my present state have wandered
　　Away from my salvation's goal.
That this too is Thy gracious doing
　　Permitted for my good by Thee
Thou in my inwardness of being
　　Hast counselled poor unknowing me.
Show me the way to win deliverance
　　Grace-giver granting Grace to all,
O Lord, in bliss beyond all thinking,
　　That dancest in high Wisdom's Hall.

---

43. NOT ONE BUT TWO **(50)**

I am not such as call light darkness ;
　　Yet I forgot the saving word
Which I from out thy gracious vastness
　　That me in it engulfs had heard

What time O Lord to me Thou camest,
The silent Teacher teaching me
The secret of the way of stillness,
How I in it might safest be.
Like children building toy sand-houses,
In fancy eat there fancy's food,
From day to day in soft contentment,
So have I chosen, Lord, as good
The half-way help of human learning
And in my mind have held as true
The daring of unbridled fancy
That Thou and I are one not two.
To curb my mind that thus rebelleth,
To keep it under right control
I do not know the way, I languish,
I faint, and long for health of soul.
When wilt Thou make me heir and worthy
Of grace, Who givest grace to all,
O Lord in bliss beyond all thinking
That dancest in high Wisdom's Hall ?

---

44. THE GURU (51)

True of tongue are the truly holy ;
Truth never from their speech is far ;
Truly within their hearts Thou dwellest :
Truth that is true, all things that are
Truth, unto them Thou truly teachest,
Truth this is true without a doubt.
Falsehood never have I abandoned ;
False one am I, within, without,
Falsehood not knowing as but falsehood,
Falsely that I should say and do
Falsehood of all falsehoods the falsest
Falsehood not seen to be untrue.
Thy doing all who in me being
My mind at Thy behest and beck
Movest. What can I do all helpless ?
Thou art the Guru round whose neck

Dark blue the ring of drunken poison
For ever burns, Siva. Thou art
The Guru who as Vishnu camest
To men Thy wisdom to impart.
Thou sittest on Thy seat of lotus
Expounder of the Vedas four,
Brahma, whose head the four-ways faceth,
Four-faced who is from evermore.
In all the creeds to calling voices
The gracious Guru comest Thou ;
And to Thy saints whose cry Thou hearest,
'Forsake us not, O, succour now,'
Thou Love, to loving ones, becomest,
Wise Counsellor in doings all,
O Source of Grace, in joy past thinking,
That dancest in high Wisdom's Hall.

---

45. WORSHIP THE INDWELLER (52)

I cannot in thy temples worship,
Or there before Thy symbols bow,
Or pluck Thee dew-kissed flowers of offering
For in the flower's heart art Thou.
How can I press my palms together,
My body bend to worship Thee,
Since it is all imperfect service,
For thou indwellest, Lord, in me ?
Thou art the vastness of the ether,
The elements, the primal sound,
The Vedas four, the goal of Vedas,
The quest beyond all seeking found,
The quest sublime, its key, its secret ;
Thou of all seeing art the sight,
And of all knowing art the knowledge,
Of sight and sense the inner light,
The word and its interpretation,
Form of the silent, saving call,
O Source of Grace in joy past thinking
That dancest in high Wisdom's Hall.

46. THE HABIT OF DYING (53)

This truth is taught in all the Scriptures,
And has been ever from of old,
That in the end the soul attaineth
To what its own attachments' hold.
Though living in the world the sages
Are merged in meditation so,
They have no thought, the ever-sleeping,
That there is Death, they do not know.
To those who know not inner wisdom
To teach this truth it is not wise,
It would but tend to disputation
And seem all foolish in their eyes.
Did not the godly-minded sages
Divinely to their goal attain,
Markanda, Suka, and the others,
Their longed-for end undying gain,
O God whom Indra and the devas,
Brahma and other gods adore;
To whom the sages of the Scriptures,
The Rishis of the Vedas four,
Unnumbered bands of gods-in-waiting
Ganesha-guided, homage give;
The nine whose fame is in the Yoga,
Who perfect in its powers live;
The sun, the moon, the constellations;
The goddesses of melody;
The servants of the god of riches,
Half-men, half-animals who be;
O God, whom these, all others, worship,
Before whom all adoring fall,
O Source of Grace in joy past thinking
That dancest in high Wisdom's Hall?

---

47. A LIVING SACRIFICE (54)

My undiscerning mind and restless
In sacrifice I've seized and slain;
My deeds the demons of my making
Shall never trouble me again.

Thy servant's love shall be th' anointing,
O God, divinity benign
My life shall be Thy full libation ;
My spirit incense at Thy shrine ;
My senses lights devoutly burning.
This worship not at times shall be,
But ever ; and oblation living
O God I give myself to thee.
O, nectar of the Veda's essence,
Be gracious, O Thou honey-sweet,
Sweetness in which divine, delicious,
The many sweetnesses all meet
And mix, O bliss of bliss uncloying,
That seekest with my sense to blend
By little and by little, openly
At last as this poor sinner's friend
In closeness of good-granting kinship,
O Source of Grace, gracious to all,
O Lord in bliss beyond all thinking
That dancest in high Wisdom's Hall.

---

48. LONGING FOR ECSTASY (55)

The body in love-languor drooping
As tho' the very bones would melt
Within because of love's great burning ;
Tears welling, for the eyes have felt
The warmth of love, its fire and fever ;
Like unto Like, soul unto Soul,
Drawn as by magnet to the needle,
Drawn with home-longings for its goal,
The heart thrilled into trembling throbbing ;
They sing, they dance in deep delight
Who love Thee, love-lit are whose faces,
As is the moon's with softening light.
Their claspéd hands like buds of lotus,
Their voices rising like the strong
Great rush and roar of unchecked waters,
And praising Thee in tuneful song,
'O Heaven, O Rain from heaven descending,
O Rain of bliss from heavens of grace.

O Flood, O over-flowing Torrent,
    Forever unto Thee be praise!'
To such art nigh ; to stony-hearted
    O source of Grace, not nigh at all,
O Lord in bliss beyond all thinking
    That dancest in high Wisdom's Hall.

---

49. SAFE INTO PORT (56)

Who hold that what is here hereafter
    Will be are wise ; good ever do ;
Lie not, nor weary in well-speaking ;
    Kill not, compassionate are, true.
Thou who in men thus truly holy
    Indwellest witness to the wise,
Boon-giving now and for the future,
    As are the trees of paradise,
Art sharaba to slay my karma
    That lion-like would prey on me.
Thou art my gloom-dispelling splendour ;
    My bark upon the boundless sea
Of love self-seeking birth-begetting,
    The bark of vast expansive grace
To bear poor helpless me to safety
    To yonder shore the heavenly place,
The bark that on self's boundless ocean,
    O Source of Grace, awaits my call,
O Lord in bliss beyond all thinking
    That dancest in high Wisdom's Hall.

VI.—LORD OF ALL

This is a selection of 54 hymns out of 389 forming the section called *Parāpara Kaṇṇi* பராபரக்கண்ணி, the most popularly used of S. Tayumanavar's psalms. Each hymn consists of two lines the second ending with the address Parāparamēy, பராபரமே, which gives the title to the whole collection. The word is rendered here 'Lord of All' which expression denotes only some of the thought covered by the original. In N.M. the whole collection in 636—1024.

50. THE MOUNTAIN (637)

Of bliss the beauteous mountain
In heaven of grace Thou art.
Who see Thee shall have never
In births and re-births part,
Lord of all.

51. RAIN OF GRACE (638)

O Rain of grace, all giving,
Foreseeing all my thought,
Lo! Thou hast come. Thy coming
Fulfilment's sprouts hath brought,
Lord of all.

52. CRY OF THE CREEDS (640)

The cry of all the creeds is,
'The Lord, Our God, who knows?'
All-Soul whose love in rivers
Of bliss unbounded flows,
Lord of all.

53. FLAME OF GLORY (641)

Thou art the flame of glory
In hearts silent to Thee,
And of the soul's unending
Bliss Thou the boundless sea,
Lord of all.

54. WITHIN ME (642)

Thou everywhere abidest,
  The goal of all Thou art.
Now sweet, O honey-welling,
  Art Thou within my heart,
    Lord of all.

---

55. INNER LIGHT (644)

O Pearl of pearls, most precious,
  O burning Gold, most bright,
O Wisdom, Understanding,
  My inmost being's Light,
    Lord of all.

---

56. HE BECAME MAN (647)

Thou art on all sides Vastness.
  That I should see Thee so
Man unto me becamest,
  Spakest the word : I know,
    Lord of all.

---

57. LOVE (649)

O love, at full-tide flowing
  Fulfillest love in me,
O God, O Bliss unbounded
  My soul's defence to be,
    Lord of all.

---

58. JEWEL OF THE SILENCE (650)

The treasure-chest of Silence
  The heaven within it hides,
Thou art the jewelled glory
  That in its heart abides,
    Lord of all.

59. IN THE VEDANTA (653)

The good in knowledge gladdened
Unceasing praises roll
To Thee, whose glory burneth
Bright in Vedanta's goal,
Lord of all.

---

60. IN THE SIDDHANTA (654)

In heaven Thy feet, fair lotus,
Thy saints adoring see,
To them Thou comest, Glory,
Siddhanta's God to be,
Lord of all.

---

61. GOD NOT KNOWN BY STUDY (672)

To boast that by book-learning
Thy footsteps I have known,
'Tis wrong, O God, vain-glory,
With contrite heart I own.
Lord of all.

---

62. MY BIRTHS (679)

O God, in bodies many
Thou knowest I was born,
Thou knowest all my sorrows,
The agonies agone,
Lord of all.

---

63. GREAT AND SMALL (700)

The life of all that liveth
As my own life to love,
Or great or small unharming,
Grant me grace from above.
Lord of all.

64. PART OF GOD (719)

Life unto all that liveth
O, all-where, Lord Thou art.
Life unto all Thou givest.
All life is of Thee part,
Lord of all.

---

65. WORDS OF MY MOUTH (754)

Words of my mouth are prayers,
I've found them so to be,
And my heart's meditations
Acceptable to Thee,
Lord of all.

---

66. INDWELLER (758)

God, Thou art with me ever,
Thou never leavest me,
And in my mind Thou dwellest,
Indwelling, makest Thee
Lord of all.

---

67. THY GAIN ? (762)

Thyself for me thou gavest ;
Giving, Thou madest me
Thine, by Thy grace prevenient.
What is the gain to Thee,
Lord of all ?

---

68. SILENCE (765)

Thou, freeing me from falseness,
Hast stillness bidden me,
Sufficient is that silence,
Bliss of the soul to be,
Lord of all.

69. YIELDING (766)

O Teacher, mute and mystic,
All Thine Thou madest me,
Sufficient is that conquest
Bliss of the soul to be,
Lord of all.

---

70. WHAT REWARD? (769)

Thine am I now, once foolish,
Of understanding none.
What reward can I render
For favours to me done,
Lord of all?

---

71. HOLY JOY (776)

'Tis gladness makes the godly,
With melody and glee
In dancing and in singing,
Rejoice, in seeking Thee,
Lord of all.

---

72. AS A LITTLE CHILD (778)

They are like little children,
The simple, the unsound,
In all they do, Thy servants,
Who wisdom's goal have found,
Lord of all.

---

73. HIGH CONVERSE (782)

With Thee, as salt in water,
Thy saints in converse are.
Words fail that bliss in telling.
All bliss surpassing far,
Lord of all.

74. I AM THEIR SERVANT (783)

To all in Siva silence
Clear-willed and pure of mind,
Thy saints, I am their servant,
Myself in bondage bind,
Lord of all.

---

75. I SERVE (784)

To those who love all others
As their own selves, and live
Lives led of grace, Thy servants,
I willing service give,
Lord of all

---

76. LET ME BE FIT (790)

O fit me for the service
Of all who truly love
And serve Thee, so shall I be
Fittest for bliss above,
Lord of all.

---

77. THE FOUR-FOLD PATH (792)

The stages of devotion,
The favoured, the four-fold,
Are bud, and blossom, fruitage
Green and then ripest gold,
Lord of all.

---

78. GOOD DEEDS (793)

Of charity, almsgiving
And prayer, penance, pain,
Deeds must they do who saving
Knowledge here seek to gain,
Lord ot all.

79. THE BODY OF THIS BIRTH (812)

Of all the deed-made many
Embodiments on earth,
Say why the best I think is
The body of this birth,
Lord of all.

---

80. THE BODY DECEITFUL (813)

This body with lies laden,
Deceitful thro' and thro',
By merely being called so
Can never be the true,
Lord of all.

---

81. BODY UNRELIABLE (814)

Fleeting as lightning-flashes,
This body of a day.
To trust it, Thee forgetting,
Is not to me the way,
Lord of all.

---

82. WATER-BUBBLE (815)

Why in this water-bubble,
This unabiding clay,
Should there be all this suffering,
And all this sorrow, say,
Lord of all.

---

83. WHY FEAR DEATH? (816)

Why do men of no knowledge
For dying bodies weep?
Why dread if one but knoweth
The happenings in sleep,
Lord of all?

84. AFTER THE BODY (817)

This bodiment dissolving,
What other frame is there ?
What burden for the bearing ?
What follows, when and where,
Lord of all ?

---

85. WHENCE THE BODY ? (818)

This load of limbs skin-covered,
This form, this living thing,
With pride assumed, yet burden,
Whence came it to being
Lord of all ?

---

86. THIS CORPSE (832)

The saints, the truly holy,
Unlonging for the lust
Of body, know in slumber
It seems a corpse for dust,
Lord of all.

---

87. FOOD-BAG (852)

Long I've laboured, breathless,
The breath of life to hold
Within this food-bag, body,
Bearer of ills of old,
Lord of all.

---

88 BOOTY (871)

There was day Thou tookest
Goods, body, being, three
Thy booty. Now, let nothing
Be lacking unto me,
Lord of all.

89. THE SEEKER (876)

O Bliss Thou bounteous camest
To me of Thine own will,
Seeking me for my gladdening,
Protecting me from ill,
Lord of all.

---

90. OFFERINGS (882)

Wouldst Thou accept a garland
Woven of words for Thee,
Or from the fields fair flowers
An offering from me,
Lord of all ?

---

91. ALLELUIA (890)

Always Thy praises singing,
Thy Grace I celebrate.
To me are thoughts none other :
The rest thy will, my fate,
Lord of all.

---

92. I WILL NOT LEAVE THEE (891)

Thro' self that ' I ', ' I ', crieth
Tho' Thou depart from me,
Yet I from Thee will never,
Never assundered be,
Lord of all.

---

93. CAST ME NOT AWAY (898)

To Thee I've come for refuge,
O cast me not away.
That Thou shouldst not give shelter
The reason to me say,
Lord of all.

94. LIGHT (912)

Thou, with all seeing blended,
Art of all eyes the light.
The eyes of all things living
In Thine Eye-light are bright,
Lord of all.

95. BELOVED (913)

If Thou to me, Beloved,
Art dearest, I should be
To Thee Thine own beloved,
As dear as Thou to me,
Lord of all.

96. ON THY HOLY HILL (923)

Intemperance, lust, murder,
Theft, anger, and ill-will
Must die in him whose longings
Are for Thy holy hill,
Lord of all.

97. I SAW (967)

Attachment and illusion
From me had passed away.
And lo ! I saw in vision
Thy glory bright as day,
Lord of all.

98. MY TEARS WIPED AWAY (968)

Illusion gone, in vision
O God, I saw, that day,
Thy hand in mercy wiping
My tears from me away,
Lord of all.

99. WHITHER CAN I GO? (973)

Where can I from Thy presence
Depart, parted from Thee,
O God who all-where fillest
With bliss abundantly,
Lord of all?

---

100. THE GUILE OF GOD (975)

Why seemest Thou unheeding,
And hearest not the while
I cry to Thee? The secret
Show me of this Thy guile,
Lord of all.

---

101. I FOLLOW (1018)

Little am I in learning,
But much there is to me
In words of holy sages,
And I have followed Thee,
Lord of all.

---

102. I GIVE MYSELF (1019)

Teacher that taughtest silence,
The saving word to me
Of joyous stillness spakest,
I give myself to Thee,
Lord of all.

---

103. IN PRISON (1023)

I know not why in prison
Of luring senses five
Thou keepest me Thy puppet:
For liberty I strive,
Lord of all.

1247—6

VII. THE SEA OF BLISS

A section of twelve hymns, Nos. 77 to 88 in N. M., is headed *Sukavári*, [illegible] meaning "Sea of Bliss." Each hymn in the original ends with this word, *Sukavári*, in the vocative case. The word is rendered here, "Of saving bliss the boundless sea." Eight of the twelve hymns are here given.

104. TO TASTE AND SEE (77)

Of Thine own self, O Lord, Thou camest
The honey-sweet of saints to be:
And sweetness all sweet sweetness passing
Thy bliss was when they tasted Thee:
Unceasing is for Thee their longing;
With love their sighing spirits melt;
Their senses with love-thinking languish;
Words fail to tell what they have felt,
Words framed in joy, a blissful babble.
In ecstasy the body faints,
And bliss they have beyond all knowing—
The rare experience of Thy saints.
Till knowledge comes of man to maiden
She has no thoughts of happiness;
When love possesses all her passions
She smiles she thought of love so less.
So I who know not but by hearing
Believing what I merely hear
Can only by Thy grace have knowledge
Of Bliss to soul-experience dear,
O God, the passionless, O Light, O Purity,
Lord over all, of saving Bliss the boundless Sea!

105. LOVE'S FULL TIDE (78)

When I, the way of love not knowing,
Was moved and stirred to love by Thee,
My spirit with love-languor fainted,
Love for Love's fulness came on me,

And, with strong yearnings for that fulness,
    My senses were with love possessed.
Thy doing all, for whom love-longing
    I pine, and pining gain no rest.
O grant me for my inmost gladdening
    The flood of Love at Love's full-tide,
Thy Bliss with all my being blending,
    Bliss-giver in my soul abide.
The fragrance in the bud is hidden,
    But to it blooming goes the bee
To petals open, cool and pleasing:
    So come, Belovéd, come to me.
Thou comest not, I cry for comfort;
    Unpitied and alone I live.
When wilt Thou grant me joy unceasing,
    As to Thy saints salvation give,
O God, the passionless, O light, O Purity,
Lord over all, of saving Bliss the boundless Sea?

---

106. THE PERIL OF WORDS (79)

Mayhap a stone may melt and soften,
    But I continue hard of heart.
He has no power, Brahma the four-faced.
    Since Thou alone supremest art,
A mind to fashion grace-resisting—
    What Thou decreest is sure decreed.
So pity me, O God, all-potent
    Show mercy to me in my need.
Behold I am become Thy burden,
    Thy care. O kindest, come to me
As rain of bliss from skies grace-laden
    Refreshing me alive to be.
An evil child a mother never
    From her as evil casts away:
What other solace but its mother
    Is left to it, O Mother, say?
In many words there is no merit,
    For oft in them a falsehood lies,

And lying lips to grace are strangers,
Outcast and alien in Thine eyes.
So, not for lofty speech, lip-service,
Wherein no profit is, I pray,
But for the bliss of holy silence
Wherein in peace my soul may stay,
O God, the passionless, O Light, O Purity,
Lord over all, of saving Bliss the boundless Sea.

---

107. THY SAINTS—AND I (80)

Bones in the body seem all breaking :
In pore and hair is thrilled the skin :
The mind within its framework melteth
As wax in fire for warmth within :
And love, responsive to love's ardour,
Rains tears of love from love-lit eyes :
Thus in Thy saints on whom Thou comest
A Rain of Bliss from grace-deep skies,
Ambrosia of the life undying :
Thus to Thy saints who love Thee well.
But wherefore Thou hast captive taken
One such as I I cannot tell,
Who have not love they have, the holy,
Yea one whose longings still are prone
To hold this frame of filth and frailty,
Of hair and muscle, skin and bone,
A lasting thing. I know its falseness,
And fain would keep my senses free
From faith in it, for 'tis the pathway
That thro' much sorrow would lead me
To ruin and my soul's undoing.
The way of worldliness I spurn,
Unwishing it, yea to its cravings
Not even in my dreams to turn,
O God, the passionless, O Light, O Purity,
Lord over all, of saving Bliss the boundless Sea.

108. FORSAKE ME NOT (83)

O Gold of heaven beyond all getting,
O Pearl of price, O Love divine,
O Love that in love-senses liveth,
And living love becometh mine,
O Flood of Love from Love o'er flowing!—
Thus, Lord, in revel and in song
Thy praises I have said unceasing,
In dances which to bliss belong,
And cried and raved with deep love-longings,
My body and my being thrilled,
My hands in worship held adoring,
And all I am with frenzy filled,
As tears from love-filled eyes in torrents
Rained votive to Thy holy name.
My heart alas! then failing, fainted,
For I grief-stricken then became
Because I knew me all unworthy
And hard of heart. Yet this I know
That ne'er from Thee have I been parted,
For lo! Thou livest: even so
My soul lives ever, yea, Thy bondman.
Forsake not poor unknowing me
But let me with Thy saints be numbered,
Their great and goodly company,
O God, the passionless, O Light, O Purity,
Lord over all, of saving Bliss the boundless Sea!

---

109. LEAD ME NOT INTO TEMPTATION (85)

The creeds are clamant disagreeing;
Therefore, to vows of silence tied,
The speechless great ones seek in silence
The calm wherein they would abide.
And Thou the heavenly Teacher camest
Three-eyed, most gracious, teaching me,
How, free from coming, free from going,
In bliss incessant I could be.

But lo! the yogins claim for Yōga
It is the path that leads to peace.
And when I seek their lonely silence
And strive to be where senses cease,
In yogic calm and contemplation
Alas! then, subtle in the mind,
Delusion makest Thou my tempter.
How can Thy slave salvation find,
O God, the passionless, O Light, O Purity.
Lord over all, of saving Bliss the boundles Sea?

---

110. WHERE DWELLEST THOU? (86)

Where is the place that is thy dwelling?
Is it creation's crown and crest,
The universe's top and summit?
Or in the great beyond unguessed?
Or midmost in the sun's bright mansions?
In fire where dwells the primal flame?
Or in the moon's ambrosial arbours?
Or where in temples to Thy name
Thy saints devoutly render worship
Before the idols in the shrine
And see, thro' symbols, there arisen
The presence of Thy form divine?
Art Thou where lead the four directions,
Or where they cease and lead no more?
Or in the splendour of the vindhu?
Or sound that soundeth from before?
Or in Vedanta or Siddhanta?
Art thou in what the eye can see,
Or where all go into non-being,
Decay and die and cease to be?
Art thou in present, past or future?
Or where beginnings have their birth?
Or rather, Lord, Thy home Thou choosest
Within the hearts of saints on earth,
The holy dead to all world-senses?
Declare, O God, Thy way to me,

Thyself the guide to lead Thy servant
In graciousness at last to Thee,
O God, the passionless, O Light, O Purity,
Lord over all, of saving Bliss the boundless Sea.

---

111. HEIR OF GRACE (87)

"O! for the day of grace that giveth
My final freedom unto me" !—
My heart within me faints thus longing
For grace to which I heir shall be.
What can I say, my doubts so many?
Behold there stalketh to this day,
Behind me and before, the peril
Whose fear I have no faith to slay.
Is bliss where throbs the mind unresting
And throbbing melts like wax in flame?
Is bliss to long to still the senses
In agonies that rack the frame?
Thou knowest all That art the knowing
Of all my knowing, Thou alone.
Why then, O God, as tho' Thou knowest
Nothing, when all to Thee is known,
Thou lettest me in sorrow flounder,
Thine own thou madest whom Thy slave?
While in the body weak, unlasting,
Let grace be mine to help me brave
The winds and waves of life's great ocean.
O safely thro' tempestuous seas
Steer this frail bark lest, wrecked and broken,
It fail to reach the port of peace,
O God, the passionless, O Light, O Purity,
Lord over all, of saving Bliss the boundless Sea.

VIII. GOD AND THE SOUL

The psalms translated in this section may well have the above heading. In the Tamil the chapter of forty psalms has the title *Áseyenum* ஆசையெனும் from the opening word of the first psalm. Those translated here are in N.M. 322, 324, 331, 341. 358, 361.

112. ATTACHMENT (322)

The mind is as a piece of cotton
    Whirled in a storm and tossed about,
When cares of life, ties, and attachments
    Grow strong, and love is lost in doubt
And disregard of holy learning,
    And goodly fellowship is far.
But God of grace and light Thou livest
    In minds that to Desire dead are.

113. DETACHMENT (324)

'Tis God who doeth as He pleaseth.
    Just as, upon a plank of wood,
A top is made to move in whirling,
    So God moves all for ill and good.
When this is known, attachment ceases,
    Since nothing here seems worth the strife.
Detached, the heart holds both as sacred
    Home life and the ascetic life.

114. THE MOTHER (331)

Thou art my father, art my mother ;
    My grief allaying camest here,
In form of Grace, O God the Guru :
    None other helper have I near
O Light whose end or whose beginning
    Unguessed, ungauged for ever lies
O God who sole the First abidest
    Yet manifest to mortal eyes,

Needs of Thy suppliant servants heeding,
    On Siragiri's holy hill,
O! Tayumanava, O! Mother,
    Thy servants' wishes to fulfil.

115. BRETHREN (341)

Who is my father, who my mother,
    Who are the people of my kin?
Thyself, Thy saving Grace, Thy servants.
    I come, unillumined within,
Lord of the mid-set eye, Thy captive,
    The lotus of Thy feet to win.

116. THE BURDEN (358)

Crown of the Vedas four, Thou knowest
    How oft I have been born, have died
How oft, reborn how often, mortal,
    Linked unto deeds, to doings tied.
Make Thine, O Lord, mind, speech and body;
    The load, I can no longer bear,
Of births the burden. Me, unknowing
    Me, Lord, Thy vassal make, and spare.

117. LIFE AND LOVE (361)

Life of my life, sense of my senses,
    O Love that in my inness art
Sweeter that sweetest fruit or nectar,
    And honey-sweet, within my heart,
With all my being blending livest
    By Grace familiar as a friend,
O let me not from Thee be parted,
    Unsundered be unto the end.
Wherefore my mind that wayward willeth
    Lead in the way, in me control,
And let Thy grace in richest measure
    Refreshing rain upon my soul.

IX. ALL-FILLING BLISS BEATITUDE

This is the translation of the heading ஆனந்தமானபரம் *Ānandamāna Param*, of a section of ten stanzas, of which four are given here in English. The English section-heading fairly represents the sense of the Tamil title which is taken from the last portion of each psalm.

118. THE ASCETICS—AND I (70)

Dry leaves and dropping fruit and water
Are all their food who hunger much,
Cave-dwellers in the darkness, stonewise
Who often sit in stillness such
As keeps them self-composed unmoving,
Eyes closed to all that calls away
From meditation; or they wander
Far in the scorching heat of day,
Till in some sacred pool or river
Devoutly they their bodies dip;
And in the quiet of cool forests
In silence sit, and sitting sip
The soma-drink whose mystic sweetness
Allays the thirst that leads to birth;
And so they sit for seasons many
As tho' deep-rooted to the earth,
Their breath subdued, their mind unmoving,
That in the tangles of their hair
Grown wild upon their head and matted
Fowls and all flying things of air
Their hiding-places have in safety.
Thus live the wise, tho' bone by bone
Is seen upon their wasted bodies
Flesh-worn with fast and feeble grown,
Because the grace that well fulfilleth
All searchings of the Scriptures rare
Is theirs to strive for, seek with striving,
Who penance do to find peace there.

But I my days pass wordly-minded,
O Lord in whose vast amplitude
The seen, the unseen, That embracest,
All-filling Bliss, Beatitude.

119. THE TILLERS (72)

The forest growths of primal darkness
Uprooted were; and wide and clear
Of weeds and noxious growth mind-spaces
Were made in stretches far and rear;
The stoniness of self was blasted
And borne away; the soil was turned
And tilled: the seed of mystic silence
For which the worldly have not yearned
Was buried there; and love's devotion
Was water for its nurturing;
By persevering labour guarded
Against delusion that on wing
Of evil over all encircleth;
And so from seed and sprout there grew
The tree of saving bliss whose fruitage
In fulness yields sustenance true
To them Thy loving ones, the saintly.
I seek their goodly company,
And, seeking, hope for good impulses
From Thy prevenient grace to me,
O God, unseen of all, who livest
In secret, and whose amplitude
The seen and unseen all containeth,
All-filling Bliss, Beatitude.

---

120. NOT BY LEARNING ALONE (75)

Whate'er I have of lore and learning,
By reading or by hearing had
Is useless, since my mind unmastered
And unsubdued remaineth bad.

The arrogance of self-assertion,
    Of 'I' and 'mine' is in me still;
The lust of things in strong attachment
    Is in possession of my will.
Compassion and the grace of giving
    Were never mine; nor any thought
Of prayer and of fast appointed;
    The Presence I have never sought
Of God within His holy temple;
    But ever lived untrue in speech
Truth never speaking, yet to others
    Wise, in mere words, to preach and teach.
Thus have I lived without an effort
    To win redeeming grace, and been
Beyond all men on earth most foolish.
    Has such as I been ever seen
Or heard of, say, Lord, who knowest
    All things and in whose amplitude
The seen and unseen That embracest
    All-filling Bliss, Beatitude?

---

121. EXPERIENCE (76)

"Of thine own self thou knowest nothing
    Thou doest nothing." Thus spakest Thou
What time Thou camest, silent Teacher,
    And claimedst me Thine own. So now
My body, being, soul Thou keepest
    Thy captive, captive from that day
When I became Thy willing bondman;
    And false things all have passed away;
Here is no continuing city;
    False is the faith in 'now' and 'here';
False is the love of wealth all fleeting;
    False is the sight that blinds the seer
To all the falseness of the body;
    Of kith and kindred bond and tie,
False is the faith in false attachments;
    And of all lies the greatest lie

Is truly that of self-assertion.
And darkness is no longer nigh,
Soul-ignorance the primal darkness :
Nor now for me the pathways lie
Of good and ill to re-births leading.
My mind is still, in peace is stayed,
And it has lost its old attachments,
Uncoming and ungoing made ;
And time is not, for all transcendent,
Transfigured are, O Amplitude
That all things in its vastness holdest,
All-filling Bliss, Beatitude !

X. THE ALL-FILLING FULNESS

Psalms 89 to 99 in N.M. are grouped under the heading *Engu Niraykinra Porul*, எங்கு நிறைகின்ற பொருள் which means "That which fills everywhere." The Tamil title is from the words with which each psalm ends.

122. WITHOUT THEE NONE (89)

" No atom moves but by His motion,"
    The sages say. What follows then ?
What is knowing, and what unknowing?
    Who knoweth, knoweth not, of men ?
Who are the silent, who the babblers
    All-mouthed and babbling such as I ?
Whence cometh mind the soul's delusion ?
    Hardness and mercy, whence and why ?
Whence is creation, whence is action ?
    And elemental changes whence ?
Falsehood and truth, fruitage and failure,
    Evil and good in consequence,
Whence come ? Whence patience and impatience ?
    Who are the great and who the small ?
Who are the foes and who the friendly ?
    Without Thee none, in Thee are all,
O Life of life That all sustainest
    For time that is and time to be,
And all-where Fulness That remainest
    For time that is and time to be.

---

123. ART THOU NOT GRACE ? (90)

Female is God is one faith's teaching ;
    Another teacheth male is He ;
A third of all beliefs will babble
    And wildly cry its creed to be

Now this, now that, is God, ever
    Uncertain and ungaining go,
Heedless of what may follow after,
    From thought to thought and nothing know;
A fourth sees God in light whose glory
    The tongue of man can never tell.
One says that God is space and vastness;
    God is the state where ever dwell
Sound and the other primal causes.
    Some say God is the atom sole
Surviving wreckage universal
    When all things into ruin roll:
That God is present, past and future,
    The threefold time is what some say.—
These thou becoming, all transcendest
    And in the gracious interplay
Of deeds Divine art Bliss eternal.
    O! marvel unto men like me
The workings of Thy grace are wondrous!
    Shall I not marvel ceaselessly,
O Life of life That all sustainest,
    For time that is and time to be,
And all-where Fulness That remainest
    For time that is and time to be?

---

124. DUAL, NON-DUAL (91)

The Vedas, Agamas, Puranas
    The Histories, all holy writ,
Teach that the soul and God 'non-dual'
    Or 'dual' are, both He and it.
While precious is the 'dual' teaching,
    The 'dual' is the fountain-head
Whence floweth forth 'non-dual' wisdom.
    Agreeing with what here is said
Reason, experience and the Scriptures
    Unite. Opposing views agree.
Therefore shall I not need hereafter
    The stages four of piety,

Because by bond and by attactment
That which I worship I would be,
And so by being drawn to Thee ward
Be least of me and most of Thee;
My thoughts of me of Thee are worship,
And I the state 'non-dual' reach.
According unto each man's seeking,
That Thou becomest unto each—
So wide Thy grace O gracious Father—
Which he in worship thinks of Thee.
Since I have come to Thee, O Fulness,
What more is needful unto me,
O Life of life That all sustainest,
For time that is and time to be,
And all-where Fulness that remainest,
For time that is and time to be?

---

125. DELUSION AND THE MIND (92)

A babe that knows not what is bidden
Is in its cradle to and fro
Rocked, and receives on thighs sharp pinchings.
Remembrance cometh even so,
And linked to it forgetting cometh
Within the budding of the soul,
That with Delusion's deadly fragrance
Is dulled, and, in the worlds that roll
Sevenfold of ignorance, is giddy,
Reels in its dances, dancing reels.
Wayward as she who from her husband,
Self-willed, departing, freedom feels,
Apart from God the soul oft dwelleth;
Than iron harder and than stone
The soul becomes, and soon believeth
That unto it are truly shown
What truly are, but all are merely
What it believes it true can call.
Anon this show will shrink and shrivel
Into nothingness smallest small.

These are the doings of Delusion
That in the mind evolveth all,
This pomp and pageant, fancy, falseness.
Help helpless me the means to find
Wherewith to curb and curbed keep under
My false Delusion-making mind,
O Life of life That all sustainest
For time that is and time to be,
And all-where Fulness That remainest
For time that is and time to be.

---

126. THE HYPOCRITE (93)

Tears from mine eyes flow down in torrents
But not because love melts my heart,
Lo ! all I do is false, is faithless,
I am untrue, I play a part.
I dance with hands held up adoring,
I sing, and ceaseth not the flow
Of tears. I, hypocrite, unceasing
Cry, feelings unfelt felt to show,
'O Brother, Light Divine, O Father,
Behold in me Thy willing slave.'
Thus in lip-service never lacking
I danced and words for praises gave.
All know this. Then much more Thou knowest
Within Thy graciousness benign.
In sweet compassion help me Homeward
To where is endless Bliss divine ;
Grant me the state of true abiding
Without attachment there to live ;
And unto me, helpless, unknowing,
The grace of Thy salvation give,
O Life of life That all sustainest
For time that is and time to be
And all-where Fulness That remainest
For time that is and time to be.

---

127. GRACE AND WORKS (94)

A single stone is strong to scatter
In hasty flight a crowd of crows.

So all past deeds, the sum of karma,
Cause never hurt or harm to those
Who for Thy grace love-thirsty longing
Its fruition and its fulness find.
That I so thirst not is no secret;
All my misdeeds, before, behind,
Oppressively beset my body;
The yoga way to ward off ills
Has failed for me. From me are distant
The thoughts of that true life that fills
Eternity. When shall my being
In love and oneness blend with Thine
What if to-day be mine that blessing
Of living in that Bliss divine,
O Life of life That all sustainest
For time that is and time to be
And all-where Fulness That remainest
For time that is and time to be?

---

128. NOT POOR IN GRACE (96)

'Tis true this body is unlasting;
Yet Thou, the Silent One, hadst given
Thy servant, once, a method mystic
In which if only I had striven
To stand, this body might be lasting.
But I, inadept, cannot learn
To train my mind to self-rejection;
The food which I by begging earn
Ill suits the body. So, for ever
In Thy pure Presence let me be,
And there in meekness render service
To those whose is the victory
Begun o'er Death, who are mind-mighty,
And serving whom I shall be strong
In power of mind and in the practice
That easily would come ere long
Of wisdom. Grant me one petition—
Keep me from this one poverty

The poverty in Thy grace poorest—
O now, compassionate, grant me.
Thou Life of life That all sustainest,
For time that is and time to be,
And all-where Fulness That remainest,
For time that is and time to be.

---

129. CONTRAST (97)

Their clothing is of barks the coarsest ;
Grain of the jungle or the hills,
And leaves that stray down from the forest
Are food their cruel hunger stills.
Both in the sun and rain they suffer
And thereby stir from heel to head
The warmth within the body latent,
A fire upon their frailty fed ;
They wash themselves in holy waters ;
They think their bodies not their own,
And do the practice of the yoga
Austerely, most desirous grown
Of saving by the way of wisdom.
Thus do Thy holy ones, while we,
The sinful, feast on food most sumptuous,
Clad in fine clothes, in luxury ;
Wear what we will, eat what we fancy ;
In lordly mansions live, in state ;
With nought to suffer seek our pleasures ;
Are sensual, insatiate.
How such as we sinful and foolish
Full worldly-living night and day
Can ever live and grow in goodness,
Be gracious unto me to say,
O Life of life That all sustainest
For time that is and time to be,
And all-where Fulness That remainest
For time that is and time to be,

130. ALL IS WELL (99)

That Thou art one with me in being
My ignorance would madly groan
In agonies of self-assertion,
Its fashion and its form unshown,
The primal taint. But like the darkness
Which hides itself before the dawn,
Hides what it holds and its own nature,
Is shrunk to nothing and is gone.
The seas are troubled in confusion,
The birth-begetting good and ill.
The waters roll away affrighted;
The storms have ceased and all is still;
Because Delusion, root and reason
Of difference, the many-made
And many-making, has been driven
To where at first its base was laid,
Nothing. The understanding ripens,
Released and undivided grows.
To more and more of wisdom's splendour,
Till Bliss that no beginning knows,
No end, no up, no down, no middle,
Is come in all its fulness, mine;
And in that Bliss to be abiding
To me is given Thine aid divine,
O God that as the soul's own Guru
In form benign of saving grace
Camest to me. Thy name be blesséd,
For ever unto Thee be praise,
O Life of life That all sustainest
For time that is and time to be,
And all-where Fulness That remainest
For time that is and time to be!

XI. THE WAY

The Tamil title *Aranm* ஆரணம் meaning "the Scriptures" is from the first word of the first of ten psalms forming the section so headed. In more than one of them there is reference to "a way", and hence the English heading. Eight of the psalms are translated here and they are 272, 273, 274, 275, 276, 277, 280, 281 in N.M.

131. THE SCRIPTURES (272)

The Vedas are the road,
The Agamas the steed,
And Thine the guiding hand.
But of Thy Form I need
Full vision, O my Light,
Lord of the mid-set eye.
Till then, with word and will,
I give Thee worship high.

---

132. A WAY OF DELIVERANCE (273)

Sakti is hid in Thee
When all things pass away,
O boundless Sea of grace.
Grant me refuge, I pray,
From all forgetting far
Beyond remembering.
To me deliverance
From births and re-births bring.

---

133. THE WAY OF BLISS (274)

Drunk with the bliss of God,
Heedless of earth and sky,
Merged in the sea's expanse
As mote to be, long I,

O Vision of the pure,
O Witness of the wise,
Tillai Dancer, heart's help,
Unseen of sinning eyes.

---

134. A WAY ASHORE (275)

Indweller, calling me
Insistent to the streams
Of Bliss, Cloud dropping grace,
O Lamp, whose cooling beams
Dispel, with holy light,
The gloom of ill, guide me
Thro' deeps of births and sin
Ashore. I trust in Thee.

---

135. THE WAY TO LIGHT (275)

O Tree of life, whose fruit
Ripeneth honey-sweet
For saints ripest in grace,
Light, Lord, lo ! at Thy feet
I lie, contrite of heart,
Grieved for the grace not mine,
Of holiness of eyes—
Illumine me with Thine.

---

136. THE WAY OF GRACE (277)

Sense of my senses, Thine
The promptings to be still ;
But I in vain unrest
Knew not ; unwisdom kill.
For Thou, and not the creeds
Of men, canst give me grace.
The Lotus of Thy feet
O Silent One I praise.

137. TO REALISE UNREALITY (280)

Grace of the silence Thou,
    Guru, hast granted me.
The womb of bodiments
    Is dead, yet I would be
Like those this body false
    Who feel, O Bliss confessed
In form and formlessness,
    And by the creeds unguessed,

---

138. WAY OF LIFE (281)

O formless Form, beyond
    All thought, Bliss without break,
Thy silence is the way
    To endless life to take,
O Lord, Thy Sakti hid,
    That satest 'neath the tree,
Light of a darkened world
    Nectar of saints to be.

XII. DELIVERANCE

"Ineffable" in Tamil *Sollatkaria*, சொற்பதங்கடந்த, is the word with which ten psalms, of which nine are translated here, begin. The Tamil title is that word. The English represents Nos. 282, 283, 285, 286, 287, 288, 289, 290, 291 in N.M.

139. HARD IS THE FIGHT (282)

O Lord ineffable, O Sea
Of Bliss, abode and flame of light—
From me in ill's bewilderment
Why hidest Thou? Hard is the fight.
Soft threads from stones who spins, the sea
Who prisons in a mustard seed,
Yaman, than night more black, is nigh—
Thy succour sorely do I need.

140. SHOW THY GLORY (283)

Lord let Thy servant have the grace
Of silence, and its secret know.
Dispel the gloom that shrouds my soul,
Once more to me Thy glory show,
O vastness into which They pass
From sin's entanglements who go,
God of the graceful Tillai dance,
Nectar whose streams unlessened flow.

141. I FOLLOW (285)

Night I forget and day, in love
And longing to be lost in Thee,
O Sea of Bliss; behold my tears;
My being melts; behold Thou me;

" Father," I cry, and follow, child,
    Crying, until, in ecstasy,
I cross the troublous waves of time,
    O Light of light, O Bliss, Beauty.

---

142. GOD IS ALL (286)

Lord, in whose hair the crescent moon
    In silver gleams, O light of light
At Tillai that in splendour danced,
    Beloved of mountain Uma bright,
Thou art my God, my Guru Thou,
    My Guide, my Father, Mother art,
Thou art my Evil and my Good,
    Life, body, being, every part.

---

143. HEAR ME (287)

In Thine own vast expanse risen,
    Thou dancest, doing all Thy will.
From bonds of births, rebirths, I flee
    To refuge of Thy Feet, from ill,
Nectar that all my thirst canst quench,
    O King of heaven, I cry to Thee,
My hands uplifted, suppliant—
    O Lord, why hearest not Thou me ?

---

144. CALL ME FROM BIRTHS (288)

Call me, Lord of the mid-set eye,
    Wearer of white ashes, call me,
From all the ties of life, the bonds
    Of births, bewilderments, to Thee,
Me, sinner moving in their midst,
    Make me Thy slave, O God whose grace,
As streams of waters, runs through thoughts
    Of saints, their prayers and their praise.

145. IS THERE NO WAY? (289)

God, who madest the heavens and all
Creation, keepest what hast made,
And canst destroy, would that Thy hands
For my saving some plan had laid,
Made known a way! Why hast Thou called
Into being one such as I?
Thy gain?—In ignorance I ask.
I trust in Thee, let grace be nigh.

---

146. IF THOU BE ALL (290)

To seeing eyes the Vision Thou,
To eyes unseeing art unseen,
All life art Thou, the body Thou,
Thou art of creeds division keen.
Lord of the mid-set eye, eight-armed
And red, if Thou be all, then, how,
I marvel, Thee Thy saints adore,
Their worship how receivest Thou.

---

147. ALL CHANGED (291)

Laying on me load of my self,
Burden of births and deeds on me,
A puppet in Thy hands, for good
And ill, Thou madest me to be.
When now, by Grace, heavenwards I go,
The world and all that is, its way
Of life, the past, is all a dream
Unwriteable of yesterday.

XIII. FROM SIN TO HIGH THINGS

Six out of ten psalms in the collection headed in the Tamil *Vambanen* வம்பனேன், are translated here. The title means "a sinner" and is from the first word of the section. The hymns translated here are 292, 293, 294, 295, 296, in N.M. The Tamil heading is not adopted.

148. IMPULSE OF GRACE (292)

A sinner, Lord, Thou knewest me,
Knewest my sin, and yet, with soft
Impulse of Grace, Thou promptedst me
To seek Thy face, O Lord, aloft
That livest, most supreme, gracious.
I live, by grace alone, I live,
Lacking nothing. And unto Thee
What reward worthy can I give?

149. THE WORD IS THE SWORD (293)

There is a way to wisdom, full,
Perfect, the bliss without a taint.
Lest on this path my footsteps slide,
Or, weary, falter, or I faint,
Sword of the Silence, flaming bright,
In secret has Thou given me,
Word of the stillness. Nevermore,
O never will I part from Thee.

150. TO SEE THY GLORY (294)

All powers and primal elements
Transcending, Thou abidest high
In the vastness of holiness.
Light in the splendour of the sky

Of Bliss, O God ineffable,
Peace-giver, when wilt Thou call me,
Sinner, unperishing to live
And fulness of Thy glory see?

---

151. MELT MY HEART (295)

I cast my cares on Thee, and trust
That Thou wouldst take corruption's core,
My soul, with all its sins, and melt
Its stoniness, and more and more,
By violence of grace, soften
It, and become its Refuge sure,
Compassionate, till holy hands
Of prayer are mine, and tear-drops pure.

---

152. SHOW THYSELF (296)

Pure light of purest bliss, whom they,
Whose minds are unafraid and free
Of ill, discern non-dual, One,
When wilt Thou show Thyself to me,
And comfort me with Thy "Fear not,"
O Secondless? When shall I be
Thy willing slave, in service glad.
And at Thy feet worshipping Thee?

XIV. PONNAI MĀTHARAI

The opening words of the first of 78 hymns give the title to the whole collection. The words literally mean, "Gold and Women" paraphrased in English into the entire first line of the first hymn. What is presented here in English is in places paraphrase-translation. There are pairs of initial rhymes and the syllabic arrangement of the original is retained. Each hymn is chantable to the tune of the Tamil. A peculiarity of the original—the last word or last but one word of one hymn becoming the first word of the next —it has not been possible to reproduce in the translation. The verses are 194—271 in N.M.

153. ONLY THOU (194)

Gain and gold-getting, laughter of love-lit eyes,
Vain I hold to be, Lord of my being, Thou.
Thee the grace-giving, luminant Lord I love,
Me the lonely one longingly Who hast sought.

---

154. THE PAST PERSISTS (195)

Mine and all I am, Lord, have I given to Thee,
Thine and only Thine gladly surrendered so.
Longings old yet are tormentful, O, my Lord;
Strongly stormed by them how can my spirit live?

---

155. TAKE ME (196)

Soul-lit knowing Thee, service I render now;
Wholly yield I my I-thinking heart to Thee,
Take me, sinful me, call me to Thee, my God,
Make me captive, Thou conquering King of Grace.

---

156. MY GARB (197)

Saintly garb and the grace that the garb adorns,
Taintless life by the gift of Thy giving, Lord—
Than that, lacking These, I can live, sooner I
Can take poison and find it to nectar turned.

157. INDWELLER (198)

Seer's seeing, Thee, seek the unseeing eyes;
He and She and It, thus Thee the soul can see.
Knower's knowing, Thee, faithless eyes seek afar—
Lo! abidest Thou, Lord, in the lowly heart.

---

158. THEIR NAME AND MINE (199)

Grace-given, God-drawn, they, mortal is not their name,
Raised to godliness, Godward who ever grow.
Name there's none for me, sin-driven raft of ill,
Aimless, tossed in an ocean of vanity.

---

159. FREEDOM (200)

Heard I wisdom in words of the Wisest One,
Stirred not grace in me, saving the soul from sin:
Bid me break through my bondage, and flee to Thee,
Rid of being else burdened with births and births.

---

160. FORMALISM (201)

Hands of worship I, head-high uplifting, Lord
Bands of faithful ones follow around Thy shrine:
Distant yet is the day when the joyous truth
Mists of darkness shall drive from deluded me.

---

161. IN ME (202)

Being who by creation unbounded art
Thee within the sky-space of my heart I hold.
There is nothing O flame of grace like the state
Where I by Thee am ill-less and good-less made.

162. THE FLESH (203)

Light of grace burning gold-red in Thy glory,
Bright, beatific, boon of the Silences,
Tho' Thy Grace had been granted to me, my God,
Lo! my being, beset with flesh-weakness, faints.

---

163. WORLDLY (204)

Gold-red Brightness, my God, O, Thou, Light Divine,
Holding fast to the fashion of worldiness,
Praise my mind does not yield to praiseworthy Thee:
Grace that calleth me, Lord, I deserve it not.

---

164. ALL-DOER (205)

Deeds I do, and the thoughts that I think are Thine—
Heeding not this truth I have lived shamefully,
Reeling in the whirl of the lie which causeth
Feelings hot of lust and hate and vanity.

---

165. THE BODY (206)

Vain this body, flesh, nerve-held, and built of bone,
Pain the profit of being so long in it.
Hurl Thy saints at it scorn, and their loathing, Lord,
Pearl of Pearls, O, Thou, unpierced Pearl found of me.

---

166. WAY AND WISDOM (207)

"This is, that is not"—argument know I not:
Wisdom have I not for this or that to speak
Thou art able to do all things; unto Thee
Now I come, save me: way there is none for me.

167. SLAVE (208)

Holy ones of Thee loving Thy saving Grace,
Lowly do I love, Lord who unknown to me
Thine hast made me be, bondman of God indeed—
Mine be name of slave and not of devotee.

---

168. LIFE OF LIFE (209)

Dweller in the soul, Life of my life Thou art,
Queller of my qualms, surely, none else could be.
Grace of God in me glowing all gloryful,
Praiséd vision, It, thought of my thought remains.

---

169. REFUGE (210)

"Fear not", said'st Thou to Markandan, much who loved;
Hearing of that grace, lo! at Thy feet I fall,
Falling, Lord, I pray grant me Thy refuge there,
All embracing Bliss, ocean of wisdom high.

---

170. IMMANENT (211)

Seas the seven, and the mountains are merged in Thee,
These and all in Thy immanent beauty are.
Need I seek to know where be the hosts of souls,
Peerless Lord who art conqueror of my own?

---

171. ALL-KNOWER (212)

Bare is all I am, Lord, to Thy seeing eyes:
Where is thought of mine that I dare hide from Thee?
Long the tale else I should tell of woes, my God;
Strong one, holding me captive, O, keep me so.

172. MORE LOVE (213)

Daily, from of old, God, have I groaned in me,
Wailing, "O my king, make me to love Thee more".
When such frail a thing shouldst Thou forsake at all,
Men would praise Thee not, praise not Thy mercy, Lord.

---

173. WIN ME (214)

Light from glory of three eyes that gladden saints,
Brightness gold-red, delight of adorers, Lord,
Win me, drawn to Thee by Thy Grace, or else I
Sinful and unregenerate must remain.

---

174. PEACE (215)

Light, O, source of Light, Fulness, Beatitude,
Right, O, Refuge, Truth, Changeless, the only First,
Seek I succour Thine, praying that, in Thy Grace,
Weak I, peace may find, peace from mind causing pain.

---

175. DEAD TO SELF (216)

He encompasseth me l'ke the open sky,
Me in bliss all beatific keepeth He,
Knowledge, wise unto saving, is His alone:
Lo I'll love Him, and, dead to self, deathless be!

---

176. DRAW ME (217)

Me to Thee draw, Lord, as does the magnet steel,
Be Thy feet to me sweetness to which to cling
Birthless, Mother-God, and with Thy fervour filled
Worthy tears to shed and joyful tremor feel.

177. LIGHT (218)

Mother, Father, the Refuge of souls, Him name
Other than the Incomparable Teacher, wise;
Call Him Light and the Source of light, who folds me
All in blissfullest splendour most beautiful.

---

178. PERFECTION (219)

First in word-revelation, world of Grace, He,
Burst, in bountiful plenty, in worlds many—
Seed and root from which fruitage of life is formed:
Heed Him, One in all Perfection, worship Him.

---

179. GOD TO ALL (220)

Six-fold faiths of men, sagest of all, their love
Fix on Him Who, to each, shows His form of Grace.
Weak I longingly love Him, the Lord of Bliss,
Seek I joy in Him, seeking I find it full.

---

180. BEAUTY (221)

Deeps I plunge into, ever-new joy of God:
Sweeps the love of God, rapturous over me,
His is timelessness, goes not He, comes not He:
Bliss His beauty is, beauty the form of God.

---

181. GOD INDEFINABLE (222)

"That is, this is He", said not the men of old;
Sat they, saints, in the silence, adoring Him.
Saints have held no distinguishing thought of God—
Faints my soul to find name for my Fount of Joy.

182. JOY UNSPEAKABLE (223)

Bliss unspeakable, me in His boundlessness
His enfoldeth He, gladness engulfing all;
Dumb men sooner declare their dreams than I can,
Humble mortal, in words of men, tell my joy.

---

183. THE ONLY TRUTH (224)

Pearl-skinned fruit in the palm of the saint art Thou:
Whirls not he in doubt, Thou art his only truth.
O, Thou truest One, truthless, my life I lead;
Show now Thyself to me as my refuge, Lord.

---

184. DYING TO SELF (225)

Mid-eyed, snake-wearer crowned with the crescent moon,
Hid the Ganga is, Lord, in Whose matted hair
When all self, in me, O Father, perisheth,
Then may I be saved, found in Thy form of grace.

---

185. THY FORM (226)

See Thy saints in all things they see only Thee,
Thee they worship in work and their words are praise:
Where all life liveth, live the five elements,
There, O, greatest One is framed Thy form of grace.

---

186. THY GREATNESS (227)

Praised I never as forms of Thee forms I found,
Gracious Father whose all-filling splendour falls,
God, whose glory lies, over all like the sky,
Lord, how can hard-hearted I Thy greatness know?

187. TO LEARN SALVATION (228)

Boundless bliss-giver, Father I have never
Found, nor followed Thee, holiest Fount of Grace.
Taints of sin in me speedily not to be
Faints my soul for the learning, O, Lord of all.

188. USELESS LEARNING (229)

Gain I get none in knowledge I gather here,
Vain and worthless the wisdom of words I read,
Knowing not in the way of the wise to walk,
O, ineffable Boast of the blessed ones.

189. PROPER STUDY (230)

Lore of word-wisdom boastfully babble I,
Store of learning begetteth no good in me,
O Abode of the mother-like Power of Grace
Show how, Core of Light, saving may come to me.

190. THE STONY HEART (231)

Light indwelling in Glory of Sakti-Grace
Bright, O, Blissful One, Ancient of days, Riches,
Touch this heart of mine, melting its stoniness,
Much which moves in ill, likest the worm in filth.

191. NOT IN TRUTH (232)

Boundless ocean of bliss, I have not in truth
Found Thee, merging myself in Thy depths of joy.
Feigning ecstatic silence of bliss-dumb saints,
Gaining grace never, shame that I pass my days!

192. RESOLVED (233)

Dark-eyed damsels shall never again find me
Mark for darts of deluding love's vanity.
Thou art real, as fruit in the open palm.
Now Thy captive, O, keep me, Lord, ever so.

---

193. AS THY SAINTS (234)

Call me Lord to Thee that I with eyes of faith
Always see Thee as see Thy saints and ever
Live unliving the life of the soul of old;
Give me grace that to mindlessness I attain.

---

194. SHOW OF RELIGION (235)

'Silence, Silence,'—thus unto the mouth I say,
Lying speak I that unto the hands also.
Nightless, dayless made when will this dog have joy,
Light, O Purity, wherein the just are merged?

---

195. PARENT OF SOULS (236)

Light, O, all-filling Splendour, the sought of saints,
Bright, beatific, Wisdom, Thou Mother art,
Bliss-begetter, O, Father, most bountiful,—
His, Hers—Thine are the numberless souls, children.

---

196. ABOVE LEARNING (237)

Vastness, yea, vastness Thou art, the Vedas say;
Past all finding out, Agamas cry amain.
Learning gauges not God, but Thy journeyed ones,
Earning Silence, hold Thee ever in their hearts.

197. ONE GOD (238)

Thou art God, and I none other worship, Lord,
Bow I not before any in thought even.
Knower, knowing all, nothing is hid from Thee,
Lo! I, truthless one, speak to Thee, Wisdom, truth.

---

198. LEARNING'S GOAL (239)

God, indwelling in glory, fulfilling all,
Lord, O Light of light, this is my learning's goal
Thee to know as the Saint 'midst the saints seated
'Neath the tree of old; knowing Thee, find my joy.

---

199. STRAYING WILLS (240)

Night-black beauty that bindeth the braided hair
Tight in bondage unending it holdeth those
Wills unwooed by the glimpse of Thy glorious feet
Thillay's sacred Courts see in Thy mystic dance.

---

200. WORSHIP HIM (241)

Grace in beauty abideth in His body,
Praiséd Grace of God, Maid of the mountains, She.
Three-eyed Peerless One, Teacher true, love Him well
Free from births to be, worship Him, O my soul.

---

201. I FEAR NOTHING (242)

Births, re-births, and the burden of being born
Earthly life to lead, hell to fear, fruit of deeds—
These I dread not since God is my Portion here,
Peace and Good-Giver, three-eyed One granting boons.

202. HIS LOTUS FEET (243)

Lord of melody mounted on milk-white bull,
God, whose eyes are three, preacher of Veda-lore;
Wisdom true is He : flee to His Lotus feet,
'Tis there, only there, soul of sin, safety seek.

---

203. SAVING GRACE (244)

Why disquieted, hard of heart, why deceived ?
High are only they, great, to whom grace He gives,
Praisèd Lord of the matted hair, mid-set eye,
Grace that maketh them wise in the Word Revealed.

---

204. THE SPEECHLESS (245)

Three-eyed, sought of the saintly ones who have crossed
Speechless the sea of delusions of the soul,
His the land of the fulness of saving grace,
Bliss is boundless there, lo ! to its deeps I go.

---

205. THE TWO-LESS STATE (246)

Three-eyed Splendour that spakest the Vedas four,
Freely all the worlds own and confess as we
Know they naught of the joy of the homing soul,
So beyond thought and hearing the two-less state.

---

206. FAVOURED (247)

Three-eyed Father high secrets that taughtest me
Free of tests hast Thou set me amidst Thy Saints,
Say what vows I had vowed to Thy holy Feet
Days agone that now I should thus favoured be.

207. PREVENIENT (248)

Praise I ever shall sing to thy Grace, O God
Grace that motherwise made itself known to me ;
Thought and thinking and longings foreseeing far,
Nought withholdest Thou, O Lord whose eyes are three.

---

208. SHELTER FROM BIRTHS (249)

Tale and total of all it is hard to tell,
Male and female my numberless births on earth :
Them I dread not now, hoping for help from Him
Gem and Jewel, O Splendour whose eyes are three.

---

209. BURDEN-BEARER (250)

Nothing know I but vision of saving Grace ;
Other refuge I have not, O, wealth of Saints ;
Cares I cast on Thee, keep Thou my mind at rest,
Bear my burden, Beatific three-eyed Lord.

---

210. SIGN AND SEAL (251)

He has taught me that Bliss is my solace here,
Me He made to know way of the speechless joy :
Mine is nought I do ; doer He, since He gave
Sign and seal mystic of Him my three-eyed Lord.

---

211. ADORATION (252)

Thee O Lord of all, grace-giver by whose side
She, the Sakti-Queen, bideth the Bride of God,
Songful worship I, spirit-eyes seeking Thee,
Longing, yearning to see Thee O King of Grace.

212. HASTEN THE TIME (253)

Lasting thought I the fashion of fleeting things,
Fast I held to it: fruitage is evil all;
Tasted Nectar, Lord, sweet in the heart of saints,
Haste the day of my merging in Mukti-joy.

---

213. LONGINGS (254)

Past and present and future are none to Thee;
Vast Thy goodness, transcending the bounds of time:
O, by grace to be likest Thee, sinful I,
So that world-life may seem but a whirling show!

---

214. IN IGNORANCE (255)

God, that gottest Thee victory over Death,
Lord, and drovest the dreaded one far from Thee,
Thee I loving not, lacking good merit's meed,
Being foolish, have ignorance as my stay.

---

215. FATE (256)

Fate Thou framedst, and me for it, free-will too,
Weighting will with desire, will to longing linked;
O, then, Lord of the herd of souls, how can I
Know the way of rejoicing in saving grace?

---

216. PRAISE (257)

Light enlightening me always to see aright,
Bright as sunbeams discovering all to sight,
Praises, praises, to Thee, O, my God be given!
Grace O! grant me to outlive my life of lies.

1247—11

217. CONTENT TO SERVE (258)

Light that dwelleth serene in Thy sweep of Grace,
Height untouched by a craving or counsel, God,
Endless births would I undergo, if, through all,
Bending knees to Thy saints, I could serve them well.

---

218. HEAVEN HERE (259)

Bright abode of bliss, Ruby-hill, by whose Light
Night of ignorance nigh to Thy saints is not,
Give me grace that I, in this my body, may,
Live in joy with Thee, losing me Lord in Thee!

---

219. SOLE REFUGE (260)

Flame unflickering, failing not, Light of light,
Framed in radiance, Ruby of Tillay-Dance,
None my refuge, or helper, or kin but Thee,
Unto Thee I come: when wilt Thou grant me grace?

---

220. DOUBT AND DARKNESS (261)

God, whose form is Thine all-filling Grace alone,
Lord o'er matter, fair dancer in Court of Gold,
Thou, enthroned in me, hast my mind-mist dispelled,
Doubt is driven far, darkness has fled from me.

---

221. KARMA (262)

Foe to me ever, fruit of ill, from of old,
Woe has worked in me, hate of good, harm to do;
Let me, Lord of the mid-fronting eye of grace,
Fetter-riven, find refuge but at Thy feet.

222. MY TAMIL (263)

Light to longing eyes, food to the famishing,
Sight alone is the solace of seeking souls—
Come, that my Tamil may to all praise Thy Name,
Humble Servant That servest Thy servants, Lord.

---

223. FATE AT WORK (264)

Lord who wearest the datura in Thy hair,
Corded Ganga-stream, crown of the crescent moon.
Sleepless sorrow I far from Thy feet's refuge,
Deep in sins of the flesh has my fate flung me.

---

224. ILLUMINE ME (265)

Thee, about whom debated men, 'Yea,' and 'Nay.
'He is wonderful,' Thou hast revealed to me,
Thou art sole, none else. O, Thou, the highest good.
Now illumine me, lighten my gloom, O God.

---

225. IN THE HOUR OF DEATH (266)

Death will send his dread angels to me at last,
Breath of life to take. Who will then help me, who,
Save He unto whom twain of the Trinity
Gave all praise, incomparable Lord of Bliss?

---

226. AFTER VISION (267)

Name and learning, love, wisdom, sincerity
Came and truthfulness lo! as mine eyes beheld
God whose grace as the rosy-red sky is spread,
Lord whose form of Love filleth eternal bliss.

227. IN SAINTHOOD GOD (268)

They are God to me who on Him meditate
Day and night drawing nigh unto Him, nigher,
Light of eye-light and innermost sense who is,
Brightly burning Truth in the broad spirit-space.

---

228. THE HIGHEST GOOD (269)

This, O, Highest Good, God over all I know,
Wisdom saving men, Bliss of the Saiva Faith,
They shall perish who preach other gods there are ;
Way of peace is theirs who have found joy in Thee.

---

229. MY HELPER (270)

Men my kith and kin can never succour me ;
When my need cometh, who can my helper be ?
He, the Lord of the matted hair, mid-set eye—
Seeking whose feet the seeker has bliss on high.

---

230. BY LOVE ALONE (271)

This is sure that by love is attainable
Bliss that unto the holy is ever true ;
Goal of bliss to gain, and in that bliss to be.
Soul, all alien faiths as false fling aside.

---

231. SAME AS 182 ABOVE (223)

The arms of Love around me are,
'Tis God embraceth me,
And in His bliss unspeakable
He holds me His to be,
Enfolded in His boundlessness,
Engulfed in ecstasy.
No tongue of man the joy can tell
The bliss beyond word's reach.
And humble I with mortal lips
Its meaning cannot teach—
Sooner the dumb their dreams declare
In joyousness of speech.

XV. GOD, SOUL, MIND

Eleven hymns, the first beginning with the word *Mandalaththin* மண்டலத்தின் which, with another word, means 'on earth,' form a section headed *Mandalaththin*. This translation gives the eleven hymns under the title, 'God, Soul, Mind.' These three subjects, in interrelation, are dealt with in them, the last three hymns being specially addressed to the Mind. The hymns are 390—400 in N.M.

232. THE ALL-UPHOLDER (390)

Men see a man perform a marvel
And wonder much how he could place
Egg upon egg in mid-air standing.
More wonderful far are His ways,
The One who all the worlds upholdeth
Within the wideness of His grace.

233. NOT ONE NOR TWO (391)

They know not one-ness nor yet two-ness
Who in yoga's seventh heaven are blest,
Full-visioned they who reach the silence
He gives, the Sole by all confessed,
The First, unending Bliss refreshing,
The Sorrowless and e'er at rest.

234. HIGH WISDOM (392)

The deathless One, the undepending,
To those above the stages three
High wisdom gives, He, darkness-render,
Beginning, Changeless, Purity,
Unseen of Faiths the six who liveth,
Seat of Silence, of Bliss the sea.

235. NOT TWO NOR ONE (393)

Great Sea of Bliss whence all life cometh
Ambrosia, Gold and Precious Stone,
Indwelling Power, to me all riches,
Not two with soul nor one alone,
All-circling Light, bliss-giving Vastness,
Unchanging e'er the same is known.

---

236. THE UNKNOWABLE (394)

Self-knowing men like Him He maketh
Who lives, unflickering flame of grace,
When all things pass away as lightning.
To know is all, the Scripture says.
The creeds are puzzled. He abideth
All-true whom gods and mortals praise.

---

237. THE LORD (395)

Beyond all praise, Supreme, the Marvel,
By all bonds bound as 'That' as 'I',
In blending so, is sweetest Wisdom,
Core of the heart to those who die
To night and day, Crown of the Vedas,
The Lord, the Bliss-bestowing Sky.

---

238. WE DO NOT KNOW (396)

Of Him, advaita's End, Eternal,
The creeds all cry, "We do not know."
Ill-less, passionless, God, Wisdom,
God-likest by His grace to grow
Who guides God-thinking men, Vastness
Of Bliss He lives, abiding so.

239. SOURCE OF DELUSION (397)

Like good things out of gold, Delusion
Within Thee springeth, O, my mind,
When free, grace-ripe, the Rest thou seekest
Love-melted. Were sins cast behind,
Then could I live, and thee, good helper,
Like God's own grace, my kin I'd find.

---

240. MIND MIGHTY (398)

The very gods, in flesh embodied,
Obedient to the mind must be.
For present powers and those hereafter
O, mind, man ever needeth thee.
Asat who art as *sat* I reverence :
That I may live be dead to me.

---

241. GOOD-BYE (399)

Tho' much I grieve, O, mind, I'm sundered
From thee, dear friend from long ago,
Thy place revere. The Silent Teacher
Has taught nor 'I' nor 'mine' to know.
For heaven I hope, and power ; and comfort
I have through thee in grace to grow.

---

242. WHEN THE MIND IS STILLED (400)

Birth-bonds that bound me long are broken,
Now in this body in this state :
Now springs the Life the soul's great secret.
O mind that changes can create
Like thee's nor cloud nor flow'ry arbour,
And in seven worlds thy fame is great.

XVI. GRACE

From the first words of the first hymn *Thanthai Thai* தந்தை தாய் "Father, Mother' this section takes its title in the Tamil. This translation condenses those words and others into "worldly kinships." The section is given a new name. The hymns are 588-594 in N.M.

243. WORLDLY KINSHIPS (588)

What time the Teacher of the silence
Gave me His grace and made it grow
How wonderous that all worldly kinships
Should seem to me a passing show!

244. ONLY THOU (589)

I counted not my gains or losses
When first I gave myself to Thee,
For, raining bliss, O cloud grace-laden
Thou Mother-wise art e'er with me.

245. I HOLD THY HAND (590)

Thy grace is all I know, O Gracious,
The ship that takest me ashore:
The hand that me into it leadeth,
Thy hand, I hold for evermore.

246. THE THREE-FOLD VISION (591)

Mine eyes have seen Thy grace e'er present,
Thee, and me. Cast me not away
From Thee for openly thus speaking
What gladness makes my lips to say.

247. SAVE ALL (592)

O God that givest joy uncloying
And in the sphere of grace art Friend,
Mix Thou with men, call all to heaven—
Would worldly life then have an end?

---

248. IF THOU WILT (593)

O Thou that holdest all creation
Within the hollow of thy hand
Thy will Thou canst perform that makest
The smallest magnified to stand.

---

249. THE HEART COUNTS (594)

Mere words! But tears of joy, love-tremor,
To know, melt thou my stony heart,
Who by the stone-grown banyan satest,
And, honey-sweet, the Three-eyed art.

XVII. GOD REALIZED

Pettavatkēy, பெற்றவட்கே, 'to her who has given birth,' is the opening word and mnemonic title of this section in the original. Its eleven hymns are 595—605 in N. M.

250. EXPERIENCE (595)

'Tis but the mother not the barren
Knows travail-pains and pangs of birth.
God's bliss who taste, not stony-hearted,
Joy tears and tremors have on earth.

---

251. STONY SOULS (596)

" Come, Lord of bliss, O Come, our Father,"
Adoring ones thus cry to Thee.
To such Thy grace Thou givest, Mother—
With stony souls how will it be?

---

252. TO LOVE THEE MORE (597)

Indweller in me poor, unknowing,
Desire and thirst Thou only art;
Thou givest Love, 'tis not my causing.
Great one grant more within my heart.

---

253. THY FEET (598)

Before I speak my needs Thou knowest
My grief. O come again to me,
And let upon my head in blessing
The lotus of Thy fair feet be.

254. WHEN? (599)

Those feet to hold, to hug caressing,
To eyes, to heart, adoring press,
Embracing them to lose Delusion,
When wilt Thou, Lord, Thy servant bless?

---

255. DELUSION (600)

From worldly friends and fleshly kinsfolk
Cut off, and kindred made to be
To saints 'tis but Delusion hinders—
In it to be why lettest me?

---

256. DOUBTS (601)

Wealth and my willing soul and body
When I surrendered, Lord, to Thee
Thou enteredst me. Why my doubtings?
O, let Delusion cease to be.

---

257. MANNA (602)

Because by little and by little
Thou dolest out the Food of Bliss,
Cared for and fed I live like cattle;
Deluded I contentment miss.

---

258. HOME (603)

What binds me back to bonds I've broken
Of home, of wealth, of women's love?
Should not now shine for me Thy glory
Of blessings of the Home above?

259. THE VISION (604)

To make me know Thou art my knowledge
Taught in the word, by teaching preached,
Pure, Life of heaven, Eye ever present,
Beyond the Sound the Vision reached.

---

260. FORSAKE ME NOT (605)

O Voice, beyond the Voice the Vastness,
The Seeing One, the Sight, the Seen,
The Scriptures, and their Secret, the Silence,
Forsake me not: from ills all screen.

XVIII. GOD KNOWN INWARDLY

The mnemonic title in the Tamil is from the opening word *Kallàlin* கல்லாலின், 'Of the banyan tree.' The 29 hymns are 606—635 N. M. This translation does not repeat the peculiarity in the original of the last word of one hymn becoming the first of the next.

261. A SECRET (606)

Beneath the banyan shade when seated,
To Four then God Thyself to be
By symbol and by sign Thou showedst.
Upon a straw to cross the sea
Were easier than to say that secret.

---

262. GOD OF ALL CREEDS (607)

" Lo! here," " Lo! there," the creeds all clamour,
But Thou above their contests art,
And yet, to each its God, Thou comest
To dwell within the human heart,
By grace the only way of knowing.

---

263. APART FROM THEE? (608)

When closely seen, what world existeth
Apart from Thee? Apart from Thee
Is sky or fire, earth, wind or water?
Apart from Thee where should we be?
Say, Lord, whose half fair Uma hideth.

---

264. THE MIND (609)

Behind a monkey devil-driven
Like one who runs I'm made to go:
My weight of body heavy dragging,
My mind I follow even so.
Why leavest Thou me thus to sorrow?

265. THOU BECOMEST I (610)

Is there to me or good or evil?
If I the meaning could but know
How Thou in me myself becomest,
Then with the holy here below
I would be as them ever happy.

266. THY LOOK (611)

From wealth and want is framed Delusion,
Of worldliness the two-fold test.
That I may tear this snare to pieces,
And, deeds not doing, be at rest
When wilt Thou look on me, O, Blissful?

267. THY VISION (612)

I cried, "Grant me Thy grace." Thou heardest
And, hearing, hastenedst to my cries;
And, hastening, me for Thee Thou tookest.
When wilt Thou, gladdening to mine eyes,
Grant what I long for, Lord, Thy Vision?

268. GRACE OF SILENCE (613)

The present, for the past repentant,
I spend in grief, and, grieving, live.
Spouse of my soul, O, Lord of Wisdom,
When comes the day when Thou wilt give
Thy grace to me of Bliss of Silence?

269. DEATH (614)

When, like the lotus softly opening,
My ready heart opens to Thee,
O, fragrant Honey therein springing,
I long the day of death to see
Of this my lust-entangled body.

270. IF NOT FOR THEE (615)

Wert Thou another world to fashion,
Thy rule and will withdrawn from this,
Justice would fail, the worlds, the scriptures;
And Truth and Order men would miss;
The deathless die; and all we perish.

---

271. TO WHOM CAN I GO? (616)

The state where self-assertion ceaseth
O Lord, sufficeth unto me;
E'en tho' it be not Home and Heaven,
Yet would I go to none but Thee,
O, Bliss that dwellest in the Silence!

---

272. THE BONDS BROKEN (617)

What time Thy fulness, Lord, abounded,
The bonds I brake of birth and change:
Sense-knowing ceased, and light, and darkness,
And, beyond all pleasure's range
And pain's, knew nothing, me not seeing.

---

273. THE WORLDLY (618)

Of all the hosts of lives Thou madest
Is there a sinful one as I
Who know this world is false and fleeting,
Yet lose myself within that lie,
With never longings other-worldly?

---

274. TAMIL PSALMS (619)

Thy Feet with kisses gods make rosy;
The sweet-toned Tamil of the Three
Thine ears delight with psalms sweet-worded;
My words from theirs how far must be,
Feeble, O three-eyed Lord, soul's honey.

275. THY FEET (620)

The life of bliss shall I gain ever
  Who for the Lotus of Thy Feet
Long not, and loveless live in sorrow,
  O Lord that givest ever sweet
The honey of the highest wisdom?

---

276. THE SIGN (621)

The fleeting all with unfixed vision
  Beholding, and beyond to see
The meaning of the Sign of Silence
  In grace Thou, Guru, gavest me
When dawns the day of deedless freedom?

---

277. THOU LIVEST. WE LIVE (622)

We live, O Lord, because Thou livest;
  We live, Thou livest, from of old;
When Thou destroyest, Thou art nothing—
  Consistently one cannot hold—
Or as Creator Thou art allness.

---

278. STATIC (623)

To know that all the world is transient
  And in that truth abiding be,
The stable stage of wisdom reaching
  Will be the day O Lord for me
When all my sorrows Thou wilt sunder.

---

279. UNLESSENED FULNESS (624)

O Time, of Time's three-foldness Framer,
  Who from unformed unforming art,
If Thou to Thee shouldst call me, gracious,
  And fill with grace my longing heart
O Lord, Thy fulness will not lessen.

280. STONE (625)

O Flame of Bliss that brightly burneth
Ineffable above all speech,
Had I but been a stone created
Then could I be above the reach
Of birth and death and all attachments.

---

281. BODY (626)

The strong in wisdom mind-untroubled,
Because they would God-seeing be,
Ignore the body, body's senses.
While I who wisdom babble free
This fleeting body feed and cherish.

---

282. SERVICE (627)

Three-eyed, unseeing why remainest
While much in me I suffer here?
Am I not servant of Thy servants
Love-melted who to Thee are dear,
O God, Light's splendour, pure Effulgence?

---

283. AFAR (628)

The hosts of darkness Thou despoiling,
My deeds, my foes, with ceaseless strife
That followed me hast Thou far scattered,
O Light, Light's Vastness, Bliss and Life.
But now from Thee afar I languish.

---

284. GRATITUDE (629)

A path to me Thou hast appointed
Where follows not delusive mind,
My deeds undone. To Thee thanksgiving
O Bliss, O Life, what can I find
But hands adoring Thee, All-Doer!

285. THE CREEDS (630)

The creeds in conflict know in common
One only God, almighty Thee;
They differ not but as thou willest;
They roll, all rivers, to the sea,
To Thee, O, Vastness of the Silence.

---

286. SALVATION (631)

Thou madest me to all united
And then, O, marvel! madest me,
Transfigured into saving knowledge,
In stillness undistracted be,
And in that state I have salvation.

---

287. DEEDS (632)

The way of being born to suffering
Is of my working, seeking, none.
Say, Mother, by what rule and reason
The deeds, misdeeds, that I have done
As fruitage past are said to follow.

---

288. WHERE? (633)

As mother that sustaineth, tender,
Why does not grace abound to me?
When thou, O, Lord from me recedest,
What worlds are there, and where, for Thee
All-Vast, All-filler, for Thy Fulness?

---

289. MERCY (634)

O, Mother-God, Thy ways are wondrous;
Ineffable the sport, the play.
That I in deeds, taint, and delusion
Should suffer, and in suffering stay,
Is surely not, O, Lord, thy mercy.

290. THE MERCILESS (635)

Mercy who does not show, O, Mother,
Nor patience has, nor piety,
Nor knowledge, nor the grace of giving,
Shrinks from Thy saints' society,
Is Iron-hearted, steely, stony.

XIX. THE BELOVED

This section consisting of stanzas 1421 to 1450 in N.M. is known as *Ánanda Kalippu* ஆனந்தக்களிப்பு *A Revel in Bliss.* It is a ballad of spiritual experience. The chorus is given at the end. In the next section will be found a rendering more nearly literal than in this section, of the 30 verses in the syllabic arrangement of the original, the English there being chantable to the ballad tune of the Tamil. The erotic realism of the original is not fully reproduced in the translation in either section.

1. TOLD IN CONFIDENCE

291. THE LOVER (1421)

He who is first, and none afore Him,
Lord of the Silence, came to me
And in the hush of softest whispers
Sayings unsayable said He.

---

292. UNSAYABLE (1422)

How can I tell His whispered secrets?
By guile He made me be alone,
In stillness sit, with nought to hinder,
Ingladdened me and made His own.

---

293. LOVE (1423)

" Cut thyself off from all attachments,
And cling to me," said softly He.
In His embrace beyond all telling
Was bliss, and in His words, to me.

2. THE SECRET

294. TRANSFORMED (1424)

Long have I been a woe-led babbler,
Till He, my Lord, deliverance gave;
And now, Desire the demon driven,
Love holdeth me God's willing slave.

---

295. ONENESS (1425)

As I from self detached was growing
My love for Him began to grow,
And He, one day, in joyous silence
Made me with Him oneness to know.

---

296. WHO IS HE? (1426)

Caste I have lost and custom broken,
Of true delights to speak were ruth.
Sister, He is no earthly lover,
My Guardian and my God, in truth.

---

297. BLISS (1427)

Bliss, like the undammed ocean rushing,
Joy-tears down gladdened eye-lids streamed,
His melting love my being thrilling—
O! sweetness as of one who dreamed!

---

3. REALIZATION

298. A MARVEL (1428)

"What in thy thought seems truth or fancy,"
He said, "be cast away from thee!"
So saying forthwith worked a marvel—
His very self He made me be.

299. SELF-DISCERNING (1429)

" Thou art not elements or senses
But Thought, a worthier, art thou,"
He said, and in His words so loving
I joyed and joyfullest am now.

---

300. DYING TO SELF (1430)

To such as love Him He is loving,
Teacher, Bliss of the Silence, He.
Upon my head His feet He rested—
Self-knowledge came: I died to me.

---

301. DELUSION KNOWN (1431)

I know how birth and death in sequence
Are linked to me. In me I find
The chain as waking and forgetting
Forged by my most delusive mind.

---

302. DEEDS UNDONE (1432)

Lord of the mystic sign and silence
Appeared beneath the banyan tree
The bondage of my deeds undoing,
In oceaned grace deep plunging me.

---

4. SEEING

303. SIGHT OF GRAGE (1433)

" See with the eye of grace," tho' bidden,
I strove with other eyes to see;
Darkness was all I saw, thick darkness;
Nor saw the seeing one, e'en me.

304. ASSIMILATION (1434)

" Be least of thee, and then thy being
From me undifferent shall be,
And secondless," He said. That saying
Is bliss untellable to me.

---

305. HE ALONE (1435)

I neared the grace of God, its vastness,
Its stretches of unending bliss
And lo! my darkness far was driven—
I saw His beauty, only His.

---

306. TRANSITORY (1436)

They laugh at life, the wise, truth-knowing;
And we have seen with our own eyes
How frail it is, as light as sleeping—
Now, say, what profit in it lies.

---

5. CONSEQUENCES

307. HOLY DESIRES (1437)

The Bliss beyond the Sound, the Silence,
To seek He deigned to give me grace
All undeserved; unrest undoing,
His feet upon my head to place.

---

308. PEACE (1438)

Me who was atom unto fulness
He changed, the Light of Bliss, by grace
Ungoing and uncoming keepeth,
O, marvel, me in His own place!

309. THE WITNESS (1439)

Untouched by all His mighty actions,
Creation, preservation, doom,
Abideth He. Behold the Witness,
And in thy thought for Him find room.

---

310. MY PLACE (1440)

There thought is born, and there it dieth
And there 'tis re-born purer where
All states exist, and I, not seeing
A second, stand the seer, yea, there.

---

311. EVER-PRESENT (1441)

He who is Being, Bliss and Wisdom
How can we say is here or there,
Or He is one or two whose glory
All-filling gloweth everywhere?

---

6. APPEAL TO ALL

312. THE BODY (1442)

O you who know not truth, you worldlings,
This body dies—why hold it true?
What answer do you hope to render
When death's dread summons comes to you?

---

313. SOLE REALITY (1443)

To think this foul and fleeting body
Is safety is but self-deceit.
The Form alone of God the gracious
Is true to own 'tis very meet.

314. BE IN STILLNESS (1444)

Away with likes, dislikes, attachments;
Those tanglements to re-births lead.
Be still, the Lord hath said, so being
Be knowledge, and His saying heed.

---

315. AS STRANGERS AND PILGRIMS (1445)

None think, "In this flesh-land a stranger
I sojourn; yet, I seek the flame
Of lust, am singed in it to losing
My high estate, unto my shame."

---

316. WISDOM (1446)

Lest I forgetting birth's causation,
Be snared by wealth and beauty's lure
The Lord has given me His pure wisdom
To sunder bonds, bright weapon sure.

---

317. MORTIFY (1447)

The god of love gave up his body
Knowing that fires of hell are fed
By lust-enkindling eyes. The holy,
Should they not to the flesh be dead?

---

318. THE WORLD (1448)

Like sun-baked saffron is the glamour,
The Agamas and Vedas say,
Of all creation: who this saying
Heed not walk but in evil's way.

319. DUTY WITHOUT ATTACHMENT (1449)

The charms of lust have no dominion
O'er holy men, the pure in heart.
God was Janaka's goal of duty,
God's bliss his portion and his part.

---

320. THE WAY (1450)

Nor 'yea' nor 'nay' to each attachment
Say, but in God's own stillness stay;
Be knowledge, bliss to gain. God teaches
This doctrine of the holy way.

Sankara, Sankara, Sambu, Siva
Sankara, Sankara, Sankara, Sambu.

XX. THE BELOVED

This is another presenting of *A Revel in Bliss* ஆனந்தக்களிப்பு given in xix above. The verses here follow the syllabic arrangement of the original Tamil, with initial rhymes and are chantable to the ballad tune of the Tamil.

1. TOLD IN CONFIDENCE

321. THE LOVER (1421)

He who is first and afore Him no one,
Light in me luminant, Wisdom and Bliss He,
See what He said to me, sister, when He
Came as the Silent One saying his secrets.

322. UNSAYABLE (1422)

Sayings unsayable said He, as He
Seating me by His side cunningly, sister,
Laying His love on me, nought to hinder,
Thrilled me with joy, yea, by making me His own.

323. LOVE (1423)

"Cast away all that you cling to within,
Cling but to me." Sister, so said He, and I
Fast as I clung to Him, knew that—can I
Say what? Unspeakable secrets then spoke He.

2. THE SECRET

324. TRANSFORMED (1424)

Woe-ridden long had I wandered, babbling
Balefully, devil-led body I, but now
Lo! the Lord driving the demon Desire
Captive me at His feet keepeth He, sister.

---

325. ONENESS (1425)

Holding my senses in, free from longings
Daily I grew in my love for His person.
Folding me close to Him one day made He
Me with Him oneness know joyous in silence.

---

326. WHO IS HE? (1426)

Me He has robbed of my birth-mark, undone;
Freely to speak of it would be but sorrow.
He is no lover mine, human, sister,
He is my Guardian and God is He supreme.

---

327. BLISS (1427)

Bliss like the bound-bursting ocean rushing,
Tears of joy streaming down love-gladdened eyelids—
His is this marvellous doing, sister,.
Melting my soul with love, thrilling my being.

---

3. REALIZATION

328. A MARVEL (1428)

"Real, unreal, whatever in thought
Hitherto hath thy heart holden most firmly
Be all away from Thee," said He, sister.
Saying so, Himself He made me be—marvel!

329. SELF-DISCERNING (1429)

" Earthy, nor elemental art thou, nor yet
Organs, nor innermost senses art Thou—
Worthier, pondering thought art. Reflect."
Blissfully spake the Lord, in His love, sister.

---

330. DYING TO SELF (1430)

Grace-giver, Lord of blest silence, Teacher,
Love unto those who love Him He is truly.
Placing His feet on my head He made me
Know myself. Knowing me died I then to me.

---

331. DELUSION DISCOVERED (1431)

" Whence came they linked to me, Birth, Death ? asked I.
Deeply considering knew I this sister,—
Sense the delusive one, bred them in me,
Guised as forgetting and waking, it working.

---

332. DEEDS UNDONE (1432)

God, for me came He not, teaching Silence,
Under the banyan shade, undoing my deeds,
Lord of the mystical mute-show sister,
Plunging me in His grace, deep in its ocean ?

---

4. SEEING

333. SIGHT OF GRACE (1433)

" See with the sight of grace," said He, but I
Sought to see with my sense, singly and apart.
Me even saw not I the seer ; darkness,
Darkness was all I saw. Why was it, sister ?

334. ASSIMILATION (1434)

Lest I deem Him from me distinct, said He,
"Secondless, undifferent, be." And from that
Best of all sayings, most blissful, sister,
O! what untellable rapture sprung in me!

---

335. HE ALONE (1435)

Where in pure infinite whiteness stretches
Siva-land's sweep of bliss boundless I drew nigh;
Tares of my darkness uprooted I saw;
Nought but the Lord I saw high in His splendour.

---

336. TRANSITORY (1436)

They who see laugh at this world-life, sister;
Have we not seen it, with our own eyes, passing?
Say is there meed in it, merit, or good,
Good in what goeth away as a sleeping?

---

5. CONSEQUENCES

337. HOLY DESIRES (1437)

Me who knew nought of grace made He seeker
Of Bliss beyond the Sound lying, the Silence,
He the most mighty One unrest undid
On my head laying His holy feet, sister.

---

338. PEACE (1438)

Light of bliss beaming upon me changed me
Atom of atom to fulness by His grace;
Right me He keepeth uncoming, ungoing,
Yea, in peace stable so wondrously, sister.

339. THE WITNESS (1439)

Much He works, mighty One, His acts countless
Making, maintaining, and marring, yet do they
Touch Him not sesamum seed-small even—
Him the true Witness O worthily adore.

---

340. MY PLACE (1440)

There is the birth and beginning of thought
In Him it dies to be re-born but purer
Where all the states exist, yea, there I am
The seer not seeing a second there I stand.

---

341. EVER-PRESENT (1441)

Being sole, Bliss is He wisdom, and lo!
All-filling gloweth the glory of our God.
Seeing this, can we then of Him declare
"Here" or "There," postulate oneness or twoness?

---

6. APPEAL TO ALL

342. THE BODY (1442)

Know ye not this body, dying, decays,
Worldlings who cling to it holding it as true?
Lo! ye of all men surely are foolish—
Can ye to death's demands render an answer?

---

343. REALITY (1443)

None so deluded as we are if we
Fancy this filth-ridden body is real;
Unsafe the safety that seek we in it;
Only the Form of the Gracious One is true.

344. BE IN STILLNESS (1444)

Let be all like and all dislike, since these
Tanglements tend but to births and to re-births.
Get to the state of the stillness He taught,
He, the Lord, and in it be thou knowledge.

---

345. AS STRANGERS AND PILGRIMS (1445)

None understandeth, and no one thinketh,
"Lo! in this alien flesh-land I sojourn,
Unknown, a stranger entangled and singed
In the flame of the flesh, forfeiting my meed."

---

346. WISDOM (1446)

Lest I forgetting the cause of re-births,
Or by the lure of love or riches be lost,
Best of all weapons, true wisdom, gives He,
Wherewith assunder to smite that great danger.

---

347. MORTIFY (1447)

Hell-fire to fulness their flesh-life feedeth
Whose days in beauty's bewilderments are lost.
Well did the god of love give up wisely
His body. Should not the knowing ones do so?

---

348. THE WORLD (1448)

Vedas and Agamas agree saying,
Like as the glamour of sun-lustred saffron,
Made but to dazzle, are all things that are.
Evil ones know not this; do they know, sister?

349. DUTY WITHOUT ATTACHMENT. (1449)

Evil allurements of love and beauty
Cling not to those that are cleanly in their hearts.
See in King Janaka goodly witness—
Gained He not God-wardly to joy endless?

---

350. THE WAY (1450)

'Yea' and 'Nay', contrasts, do these exist?
Seeker of saving Bliss stand but still and see
Way of the knowing one, knowledge be thou—
Goal of the Vedas, God, teacheth this, sister.

(*Chorus*) *Sankara, Sankara, Sambu, Siva*
Sankara, Sankara, Sankara, Sambu!

XXI. HERE AND THERE

Portions and whole hymns from different sections of the Tamil are grouped here under the above heading. The first translated is a whole hymn in the section entitled in Tamil உடல் பொய்யுறவு, *Udalpoyuravu.* The second is a portion of what is translated in section xviii above, and numbered 279, which is 624 in N.M. The next is a part of what is 2 in section 1, above. The fourth, a part of the fifth which is the whole of 60 in N.M. The last in this miscellaneous collection is the opening hymn of the section entitled in the Tamil *Panmalai*, பன்மாலை, "Garlands."

351. THE GURU (541)

He is the Guru who granted me grace to gain
 Good for the life that is, good for the life to be,
Being most worthy to show me true wisdom's way
 How best to be but the doer of good only;
Me He with mother-like tenderness draws to him
 And in my heart-temple dwelleth the Guru, He.

352. TIME AND FORM (624, PART OF SEC. XVIII, NO. 279 ABOVE)

 Thou art all Time,
And Time's three-foldness framest Thou
Its Past, its Future and its Now,
 Thou framest all,
Framer untouched by what Thy hand
Fashions in air, in sea, on land,
 Thou art all Form—
Thou formest seed and fruit, their laws,
Yet hast nor consequence nor cause.

353. MANY BIRTHS (2, PART OF SEC. I, NO. 2 ABOVE)

Many the lands of my birth,
Many my places on earth,
Many the names I have borne,
Many the marks I have worn,
Many my kith and my kin,
Many my bodies of sin,
All by deeds begotten, all fresh deeds begetting.

---

354. THE BEST (60, PART OF NO. 355 BELOW)

Birth follows birth,
And the tale baffles numbering.
Of births on earth
The rarest, worth remembering,
Most opportune, is this the present
Which missed this chance of grace is misspent.

---

355. THE BEST OF BIRTHS (60)

Of births and bodies without number
This present human is the best.
This missed, who knows what I may suffer
In births to be, and go unblest?
While in this birth and in this body
My spirit's shelter, halting place,
'Tis best that I in joy be blended
With bliss that from the sky of grace
A cloud with bounty laden raineth
Beatitude. Before the day
When this my body's frame and fashion,
Belike a show, shall pass away,
I pray that by the grace of Sakti
The blessedness may here be mine
To drink the mystic moon-drawn Soma,
Incessant drink the draught divine,
Ye holy ones who have the wisdom
That holds in balanced harmony
Vedanta and Siddhanta teaching
And finds in two oneness to be!

356. GARLANDS (175)

Of flowers many, flowers rare,
Are garlands woven, garlands fair,
But these, Thy holy ones declare,
Delight not Thee.

Delight Thee more the garlands strung
Of syllables of praises sung
By those who sing with heart and tongue
Of piety.

Self-knowers they who so can sing.
Unlearned I weave many a string
Of pearls of tears, and Lord I bring,
Love melting me,

Word-garlands woven for Thy praise.
Call me, Need-Knower, by Thy grace,
That praising Thee I all my days,
May with Thee be.

XXII. LONGINGS

Twenty-three couplets are chosen to represent the section consisting of 226 and entitled in Tamil *Enndll Kanni*, எந்நாட்கண்ணி, a title taken from the last words எந்நாளோ of each couplet. The last words mean, "When ?' and are rendered here "When will it be ?" and "When comes the day ?" "Oh for that day !' "When dawns the day ?" and once, "When will it come ?" The couplets express deep longings. This section,—two lines of Tamil forming in translation five lines—is headed "Longings." The whole section in N.M. is 1083-1314.

357. HERE IS GRIEF (1177)

The longer here we linger
'Tis only grief we gain,
There is a heavenly City
Where we shall have no pain—
When will it be ?

358. ALL IS VANITY (1178)

Here all is false and fleeting
This land of vanity.
There is a land of vision
Where grace our lot shall be—
Oh ! for that day !

359. THE SKY-WIDE SEA (1179)

Nowhere begins its vastness,
Nor ends the sky-wide sea.
To reach that sea most spotless
Of grace, and in it be,
When comes the day ?

360. STREAM OF GRACE. (1180)

There is a stream whose waters
Of grace run everywhere,
I fain would wash my body
In it that river rare—
When will it be?

---

361. THE MOUNT OF GOD (1181)

"A place of mystic secrets,"
The books bewildered cry.
I long to climb that holy
Mountain of God most high—
When will it be?

---

362. REFRESHING RAIN (1182)

The fire of all my longings
Of mind is burning pain.
I pray for grace of quenching,
God's own refreshing rain—
When will it come?

---

363. THE CITY OF GLORY (1183)

Nor sun, nor moon there shineth,
Nor star where God is Light:
I long to reach that City
Of glory, heavenly bright—
When will it be?

---

364. HEAVENLY WATERS (1187)

At the feet of God moonbeams
Unceasing brightness give.
I thirst for heavenly waters,
And unreborn to live—
When will it be?

365. FROM THE WORLD (1188)

The world, awake and weary,
In cares, unresting keeps me.
O, in the soothing slumber
Of grace, asleep to be,
When comes the day?

---

366. FROM BIRTH-BONDS (1189)

The heat of birth-bonds burneth.
I long to reach that place
Where at the feet of God is
The shadow of His grace—
When will it be?

---

367. FROM SORROW (1190)

Dark is the sea of sorrow,
It spreads behind, before:
I long to cross its waters,
And reach the heavenly shore—
When will it be?

---

368. SWEET WATERS (1215)

The pure in heart have vision
Of Bliss the boundless sea!
I long for its sweet waters
And therein merged to be,—
Oh! for that day!

---

369. AS THE LOTUS (1228)

As laughs with joy the lotus
Before the rising sun,
By grace shall I be gladdened
Grace of the Holy One—
When will it be?

370. AS THE PEACOCK (1229)

At sight of clouds the peacock
In dance of pleasure reels.
To see the heavenly Dancer
My heart high gladness feels—
Oh! for that day!

---

371. AS THE NIGHTINGALE (1230)

For mellow light of moonbeams
As longs the nightingale,
Sun in the soul arisen,
Thy heavenly light to hail,
When comes the day?

---

372. ONE WILL (1232)

To Him the heavenly Dancer,
Myself, my all to give,
My will to His surrendered,
His willing slave to live,
When comes the day?

---

373. COME TO ME (1234)

O God whom gods and devas,
For glory cannot see,
To cry with love and longing
"O come, O come to me,"
When dawns the day?

---

374. ALL-DOER (1235)

To think that all my actions,
Have Thee, O God, for goal,
So thinking, for all doings,
Invoke Thee in the soul,
When comes the day?

375. JOY (1238)

As breaks its bounds the ocean,
So ecstacy to flow
In melting tears, and thrilling
Rapture of soul to know,
When comes the day?

376. FLAME ON CAMPHOR (1278)

As burns a flame on camphor
Unquenched of any wind,
Oneness of soul, unsinning,
With God by grace to find,
When comes the day?

377. LAMPLIGHT IN SUNLIGHT (1280)

Evil to God's pure presence
Goes not. Oh! there to be,
As light of lamp by sunlight,
His love absorbing me,
When comes the day?

378. MILK IN WATER (1293)

He has nor up nor under,
Beginning nor an end.
Mingled, as milk in water,
In Him in bliss to blend,
When dawns the day?

379. AT LAST (1279)

To rest beneath the shadow
Of God's own feet of gold,
The God unseen of mortals,
Marvel of grace untold,
When dawns the day?

Notes.

The following annotations are numbered, and the passage, word or phrase annotated is indicated by reference to the page of this book and to the numbering of the English rendering of the psalms. The system of reference indicated at page 1 above is retained, that is, the numbering refers to the English, and the Tamil original (especially where not translated for inclusion in this book) is referred to as N.M. Thus No. 3 = the English rendering in the continuous left-hand numbering. N.M. 570 = (in these notes) the verse so numbered in the Tamil original in N.M. edition (see page 1 and Introduction, *ad. fin.*). In the footnotes the figures in the *Tamil* references are to stanzas, except where page is expressly indicated as in the case of annotated editions.

1. PLACE. (Page 3, No. 1).

The Tamil of 'Place has no power . . . . delimit' literally means 'Being neither here nor there.' See No. 3 (at page 4) where the first four lines are a paraphrase of this idea, and compare with it No. 341 at page 111. The expression 'Nor here nor there' has a deeper sense than that of mere omnipresence of God, and that is brought out by the poet in N.M. No. 524, "Abide in the two-less state and thou shalt realize Sivam, and think not of God as here or there." To the man who is willing to see *God* only everywhere, the two-less state (see *Introduction*, part v) is natural. The surface sense, however, that is, of God's omnipresence, is obviously intended in the hymn under comment to be emphasized, particularly by the words translated "*all-filling* splendour." There is a great deal in the saying of the Jewish Rabbis, "God is not in place, but place is in God."[1] In speaking of God realized in the soul, S. Augustine ignores space-thoughts of God when he says, "Where did I find Thee that I might learn Thee, but in Thee above me? Place there is none; but we go backward and forward, and there is no place."[2] It has been remarked that the *Confessions* is full of the noblest expressions as to the non-spatial character of God, of the soul's dispositions, and of the relation between God

[1] Quoted in Farrar's *Lives of the Fathers*, ii. 471.

[2] *Confessions*, x. 26.

and the soul.[1] Eckhart, with a strong monistic trend in his thoughts of Deity, non-spatially and non-temporally says, "Reason severs us from *here* and *now* . . . *Here* is indeed a small space . . . . but it must go if I am to see God."[2] The conception of Deity in terms of space, as immanent and yet transcendent as in the case of S. Tayumanavar, is well illustrated by the philosophical biographer of S. Catherine of Genoa :

> These three categories of within and inward, outside and outward, above and upward, position and movement can lead and do actually lead in Catherine's case to two separate lines of thought and feeling......the Negative [God's transcendence]......the Positive [God's immanence]......Those experiences of God's presence as apparently, in a special manner within us, and without us, above us, also lead by means of another connection of ideas......to a positive result. For those experiences can lead us to dwell, not upon the difference of the 'places', but upon the apparent fact that He is in a 'place' of some sort, in space, somewhere, the exact point of which is still to find; and, by thus bringing home to the mind this underlying paradox of the whole position they can help to make the soul shrink away from this false clarity, and to fall back upon the deep, dim, true view of God as existing, for our apprehension, in certain states of soul alone, states which have all along been symbolized for us by these different "places" and "positions." And thus what before was a paradox and mystery *qua* space, because at the same time within and without and because not found by the soul "within" unless through getting "without" itself, becomes now a paradox and mystery *qua* state because the soul at one and the same time attains to its own happiness and loses it, indeed attains happiness by deliberately sacrificing it. And thus we come to the great central secret of all life and love, revealed to us in its fulness in the divine paradox of our Lord's life and teaching......If God be in a place, we cannot well conceive of Him as other than outside of and above the soul, which itself, even God being in a place, will be in a place also...... And then that "place" in which God was pictured as being, is found to be a state, a disposition of the soul......And God being thus not without nor indeed in space at all, she [S. Catherine] can love Him everywhere, indeed the *what* she is now constitutes the *where* she is.[3]

There is thus the possibility of a 'place' conception of God as well as of a 'state' conception of God. In the writings of most mystics the

---

[1] Baron von Hügel's *Eternal Life*, 87, 88. Among editions of the *Confessions* may be mentioned Pusey's, Arthur Symons's, the volume in the series of Ancient and Modern Library of Theological Literature, and Pilkington's, all in English. The two volumes in the Loeb Classical Library series contain the Latin also. Pilkington's (T. and T. Clark) has copious notes. Mention must also be made of Bigg's edition also that of Marcus Dods.

[2] Translated in *Eternal Life*, 115.

[3] Baron F. von Hügel in *The Mystical Element of Religion*, i. 276—279 The two volumes are a work of immense indispensability to the student of mysticism.

stress is sometimes on one and sometimes on the other. In S. Táyumánavar, what is in S. Catherine a 'state' idea is given prominence in the thought of the indwelling God. The Bible is clear as to the omnipresence of Deity, "Whither shall I go from Thy spirit? Whither shall I flee from Thy presence?"[1] On the 'place' and position idea we may note Solomon's words, "But will God indeed dwell on the earth? Behold the heaven, and the heaven of heavens cannot contain Thee; how much less this house I that have builded?"[2] God is not to be located.[3] S. Paul's words to the Athenian thinkers seem to be apt here, "The Lord of heaven and earth dwelleth not in temples made with hands ......He giveth to all life and breath and all things......He is not far from every one of us, for in Him we live, and move, and have our being."[4] The 'place' and 'state' conceptions find mention in a great Jewish utterance, "Thus saith the high and lofty One that inhabiteth eternity, whose name is Holy, 'I dwell in the high and holy place, with him also that is of a contrite and humble spirit.'"[5]

2. GRACE......WILLETH. (Page 3, No. 1).

The subject of Grace is dealt with in the *Introduction*, part vii, above. The thought of God's *willingness* to be associated with all life is represented in the Siddhanta by the idea of that aspect of Grace known as *Ichcha Sakti* which "may be defined as supreme Love desiring the welfare of all creatures."[6] "At the sight of jivas," says the English translator and commentator of the *Siddhiyar*, "weltering in sin and suffering, God's love is stirred, and He *wills* to save souls."[7] God is essentially Love, not simply loving, as a Hindu Saint[8] had well said before our poet, and long after S. John—

> That God and Love are twain,
> In ignorance do men exclaim,
> Not knowing Love is God's own Name.
> Once knowing Love and God are same,
> In Love they rest from pain.

---

[1] Ps 139:7.
[2] 1 Kings 8:27.
[3] S. John, 4:21, 23, 24.
[4] Acts, 17:24—28; See Acts, 7:48.
[5] Isaiah, 57:15.
[6] *Siddhiyar*, 3. 1. 63.
[7] Nallaswami Pillai's *Siddhiyar*, p. 159. See *Sivapragasam*, Stanzas 2, 14, 15, and the excellent notes at pp. 4, 25, 27 in Tiruvilangam's Tamil edition.
[8] Tirumular, *Tirumantram*, Stanza 270; 1 John 4:16.

It is the property of God ever to love, and so it is that the Bible postulates active Love of God in eternity. "Thou lovedest me before the foundation of the world."[1] As in Hindu thought, so in the Christian, it is rightly believed that God's love is stirred at the sight of human sin. God's solicitude for man is part of His eternal purpose of love.[2] In the *Introduction*, part vii, I have gone at length into the thesis that God's Love *willing* the salvation of souls, His *Ichcha Sakti*, is seen in the Christian conception of the Cross as the furthest limit of Love, sacrifice—" God *so* loved the world."[3]

3. LIFE, LIFE OF LIFE. (Page 3, No. 1; Page 4, No. 3).

The expression 'Life of Life', varied at times into 'Lord of Life' (N.M. 155) or 'Sense of the Senses' (N.M. 315), or 'Guardian of Life' (N.M. 378), occurs in numerous places in the writings of our poet-saint.[4] It may be rendered "Soul of Souls" as in the English translation by Mr. Nallaswami Pillai of the *Siddhiyar*.[5] A Persian mystic, Rumi, addresses God as "Soul of Soul of Soul."[6] All expressions and renderings are intended to convey an idea of the closeness of the relation of God to the human soul. The meaning is not exhausted by stating that the conception "consists in the comprehension of God as the Infinite including all finite existences, as the Immanent Absolute who progressively manifests His character in the ideals of Truth, Beauty, Righteousness and Love."[7] God is absolute Being. The ancient Hebrew conception of God as Life is indicated in the name made known to Moses, "I am That I am."[8]

---

[1] S. John 17 : 24.

[2] Eph. 1 : 4; 1 Peter, 1 : 20.

[3] S. John 3 : 16. See above, *Introduction*, Part vii.

[4] See Nos. 19, 21, 23, 25, 117, 122-130, above, for examples.

[5] The *Siddhiyar* 3. 5. 5; 3. 8. 28; 3. 9. 5; original is in each place உயிர்க்குயிர் literally 'Jiva of Jiva' or 'Life of Life.'

[6] Davis, *Persian Mystics* i. 44.

[7] Pringle Pattison in *Hibbert Journal* (1902), p. 458. "Man is not a particle of God so that the requisite number of particles of human souls will make up one God." (Nallaswami Pillai, *Bodham*, 58.)

[8] Ex. 3 : 14. On the purposeful use of "I am" by our Lord in S. John 8 : 58 see Watson's *Mysticism of S. John's Gospel*, 81, 82, and for the Ignatian inference of timelessness from S. John 8 : 58 see *Journal of Theological Studies* [1913], p. 208.

In the hand of God is the life of every living thing, and the breath of all mankind.[1] "The being of the creature is rooted in the Godhead, its Creator; its continuance is being grounded in the Godhead, its Conserver. Without the Divine Conservation and Co-operation the being and the action of the creature would cease. Thus is the life of the creature wholly in God."[2] The unnamed author[3] of a classic of Christian mysticism well observes, "God is the Being of all that are, and the life of all that live, and the wisdom of the wise, for all things have their being more truly in God than in themselves, and also their power, life, knowledge and the rest, for, if it were not so, God will not be all-good." S. Augustine in addressing himself states the same truth, "Now, to thee I speak, O my soul, thou art my better part; for thou quickenest the mass of my body, giving it life, what nobody can give to a body; but thy God is even unto thee the Life of thy life."[4] In the great Gospel utterances all this and more are contained: "As the Father hath life in Himself, so hath He given the Son to have life in Himself. . . . . I am come that they might have life, and that they might have it more abundantly."[5] The experience of Christian and non-Christian mysticism is in accord with the realization of the Hebrew poet who owned, "With Thee is the fountain of life."[6] The devotional context in which poet-saints and mystics speak of God as Life of Life, Soul of Soul, lifts the conception above the plane of a pure academic assertion. It assumes the nature of a discovery in spiritual realization. "Life is more than physical existence; it is fellowship with the Unseen. Since God alone possesses life in the highest sense, fellowship with Him is the one condition on which man can obtain it."[7] Fellowship with God issues in practical conduct.[8]

---

[1] Job 12: 10.

[2] Watkin, *Philosophy of Mysticism*, 36; see Ruysbroeck, *Spiritual Marriage*, ii. ch. 37.

[3] *Theologia Germanica*, 'written in the 14th century by a priest and warden in the house of the Teutonic Order at Frankfort, and nothing more than this is known about its author. His very name has perished.' (Inge, *Faith and Knowledge*, 263). The passage quoted in the text, above, is from Miss Winkworth's translation, p. 188.

[4] *Confessions*, x, 6.

[5] S. John 5: 26; 10: 10.

[6] Ps. 36: 9.

[7] Scott, *Fourth Gospel*, 235.

[8] I John 5: 7.

4. NOR BY SPEECH SEARCHABLE. (Page 3, No. 1).

Language is a poor vehicle to convey any adequate idea of God. In many places our poet-saint acknowledges that God is above the reach of words.[1] It has been well remarked by a modern thinker[2] commenting on Eckhart's distinction between *God* and the *Godhead*:

> No word that voices distinctions or characteristics, then, may be spoken of the Godhead............The reader who finds himself somewhat dazed in this height of speculation would run up into the same difficulty himself if he should undertake strenuously to think out what is involved in the word *Infinite* which he, without giving it much thought, applies to God. He supposes he glorifies God by calling Him 'infinite' or 'absolute,' but in doing it he has, whether he realizes it or not, raised Him above 'knowledge' and has 'reduced' Him to an empty indeterminate abstraction which for thought is as truly 'nothing' as it is 'everything.' "Infinite-Being" is the emptiest of all conceptions. It is, however, a method of thought by no means confined to ancient mystics......We avoid many difficulties because we do not feel the necessity of universalizing our concepts. We rest satisfied with bare words and save ourselves a deal of trouble by not asking the further questions which are involved in our words about God.

To speak worthily of God, says S. Basil the Great, one must transcend all one's senses, all times, all space, the universe, and angelic natures and contemplate the 'Ineffable.'[3] An old Upanishad, belonging to the early post-Vedic age, describes Deity in a series of negations, "He is not this," "He is not this," quite in contrast to the Rig-Vedic knowledge of God by affirmatives.[4] Dean Inge considers that the eliminatory and negative way of approach to descriptions of God is neither Greek nor Christian but Indian.[5] We may infer from its presence in mediæval mystical thought that it had travelled from the East into Europe and found acceptance there. It has been much criticized as the way of reaching God "with empty hands" and "a deification of the word 'not'"[6] An exponent of the mysticism of S. John of the Cross defines and justifies the negative method:

---

1 *E.g.* in Nos. 22, 24, 33, 41, 280, above.

2 Dr. Rufus M. Jones, *Studies in Mystical Religion*, 226, 227.

3 The whole passage from his homily on Faith is translated in Underhill's *Mystic Way*, 293, 294.

4 *Brihad Upanishad*, 3. 9. 26; 4. 4. 22; 3. 8. 8; 2. 3. 6.

5 *Christian Mysticism*, 111.

6 Herman, *Meaning and Value of Mysticism*, 298, quoting Edward Caird's *Evolution of Theology in the Greek Philosophers*, ii. 215, and Watson's *Interpretation of Religious Experience*, i. 73. Dean Inge (*op. cit.* 112) refers to Sir William Hamilton's *Discussion*, p. 21, on the hypostatising of the zero.

We know that all that is positive being in the creature is in Him—but in another way—without the limitation of the creature and therefore with an infinite transcendence . . . The negative way is the complement of the other. God *is* all the positivity of creatures, *is not* their essential negativity. *Thus this negative way is really ultra-positive—it denies nothing of God, except limitation which is non-entity. This point cannot be urged too strongly since the failure to understand it is the root of all the attacks on mysticism, alike its theory and its practice.*[1]

So, if we concede that the negative method "consists in denying of God any attribute or perfection whatsoever, *to whose knowledge we can attain*", and allow that the language of absolute negation "is employed to bring home the fact that the distance between our limited concepts—even the highest and most spiritual—and the unlimited being of God is *infinite,*"[2] then, we shall be able to appreciate the value of many statements which, mostly torn from their contexts, seem extravagantly negative: Despite all the negations in which mystics revel they do not disguise their spiritual convictions based upon spiritual acquaintance, friendship, intimacy, love. S. Augustine's love bubbles up through his very questionings, "Where art Thou, then my God? . . . What can I say, my God, my life, my holy joy? Or what can any say who speaks of Thee?"[3] The God formally unknowable is withal the God of personal attachment and adoration.[4] So Richard Rolle rejoices in his agnosticism:

There is none other God but He that none may know, which may not be known . . . He only is my God of whom none can one word say, nor all they of Paradise one only point attain nor understand, for all the knowing that they may have of Him.[5]

S. Tayumanavar, like all the great mystics of the world, realized that where knowledge fails love succeeds, and that though the mind cannot measure, nor speech reach the heights [p. 4, No. 3 (5)], where the Eternal One is, yet, out of the abundance of personal sensing of God, he hesitates not to call God, Father and Mother (p. 48, and No. 114), Need-Knower and Kinsman.[6] In his *Confessions* we see

---

[1] Watkin, *Philosophy of Mysticism*, 61, 62, (italics his).

[2] Watkin, (*op. cit.* 62). Erigena explains; (see Inge, *Christian Mysticism*, 135, note) affirmations about God are made *non proprie sed translative* and all negations *non translative sed proprie.*

[3] *Confessions*, i, 4. See eliminatory epithets in S. Tayumanavar, *e.g.*, N.M. 33.

[4] See Herman, *Meaning and Value of Mysticism*, 299, on this line of thought.

[5] *Mirror of Simple Souls*, ch. iii.

[6] See above p. 116, and N.M. No. 361. See *Rig Veda*, 1-10-6; 1-15-5; 1-30-7; 1-139-9; 2-29-4; 3-53-5; 6-29-1.

S. Augustine's setting forth of the love of his soul for God in terms of even passionate tenderness,[1] and yet, he is the same man whose thoughts[2] of God run in these lines:

> God is above all that can be said of Him. We must not even call Him ineffable.[3] He is best described in silence, best known by nescience, best described by negatives.

The principle of negation as applicable to human efforts at knowing God may be stated best in the words of Richard Hooker:

> Dangerous it were for the feeble brain of man to wade far into the doings of the Most High; whom although to know be life, and joy to make mention of His name; yet our soundest knowledge is to know that we know Him not as indeed He is, neither can know Him; and our safest eloquence concerning Him is our silence, when we confess without confession that His glory is inexplicable, His greatness above our reach.[4]

God is unsearchable, and also "the Quest beyond all seeking found," (p. 27, No. 45).

5. Claim and the Contest of all Creeds, (Page 3. No. 1).

In our poet's utterances the creeds are represented as bewildered;[5] that God is above their contests;[6] that God causes the very differences in the creeds[7] and that in all religions it is the One God who is worshipped.[8] That those who worship other gods with sufficient faith and sincerity worship the One is also taught in the *Bhagavad Gita.*[9] In S. Tayumanavar, while we find verses suggestive of immense tolerance and catholicity as to different creeds, we also find utterances in which Saivism, that is, the Siddhanta, is considered *the* religion, in the midst of "alien" faiths. It is *the* Faith,[10] known also as Vaidika Saivism;[11]

---

[1] Take for instance the beautiful passage in *Conf.*, x, 5, beginning, "What do I love when I love Thee?"

[2] Summarised in Inge's *Christian Mysticim*, 128, Aug. *De Trin*, vii. 47; *De Doct Christ*, i. 5.5., *Serm*, 52, 16; *De Civit. Dei*, ix, 16; *Contra Adiam. Man.* ii; *De Ord.* ii, 16, 44, 18, 47. *In Ps.* 85, 12.

[3] Following Basilides. See Herman, *Op. Cit.* 298.

[4] *Ecclesiastical Polity*, First Book, ii, 2. See Job 11: 7, Eccl. 3: 11; Ps. 145: 3; Is. 40: 28; 55: 8; 1 Cor. 2: 1.

[5] *E.g.* See Nos. 2, 52 above, and N.M. 135, 280, 386, 394, 396, 640.

[6] *E.g.* See Nos. 1, 262, and N.M. 140, 182, 220.

[7] *E.g.* See above Nos. 146, 285, and N.M. 290.

[8] *E.g.* See above No. 44, and N.M. 69, 1088, 1103, 1210, 1211.

[9] *E.g.* vii. 21, ix. 23. See same in *Siddhiyar*, 3. 2. 24.

[10] See N.M. 554.

[11] N.M. 1105, 474, 479.

excludes other religions,[1] is the religion of the elect,[2] and yet includes in it al' other religions.[3] In ascribing supremacy and universality to Saivism, that is, the Siddhanta, our poet follows the *Siddhiyar* which lays down:

> Religions and postulates and text-books are various and conflict one with the other. It is asked which is the true religion, which the true postulate and which the true book. That is the true religion, postulate and book, which, not conflicting with this or that, comprises reasonably everything within its folds. Hence all these are comprised by the Vedas and Saivagams. And these two are imbedded under the sacred feet of Hara.[4]

It is a favourite thought in S. Tayumanavar that all the religions are like so many rivers, and God the great ocean into which they all run and are swallowed up.[5] By another figure God is the cloud watering the creeds.[6]

6. Bliss. (Page 3, No. 1.)

See above, *Introduction*, part iv on the poet's conception of God.

7. Day......Night. (Page 3, No. 1).

In the English there is added to the translation the explanatory words, 'remembering, forgetting' a sense found expressed in other places.[7] Sometimes all four terms, 'day, night, remembering, forgetting' occur together.[8] Usually, however, the occurrence of 'day, night' without the explanatory pair 'remembering, forgetting' is more frequent in this poet.[9] Associated with 'night and day,' 'forgetting, remembering,' is the pair, 'going, coming'.[10] According to the Saiva Siddhanta it is one of the limitations to which the soul is subjected by its deeds to be born in bodies which die, and to be re-born, and this undergoing of birth, deaths, re-births, is known as 'coming, going'.[11] It is 'remembering, forgetting' 'day, night.' God, in

---

[1] See above, Nos. 228, 230. See *Introduction*, part ii.

[2] See N.M. 141, 142.

[3] N.M. 143, see Nalla. *Studies in Saiva Siddhanta*, p. 360.

[4] 3, 3, 14. See 3, 8, 16 on the glory of the Siddhanta. Hara is Siva.

[5] See N.M. 134, 411, 578, 630 for example.

[6] See N.M. 585. See above, *Introduction* part ii on 'warring religions.'

[7] *E.g.* N.M. 336 where the special terms [illegible], [illegible], (*Sakala Kēvala*) occur.

[8] *E.g.* N.M. 395.

[9] See N.M. 31, 44, 113, 187, 190, 702, 780.

[10] For examples of the last see above Nos. 121, 180 (pp. 53, 74) and N.M. 29, 33, 35, 85, 109, 192, 314, 570, 1198.

[11] *Sivapragasam*, 19.

the Saiva Siddhanta philosophy, is not subject to this limitation.[1] He is "the Blessed One whom bonds bind not, and to whom is not any coming, or any going"[2] the "expanse of Bliss where is nor night, nor day"[3] and the One "to whom is nor night, nor day, nor going, nor coming, nor in, nor out."[4] Following this line of thought one rightly reaches the idea that God is not conditioned by time, or space. What Plotinus says in a different context is apposite here, "The One is everywhere and nowhere."[5] Delacroix is thus quoted as commenting on Eckhart's ideas of God:

> In God progress and regress, coming and returning, are closely united; they are at bottom one and the same act, the act by which God penetrates Himself and finds Himself wholly in Himself. Thus Divine movement is at bottom repose. Becoming is eternal; that is to say, its change alters nothing in eternity. God is immobile in Himself and so abides.[6]

God is not fettered by the incidents of time. God possesses, it has been well said, the splendour of ever-tarrying eternity which is incomparable with never-tarrying times, since in it nothing passes, but the content of everything abides simply present.[7] "Thy years neither come nor go...All thy years abide together......Thy years are but one day, and this thy to-day is not every day but to-day. This Thy to-day is eternity."[8]

8. In the Still Sweep of His Silence. (Page 3, No. 1).

The original context of this expression may be literally rendered, 'Let us consider all that we see as the form of the vastness of His Silence.' An early translator[9] gives, 'All that we see is His form; let us think of Him as He is revealed in the form of Silence.' Terser

---

[1] See Nallaswami Pillai's *Bodham*, p. 88; *Siddhiyar*, p. 170; and his *Studies* pp. 83, 85, 242, 299. On the Incarnation of our Lord, and the Saiva idea, see above *Introduction*, part vii.

[2] *Tiruvachagam* i. Line 77, *cf.* S. Tayumanavar (N.M. 29), போக்கு வரவற்ற பொருளே.

[3] *Tiruvuntiar*, 20.

[4] *Kanthar Alangaram*. See *Tirumantram* 1528, and S. Pattanattar's *Kailayam* 3.

[5] *Enneads*, 5.5.8.

[6] Inge's *Philos. of Plotinus*, ii. pp, 72. 73.

[7] Hügel, *Myst. El. of Religion*, ii, p. 248.

[8] Aug. *Confessions* xi, 13, 24. *In Ps.* 90. *cf.* 2 Pet. 3 8 Heb, 13 8. See Hügel's *Eternal Life*, 383; Taylor's *Select Works of Plotinus*, 135; Inge's *Phil. of Plotinus* ii, 97-103, and *Christian Mysticism* 52; Alexander's *Spinoza and Time*, ch. v. "All time is nothing more than a single night" (Plato. *Apology* 40-E).

[9] Rev. G. E. Phillips in *The Madras Christian College Magazine*, xxvii, 505.

is the Rev. G. Mackenzie Cobham's rendering, 'The Silent, the soul of all we gaze on'[1] In *Prabuddha Bharata*[2] the equivalent is 'The expanse of Peace that circles all.' In the present writer's 'imaged in all we see in the still sweep of His silence', varied at page 4 into, 'who has to all made known, in the still sweep of His silence, the way', the word 'imaged' is intended to cover the conception of the Tamil, that God is 'knowable' in the உரு, 'form,' which the poet says is manifested in all that is seen. The poet, elsewhere, speaks of the silence of "the formless Form" as the way of life,[3] and God is "of the great silence the Treasure,"[4] the "Silence told not in height or depth known not or otherwhere;"[5] the "Form of the silent, saving call;"[6] "the seat of Silence;"[7] "beyond the sound the Vision;"[8] the "Voice, beyond the Voice the Vastness......... the Silence;"[9] and "the Bourne of the Silence of Saints."[10] We have next the poet's references to the humanly manifested God as the "Guru of the Silence", "the Silent Teacher."[11]

The conception of Deity in terms of silence finds indication in early Upanishadic philosophy:

> The Sound-Brahma is the Syllable *Om*. That which is its acme is tranquil, soundless, fearless, sorrowless, blissful, satisfied, steadfast, immovable, immortal, unshaken, enduring, named Vishnu [the Pervader].[12]

Perhaps from the East, or from some source common to both East and West, the idea of God as silence finds expression in Christian writings in the West.

> In the language of early and mediæval devotion *The Silence* became even a name of God, the First Person of the Blessed Trinity. The Eternal Word was said to be generated by the Eternal Silence. "Within the Silence alone (that is within the Divine Nature) may God be searched into. If the Angels had come to search into God, they had met the Silence, and been restrained. Blessed is he that hath learnt that the seraph crieth, 'Holy,' and is still. Blessed is he that hath been a mariner for his faith, and from the storms of controversy hath fled into the port of Silence."[13]

---

1 *Madras Christian College Magazine*, July 1884.
2 June 1913, by A.K.
3 Above, No. 138.
4 Above, No. 2.
5 Above, No. 11.
6 Above, No. 45.
7 Above, No. 234.
8 Above, No. 259.
9 Above, No. 260.
10 Above, No. 24.
11 See above, *Introduction* part vii, where principal passages are noted.
12 *Maitri Upanishad*, 6, 23.
13 Father Congreve's preface, p. xviii, to Hepher's *The Fruits of Silence*, quoting S. Ephraim, *R.* iii, 4.

S. Ignatius, an Apostolic Father, may have been aware of this name of God and had it in mind when he wrote, "There is one God, who manifested Himself through Jesus Christ His Son, who is His Word proceeding from Silence." [1] The "Alone" of Plotinus [2] is analogous to the Gnostic conception of Him who is the Abyss and whose consort is Silence and Grace.[3] "The Plotinian God is, in the mystic's phrase, the Silence, the final stillness beyond all the sound and fury of the world of particular things. But the silence and stillness are positive, are more than absence of noise and change, though we are able only to describe them as such." [4] Ruysbrœck thinks of God as

> the omnipotent and ever-active Creator of all things, an immeasurable Flame of Love perpetually breathing forth His energetic Life in new births of being and new floods of grace, and drawing in again all creatures to Himself. Yet this statement defines, not His being, but one manifestation of His being. When the soul pierces beyond this 'fruitful' nature to His 'simple' essence—and simple is here......to be understood in its primal meaning of 'synthetic'—He is that absolute and abiding Reality which seems to man Eternal Rest, the 'Deep Quiet of the Godhead' the 'Abyss' the 'Dim Silence'; and which we can taste indeed but never know.[5]

With the thought of the "form of silence" may be compared the suggestive observation made in a different context:

> Music is the silence of heaven, the old saying tells us, and colour is its speech.........Can silence have a colour?
>
> Then you mean that silence is coloured by its surroundings? Is that the idea of the colour of silence? Partly, but not altogether .... The material becomes insensibly tinged and dyed with the spiritual; the spiritual functions through the material, until they blend in one inseparable Reality .... Blue is the creative silence in the world of thought .... Gold is the silence of conquest, of victory, of harvest and completed life .... Green is the silence of youth ....of strength, of energy, of vigour .... The perfect silence is the white silence of completed praise.[6]

On the mystical practice of silence see below.

9. In Many Bodiments to be Born. (Page 3, No. 2).

On births and re-births, see above, *Introduction*, part vi.

---

[1] *Epistle to the Magnesians*, 8 : 2.

[2] *Enneads*, 5.1.6.

[3] Legge, *Forerunners and Rivals of Christianity*, ii. 96, 98. On the thought of *Grace* as consort in Saivism see above, *Introduction*, part vii.

[4] Fuller, *Problem of Evil in Plotinus*, 61, 62.

[5] Underhill's *Ruysbroeck*, 60.

[6] L. V. Hodgkin in *The Fellowship of Silence*, 213, 219.

10. GRACE. (No. 2, page 4).

On *Sakti* which prompts the soul to good impulses, see above, *Introduction*, part vii, and above, page 124.

11. *Turiya*. (No. 2, page 4).

This is the highest state of existence, and it is postulated as peculiar to Deity. It is approachable by the soul. On this see below note on *Turiya* to No. 19.

12. TRANSCENDANT GOD. (No. 2, page 4).

See above, *Introduction*, part iv. It is the word கடவுள் of the original which is here rendered, 'Trancendant……liveth Lord.' The Tamil word denotes that Deity is above the numerous limitations named in the text, and above *all* limitations.[1] The ordinary meaning of கடவுள், 'God' is also retained in the English rendering.

13. MANY-NAMED. (No. 2. page 4).

See above, *Introduction* part iv, on some of the names given to Deity in the Hindu sacred books.

14. BEING, BLISS, WISDOM. (No. 2, page 4).

The attributes 'ineffable' and 'endless' go with 'Being, Bliss Wisdom.' God is unending and eternal Being, and Bliss and Wisdom. The word rendered 'Being' is பதம் (*padam*). See below, note on *Sat-Chit-Ananda*.

15. PRACTICELESS, INADEPT. (No. 4, p. 5).

The Upanishadic precept for effecting union with the One is this: restraint of the breath, withdrawal of the senses, meditation, concentration, contemplation, absorption.[2] By restraining voice, mind and breath one sees Brahma through contemplation.[3] The poet says in the verse under comment that he is inadept in the art suppressing thought and repressing the breath. He has elsewhere references to this breath-repression process.[4] The repression of the breath is considered in leading Saivite books of teaching as an indispensable to

[1] *Siddhiyar*, 3. 1. 73. Ramayogi's *Tayumanavar*, pp. 59-61

[2] *Maitri Upan*, 6. 18.

[3] *Ibid*, 6. 20.

[4] Above, Nos. 38, 118, and see N.M. 105, 347, 428, 586. 1175.

yogic calm.[1] The Upanishadic six-fold yoga[2] as noted above is eight-fold in most Saivite books, the two exercises added to the Upanishadic list being *Yamam and Nyamam.*[3] In the Gita, yogic exercises are mentioned,[4] including that of the constraint of breath.[5] See further notes under No. 38.

16. WORSHIP......LIP-SERVICE. (No. 4, p. 5).

Ecstacy in worship is described by the poet in Nos. 36, 48, 107, 108. In No. 126 lip-service is deplored. On worshipping in spirit and in truth see Nos. 45, 47.

17. STILLNESS. (No. 4, p. 5).

The goal of Hindu mysticism is a state of stillness attained by the restraint of "sense-instruments from sense-objects."[6] It is a state where the mystic "closing eyes, in the quietness, sense-stilling"[7] is "incessantly stayed in the peace of the silence"[8] his "mind right-centred."[9] He sits "in silence, dead unto speech."[10] Such men "merged in meditation, the ever-sleeping"[11] become "famed as men of the silence."[12] They, however, have their "lapses"[13] because even in that condition of "lonely silence where senses cease in yogic calm and contemplation" the mind may be powerless to resist Delusion.[14] Therefore, for ensuring security in the state of silence something, above all other aids and accessories to physical stillness, is needed wherewith "to curb and curbed keep under the false Delusion-making mind."[15] Hence we find in our poet frequent prayers for some means

---

1 *Sivatarumotram*, 10. 67. *Tiruvantiar*. 22. *Tirumuntram*, 564—577.

2 See Hume, *Thirteen Principal Upanishads*, p. 435.

3 *Tirumantram*, 552. The verse names the eight—*Yamam*, *Nyamam*, *Athanam*, *Pranayamam*, *Pratyaharam*, *Dharanam*, *Dyanam*, *Samadhi*. The fourth deals with the breath. The retention of breath is called *Kumbhakam*.

4 *Gita* iv. 28—30 ; vi. 10—14.

5 *Gita* iv. 29. v. 27.

6 *Gita* ii. 68.

7 Above, No. 7 at p. 7.

8 No. 11, at p. 9.

9 Above, No. 12 at p. 9.

10 Above, No. 38 at p. 21.

11 Above, No. 46 at p. 28.

12 Above, No. 6 at p. 6.

13 Above, No. 6 at p. 6 and No. 109 at p. S.

14 Above, No 109 at p. 46.

15 Above, No. 125 at p. 57.

whereby the mind may be stilled.[1] He seems to have realized such a conquest over his mind, having found true his confidence, "with the Weapon of Grace I shall slay thee O my mind"[2]. By Grace[3] the saint becomes "mind-mighty"[4] in a state of "mindlessness"[5] in which the mind is deemed "dead."[6] The result is that "the storms have ceased and all is still,"[7] "birth-bonds are broken"[8] a path is opened "where follows not delusive mind,"[9] and all "the past is a dream, unwriteable, of yesterday.[10]"

18. TREE OF GRACE. (No. 4, page 5).

The *Rig Veda*[11] mentions a "tree clothed with goodly leaves where Yama drinketh with the gods, the Father, Master of the house, tendeth with love our ancient sires." The *devatharu*[12] is one of the five trees of Indra's paradise. Our poet speaks of God as the *devatharu*, as here, as "the tree with gifts of graciousness,"[13] "the fragrant tree which sheds blossoms of grace"[14] the tree of heaven, called *Kātpagam*[15] and "the *Katpagam* beneath the banyan shade."[16] In Jewish literature references occur to "a tree which had a fragrance beyond all fragrance, and its leaves and blooms and wood wither not for ever."[17] The pious ones of God are called "the Paradise of the Lord, the trees of life."[18] The canonical mention suggests itself in this context: "The Tree of life......The leaves of the Tree were for the healing of the nations."[19]

---

1 Above, No. 12, No. 264, for example.
2 N.M. No. 450.
3 See N.M. No. 413.
4 Above No. 58.
5 N.M. Nos. 33, 118, 185, 412.
6 N.M. Nos. 499, 539.
7 Above. No. 130.
8 Above, No. 242.
9 Above, 284.
10 Above, No. 147, See above, *Introduction*, part vi.
11 1C. 135. 1.
12 Word used in No. 4. under note. The *Tiruvachagam*, 9, 10, speaks of "*Indra's Katpagam.*"
13 N.M. 276.
14 N.M. 301.
15 N.M. 345.
16 N.M. 1392.
17 1 *Enoch* 24: 4. See 4 Ezra 7: 123. *Apoc. Mos.* 19: 2.
18 Psalms of Solomon, 14: 2.
19 Rev. 21: 2.

The tree is said to confer on men every blessing. Hence God, the all-bestower, is compared to, and called, the Katpagam Tree. A beautiful reference in S. Appar may be thus rendered:

Thou art my never-failing treasure,
  The fulness of my wealth Thou art;
Thou art my kin and Thou my kindred;
  Within my flesh Thou art my heart;
Within my heart Thou art the vision;
  The Light that livest in mine eye,
The image in mine eye-light mirrored;
  The glory of the gods on high;
Thine are all blessings, boon-bestowing Tree,
My Katpagam: from sorrow keep me free.

19. TANGLEMENTS OF SIN (No. 4, page 5).

The original is literally "the forest of attachment." It is A. K's "jungle of desire"[1] and Cobham's "jungle of earth's care."[2] Some Tamil commentators[3] explain it to mean attachment to ties of earthly kinship. Of our poet-saint's utterances a few may be taken as typical of his view-point on this subject. "Where cares of life, ties and attachments grow strong," the mind is unbalanced.[4] Under the influence of Divine grace he realizes that "all worldly kinships seem a passing show."[5] Sometimes he feels drawn to the bonds he had once broken "of home, of wealth, of women's love."[6] Wife, children, wealth and all material good do not follow one in the hour of death.[7] "Father, mother, wife, children, kinsfolk are like casual acquaintances of the market-place".[8] God, His grace, and His saints are the true devotee's father, mother and kinsfolk.[9] Nevertheless, the poet does not seem to imply that earthly kinships are essentially bad. They are good or bad according to the degree of one's attachment, and so "detached, the heart holds both as sacred, home-life and the ascetic life."[10] The belittling of earthly ties, however, is

[1] *Prabuddha Bharata*, July, 1913.

[2] *Madras Christian College Magazine*, July, 1884.

[3] *E.g.* K. Sundara Mudaliyar in his edition, p. 17; Ramayogi's edition, p. 6.

[4] Above, No. 112.

[5] Above, No. 243.

[6] Above, No. 258, See No. 153.

[7] N.M. No. 417. *cf.* Job 1:21; 1 Tim. 6:7.

[8] N.M. No. 113.

[9] Above, No. 115. *cf.* Our Lord's words in Luke 8:21.

[10] Above, No. 113. Home-life and ascetic life are commended in *Kural*, parts ii and iii, respectively.

generally insisted upon in the bulk of Tamil religious literature. Thus, the *Tiruvachagam* :[1]

> Each unto him his kith and kindred be ;
> None other unto each be tied ;
> Each unto him be doom and destiny ;
> To 'me' and 'mine' each having died,
> Let bonds be broken and attachments flee.

Similar disparagement of domestic ties is found in other religious writings.[2] The right principle underlying the insistence upon the abandonment of ties of kinship is that implied by our poet in the passage quoted above[3]—*detachment.*[4] Every attachment should be subordinate to one's love for God, and if it be not possible to have the love of friends and kinsfolk in a spirit of *detachment*, if, indeed, such lesser love is likely to endanger one's salvation, then such lesser attachments have to be given up. This principle, enunciated on a higher plane, is expressed in the teaching of our Lord Jesus Christ. "He that loveth father or mother *more* than Me is not worthy of Me; he that loveth son or daughter *more* than Me is not worthy of Me."[5] "If thy right eye *offend* thee pluck it out and cast it from thee .... If thy right hand *offend* thee cut it off and cast it from thee."[6]

20. Wisdom of Vedas, Vedanta (No. 5, page 5).

This phrase is in Tamil வேத வேதாந்த ஞானம் (*Veda Vedanta Gnanam*). Cobham has translated it, "The Veda and Vedanta's mystery."[7] The Tamil literally means, "Wisdom of the Vedas and of the Veda's end." The Vedas are the four collections of hymns and prose utterances of which the *Rig Veda*[8] is the chiefest and most ancient. The Vedas' End is usually said to be the essence of the religious and

---

[1] *Tiruvachagam*, 45 lines 9—12 *cf Ibid*, 8 : 118—128.

[2] *Sivatarumotram*, viii. 90; *Olivilodukkam*, vii. 4; *Kanthar Anupoothi*, 4. Passages setting forth the duty of abandoning earthly ties occur in the writings of Apparswami and Pattanattu Pillayar.

[3] See Note 10 at p. 137.

[4] "Fulfil ever without attachment the work that thou hast to do." (*Gita* iii. 19), See *Gita* iii. 7 ; iv. 20 ; xiii. 9 (" unattachment, independence of wife child, home, and the like, everlasting indifference of mind"); xv. 3 ("Stout axe of unattachment"); xv. 5 (" taint of attachment ") ; xviii. 6, 9.

[5] *Mt.* 10 : 37, See *Mt.* 19 : 29.

[6] *Mt.* 5 : 29, 30 ; 18 : 9.

[7] *Madras Christian College Magazine*, July 1884. A. K. in *Prab. Bh.* July. 1913, gives, " Wisdom of Vedanta lore."

[8] The present writer's thesis as to the great antiquity of the Rigveda, its monotheism. etc., may be seen in ch. iii. iv of his *Foregleams of God.*

philosophical teaching contained in the *Upanishads*.[1] Now, the religion[2] of Tayumanavar is the *Saiva Siddhanta* and not the Vedanta. He expressly says சைவ சமயமே சமயம், 'The Saiva Faith is *the* Faith,' and his meaning is clear from other passages.[3] He must therefore be taken to mean that God is the wisdom, hence the soul's goal, of the Vedas and the Siva Agamas. The combination *Vedas and Siva Agamas* occurs in our poet's writings.[4] It is the same as 'Vedas and Agamas.'[5] Considering the context in which the word 'Vedas' above is found it is sometimes justifiable to add 'Agamas' in translation or exposition. The word 'Vedas' has added to it the word 'Agamas' in my paraphrase-translation in No. 21 (same as No. 29) for instance. In an authoritative work on the Saiva Siddhanta it is laid down:

> Religions and postulates and text books......are comprised by the *Vedas* and *Saivagamas*......The *Vedas* and *Agamas* are called......' revealed books '...... The *Smirtis*, and *Puranas* and *Sastras*......are 'Guide books.' The *Vedanta* and *Upangas* form......' aid books.' Nothing can compare with the *Vedas* and *Agamas*......The only real books are the *Vedas* and *Saivagamas*. All other books are derived from these .....The *Vedas* are *general* and given out for all; the *Agamas* are *special* and revealed for the benefit of the blessed, and contain the essential truths of the Vedas and Vedanta......The *Sivagamas* alone are Siddhanta works.[6]

"Our contention is," urges one of the most erudite of modern Tamil scholars, "that all the Vedas and Upanishads and Agamas established the Saiva religion and Siddhanta philosophy."[7] The Agamas are distinct from the Upanishads, though they have the affinity of Vedic origin with the Upanishads. "The Agamas constitute the truest exegesis of the Vedas and their origins are certainly as ancient as those of some of the classical Upanishads."[8] The association of the Agamas with the Vedas is expressed by Tayumanavar thus: "The Vedas are the road, the Agamas the steed."[9] The literature culminating in the philosophic Tamil work of Meykanda Deva is thus eulogised in a Tamil stanza:[10]

---

[1] The latest edition of the Upanishads in English is Hume's *Thirteen Principal Upanishads.*

[2] See full treatment in *Introduction*, above, part ii.

[3] N.M. 554. See N.M. 141, 142, 143, 269, 474, 479, 1105.

[4] N.M. 475, 339.

[5] Above, Nos. 124, 131, 196, 318, and N.M. 425, 470.

[6] *Siddhiyar*, 3. 8. 13—15. See *Tirumantram*, 2397.

[7] J. M. Nallaswami Pillai in his English edition of the *Siddhiyar*, p. xiv.

[8] J. M. Nallaswami Pillai, *Studies*, pp. xii. xiii. Dr. Farquhar (*O.R.L.I.* 194) assigns the earliest Agamas to the seventh and eighth centuries of our era. For reasons in favour of the high antiquity of the Agamas, see Nalla. *Bhodham*, p. v.

[9] Above, No. 131.

[10] Quoted in Nalla. *Bhodham*, p. xix.

The Veda is the cow that yieldeth
    The milk of rich Agamic lore;
Churn the milk for ghee most goodly—
    The Tamil of the Saintly Four; [1]
The essence of this ghee delicious
    Is in the Tamil of renown
And skill of sage Meykanda Deva [2]
    Born in Nallur the Butter Town.[3]

12. In my fulness of time (No. 5, page 6).

The fulness of time is from the point of view of the soul The Guru was seen when the seer was ripe for the manifestation. See above *Introduction*, part vii.

22. Soughtest me Loving (No. 5, page 6).

See above, *Introduction* part vii, on God's quest of man.

23. Thine are all doings (No. 6, page 6).

The meaning of this verse is that the soul, even each of the high gods being reckoned a soul, knows nothing of itself, does nothing of itself. "The soul understands only with the Supreme Intelligence, and cannot understand by himself, inasmuch as this knowing soul knows only through some sense or other, forgets what it has learnt, and learns from others, and does not know himself the knower." [4] The soul is not self-luminous.

24. None even of Devas (No. 6, page 6).

At page 10, above is given a second rendering of No. 6. There the statement, "even the devas too, Brahma and others, lack not impulses, direction and lead" explains 'devas' by the literal rendering of the Tamil, 'Brahma and others.' The gods [5] Brahma, Vishnu, and the conditioned Rudra are all subject to the direction and lead, and the acts permitted, of God.

---

1 See below, notes under No. 274.

2 See above, *Introduction*, part ii.

3 The birth place of Meykanda Deva is reputed to be Tiru Vennai Nallur, The middle of this name means 'butter'. See *Iruppa Irupaktu*, opening verse.

4 *Siddhiyar*, 3. 5. 3.

5 See above, *Introduction*, part iv.

25. Moon-Perfect (No. 6, page 6).

These are those who are of even mind calm and serene as the moon. Even such, this verse says, have their lapses into conduct not placid.

26. Siva's Night-Vigil (No. 6, page 6).

A night in February—March is set apart for fasting, meditation and prayer in remembrance of Siva having drunk [1] poison. The rarer opinion is that every month a night becomes 'Siva's night-vigil.[2]

27. Maya (No. 7, page 6).

"All this universe is spread out and multiplied from the primal invisible and subtle *maya* into visible and grosser and grosser forms, as life and body, and these forms again are resolved in the same order and they appear as one, different, and one-and-different. The one Supreme Being also, is one, different, and one-and-different from the world." [3] For a fuller treatment of *maya* see above, *Introduction*, part v.

28. Self-Sundered (No. 7, page 7).

The original literally refers to a state 'where the assertiveness of *I* is destroyed.' This assertiveness, centering in ideas of 'I', 'mine,' is referred to by our poet in numerous places.[4] It is a demon possessing the soul and needs exorcism.[5] It springs up within the mind.[6] It is called *Ahangkaram* (அகங்காரம்) when it expresses itself as 'I,' and *Mamakaram* (மமகாரம்) when its force is in thoughts of 'mine.' Ahangkaram is one of the internal senses, faculties of perception.[7] "*Buddhi* gives rise to *Ahangkara* which is the seed of 'I'-ness in man, and which says, 'who is there to compare with *me*?' and says

---

[1] See below notes under No. 13.

[2] See M. D. Press edition of *Tayumanavar*, p. 18. See *Abidhana Kosam*, *s. v. Sivaratri*.

[3] *Siddhiyar*, 3. 1. 27. On one, different, one-and-different see Nalla. *Bodham*, p. 15.

[4] Above, Nos. 119, 120, 130, 184 and N.M. 129, 145, 291, 376, 414, 527, 794, 851.

[5] N.M. 330.

[6] N.M. 533.

[7] *Bhodham*, 4; *Siddhiyar*, 3. 4. 1. The others are *Manas* (mind), *Bhuddhi* (intellect), *Chitta* (thought). See *Prasna Upanishad* 4. 8; *Svet*, 5. 13; *Maitri*, 6. 5; *Sivapragasam*, 26; 43.

'I' and 'mine', and is inseparably associated with man."[1] Self-assertion is 'the first warder at the door to Brahma,' and must be slain 'with the arrow of freedom from self-conceit.'[2] It has been truly remarked that we seem unable even to think except in terms of proprietorship.[3] The language of daily life is so full of the obsession of 'I,' and the possessoriness of 'my' that the wisdom of self-obliteration has no room in our philosophy. It is one of the most remarkable truths about the genius of the Hebrew language that in its grammar the first person is *he*, and the third *I*. Hebrew is the language of self-effacement, and so there is, in a spirit of complete self-forgetting, given to God all the majesty and the grandeur and the glory in the opening words of the Hebrew Bible: "In the beginning God."[4] It is He and not I.

29. Quietness, Sense-Stilling (No. 7, page 7).

The Tamil means 'cessation of the senses, and of the four perceptions, *manas*, *bhuddhi*, *chittam*, *ahangkaram*.' See above, last note. The 'senses' and 'perceptions' are respectively *karuvi* (கருவி) and *karanam* (கரணம்), the words used in the original here. References to *karanam* occur elsewhere in Tayumanavar.[5] In one hymn[6] is mentioned the number of forces that war against the soul—the two *karmas*,[7] the three *gunas*, the four *karanam*, the five senses, the six desires, the eight arrogances. Hints on the methods of liberation from *karanam* are given in *Sivapragasam*.[8] Our poet-saint himself after describing some processes of training and discipline, asks:[9]

Can all this liberation bring,
Achieve salvation of the soul,
Except by knowing Thee, O Lord,
The Ever-First, Siddhanta's Goal?

S. Paul speaking of carnality 'warring' against the law of his mind asks and answers: "Who shall deliver me from the body of death? I thank God through Jesus Christ our Lord."[10] The answer sufficeth.

---

1 *Siddhiyar*, 3. 2. 59.
2 *Maitri Upanishad*, 6. 28.
3 Dr. L. P. Jacks, quoted in Inge's *Phil. of Plotinus* ii. 244.
4 Gen. 1: 1. In the Hebrew text there is a pause-mark after the word 'God', so that the devout reader may reverently pause there, and think of the significance of the pause.
5 N.M. 123, 149, 176, 346, 448, 625, 728.
6 N.M. 176.
7 See above, *Introduction*, part vi.
8 81, 82.
9 Above, No. 38, at p. 22.
10 Rom. 7: 23—25.

30. KARMA (No. 7, page 7).

See above *Introduction*, part vi, on Karma and the soul.

31. SOUL'S PRIMAL LOAD (No. 7, page 7).

According to the Saiva Siddhanta the soul starts its career with a handicap. There is attached to it from the first a 'primal load,' its old karma. It is sufficient to note here that the poet expressly refutes the heterodox view that the initial karma of the soul is God. There are, he says, 'the warrings of karma but this will not lead one to deem the soul's primal load mighty to be the soul's master.'

32. THOU ART THE DOER OF ALL I DO (No. 8, page 7).

It is Saivite teaching that the soul is at first in a condition of sleep and inaction and that God gives it the initial impetus to action. He gives "knowledge to the soul by means of the senses, perceptions, the luminaries, time, karma, and bodies and by means of books...... and by the word of the Guru, inasmuch as the soul in the *kevala* [1] condition is formless and non-intelligent." [2] The soul's primal condition of obscurity is like that of 'copper covered with dross.[3] It is again compared to that of a babe 'rocked to and fro in its cradle.' [4] Our poet-saint claims to have been taught by God, "Of thine own-self thou knowest nothing, thou doest nothing." [5] The attribution of the soul's acts after maturity to God is the logical outcome of the doctrine that God is the all-mover. Statements to the effect that He is the mover of all things and in all things occur in our poet's psalms. 'No atom moves but by His motion.' [6] He is the mover and He witnesseth what He moves.[7] God, having framed the body, put the soul there, and giving its faculties impetus and initiative, is the originator of the soul's deeds, His sport.[8] He is the mover of the Sakti-powers in man just like a snake-charmer makes the snake do his bidding.[9]

---

[1] See above, p. 130.
[2] *Siddhiyar*, 3. 5. 4. *Sivapragasam*, 19.
[3] See above, No. 37 and notes on that hymn.
[4] See above, No. 125.
[5] Above, No. 121.
[6] Above, No. 122.
[7] N.M. 109.
[8] N.M. 448.
[9] N.M. 1231.

God 'lays on the soul the burden of the body makes the soul the burden-bearer and makes the soul dance in the way of good and bad actions.'[1] Therefore He is 'the crafty One concealed within the soul's senses, and moving them to deeds.'[2]

'Tis God who doeth as He pleaseth.
Just as, upon a plank of wood,
A top is made to move in whirling,
So God moves all for ill and good.[3]

From this point of view the thinkers of the Siddhanta school are led on to the associated, and inferential notion that God is the doer of all deeds.[4] Even the very thought that all deeds are God's is prompted by God.[5] It was not pushing the idea of God being the all-doer beyond the limit of reason to postulate that His activities in the sphere of deeds are not restricted to good actions alone. It is God, and not the soul, that selects appropriate bodies for the good karma as well as for bad.[6] Justly then may the poet say:

Thou art my God, my Guru Thou,
My Guide, my Father, Mother art.
Thou art my Evil and my Good
Life, body, being, every part.[7]

His view-point is clear in the complaint:

Why hast Thou placed within my being
Unbending pride,
The pride that from of old has cried,
Incessant crieth, "I"?
Why midmost in it hast thou planted
Deed-bearing seed,
Whence cometh merit, cometh meed,
The fount of good and ill?
Why hast Thou laid on me my body,
Burden to bear,
And why, a living something, there,
Hast Thou put me?[8]

The sequence to this line of thought, so frequent as a reiterated fundamental, in the Saiva Siddhanta writings is that all acts of the soul are God's, and there is a stage of spiritual discrimination at

---

1 N.M. 291.
2 N.M. 562.
3 Above, No. 113. See. N.M. 302, 445.
4 Above, Nos. 42, 147, 164. N.M. 279, 362, 363, 445.
5 N.M. 970.
6 *Sivapragasam* 24.
7 Above, No. 142.
8 N.M. 179 (first part). See above, Nos. 147, 215 and N.M. 632, 746.

which even evil deeds of a soul are ascribeable to God. Thus the hard saying in a Siddhanta classic finds its place in this context:

The good or evil which he performs will redound only on those who do good or evil to him. His faults will vanish when......he becomes one with God and *dedicates all acts* to Hara, and stands fixed in this posture. And God also will hold all his acts as His own and everything done to him as done to himself and will remain united to him driving away his faults. The greatest sins when committed in this condition of all love will only be good service and not otherwise.[1]

Harder than the last sentence in the above excerpt is this:

When they possess Siva-wisdom, then, even though seen sporting with damsels very fair, decked in fragrant flowers, their heart will be imbedded in the feet of the Blessed Lord and will rest in bliss.[2]

The principle of this position of sanctity in the midst of not simply aesthetic, but grossly sensual, environment, is that "the soul perceives all its actions to be God's." [3] The startling sayings above cited do not suggest mere environment of sensuality but actional correspondence and contact with such environment. They may be taken to denote an intense manner of stating the truth, about which there can be no question, that, when God's will is paramount, all acts of the soul are God-directed. For, until there is such a complete surrender of the human will to the Divine as will efface differentiation [4] there must be much contrariness of purpose, a warring of wills, and such contrariness is sin. S. Tayumanavar's experience [5] vividly recognizes this contrariness as a fearful reality, and in numerous places [6] repels any suggestion of liberty unto licentiousness. We do not, therefore, marvel at his prayers against sensual distractions. When he prays that it may be given him ever to remember God's grace at all times, and in all circumstances of acts and occupations, some of which in themselves not sinful, and in wordly pleasures some of them sensual, he owns the dreadful possibility of spiritual peril in such occupations and pleasures:

What time the fragrance falls on me
Of full and fresh-blown flowers
Which make the shady bowers
Wherein I rest;

---

[1] *Siddhiyar* 3. 10. 1.

[2] *Siddhiyar* 3. 10. 5. See *Siddhiyar* 3. 2. 29; 3. 8. 33.

[3] *Bhodham* 10; *T.A.P.* 7. 7.

[4] The fire of wisdom burns away 'I', 'Mine', (*Siddhiyar* 3. 10. 2,)

[5] See above, *Introduction*, parts iii and viii.

[6] See above, Nos. 199, 315, 316, 317, 319 and N.M. 306, 433, 435, 579 for instances.

What time of waters cool and clear
Delicious draughts I drink
And in them float and swim and sink
In pleasing sport;

What time scent-laden breezes blow,
Soft as the tread of feet
Of damsels fair, all sweet
To listening ears;

What time the moon most gladdens me,
Full-orbed and silver white
In splendour of the light
That makes night day;

What time I wonder if my food,
Most dainty, may not be
Ambrosia of the sea
In very sooth;

What time I chew green leaf and nut,[1]
And, gay with flower and scent,
My night in pleasures spent,
I fall asleep;

At all times, Lord, grant me to be
Most mindful of Thy Grace,
Most mindful all my days,—
And so save me.[2]

A man may so do his duties without attachment and fulfil the obligations of earthly ties "though never so implicated in those relations as to forget for a moment the grace of God." [3] What the poet in the passage above translated prays for is not merely to remember [4] God's grace at all times, but to realize its sustaining power and such realization would exclude pleasures which vitiate the soul. It cannot, therefore, be true that "the greatest sins when committed in the condition of all love will only be good service and not otherwise."[5] The

---

[1] Betel-leaf and areca-nut chewed with other ingredients have not only hygienic effects but also act as a pleasant stimulant.

[2] N.M. 110.

[3] Sir P. Ramanathan, *Mystery of Godliness*, p. 5.

[4] Augustine in his sins did not *forget* God (*Conf.* 3. 1; 3. 4; 3. 6.)

[5] *Siddhiyar* 3. 10. 1, quoted above. Mr. Nallaswamy Pillai in his *Siddhiyar* notes under 3. 10. 5 S. Tayumanavar's psalm I have here translated and gives both the Tamil and Sir P. Ramanathan's English prose rendering. In the *Siddhiyar* passage are the words "even though seen sporting with damsels fair," the realistic original disguised in the English. If our poet had, as it is highly probable, these words in mind, he has summarised them in words which I have, less pointedly than the Tamil, paraphrased, "My night in pleasure spent," and which my distinguished countryman (*Mystery of Godliness*, p. 6) has toned down to "much merriment."

surface sense of these words is very unethical. If they are not, as I have already observed, but an intense manner of expressing co-ordination of the human will to the Divine, then, they are of dubious moral value. Non-Hindu mystics too have said extravagant things and even erroneous things on the soul's freedom of action. Such are referred to by mediæval mystics in terms of dispraise:

> There are persons who say, 'I have God and His love, I can do what I wish.' This view shows an ignorance of true liberty. When thou wishest to do a thing contrary to the will of God and His law, thou hast not the love of God, even though thou endeavourest to make the world believe thou hast. That man who has established himself *in the will of God* and in the love of God does what God loves and leaves undone what He forbids. It is as impossible for him to do what God does not will as it is not to do what He wills. The man whose feet are bound cannot walk, and the man who lives in the will of God cannot sin.[1]

Conformity to God's will is possible to those who are born of God. "Whosoever is born of God doth not commit sin for His seed remaineth in him; and he cannot sin because he is born of God."[2] It has been observed[3] that discerning souls should read with a holy smile such statements as, "Virtues, I take leave of you for evermore,"[4] or "He only is a contemplative who is the slave of nothing, not even of his virtues,"[5] or S. Augustine's "Love God and do what you like." Sentiments such as these, on the same footing as the *Siddhiyar* passages I have quoted already, are only an excessive way of expressing complete subordination of the human will, not in slavery but in love to God's own will. If they do not mean this, then, whether Christian or non-Christian, they are wanting in moral elegance, and come under condemnation. It is really complete identification in will with God that is implied in the sayings of many mystics. Of S. Catherine of Genoa it is reported that, at a certain stage of spirituality, "she no more strictly recognized her human acts whether they had been done well or evilly, but she saw all in God."[6] More nearly akin to the *Siddhiyar* sentiments and as daring are Jacopone da Todi's exclamation:[7]

---

[1] Eckhart, quoted in Jones's *Studies in Myst. Rel.* 212.

[2] 1 John 3: 9.

[3] Herman, *The Meaning and Value of Myst.* 80. See Underhill, *Mysticism* 263; Coats, *Types of English Piety* 220-222.

[4] The *Mirror of Simple Souls.*

[5] Ruysbroeck, *Flowers of a Mystic Garden*, p. 45.

[6] Hügel, *Myst. Element* i. 392.

[7] *Myst. Element* ii. 107.

Since my soul has been transformed into Truth, into Thee, O Christ alone, into Thee who art tender, loving,—not to myself but to Thee can be imputed what I do. Hence, if I please Thee not, Thou dost not please Thine Own Self, O Love!

The ascription of human actions to Divine impulses, indeed the identification of man's deeds with God's, finds parallels in Islamic mysticism:

My servant draws nigh unto Me, and I love Him. When I love him I am his ear so that he hears by Me; and his eyes so that he sees by Me; and his tongue so that he speaks by Me [1]

It is laid down by a high Islamic authority:

Fana is the passing away of a man's regarding in his actions that which he does God's taking his place therein ...Those who inculcate the doctrine of *Fana* mean the passing away of regarding one's own actions and works of devotion through the continuance of regarding God as the doer of these actions on behalf of His servant.[2]

Less open to misunderstanding, and more in accord with New Testament purity, is what the *Theologia Germanica* says:

Whatever cometh to pass in a man who is truly Godlike, whether he do or suffer, all is done in this Light and this Love, and from the same, through the same, unto the same again. In his heart there is a content and quietness, so that he doth not desire to know more or less, to have, to live, to die, to be, or not to be, or anything of the kind; these become all one and alike to him and he complaineth of nothing but sin only. . . And sin is to desire or will anything otherwise than as the One Perfect Good and the One Eternal Will . . And what is done of sin, such as lies, fraud, injustice, treachery and all iniquity, in short all that we call sin, cometh hence, that man hath another will than God. . .[3]

There is a great distance in thought and outlook between the *Siddhiyar*, the mediæval mystics already noted, on the one hand, and on the other S. Paul who says, "I live, yet no longer I, but Christ liveth in me."[4]

33. The Harmony (No. 8, page 7).

On the word சமரச (*Samarasa*) rendered here 'the harmony balancing...' see above, *Introduction*, part ii.

---

[1] Nicholson's *Mystics of Islam*, 100. See his *Studies in Islamic Mysticism* 50, 126, 151.

[2] *Luma*, 151 (a). *Risalat*, 43: 13-45, translated by Dr. Nicholson in J. R. A. S. 1913, pp. 57, 60. Jami of Persia says—"Deem not your actions by yourself are done." (Davis, *Persian Mystics*, ii. 66.)

[3] Winkworth's Translation, 169, 170.

[4] Gal. 2: 20.

34. The Weapon (No. 8, page 7).

The weapon is heavenly wisdom: "By knowing God one is released from all fetters."[1] The *Maitri Upanishad* speaks of a 'bow and arrow' for use in effecting an entrance into the hall of Brahma.[2]

35. Cause of All (No. 9, page 7).

As to conjectures, similar to those stated in this verse, see *Svetasvatara Upanishad*, 1: 1-3. See *Siddhiyar*, 3. 1, 1-28. This verse gives the views held by various schools of thought. See above, *Introduction*, part ii, *Refutations*.

36. Elements (No. 9, page 7).

On *Maya* see above, *Introduction*, part v. The elements are ether, air, fire, earth, water.[3]

37. Three Principles (No. 9, page 7).

The Tamil குணம் (*kunam*) is the Sanscrit *guna*. The three 'principles' or 'qualities' are pureness (*sattva*), passion (*rajas*), and darkness (*tamas*). It is 'the red, white, black' of the *Svetasvatara*.[4] Each of these three 'qualities' has its own characteristics. Readers of the *Gita* will re-call the detailed exposition of the 'three qualities' their characteristics and activities.[5]

38. Sound . . . Energy (No. 9, page 7).

Sound, *Nātham*, is "the Deity as representing the sound of the Pranava;[6] God as present in the universe when at the very beginning of evolution, the great sound or Sabdam or Natham burst forth; cosmic matter in the state of sound,"[7] This is hardly a definition of what is not very easy to understand. What is translated 'energy' is in

---

[1] *Svet. Upan*. 1. 8; 1. 11; 5. 13.

[2] *Maitri* 6. 28.

[3] *Siddhiyar*, 3.2.65. *Ait. Upanishad*, 5.3. *Maitri*, 3.2.

[4] *Svet*. 4. 5. That the *gunas* are three is stated in *Svet*. 5. 13, *Maitri* 6. 10. The three are named in *Maitri* 5. 2.

[5] *Gita* xiv. 5—27; xvii. 4-22; xviii. 7-40. The characteristics of two 'qualities' are detailed in *Maitri Upanishad* 3. 5.

[6] The highest Hindu mantra (*Mundaka Upan*. 2. 2. 4).

[7] Nalla. *Bodham*, p. 123.

Tamil விந்து *Vindhu.* The orthodox sign of *Vindhu* is a circle and of *Natham* is a straight line.[1] *Vindhu* is also known as *Suddha Maya Sakti,*[2] and so is here rendered 'energy.'

39. NON-DIFFERENT FROM GOD (No. 9, page 8).

On the *betha*-less state in which the soul stands "non-different from God" see above, *Introduction*, parts iv, v.

40. NOTHINGNESS (No. 9, page 8).

The void, சூனியம், *Sūnya*, which is beyond the three great abysms. The three are the abysm of life, the abysm of space, the abysm of the Deity. In Tamil they are சீவப்பாழ் (*Seevappārl*), பரப்பாழ் (*Parappārl*), சிவப்பாழ் (*Sivappārl*).[3] It is strictly not 'nothingness.'

41. DARKNESS (No. 10, page 8).

See above, Note 28. The soul, according to the Siddhanta, is from eternity covered with imperfection, *mala*, மலம். "The three *malas* namely *Anava* (darkness of ignorance), *Maya* and *Karma*, delusive in their character, veil the true nature of the soul and produce illusory pleasures, bondage and capacity for experience."[4] This *Anava Mala* is the darkness, 'the dwelling place of the soul.'[5] This darkness is so adherent to the soul 'as the dross in copper.'[6] It veils the soul in ignorance.[7] The eternal adherence of the *malas* to the soul is illustrated by the 'sprout, bran and chaff in paddy.'[8] "A grain of paddy appears as one; still it is composed of husk, bran, rice and the sprout,·· united together at the same time. The husk conceals the rice...There is one more thing which conceals the whiteness and purity of the rice (*soul*) and that is the dark bran (*anava*) more intimately connected

---

[1] See *Bodham*, 4, in *Nalla*, edition p. 46, also pp. 48-50. *Siddhiyar* 3. 1. 19—28.

[2] *Siddhiyar* 3. 1. 25. For a criticism of *Maya* views see Gnanapragasar's *Philosophical Saivism*, p. 44. See above, *Introduction*, part v.

[3] *Vedasrotayam* quoted in K. S. Mudaliar's edition of *Tayumanaswami* p. 35.

[4] *Siddhiyar* 3. 2. 86.

[5] Among other references to this in the poet may be noted N. M. 174, 573, 1370, 1162, 1319. See above, Nos. 37, 119, 125, 130.

[6] *Siddhiyar* 3. 2. 80. See above, No. 37. *Sivapragasam* 20.

[7] *Sivapragasam* 20. *Siddhiyar* 3. 2. 84.

[8] *Siddhiyar* 3. 2. 86. *Sivapragasam* 25. *Tirumantram* 468. *Bodham* 2, Argument 2, (c).

with it. Then there is a sprout (*karma*) but for which the grain will not germinate (*attain bodies.*)...When you want to get at the rice, (*the real self-soul*) the husk helps by friction (*successive births, evolution*) to remove the dark bran (*anava* ignorance)."[1] Our poet-saint in No. 37, above, uses the other Siddhanta analogy of dross and copper in speaking of the soul and its primal taint of *Anava Mala*, ignorance, and speaks of the alchemic process of the purification of the dross-covered soul into gold.[2] See further, *Introduction*, part v.

42. CHARACTERED (No. 10, page 8).

Destiny is believed to be inscribed by Brahma on each man's *skull*. On this 'fate to hold fast to what I grasp' see above, *Introduction*, part v.

43. BODY (No. 10, page 8).

See above, *Introduction*, part vi.

44. HIGH MYSTICAL MEANING (No. 10, page 8).

To inquire as to the soul's state and man's lot and to make guesses as to this or that being the cause of it is to miss the true significance of the relationship of God to the soul and to the soul's condition. See above, *Introduction*, parts v, vi on God, Soul, Karma. No. 11, above, gives a hint of an answer to the question asked in No. 10.

45. HARMONY (No. 11, page 8).

On சமரச, *Samarasa*, translated 'holden in harmony' see above *Introduction*, part ii.

46. UNDAMMED (No. 12, page 9).

"He hath encompassed the waters with bounds"[3]

47. BANE, AMBROSIA (No. 12, page 9).

There is a legend that the devas were once churning the Sea of Milk for the food of the gods, ambrosia, and found a deadly poison. Siva coming to their help swallowed the poison in the churned sea

---

[1] Nalla, *Bodham*, pp. 26, 27. One is not sure whether in his *Siddhiyar* p. 187, the learned commentator of that classic does not suggest that *anava mala* is the chaff, *maya* is the bran, *karma* is the sprout.

[2] This analogy is explained at length in Nalla, *Bodham*, p. 27.

[3] Job, 26 : 10.

and gave the devas ambrosia. It is owing to this that Siva is named *Nilakanda* 'blue-throated'[1] There is more than one version of this story.[2] Modern Hindu writers allegorize it.[3] Rev. Father Gnanapragasar, my eminent countryman, has a brief critical inquiry into the origins of this poison legend.[4]

48. Deep Ocean Fire (No. 12, page 9).

It is believed that there is fixed in the sea somewhere a mare-shaped figure of fire, the object of which is to keep the waters within their bounds.[5]

49. The Seven Clouds (No. 12, page 9).

Indra, the god of thunder, whose weapon is thunder, exercises his will over seven clouds—pearl-cloud, rain-cloud, gold-cloud, flower-cloud, sand-cloud, stone-cloud, and fire-cloud.

50. Meru (No. 12, page 9).

Siva's 'bow victorious is the mighty mount.'[6] He is said to have used this on the occasion of his waging war against the three cities which were being held by three powerful *Asuras*, giants. In the earliest form of the story[7] the bow is described as Mount Meru, but the arrow is said to have been made of Vishnu, Agni and Soma. The Puranic form[8] filled in details, made Mount Meru the bow, and furnished material for the later esoteric sense in which the story came to be expounded, 'that the three cities are the product of the triple *mala*'.[9] The esoteric sense seems to be implied in the title *Gnanavetti*, 'spiritual conquest', given to the section in the *Tiruvachagam*[10] where Siva's five great acts are celebrated. Mr. Nallaswamy

---

[1] See above, No. 44 at pp. 26, 27.

[2] See Pope's *Tiruvachagam*, p. 162. Muir's *Sanskrit Texts*, iv, 366. *Kamba-Ramayanam*, ix. 17. Wilson's *Vishnu Puranam*, ch. ix.

[3] See, *e.g.* Sabaratnam, *Essentials of Hinduism*, 276.

[4] *Philosophical Saivism*, 158—160.

[5] See Wilson, *Sanscrit Dictionary* S. V. *Badavagni*. In my *Foregleams of God*, iv § 13, I have identified this fire with Agni the *Samudra-vasas* of *Rig Veda*, 8. 91. 4.

[6] *Tiruvachagam*, vi. line 114; xxix, line 21.

[7] *Yajur Veda*, 6. 2. 12.

[8] *Matsya Purna*, ch. 129--140. *Skanda Purana, Upadesa Kanda*, ch. 70—72.

[9] *Tirumantram*, 343.

[10] xiv. lines 1—12 refer to the destruction of the Three Cities.

Pillai is right in urging [1] that the allegorizing of the story of the cities is ancient. In the *Upanishads* the analogy of bow and arrow in meditation occurs.[2]

51. WOMAN. (No. 12, page 9).

The allusion is here to Ahalyagai, the wife of a rishi called Gautama. Owing to a suspicion of infidelity he cursed her and she was turned into stone. Being later sorry for her lot, he said, " Live when Rama's foot touches thee." Rama, the hero of the Ramayana, happened, when on a march, to tread on 'the slab of stone that once was a woman' (p. 11) and it became Ahalyagai again.

52. DESIRE. (No. 13, page 9).

Desire is, in the Saiva Siddhanta and in philosophic Hinduism generally, a great factor in determining the soul's destiny. It is an aspect of *pāsam*. Our poet speaks, of the 'forest of desire,' [3] 'the flood of desire,' [4] 'the stormy sea of desire,' [5] and 'the tempest of desire.[6] "As is a man's desire, such is his resolve; as is his resolve, such the action he performs; what action he performs, into that does he become changed." [7] Desire brings on re-births.[8] Desire is a link in the Buddhist 'chain of causation' since 'by desire is sensation and by sensation is attachment, and by attachment is renewed existence, and by renewed existence birth, and by birth is sorrow, decay, death'.[9] In the *Gita* it is taught [10] that "the man who casts off all desires and walks without desire, with no thought of a *Mine* and *I*, comes unto peace." The disease of desire is thus spoken of in the *Mahabharata*: "Desire is a sickness that is hard for the foolish to abandon, which ages not with man's ageing, which only ends with life itself. Blessed is he who frees himself from it." [11]

---

1 *Siddhiyar*, pp. 146—150; *Studies*, pp. 278, 279.

2 *Mundaka*, 2. 2. 3; *Maitri*, 6. 24; 6. 8.

3 N.M. 284. The expression is பாசடவி *pāsadavi*, rendered 'tanglements of sin' in No. 4 above. See p. 137.

4 N.M. 302.

5 N.M. 1363.

6 N.M. 322.

7 *Brih. Ar. Upanishad*, 4. 4. 5.

8 *Brih. Ar. Upanishad*, 4. 4. 6; *Mundaka* 3. 2. 2; *Maitri* 6. 30.

9 Hardy's *Buddhism*, 391, 392. Rhys Davids' *Buddhism*, 100, 101.

10 *Gita*, ii. 71

11 xii. c. 174, translated in Barnett's *Heart of India*, 33.

53. God of Wealth. (No. 13, page 9).

The Hindu Plutus (page 13) is Kwēra (page 12) and his name in the text here is Alagēsan.

54. Life. (No. 19, page 14 ; No. 26, page 16).

What is rendered 'Life of life; non-dual' (page 14) and 'lasting non-dual the life in all' (page 16) is in the original: 'He who in all things, at all times, unseparate from anything, energizes everything'. On 'Life of life,' see above, page 125, and on 'non-dual' (which is intended to be correcter, far more expressive, than 'one with') see above, *Introduction* part v.

55. Turiya. (No. 19, page 14 ; No. 26, page 16 ; No. 2, page 4).

Turya, varied in some Upanishads into *turiya*,[1] is the fourth and highest condition of existence. The four states of the soul are *Jagra* (being in conjunction with the fourteen senses and sensations), *Svapna* (being in conjunction with four organs of perception), *Sustrupti* (being in conjunction with *chitta* only), and *Turya* in which there are no sense-enjoyments.[2] The description of the Turya state in one of the Upanishads[3] is as follows :

> Not inwardly cognitive, not outwardly cognitive, not both-wise cognitive, not a cognition-mass, not cognitive, not non-cognitive, unseen, with which there can be no dealing, ungraspable, having no distinctive mark, non-thinkable, that cannot be designated, the essence of the assurance of which is the state of being one with the Self, the cessation of development, tranquil, benign,[4] without a second.[5]

Tayumanaswamy speaks of Turya not only as the state in which Deity dwells to be spiritually discerned by the devout[6] but also as a condition attainable in this life on earth by the devout.[7]

---

[1] *Brih. Ar. Upanishad* 5. 14. 3.

[2] *Siddhiyar*, 2. 5, 11. These are the waking state, the dreaming state, the deep-sleep state, and 'the fourth state' of *Mandukya Upanishad*, 3—7. On the number of senses and sensations, whether 14 or more or less, and Sankara's opinion see Hume's *Upanishads*, p. 391.

[3] *Mandukya*, 7. Turya is referred to in *Maitri*, 6. 19; 7. 11.

[4] The original is *Siva*.

[5] The original is *Advaita*, in the sense of 'non-dual.'

[6] N.M. 926.

[7] N.M. 764. For a learned exposition of *Turiya* see *S. Deepika*, xii. 158 and xiii. 176.

56. FRAGRANCE, OIL, SPIRIT. (No. 21, page 15; No. 29, page 17).

The *Svetasvatara* Upanishad [1] has these words:

As oil in sesame seeds, as butter in cream,
As water in river-beds, and as fire in the friction-sticks,
So is the Soul apprehended in one's own soul,
If one looks for Him with true austerity.

A great Saiva Saint, Tirumular, says, "My Lord and my King is present, united to all, like feeling in air, sugar in the cane, butter in milk, the sweet juice in the fruit, and the fragrance in the flower."[2] Another Tamil Saint, Appar, tells us:

As fire in wood, as ghee in milk,
The Luminious One lies hid within.[3]

The figure of fragrance is employed by Tayumanavar in a hymn which deserves to be fully given:

The wide, wide world, this sweep of space,
Are to Thy saints expanse of grace;
By Thy one word the mystic state
Of Yogic calm is theirs, the great,
To whom Thou grantest, Lord, thine aid,
Helper on Whom their hope is stayed,

Who love Thee best Who lovest me
Friend of my lowly self to be,
O Hill of Heaven whose form of Bliss
Beginningless, unending, is.
O Lord that livest in Thy Light
O Life that shinest ever bright,

Yet with all worlds and bodies willest e'er to be,
And with all beings, blended joyously,
As full as fragrance in the half-blown flower dwells,
Half-blown as are half-parted mouths of tinkling bells.[4]

There are, as will be seen, in the above illustrative passages, five figures employed to show the relationship of God to the soul and the world—oil, butter, water, fire, fragrance. For other analogies, see above, *Introduction*, part ix.

---

[1] 1. 15.

[2] *Tirumantram*, 2639.

[3] Nallaswamy Pillai's *S. Appar*, p. 4. See Nalla. *Studies*, p. 1.

[4] N.M. 132. The lines 'O Lord that livest .... ever bright' represent the sense of two words சோதி நிலை, such is the marvellous terseness of the Tamil of our poet. See also N.M. 62, and above No. 105, 110.

57. INDWELLER. (Page 16, No. 24).

See above, Note 1, at page 123. God is the Inhabitant of the soul. Our poet has numerous references to God as the Indweller [1]

......Thy home Thou choosest
Within the hearts of saints on earth
The holy dead to all world-senses.[2]

Again he prays:

Life of my life, Sense of my senses,
O Love that in my inness art
Sweeter than sweetest fruit or nectar,
And honey-sweet, within my heart,
With all my being blending livest.
By grace familiar as a friend,
O let me not from Thee be parted,
Unsundered be unto the end. [3]

Other Siddhanta poets give expression to the thought of the indwelling God. Thus Kaduvali Sittar:

All bright in glory lo! He shines
Who deigns in loving hearts to live;
The servant of His servants, He
Heaven to His worshippers will give. [4]

S. Sundaramurthi in one of his psalms says:—

The mind He rids of vain delusions
And in the midst of it abides;
He frames the frailty of the body;
In fire and wind Himself He hides
That they may cease; He sends diseases
To hasten death; He dispels ills,
The strong, the King of Needur City—
Adore Him in your inmost wills. [5]

An anonymous poet philosopher asks:

'Tis in the heart the Teacher is,
And in the heart deceit is seen;
Not knowing where the thing may be
How can you seek to make it clean? [6]

---

1 See above, Nos. 24, 31, 37, 49, 53, 54, 66, 105, 110, 117, 134, 157, 252, 262, 351.

2 No. 110, above, p. 46.

3 No. 117, above, p. 49.

4 *Ananthakalippu*, last verse. Except where otherwise stated all translations from the Tamil are the present writer's.

5 *Tevaram*, Tiruneedur section. No. 8. See *Tiruvachagam*; i (line) 33; v. 187; xvii, 5-8; xix, 33/34; xxxiv. 36; xlix. 17.

6 *Gnanakummie*, stanza 134.

S. Pattanattu Pillayar, like other Puritans among Saivites, says thus on worshipping the indwelling God outside temples and apart from idols:

> I cannot worship such as these,
> But make my lofty boast
> That in my heart I set the feet,
> The golden feet of God,[1]

Severer than he is S. Sivavakiar[2]:

> Ye whose feet to temples often hasten in the heat of day,
> See ye not within you stands the sanctuary of the Lord?
> Sin to wash away ye wander daily to all water-pools,
> Into you ye look not for the Laver for the erring soul!

The Lord, says the *Gita*, dwells in the hearts of all born beings.[3] The Persian mystic, Rumi, exclaims, "I gazed into my heart and there I saw Him who was nowhere else."[4] Likewise the Greek thinker says, "The One is not far away from any one, and yet is liable to be far away from one and all, present though It be. It is present only to such as are capable of receiving It and are so disposed as to adapt themselves to It."[5]

One of the most learned of Christian thinkers well remarks:

> Great is the blindness and exceeding great the folly of many souls that are ever seeking God, continually sighing after and frequently desiring God, whilst all the time they are the tabernacles of the Living God . . since their soul is the seat of God, in which He continually reposes.[6]

It is recorded of S. Catherine of Siena that she cried out once, like the tempted S. Anthony, "Where wert Thou, Lord, when my heart was so vexed with foul and horrible temptations?", and received the answer, "Daughter, I was in thine heart."[7] St. John of the Cross exhorts:

> We must remember that in every soul God dwells secretly and veiled in their substance, for were it otherwise they could not endure in existence. There is, however, a difference as regards this inhabitation between one soul

---

1 Barnett's translation in his *Heart of India*, 89.

2 *Padal*, Stanza 34. Some scholars think that there was no saint by name Sivavakiar.

3 xviii, 61; xv. 15.

4 Davis, *Persian Mystics*, i. 53

5 Plotinus, *Ennead*, 6. 9. 4.

6 S. Thomas Aquinas, *De Beatitudine* iii, 3, quoted in Hügel, *Myst. Elem. of Rel.* ii. 152.

7 Richardson, *The Mystic Bride* 85. *cf.* "Thou wert within, and I without, and there I sought Thee." (*Confessions* x. 27.)

and another, and a great difference it is. In some souls He dwells alone; in others not alone; in some pleased, in others displeased; in some as in His house, commanding and directing everything; and in others as a stranger in a house not His own, where He is not permitted to order or do anything.[1]

The realization of the fact of the indwellingness of God is highest in the conception of the incarnation of God. "Incarnation is a universal principle and Jesus Christ is the specialization in absolute perfection."[2]

God's immanence in nature, we reasonably assert, reappears as inspiration in man. Meanwhile our spiritual character reacts upon the material instrument of its realization, moulding the brain and nervous system, and thence the entire bodily organism, into gradual accordance with itself; till the expression of the eye, the lines of the face, the tone of the voice, the touch of the hand, the movement and manners, and gracious demeanour, all reveal with increasing clearness, the nature of the spirit that has made them what they are. Thus the interior beauty of holiness comes by degrees to be a visible thing; and through His action upon our spirit, God is made manifest in our flesh. While in proportion as we are enabled to recognize this progressive manifestation of God in matter, we are prepared to find it culminate in His actual Incarnation, the climax of His immanence in the world.[3]

The fact of the indwellingness of God is capable, in the light of the Incarnation of the Lord Jesus Christ, of the highest personal appropriation and realization. Mysticism is the practice of the Incarnation.[4] The Incarnation is 'redemptive immanence.'[5] The practice of the presence of God issues in works which testify to the concreteness of the doctrine of the indwellingness of God.[6] The "doctrine of Christ in every man[7]" is translated into the facts of life in the atmosphere of the Holy Ghost. "Hereby we know that He abideth in us, by the Spirit which He has given us"[8] "The spirit of mysticism is the true and essential Christianity. . . It is in fact the doctrine, or rather, the experience of the Holy Ghost. . . All

---

[1] *Living Flame of Love*, 4.

[2] Wilberforce, *Mystic Immanence* 60.

[3] Illingworth, *Divine Immanence*, ch. iv.

[4] Watson, *Myst. of S. John's Gospel* 104.

[5] Herman, *Meaning and Value of Mysticism* 321,

[6] "Nothing is more beautiful, or more reassuring of God's indwelling in the human soul than to see a life, a career and a character developing along lines of natural growth from small beginnings to great issues." (Mrs. Richardson, *The Mystic Bride* 144. See also S. Francis DeSales, *Devout Life*, Part ii. ch. 2.)

[7] Charles Kingsley in Preface to Winkworth's (Translation of) *Theologia Germanica*.

[8] 1 John 3 : 24.

Christians profess belief in the Holy Ghost. Had only all Christians understood and tried to use their belief they would have been mystics: or, in other words, there would have been no mysticism."[1]

58. FLAVOUR, THREE-FRUITED, SWEET. (Page 16, No. 25).

The three fruits here alluded to are the jack, the mango, and the plantain. To the joint sweetness of the three fruits reference is made by the poet in other places.[2]

59. TEARS. (Page 16, No. 25).

Tears of joy as evidence of true devotion find mention in many hymns of our poet.[3]

60. SKY, SOUL-SPACE. (Page 17, No. 31).

God fills, the commentators say, the visible sky, the sky of the soul, and the sky of spiritual wisdom. In the *Chandogya Upanishad* [4] it is written, "As far, verily, as this world-space (*ayam ākasā*) extends, so far extends the space within the heart .... That is the real city of Brahma . ."

61. MOTHERLIKE. (Page 18, No. 32).

The Motherhood of God is one of the outstanding features of the Siddhanta. *Thāi* in Tamil is 'Mother' and is part of the name *Tayumanavar*. See above *Introduction*, part iii. At p. 48 is given a rendering of a hymn in which God is addressed as Mother and by the name Tayumanava, that is, 'He who became a Mother,' to minister (so runs the tradition current in Ramanad) to a woman in travail. Two hymns are specially addressed to the God so manifested, 'Tayumana, the Lord most gracious.' [5] References to God as Mother are numerous in our poet.[6] This thought of God as Mother is to be distinguished from the conception of a consort [7] of Deity. A Vaish-

---

[1] Moberly, *Atonement and Personality*, 312. 315. 316.

[2] See above No. 117 and N.M. 64, 314, 370. For other figures expressing sweetness see above No. 104 and N.M. 138, 192, 466, 508, where the words honey, nectar, sugar' occur.

[3] See above Nos. 31, 36, 48, 107, 126, 141, 249.

[4] 8, 1, 3.

[5] N.M. 556, 557. The second closes with the words, 'Father and Mother, Thou becamest, O Lord most gracious, Tayumanava made known on Siragiri.'

[6] *E.g.* see above Nos. 106, 114, 115, 142, 176, 177, 195, and N.M. 318, 306, 490, 495, 548, 577, ('more than mother') '1329' ('more than mother').

[7] See above, *Introduction*, part. vii.

navite scholar [1] points out, "As Father, God is the Judge, as Mother He is the Forgiver." It would be incorrect to say that Christianity has no idea of the Motherhood of God. "Can a woman forget her sucking child, that she should not have compassion on the son of her womb? Yea, these may forget, *but I will not forget thee.*".[2] This is the love of God passing the love of a mother. The motherly tenderness of God's love is compared again to that of an eagle bearing her brood across to safety,[3] and a similar thought, full of inexpressible motherliness, is in the words of Our Lord spoken to unrepentant Jerusalem: "How often would I have gathered thy children together, even as a hen gathereth her chickens under her wings!".[4] It has been pointed out that the motherhood of God is present in the words of St. James, "Of His own will He brought us forth." [5] Cobb follows the thought of the Motherhood of God through theosophic channels into conclusions almost Gnostic.[6] If we turn to the language of Christian piety we shall find the idea of the Motherhood of God stated in clear terms:

> As verily as God is our Father as verily is God our Mother, and that sheweth He in all .... I understand three manner of beholdings of the Motherhood in God. The first is the ground of our natural making. The second is taking of our nature and there beginneth the Motherhood of Grace. The third is Motherhood in working: and therein is a forth-spreading by the same Grace, of length and breadth, of height and deepness without end, and all is one Love.[7]

The Christian conception of the Motherhood of God is clearer than the Siddhanta one, in the light of the Incarnation and the Cross—motherhood being inseparable from sacrifice.[8]

---

1 Govindachariya, *Divine Wisdom of Dravida Saints*, pp. 19, 20. See also *Ibid*, p. 151.

2 Isaiah 49: 15. See 66: 13.

3 Exodus 19: 4.

4 Matt. 23: 37.

5 James 1: 18. 21, commented on by Archdeacon Wilberforce in his *Mystic Immanence* pp, 50—68. His observations on God as Mother-soul, Mother-mind are interesting.

6 *Mysticism and the Creed*. 152. "God the Father-Mother .... the Heavenly Mother .... the Blessed Virgin Mary" are his doubtful equations.

7 Julian of Norwich, *Revelations of Divine Love*, chap. lviii, lix. A book of selections from her writings is Father Congreve's *The Shewing of a Vision*.

8 See Griffith-Jones, *The Ascent through Christ*, Book ii. c. iii, sec. 2.

62. 'A' OF ALL VOWELS. (Page 18, No. 33).

The association of God with the world is expressed by various figures, for example those noted above at p. 156. See *Introduction* part ix. The illustration here is from Grammar, from the vocally blending character of the அ sound.

A, as the first of letters, every speech maintains;
The 'Primal Deity' is First thro' all the world's domains.[1]

"Like the letter அ the Incomparable Lord is all intelligence and pervades everything without change."[2] *The point to be noted is not the fact of the first place of அ in the order of letters* but its going into the composition of *all* letters. It is inherent in all the letters of the Indian Alphabets.[3] "As we say that without அ no other letter will sound, so the Vedas say, 'Apart from the Lord nothing exists.'"[4]

63. ALL YET NOT ALL. (Page 18, No. 33).

This follows from what has been said in the last note. "God is all but all is not God. He is immanent in everything and yet above everything. The doctrine is very popular in nearly the whole of Tamil literature, and it is most vividly expressed in the favourite phrase எல்லாமாய் அல்லவுமாய் [All yet not all]. The Hindu idealists stop at எல்லாமாய் (He is all) and do not proceed to postulate அல்லவுமாய் (He is not all or He is above all)."[5] Our poet employs here this much-used expression எல்லாமாய் அல்லவுமாய். The thought is amplified in a whole hymn:[6]

The clearness of the mind, its dimness,
And its bewilderment Thou art;
Within the mind Thou art its knowledge,
Of knowledge its divinest part;
Thou art all form and change most wondrous,
Reality change cannot reach;
Thou art all objects known in Nature,
Thou art the means of knowing each;
The senses five art and five primals,
Outness Thou art, inness of all;
Art closest nearness, furthest distance,
Rise and increase, decrease and fall;

---

[1] *Kurral*, 1. 1, 1, (Pope's Translation).
[2] T. A. P. 1, 1.
[3] Barnett, *Gita* p. 199, note on *Gita* x. 33, "Of letters I am the syllable A."
[4] *Bodham* ii. 1 (b). See Nalla. *Bodham* p.p. 12, 19, 20; Nalla. *T.A.P.*, pp. 7.18; and Nalla. *Studies* pp. 53-62, for a learned disquisition on 'vowels and consonants.'
[5] Nalla. *Bodham*, p. 17.
[6] N.M. 68. See N. M. 71. In *Isa Upanishad*, verses 1, 4, 5, we have the idea of God being all yet not all, particularly verse 5 which says, "It moves not; is far, is near, is within all this, and is outside of all this."

Evil and good, and light and darkness;
The present and the times to be,
To-day, to-morrow, and all ever;
The one, the many, all we see.
That Thou art all, nor all art ever,
They only know who have Thy grace;
That Thou art all, yet all transcendest,
All things that are in time and space,
They know the wise in God, grace-gifted,
O God in whose great amplitude
The seen the unseen That embracest,
All-filling Bliss, Beatitude.

The idea of God being all and yet not all is best explained by the figures given above of vowels and consonants, fragrance, etc. So far as the mind and its acts are concerned, God is, according to the Siddhanta,[1] identified with the acts as Doer, to the extent that they are done in His presence and permitted by Him.

64. Lord of the herd of souls. (Page 10, No. 33).

The original here, and elsewhere[2], is பசுபதி *pasupati*. The history of this word is interesting. In the *Rig Veda* one of the titles of Rudra is *pasupa*, 'protector of cattle',[3] and in later literature Rudra is called *pasunam patih*, 'lord of cattle'[4] *Patih* 'lord' occurs in the Rig Veda with names of gods, as *Prajapatih* 'lord of creatures,'[5] *Idas patih*, 'lord of oblations',[6] *Brihaspatih* 'lord of prayer,'[7] *Brahmanaspatih* 'lord of prayer.'[8] Rudra is addressed in an early hymn as *Medhapatih* 'lord of the sacrifice.'[9] Mr. Nallaswamy Pillai observes that "*Medhapatih* is the same word as the more popular *Pasupati*, *pasu* meaning the animal offered in sacrifice, *yajna-pasu*, and symbolically representing the bound soul-jiva. As the *pati* of all sacrifices, he is the fulfiller of sacrifices".[10] In another place the

1 K. Sundara Mudaliyar's edition of *S. Tayumanavar* p. 165.

2 See above No. 215.

3 R. V. 1. 114. 9.

4 See Bhandarkar's *Vaisnavism and Saivism*, p. 102, 103, In the *Atharvaveda* 11. 2. 1, occurs the name *pasupati*.

5 R. V. 9.5.9, and other places.

6 R. V. 5. 43. 14.

7 R. V. 1. 14. 3, and other places.

8 R. V. 1. 18. 1, and other places.

9 R. V. 1. 43. 4.

10 *Studies* 112, *quoting* R. V. 1. 114, 4, and 3. 2. 5. On R. V. 3.2.5 Griffith points out that Rudra there is a synonym for Agni.

same scholar observes that *pasu* in *pasupatih* means 'souls' and not 'cattle.' [1] It has been remarked that "the transition of meaning from lord of animals to lord of souls fettered like animals by the bonds (*pasa*) of sin—which is the sense the word *Pasupati* bears now in the Saiva Siddhanta—was a very natural one."[2] To the student of Comparative Religion the present contents of the term *pasupati* 'lord of the herd of souls,' are significant. The term is used in all Saiva Siddhanta references as a title of Siva.[3] It is interesting to note that Krishna is addressed in the *Gita* 'Lord of the Herds.'[4] I may be permitted to refer to what I have elsewhere [5] remarked on the great thoughts of the *Gita*: "Another great ideal, the evolution of which is traceable from the age of the Rig Veda, is that which is suggested in Krishna's name 'Lord of the Herds.' It is the Vedic *pasunampatih*, the Siddhanta *pasupati*, 'Lord of the herd of souls.' It is a title (the *Gita* 'Lord of the Herds' in its spiritual setting and apart from any association with a Krishna the cowherd) [6] rich in the contents of such tenderness, of the relationship of God to the human soul, as finds its final and full expression in Him who is the Shepherd and Overseer [7] of our souls, the Good Shepherd [8] Who has laid down His life for His sheep."

65. Sankara, Suyambu, Sambu. (Page 20, No. 36).

These are much used words of Saiva adoration. They occur in the chorus to the verses forming the section entitled, above, *The Beloved*, (see, page 106).

Sankara means 'the Beneficent.' As doer of good God is called Sankara.[9] In Saiva devotional literature it is a name of Siva.[10] Long before the composition of the *Gita* the name Sankara had become a well-known title of Siva and the cult of Siva well-established. The author of the *Gita* desirous of asserting the supremacy of Krishna-

---

1 *Siddhiyar* p. 144.

2 Father Gnanapragasar, *Philosophical Saivism* 153.

3 See above, *Introduction*, part iv.

4 *Gita* 1, 32.

5 *Foregleams of God*, ch, ix § 12, *ad fin*.

6 On *Govinda* 'finder of lost cows' see Bhandarkar *V, S*, 36.

7 1 Peter 2 : 25.

8 S. John 10. 11.

9 *T. A. P.* 1. 9. The sense of 'destroyer' from Sanscrit *Samhri* has been suggested.

10 "Hail! Ganga-wearing Sankara," *Tiruvachagam* V. 256.

Vasudeva over the gods of other cults makes Krishna say, "Of the Rudras I am *Sankara*." [1]

Suyambu is the *Svayam-bhu*, meaning 'self-existent,' of the Upanishads. It is an attribute of Deity.[2] *Sambu* which may be rendered 'the beneficently happy' is the *Sambhu* of the Upanishads. It occures as one of the many names of God, referred to as the Soul.[3] Our poet has a list of over twenty titles of Siva, including the three under comment, in one of his hymns.[4]

66. The Four. (Page 20, No. 36).

Sanakan, Sanantanan, Sanātanan, and Sanatkumāran, were according to legerd, four sons of the god Brahma of the Puranic Triad. These four had studied the Upanishads and other writings of the Hindu religion for years but did not find rest of soul. They then prayed to Siva, "Lord, give us the grace to find peace of mind," and Siva appeared to them, under a banyan shade, and sat down in the posture of an ascetic. He showed them a secret by the mystical sign indicated by the figure of the thumb joining tip of the pointer, and gave them the saving word.[5]

The four are alluded to by our poet in many places.[6]

67. One Word. (Page 20, No. 36).

The four are said to have received the knowledge of salvation 'by one brief word' spoken by Siva. A very sensible comment on this word is that 'as it was spoken by the Teacher for the cars of the disciples alone it is not revealed to others.'[7] Tayumanaswamy himself, when he refers[8] to the 'one saving word' spoken to him by his Guru, seems to support the view that the 'word' was a secret communication to the disciple personally, and 'suddenly.'[9] It was a secret:

> Upon a straw to cross the sea
> Were easier than to say that secret.[10]

---

1 *Gita* x. 23.

2 *Brih. Aran. Upanishad* 2, 6, 3; 4, 6, 3; 6, 5, 4.; *Katha* 4. 1; *Isa* 8.

3 *Maitri Upanishad*. 6. 8; 7. 7. Among the names are Lord, Rudra, Truth, Life, Teacher Vishnu and *Narayana* which, in the rendering 'Son of Man'(Hume *Upanishads*, 429) arrests Christian attention.

4 N. M. 47.

5 *Parthasarathi Naidu* (M.D. Press) edition of *Tayumanavar*, page 42.

6 See N. M. 120, 131, 174, 182, 310, 420, 509. Above No. 261.

7 V. V. Series edition of *Tayumanavar*, p. 33.

8 See N. M. 46, 48, 50, 116, 132, 184, 186, 325, 449, 460, 469, 504, 515, 527, 528, 529, 647.

9 N. M. 46 ஒரு மொழி [illegible], 'when one word was suddenly uttered.'

10 Above No. 261.

This is the poet's own experience. The *Siddhiyar* teaches that "God graciously grants the *higher knowledge* as Guru and grants the supreme seat;"[1] that as Guru "He removes sins by means of the four methods of grace-giving";[2] that among the means of illumination employed by the Guru are imparting of instruction and imparting of Himself;[3] that "knowledge of God can only be secured by the grace of the Guru;"[4] and that "when the Divine Guru appears before a man then will arise heavenly wisdom in him,"[5] grace being given "by touch, by thought, by sight"[6] On our poet-saint's experience see above, *Introduction*, part iv.

There have been conjectures as to what the 'one word' spoken to the Four and to our poet was. Was it "the mystic syllable *Om*[7] from which darts the soul as an arrow to Deity its mark"? This *Om* is known as the *pranava*. There is a very full treatment of "The secret of *Om*" by a modern Siddhanta scholar.[8] The guess that *Om* was the 'one word' is weakened by the fact that it was no *secret* word in the time of Tayumanavar, having been known from early days to many. Was it the Great Text[9] of the Upanishads, 'That thou art'? Our knowledge of the wide range of our poet's learning shuts out the supposition that he was not aware of the *Upanishadic* 'great text' till the arrival of his Guru. A section of the *Tirumantram* of S. Tirumūlar, 'of whose line'[10] was the poet's Guru, is headed

---

1 3. 5. 8.

2 3. 8. 2. Four methods are termed *Saktinipāda*, "descending of grace or light."

3 3. 8. 3. *Sastra diksha, yoga diksha.*

4 3. 12. 6.

5 3. 8. 28.

6 3. 12. 7.

7 *Mundaka Upanishad* 2. 2. 4.

8 Vedasalam Swamy, *Saiva Siddhānta Gnāna Bodham*, chapter headed *Pranava Irgasiam.*

9 *The* [illegible], *mahāvākya*, 'great text,' of the Upanishads is found in *Chandogaya* 6. 8. 7, 6. 9. 4, 6. 10. 3, 6. 11. 3, 6. 12. 3, 6, 13. 3, 6. 14, 3, 6. 15. 3, 6. 16. 3. Its Sanscrit form is *Tat twam asi*. Three other great texts are known (1) 'Intelligence (*prajnāna*) is Brahma,' *Ait. Upan.* 5. 3; (2) 'This self (*atman*) is Brahma' *Mandūkya Upan.* 2; (3) 'I am Brahma,' *Brih Aran Upan.* 1. 4. 10. In the Tamil magazine called *Siddhantam*, March 1912, p. 73 is a short account of these four Great Texts and their alleged harmony with the Siddhanta. A fifth Great Text is sometimes mentioned, 'One only without a second,' (*Channdog.* 6. 2. 1.)

10 N.M. No. 37—46.

Prānavasamāti[1] 'the state of meditation of Om' and it has a statement, "*One word* within the Om".[2] A comment[3] on 'one word' is that it is the *mahāvakgam*. S. Pattanattar speaks of "the unuttered *mantra* of the Guru and the unceasing worship within the heart".[4] The true nature of the 'one word' is, as has been well observed,[5] 'something which the Guru spoke without speaking, and the faithful disciple knew without knowing.'

68. Siragiri. (Page 20, No. 36).

The hill of Sira named so after a former ruler of the district in which it stands. It is the modern Trichinopoly.

69. Lord of the Southern Shrine. (Page 20, No. 36).

I have so rendered the original '*Dakshanā mūrti*,' which may be more literally translated, 'The south-facing theophany.' Elsewhere[6] the poet refers to, 'the Beatitude manifested south-facing' (தென் பாலின் முகமாகி) and says he will 'worship in all places the manifestation seen in the south,' (தென் முகத்தின் முகமாயிருந்த கோது).[7] In the *Tiruvachagam* Siva is named, 'Lord of the south-land's clustering cocoanut-groves and Perinturai's shrine',[8] and generally 'Lord of the South'.[9] He is also described as 'He of the Southern Pandya Land'.[10] Siva as *Dakshanāmūrti* is usually viewed in four different aspects, namely, as teacher of *yoga*, teacher of *jnana*, teacher of *vina* (music), and as expounder of *Sastras*. The *Dakshanāmūrti Upanishad* gives an esoteric meaning of the name, and Siva's figure in temples, and it is that since *jnana* is known also as *dakshina* and since *dakshina* is ever in front of Siva and is gazing at him, he is called 'South-facing,' *dakshinamukha*.[11]

---

1 *Tirumantram*, verses 2675—2680.

2 *Tirumantram* 2676.

3 Ramanatha Chettiyar's edition, p. 566.

4 In *Kalignani malikai* series edition, No. 3 p 38.

5 K. S. Mudaliyar's edition of *Tayumanavar*, p. 65.

6 N. M. 120.

7 N. M. 131.

8 *Tiru* 8.4 (Pope's Translation).

9 *Tiruvachagam* 7. 26; 11. 36; 15. 30; 47. 14. The word used is தென்னவன், of the South,' a Tamil equivalent of the Sanscrit *Dakshana*.

10 *Tiruvachagam* 1. 90; 19. 8.

11 Gopinatha Rao, *Hindu Iconography*, ii. 277.

70. GRACE MATURED. (Page 20, No. 36).

In No. 37, at page 21, is the poet's account, in figurative language of the 'maturing' of the soul and its receipt of grace. A soul, it is taught in the Siddhanta, is of one of three kinds. The classification is according to the soul being attached to one or more of the primal impurities, *mala*. The *ānava mala* (see above, p. 150) is common to all classes, and the class which has only *ānava mala* is called *vijnāna kalar*. The class which has *ānava* and *karma* is *pralayā-kalar*. The class which has *ānava*, *karma* and *maya* is *sa-kalar*.[1] Human beings belong to the class of *sa-kalar*[2] that is, are united to all the *kalai*, which, literally means, 'sense-deceptions.' The *sakalar* may gradually become free from their disabilities and reach the stage of being *akalar*,[3] 'those without kalai.' To each class God has to manifest Himself, to the *sakalar* as Guru, and to the others in their inner consciousness.[4]

The appearance of the Guru to one is when he has undergone the processes of preparation for the Guru. He is then 'grace-matured' in a state of ripeness, பக்குவம், as the Tamil in the hymn under comment has it. It is his fulness of time.[5] When deeds are balanced, then the Lord shows Himself to the *Sakalar* as Guru, and puts an end to their *mala* (taints) by the fourth *saktinipatham*[6]

---

[1] *Siddiyar* 3. 8. 2. and Gnānaprakāsa Tambiran's notes in Tamil on the verse; *Sivapragasam*, 8; *T. A. P.* 2. 2; 5. 8. Sabīratnam, *Essentials of Hinduism* 71. Father Gnanaprakasar in a learned criticism (*Philosophical Saivism*, 180, 181) of *Essentials* points out, "The three classes of souls in the Siddhanta are merely the phenomenal individualization of the Saguna Brahma in his three successive states as Isvara, Hiranaya-garba, and Vaisva-nara. The Siddhanta states (*avastha*) of the souls also correspond exactly to those of the Vedanta excepting the last, *Turiyatita*, which is superadded to the former without any practical utility." See, for a lucid statement of Siddhanta views, Nalla, *Studies* 39.

[2] *T. A. P.* 2, 3, and Nalla. *T. A. P.* p. 11; Tiruvilangam's *Sivapragasam* p. 14; Gña. Tambiran's *Siddhiyar*, notes on 3. 8. 2. Nallaswami Pillai translates *T. A. P.* 2. 3 second line "The *sakalar* alone are not conscious that they are in *bantha* (bound) condition," while Pope (*Tiruvachagam*, p. lxxx) renders it, as he says, literally, "To those who cling to Him the unseen Lord is help." The two lines in Tamil are:

> முன்னிற்றத் துன்னாரு முலைலத் துன்னாக
> பேரன்புள்ளொரத் துன்னார் துணை.

[3] *T. A. P.* 5. 8.

[4] *Siddhiyar* 3. 8. 2.

[5] See above, pp. . . .

[6] *Siddhiyar*, 3. 8. 2; 3. 2. 33.

Deeds, that is good, *Karma* and evil *Karma*, must first have been 'balanced.' The Tamil for 'balancing' here is ஒப்பு. What is balancing?

After performing evil and good, he attains to இருவினை யொப்பு [*Iru vinay oppu*] becoming balanced in good and evil, pain and pleasure. This does not mean that he should so perform actions that all his good actions will weigh as much as his bad actions, or doing as much *punyam* [good] as *papam* [evil], but *it is attaining to a condition of viewing deeds either good or bad* without either liking or disliking, a condition of being described as வேண்டுதல் வேண்டாமையிலான் [He that has neither likes nor dislikes].[1]

S. Tayumanavar speaks of that stage with longings. He calls it the time of being purged of '*mala*,' மலபரி பாககாலம், (*mala paripāka kālam*).[2] He refers to the need of being spiritually fit for that time.[3] "He having become 'balanced' in the two-fold *karma*, plunges into the power of God, obtains the grace of the Guru, reaches the stage of *jnana yoga* and is freed from the triple *mala*. Then his knowledge ceases to be little, and wisdom abounds, and he is led to the Feet of the Lord".[4] *Saktinipatham*[5] is, according to the spiritual capacity of the soul, of four stages corresponding to the acts and disciplines in *sariyai, kiriyai, yōgam, jnānam,* (see below notes under No. 41) respectively. The stages are *mandham, mandhataram, teeviram, teevirataram.*[6] The personal manifestation of the Guru is to those who reach the fourth stage, and it is the fourth stage that is known as திருந்திய சத்திநிபாதம் (*tiruntiya satinipatam*), 'the excellent way.[7] Of this 'excellent' stage the poet-saint Tirumūlar says, "When the two kinds of karma are 'balanced,' the gracious power of God manifests itself as Guru, casts away all taints, and gives wisdom by which the soul becomes indifferent to deeds and has the triple *mala* destroyed and reaches God."[8] One of the signs of having passed the third stage

---

[1] Nalla, *Studies*, 200. *Sivapragasam* 48, and Tiruvilangam's notes p. 101.

[2] N. M. 454, 583.

[3] "In my mind there is no good that I may be ready for the time of putting off my *mala*" (N. M. 583, See above, No. 127).

[4] *Siddhiyar* 3. 4. 40.

[5] *Siddhiyar* 3. 8. 2. Pope (*Tiruvachagam*, p. xlvi) while rightly giving this word the sense of 'cessation of energy' which indeed covers the idea of indifference to likes and dislikes is misled into the error (p. xlviii) of explaining இருவினையொப்பு as an *equalising of evil and good deeds*, a setting off of one against the other.

[6] *Tirumantram* 1514—1529.

[7] *Sivapragasam* 48.

[8] *Tirumantram* 1527. The concluding portion in the Tamil is: கர்மமும் அறுத்துத் திவ்விய சித்த சிவமாக்கவே. See, for a full and lucid treatment of *Sattinipatam* the March 1912 issue of *Siddhantam*, pp. 77—86.

is a very intensive longing for the vision of the Guru, and souls in that condition are referred to by Tayumanavar as those who for God's grace "love-thirsty longing, its fruition and its fulness find."[1]

71. BANYAN. (Page 20, No. 36).

The appearance of Siva to the saints under the shade of a banyan tree is frequently mentioned by our poet.[2] The expression கல்லால் (*kallāl*) 'stone-grown banyan' means in these hymns, as in other Tamil writings,[3] the *ficus indica* which grows on any soil chiefly on stony ground. A Tamil annotator[4] of what is No. 332 (above p. 109) seems to read the first line to mean, "my mind is stony," and so shuts out all reference to the banyan tree. This interpretation is not in accord with all the கல் ஆல் references in the hymns. In this context reference may be made to the opening passage of the *Bodham*[5] a part of which Mr. Somasundaram Pillai renders:[6] "He who sat under the banyan tree," adding, "There is nothing here to show that the god who sat under the mountain banyan tree removed the doubts of Nandi or those of anybody else as the commentators including Mr. Nallaswamy Pillai[7] would have it." The criticism may be understood to go no further than this—that the *Bodham* text does not say why the Guru was seen under the banyan tree and that Mr. Nallaswamy Pillai's rendering is not warranted by the bare text.

72. COPPER......GOLD. (Page 21, No. 37).

It is Siddhanta teaching that, as the capacity for rust is in the very core of copper, even so the primal taint (see above pp. 141, 150) is associated with the soul from eternity. Births bring the soul (copper) into use, and *maya* is friction which rubs and polishes it. Then rust covers it again. After considerable purification and refinement it is touched by the alchemist's stone (grace) and it becomes gold (divine). "Our belief is that after we have undergone a sufficient number of births, and reached *malaparipāgam* (மலபரிபாகம்) God's grace (சத்தி

[1] Above, No. 127, at p. 58.

[2] Above, Nos. 37, 261, 332. N.M. 135, 182, 281, 345, 419, 420, 425, 430, 435, 504, 509, 520, 1392, 1415. In some of these the poet speaks of his own experience.

[3] *E.g., Tiruvachagam*, xii. 62, 63, 77 ; xiii. 49.

[4] K. S. Mudaliyar's edition, p. 713.

[5] *Invocation.*

[6] *Third Saiva Conference Addresses*, 1914, p. 20.

[7] Nalla. *Bodham*, p. xxx.

பாதம் *satinipālam*) will touch and convert us into Himself. There is no harm for us if we believe that we will reach perfection, Divinehood. At any rate we are sure of reaching perfect manhood." [1] With this may be compared the Islamic statement, "Our copper has been transmuted by this rare alchemy." [2] It is well to note that in Hindu religious literature analogy plays an important part and in a subtle manner becomes a substitute for argument.[3]

73. Six Great Ends. (Page 21, No. 37).

The six *antas*, 'ends' are Vedanta, Siddhanta, Nādhanta (end of sound), Bōdhanta (end of knowledge), Yōganta (end of yoga), and Kalanta (end of all philosophy). The poet associates *bodhanta*, whose end is knowledge, with the Vedanta.[4] All six are alluded to in one short verse.[5] In association with the Siddhanta, the Saiva religion he professed, he uses what he calls *muttānta*.[6] This is a seventh great 'end', the 'goal of *mukti*', heaven, deliverance.

74. Advaita. (Page 21, No. 57).

See above, *Introduction*, part v.

75. Nine Continents. (Page 21, No. 38).

The 'nine continents' which cannot be geographically located anywhere are named and described in terms of incredible exaggeration in *Sivatarumōtram*.[7]

76. Bathe. (Page 21, No. 38).

Bathing in the sea or in rivers at stated seasons is a meritorious act.[8] A puritan view of this religious duty is contained in some beautiful verses in *Tirumantram*.[9]

---

[1] Nalla. *Bodham*, p. 13, 27. On Christian "perfection" see Sacramelli, *Dir Ascet.* i. ›. 1. § 10. Belief in alchemy is seen in No. 13, above, and N.M. 58.

[2] Nicholson, *Mystics of Islam*, 118.

[3] See above, *Introduction*, part ix.

[4] See above, No. 59 (at p. 33).

[5] N.M. 1253.

[6] Above. No. 60 (at p. 33) and N.M. 1000.

[7] xii. 51-65. See *Vishnu Purana*, Book ii, ch. 2.

[8] *Sivatarumotram*, iii. 47-54.

[9] Verses, 509-514.

77. Seven-Forked Fire. (Page 21, No. 33).

Fire is seven-forked.[1] The context in which ascetics are said to stand in the seven-forked fire, namely, that, while so standing, they eat dry leaves and drink water or air to still their 'pangs of hunger' suggests that the reference is not to any literal standing in the midst of fire. The passage means that they *fast*, eating dry leaves at most. In the Upanishads we read of a digestive fire.[2] There is 'a fire in the stomach which cooks food'.[3] The 'digestive fire should be built up'.[4] Associated with food and digestion is the *Samāna* breath 'from which arise the seven flames'.[5] It is taught that 'from the Imperishable come forth the seven life-breaths, the seven flames, and their fuel'.[6] Sankara's comment on the 'seven life-breaths, *prāna*' is that they are the seven organs of sense in the head, and their locations are the two eyes, the two ears, the mouth and the two nostrils.[7]

A Tamil commentary on Tayumanavar has this note on the passage under comment: "When yogis perform austerities (தவம்) in the midst of the five fires (பஞ்சாக்கினி *panjāgni*) they eat, when necessary, dry leaves, etc."[8] The fire of the five senses is not to be identified with the fires of the Five-Fire Doctrine, *panjāgni vidyā*.[9] Mr. Shanmuga Mudaliyar's paraphrase-translation of the passage bears out the line of annotation I have here adopted. He has:[10] "Curing the pain of hunger with dry leaves or water or air, or keeping the stomach empty withal (*sic.*) its fire of digestion arising in seven flames". It is to the pangs of hunger we may take it that the poet refers elsewhere:

How often have I longed to live alone
  With lips unspeaking and unseeing eyes,
Dead unto all things living, dumb and blind,
  And, for the quenching of the fires that rise
Within, dry leaves from forest trees my food
  Of fallen fruit ripest to eat or green,
Or root my fingers rend from tree or herb,
  Or bulb that groweth underground unseen.[11]

---

[1] *Rig Veda*, 1. 141. 1; 4. 50. 4. *Mundaka Up.* 1. 2. 4. speaks of 'the seven flickering tongues of flame.

[2] *Brih. Aran. Up.* 5. 5. 9; *Maitri* 2. 6.

[3] *Maitri*, 6. 17.

[4] *Maitri*, 6. 34.

[5] *Prasna*, 3. 5; 4. 4..

[6] *Mundaka*, 2. 1. 8.

[7] Sashachari, *Upanishads* i, p. 131. Hume, *Upanishads*, p. 371.

[8] K. S. Mudaliyar's edition, p. 91.

[9] *Chandog. Up.* 5. 10. 10. Hume, *Upanishads*, p. 60.

[10] *S. Deepika* i. 33.

[11] N. M. 104 (a part). See above No. 118 and N. M. 126, 156 where mention is made of dry leaves, etc.

78. Mountain's Cave. (Page 21, No. 38).

A cave of some lofty mountain is considered a spot congenial for ascetic meditation.[1]

79. Veins, Spark, Breath, Moon, Soma. (Page 22, No. 38).

It is taught that there are 72,000 veins, called *hita*, leading from the heart to the pericardium;[2] as a hair sub-divided a thousand fold, so minute are they, full of white, blue, yellow, green and red.[3] More relevant to the hymn under comment is the statement that of the 'hundred and one arteries of the heart, one passes up to the crown of the head, and going up by it the soul reaches immortality.'[4] An Upanishad explains the total of arteries thus, namely that to each of the hundred and one arteries of the heart belong a hundred smaller arteries and to each of these belong seventy-two thousand branching arteries.[5] The veins to which attention is limited in this hymn are the ten[6] *tasai nādi* (தசை நாடி) one of which is known in the Upanishads as *sushumna*.

> There is an artery called the *sushumna*, leading upwards conveying the breath, piercing through the palate. Through it, by joining the breath, the syllable *Om*, and the mind, one may go aloft. By causing the tip of the tongue to turn back against the palate and by binding together the senses, one may, as greatness, perceive greatness. Thence he goes to selflessness .. . . After having first caused the breath that has been restrained to stand still, then, having crossed the limited, with the unlimited one may at last have union in the head.[7]

The Yogic process which Tayumanavar in this hymn mentions as inefficacious to secure 'liberation' is what he gives elsewhere[8] with greater detail—'restraining of the primal breath, driving the primal fire up to the moon's region, in the head, and tasting the resultant moon-drawn food.' The breath and the primal fire, *mulāgni*, find mention in other places in the hymns.[9] The *Gita* has directions as

---

[1] N. M. 105, 125. See above No. 118. For the *Gita* rules for Yogis see vi. 10.

[2] *Brih. Aran. Up.* 2. 1. 219.

[3] *Brih. Aran. Up.* 43, 20; *Kaushitaki Up.* 4, 19.

[4] *Chandog.* 8. 6. 6; *Katha* 6. 16.

[5] *Prasna* 3. 6.

[6] The ten are *sushmna, idaikala, pingkala, kāntāri, anti, singuvai, alampuiai, purusha, sangini, kuku.*

[7] *Maitri Up.* 6, 21.

[8] N.M. 111.

[9] N.M. 58, 63, 105, 108, 114, 127, 347, 428, 788, 1175.

to the repression of the breath.[1] The primal breath is the same as *prāna*, 'one of the heart's five openings for the gods, the five gatekeepers of the heavenly world.'[2] The suppression of the vital breath is a yogic sacrifice.[3] The 'fire' the poet speaks of is probably the heat described in the *Maitri Upanishad*, as 'the heat of Brahma . . the warmth of the body'.[4] 'The *prāna* breath as fire gives warmth'.[5] According to text-books on Yoga asceticism an important part of Yoga is the *prānāyāma*,[6] which has "as its chief object the mixing of *prāna*, the upper breath, and *apāna*, the lower breath, and raising them upwards by degrees and stages, till they subside in the head. The practice awakes a peculiar force which is dormant about the navel . . . It is this force which is the source of all occult powers".[7] This force, believed to be situated in the region of the navel, is the 'fire,' 'spark' the poet mentions. 'The moon' says a Hindu writer,[8] 'is said to remain in our forehead for our benefit.' This combines the thought of union at last in the head' in one Upanishad [9] with that of another [10] that "the moon is the door of the heavenly world." The moon is in the Upanishads spoken of sometimes as the food of the gods,[11] once as semen,[12] and once as 'a sprout, as is prāna, of the bright power . . . which is the nectar in the midst of the sun.'[13]

The yogic practice of *prānāyāma* is believed [14] to confer deathlessness, 'to live undying unto length of days,' as our poet suggests in this hymn. With the poet, it may yet be asked, even when one has mastered all the learning on this subject, "Can all this liberation bring?"

80. Frame of my Frailty. (Page 24, No. 41).

On the body in the Siddhanta scheme of salvation see above, *Introduction*, part vi.

---

1 *Gita*, iv. 29; v. 27; viii. 12, See vi. 10.

2 *Chandog. Up.* 3. 13, 1-6, where the five breaths are named and located. See also *Tait. Up.* 2. 2; *Prasna* 3, 4-12; *Brih. Aran.* 3. 9. 26; 4. 2. 4; *Maitri* 6. 33.

3 *Maitri*. 6. 26, and *Gita*, iv. 27. See also *Kaushitaki Up.* 2. 5.

4 *Maitri*. 6, 27.

5 *Prasna*, 2. 5.

6 'Restraint of breath' *Maitri* 6. 18.

7 Manilal Drividi, *Yoga Sastra*, 32.

8 Shanmuga Mudalyiar, *S. Deepika*, 1. 34.

9 *Maitri*, *Up.* 6. 21.

10 *Kaush.* 1. 2.

11 *Chandog.* 5. 10. 3.

12 *Brihad.* 1. 4. 6.

13 *Maitri*, 6. 35. On the moon in connection with the passage of souls after death see my *Foregleams of God*, ch. x.

14 *Maitri*, 6. 25; *Kaushitaki*, 3. 2.

81. Sariya, Kiriya, Yoga. (Page 24, No. 41).

There are four stages of religious growth. The first is *sariya* which includes all devotional and moral exercises in which the practiser surrenders his body to Siva. The second is *kriya* consisting mainly in ritual duty and conformity to institutional religion. The third is *yoga*. The fourth in *jnānam*, where the Guru appears to the matured soul (see above, p. 167.) In the *Gita* yoga is of three kinds, *jnāna-yoga*, the Rule of Knowledge [1] *kriya-yoga* in which social duties are done without attachment,[2] and *raja-yoga* in which the yogin becomes the man of the Rule.'[3] Tayumanavar speaks of *siva-raja-yoga* [4] and simply of *raja-yoga*.[5] A Tamil commentator [6] of the poet's hymns identifies *siva-raja-yoga* with the *pranayama*.

82. Dancest in Wisdom's Hall. (Page 25, No. 42).

In the *Rig Veda* it is suggested that the earth was formed from the dust of Vishnu's strides.[7] In a Hymn [8] addressed to "the gods" generally, creation is ascribed to the dancing of the gods and to the 'thickening cloud of dust' arising from their feet. Indra is spoken of as the 'Dancer.'[9] The Maruts, sons of Rudra, are 'dancers breast-adorned with gold.'[10] Whether the idea of dancing is borrowed by the Siddhanta writers from the Rig Veda, or from other sources, it is associated in their writings, with Siva who, accordingly, is named *Nadarajah*, 'Lord of the Dance.' His acts are compared to a dance, 'the dance of creation, development, destruction, veiling and grace.'[11] In an especial manner for the benefit of the devout, Siva is said to be dancing in the Hall of Sidambaram, one of the most famous of Saiva

---

[1] ii. 39.

[2] ii. 45; iii. 6; v. 27.

[3] ii. 55; vi. 3.

[4] N. M. 62

[5] N. M. 586. This hymn gives what the results are of *Raja-yoga*.

[6] K. S. Mudaliar's edition, p. 180. See *Tirumantram*, 564 577. On *Sariya*, etc., see *Sivapragasam*, 10.

[7] R. V. 1. 22. 17.

[8] R. V. 10. 72. 6.

[9] R. V. 1. 130. 7; 2. 22. 4; 3. 22. 6; 8. 24. 12; 8. 57. 7; 8. 31. 3. Some commentators take, 'dancer' to mean 'dancer in war.' Sayaṇa explains 'dancer' as applied to Indra owing to his 'faculty of internal impulse in all things' Griffith, *Rig Veda*, Vol. ii. 157.

[10] R. V. 8. 20. 22.

[11] *Siddhiyar*, 3. 5. 8. also 3. *Invocation*; *Tirumantram*, 2789. On the dance of Siva see S.P.G. Rao's *Hind. Icon.* ii, part i, p. 231.

shrines in South India. S. Tayumanavar refers to this in many places.[1] The scene of this dance is named Tillai, Pundarika, Kanagasabai, equivalents of Sidambaram. The Dancer in the universe is the Dancer in Wisdom's Hall in Sidambaram, and by transition of thought into the plane of mysticism, he is also the Dancer in the shrine of the human heart. Devout references to this last idea are found in Tayumanavar.[2] See above p. 156, on the Indwelling God. The conception of the heart as the House of God forms the subject of a thoughtful essay by Mr. Nallaswami Pillai.[3] The idea of God taking part in the dances of the devout is traceable in the writings of the neo-Platonists.[4] High spiritual relationship of the soul to the soul's Lover is sometimes expressed by the imagery of a dance.[5]

83. ONE NOT TWO. (Page 26, No. 43).

See above, *Introduction*, part v. on Advaita.

84. DRUNKEN POISON. (Page 27, No. 44).

On Siva's blue neck due to poison see above, Note 47, page 151.

85. SIVA, VISHNU, BRAHMA. (Page 27, No. 44).

See above, *Introduction*, part iv. In this Hymn the poet eclectically makes the Guru-God identical with each person of the Triad. Vishnu's great incarnation as Krishna is the theme of the *Gita*. Brahmā 'the four-faced' is said to have expounded the Vedas from his seat on a lotus.

86. THE SOUL ATTAINETH. (Page 28, No. 46).

On this nature of the soul see above, *Introduction* part v.

87. MARKANDA, SUKA. (Page 28, No. 46).

Markanda was a young devotee owing to the strength of whose faith Siva overcame for him the god of death.[6] Suka was a great

---

1 See above, Nos. 42-49, and N. M. 169. 182. 259. 260. 261. 284. 285. 287. 299. 306. 310. 328.

2 For instance in N. M. 373. 378. 439.

3 *Studies*, pp. 1-20. See *Unmai Vilakkam*, 32.

4 Hügel, *Myst. Elem.* ii. 97. *cf.* Underhill, *Mysticism* 281, *note.*

5 See extracts from Mechthild's *Book of the Flowing Light of the Godhead* given by Evelyn Underhill in *The Quest*, July 1913, pp. 629–652.

6 See above, No. 169, at p. 72, also N.M. 502, 763 and see below, p. 192.

ascetic who was never touched by the love of women. He is one of the twenty-one great saints.[1]

88. Other Gods Adore. (Page 28, No. 46).

See above, *Introduction*, part iv.

89. Rishis of the Vedas Four. (Page 28, No. 46).

The sages to whom are ascribed the Rig Veda and the other Vedas, or sages skilled in the Vedas. The former sense is more appropriate to the context which excludes living sages who may happen to be skilled in the scriptures.

90. Gods-in-Waiting. (Page 28, No. 46).

The original கணநாதர் is paraphrased into what it means, gods-in-waiting ' at whose head is Ganesha.

91. The Nine. (Page 28, No. 46).

The original is simply 'the nine siddhars' நவநாத சித்தர்கள். A collection of hymns is specially addressed by our poet[2] to the *siddhars*, men who had acquired marvellous powers psychic and physical. Sattyanātar and eight others were the most renowned of these *siddhars*.

92. Goddesses of Melody. (Page 28, No. 46).

The original கந்தருவர் is paraphrased here.

93. Servants—Half-Men, Half-Animals. (Page 28, No. 46).

This is the paraphrase of the one word கின்னரர்கள் in the original.

94. This Worship. (Page 29, No. 47).

The poet finds a spiritual parallel to the essentials of ceremonial worship—sacrifice, anointing, libation, incense, lights. A similar spiritual outlook is seen in No. 45, above

95. Seekest. (Page 29, No. 47).

See above, *Introduction*, part vii on God's quest of man.

---

[1] See N.M. 43, 154, 163, 329.

[2] N.M. 59-66. N.M. 60 is No. 355, above, at p. 115.

96. TREES OF PARADISE. (Page 30, No. 49).

See above, Note 18, pages 136, 137.

97. SHARABA. (Page 30, No. 49).

This is supposed to be an eight-legged bird ever the most feared foe of the lion.

98. BARK. (Page 30, No. 49).

Mr. Shanmuga Mudaliyar translates the lines, I have paraphrased, about 'the bark' thus: "Thou art the safety-boat regularly plying in the celestial sphere of Thy Grace and anchoring to take me in at the harbour of my undying love of devotion to Thee."[1] A. K. renders differently:

> O ship that doth traverse the space of Grace
> To cross the flood of man's limitless greed
> And help my humble self to reach the shore.[2]

My paraphrase rendering, like A. K's translation, is justified by the original which speaks of the 'boundless sea (flood) of self-love', கைதற்ற பேராசை வெள்ளத்தின், etc. I think that the learned Shanmuga Mudaliyar's 'my undying love of devotion to Thee' gives quite the opposite sense. I have expanded the Tamil meaning and emphasized it by repetition: 'the boundless sea of love self-seeking, birth-begetting. . . self's boundless ocean'. The sea of self is according to the theology of our poet, the sea of births and re-births.[3]

99. KNOWLEDGE. (Page 33, No. 59).

Bodanta is 'the end of knowledge'. See above, page 170. In this verse the Vedanta is praised as the way of knowledge, while in the next the Siddhanta is named as the way of love and devotion.

100. IN HEAVEN. (Page 33, No. 60).

The original is முத்தாந்த வீதி, 'the procession yard of Muktanda' which is beyond the six great ends (see page 170) and means 'the end of mukti', the soul's home-coming.

101. AS CHILDREN. (Page 35, No. 72).

The thought that saints are comparable in their simplicity to children and the insane occurs in other places.[4]

---

[1] *S. Deepika*, i. 107.

[2] *Prabuddha Bharata*, November 1913, p. 209. *cf.* 'Brahma-boat', in *Svet.* 2. 8.

[3] N. M. 285.

[4] N. M. 130, 199, 776. Ruysbroeck refers with disapprobation to acts, like those of the insane and the drunkard, supposed to be signs of rapture (Underhill's *Ruysbroeck*, 125.

102. Salt in Water. (Page 35, No. 73).

The soul's relationship to God, at a certain stage of spirituality, is expressed by the analogies of salt in water, flame on camphor (page 121), lamplight in sunlight (page 121), milk in water (page 121). See above, *Introduction*, parts v, ix.

103. Booty. (Page 38, No. 38).

A definite spiritual experience, the three-fold surrender, is of frequent mention by our poet.[1] This surrender is made to the God-man Guru. The poet speaks thus of this experience :

When I in glad surrender gave
Myself, my God, to Thee,
The boundlessness of bliss became
In fulness food to me ;
The life that knows nor night nor day,
Unending, I attained,
And every blessing, every boon,
In richest measure gained ;
And to Thy lowly devotee
God Thou hast given the grace
Beyond the bonds of births to be,
Untreading troublous ways.[2]

Full surrender is confessed by other Siddhanta saints. It is attested by the experience of Christian mystics as a definite and dateable fact :

On Saturday, November 17th, 1534, having, before Holy Communion, a great desire to die to all things, I prayed with all my heart that God, in the most perfect manner possible, would slay me and unite me with Himself. And in so doing I renounced into His hands all myself and everything existing under heaven, whilst electing God anew as my only Love, my only solace, my only comfort, and my All.[3]

Fulness of surrender is a commonplace of Christian experience, it is at least demanded of all Christians, as evidenced in the Church's highest worship :

We offer and present unto Thee, O Lord, ourselves, our souls and bodies to be a reasonable, holy and lively sacrifice unto Thee.[4]

This follows from the great truth thus stated by a Christian mystic :

---

[1] N. M. 76, 149, 321, 362, 440, 500, 529, 535, 556. See above, No. 195.

[2] N. M. 500.

[3] Battista, in *Myst. Elem.* i. 346.

[4] The Prayer Book, H. C. Service.

It is the property of love ever to give and ever to receive. Now, the love of Jesus is both kind and generous. All that He has, all that He is, He gives: all that we are, all that we have, He takes. . . He would absorb our life in order to change it into His own: ours full of sin, His full of grace and glory, all ready for us, if we will but renounce ourselves. [1]

104. SEEKING ME. (Page 39, No. 89).

See above, *Introduction*, part vii.

105. GUILE. (Page 41, No. 100).

Elsewhere the poet says that to the matured soul God appears as Guru 'taking the form of man to save man, even as a decoy deer is used for capturing other deer.' [2] This is a form of 'the guile of God.'

The selfishness of man is so contrary to God and rebellious against Him, that God Himself cannot induce the soul to do His will except by certain stratagems: promising it things greater than those left, and giving it, even in this life, a certain consoling relish, and this He does, because He perceives the soul to love things visible so much, that it would never leave one unless it saw four. [3]

Crashaw, one of the poets of English mysticism, says:

> Let not my Lord the mighty Lover
> Of souls, disdain that I discover
> The hidden art
> Of His high stratagem to win your heart.[4]

In the book of a great Jewish mystic, the prophet Hosea,[5] the Lord is represented as saying: "I will allure her, and bring her into the wilderness, and speak comfortably unto her. I will even betroth thee unto Me in faithfulness."

106. ECSTASY. (Page 42, No. 104).

The physical effects of inward feelings are more fully described elsewhere by the poet.[6]

---

[1] Ruysbroeck, *De Contemplatione* (Hello) pages 152, 153.

[2] N. M. 148, See N. M. 58, 562, 1082. *Sivapragasam* 8.

[3] S. Catherine of Genoa in *Myst. Elem.* i. 271.

[4] Crashaw's *Poems*, page 283.

[5] Hosea 2: 14, 20. "Hosea was one of the first one of the noblest of the not very large family of mystics who dare to make their own thoughts, feelings and action the norm of divinity." (The Rev. J. Strahan in *The Expository Times*, August 1912, page 522.)

[6] See above, Nos. 36, 48, 107, 108, 126.

107. KNOWLEDGE OF MAN TO MAIDEN. (Page 42, No. 104).

The thought that as love comes to a maiden when she is fit for it so does the love of God reach the matured soul occurs elsewhere.[1] Under a different figure the same idea is expressed in No. 105.

108. BRAHMA. (Page 43, No. 106).

Brahma, the creating God, is not supreme. See above *Introduction*, part iv.

109. THIS FRAME. (Page 44, No. 107).

On the body see above, *Introduction*, part vi.

110. MY BODY AND MY BEING THRILLED. (Page 45, No. 108).

In Catholic theology the fourth degree of contemplation is called 'the inebriation of love'[2] It is the Islamic *sukr*, 'intoxication.'[3] "It is a jubilation excited in the soul by an excess of love, and the joy of the soul overflows to the senses and reveals itself externally by sallies and eccentricities that resemble the results of material inebriation."[4] That inebriation, has, in some cases, the likeness of hysteria.[5]

111. THOU LIVEST, MY SOUL LIVES EVER. (Page 45, No. 108).

The soul, according to the Siddhanta, is co-eternal with God. See above, *Introduction* part v, and No. 277 at page 96.

112. THREE-EYED. (Page 45, No. 109).

Siva is the Lord of the mid-set eye,[6] the third eye being in the forehead, midway between the eye-brows. The red, white, or black mark worn by Hindus on the forehead, between the eye-brows, is symbolical of this third eye of Siva. It is taught that the third eye is only an allegory and is not a physical reality. Thus we read in the *Siddhiyar* :

When Uma out of playfulness shut the eyes of the supreme Lord, all

---

[1] N. M. 192, 1064.

[2] Devine, *Mystical Theology*, 409.

[3] Nicholson, *Studies in Islamic Mysticism*, 248.

[4] Devine, *Mystical Theology*, 409.

[5] S. Teresa, *Interior Castle*, Sixth Mansion iv, 18, vi. 15. S. Teresa's *Life*, c. xvi.

[6] See above, Nos. 144, 146, 184, 206—210, 282.

the worlds were darkened, and the darkness was removed by his third eye. They know not that by this tradition it is meant that all the lights of heaven are but reflections of Siva's supreme jyoti form.[1]

Along lines of interpretation similar to the above is the teaching that the three eyes are the sun, the moon, and fire, or again that the third eye is wisdom.[2]

113. COMING, GOING. (Page 45, No. 109).

See above, notes at page 130.

114. VINDHU. (Page 46, No. 110).

See above, Note 38, page 149.

115. WHILE IN THE BODY. (Page 47, No. 111).

The conviction that of all births the human is the best is very strong in the poet.[3] "What if *to-day* be mine the blessing?", is his longing.[4]

It is this birth, this life, *this body* that is most opportune, and not to find salvation *in this body* is to miss much that is certain for the chances of the unknown hereafter. This belief is very marked in the poet.[5]

While in this birth and in this body
My spirit's shelter, halting place,
'Tis best that I in joy be blended
With bliss that from the sky of grace
A cloud with bounty laden raineth
Beatitude.[6]

116. GOD MOVES ALL. (Page 48, No. 113).

See above, Note 32, page 143. The arbitrariness of God doing what He wills, is a fact which must be humbly acknowledged by the intellect of man. Human reason has to own the supremacy of Divine unreason. God has His reserved rights.[7] "Shall the clay say to

---

[1] *Siddhiyar*, 3. 1. 52.

[2] See Ramaswamy Iyer's notes to *Tirumantram* in *S. Deepika*, i. 76.

[3] See No. 355, at page 115.

[4] No. 127, at page 58, also N.M. 108, 126.

[5] N.M. 126, 259, 297, 400, 438, 555, 812, 930, 1341, 1346.

[6] Above, p. 115. See *Siddhiyer*, 3. 8. 16 and 3, 2. 89 on the human birth as the best of births.

[7] See the Rev. H. J. R. Marston's paper in *Transactions of the Victoria Institute*, vol. 50, page 74.

him that fashioneth it, what makest thou?"[1] "O house of Israel cannot I do with you as this potter?"[2] A wise thinker confessed, "We are the clay, and thou our potter."[3] S. Paul[4] recalls these thoughts:

O man, who art thou that disputest with God? Shall the thing formed say to him that formed it, why hast thou made me thus? Hath not the potter power over the clay, of the same lump to make one vessel unto honour and another unto dishonour?

This idea was a Jewish commonplace, even outside the Old Testament. In the *Wisdom of Ben Sira*, probably of B.C. 190—175, we read, "As the clay is in the potter's hand to fashion it at his pleasure so man is in the hand of Him that made him."[5] The arbitrariness of God to do what He will with what is His own to give or refuse[6] is consistent with all that is revealed to us of His character generally, and particularly as the Father who is solicitous for the well-being of a sparrow and whose providence covers the very hair of our heads.[7]

It is in some way, I take it, to the reserved rights of Deity that the thinkers of the Siddhanta refer when they say, in the terse words of our poet, "'Tis God who doeth as He pleaseth."[8] Tayumanavar discusses in a hymn the logical consequence of the doctrine that God is the mover of all.[9] He speaks of God as moving souls like figures in a puppet show;[10] the Maya maker;[11] and the poet adopts the language of his age in speaking of all God's acts as His sport.[12] The acts of Siva in the universe are called the சேட்டை, '*sēttai*' of Siva, 'mere playfulness.'[13] A great Siddhanta thinker, the author of *Sivapragāsām*, lifts this idea of 'sport' above the conception of capricious and wanton playfulness by corrective and cautionary exposition that the acts of God should be more properly called 'acts of grace' than 'sport.'[14]

---

1 Isaiah, 45: 9

2 Jeremiah, 18: 6.

3 Isaiah, 64: 8.

4 Romans, 9: 20, 21.

5 xxxiii. 13.

6 S. Matt. 20: 15.

7 S. Matt. 10: 29, 30.

8 No. 113, page 48.

9 No. 122, page 54.

10 No. 147, above.

11 N. M. 562, 570.

12 N. M. 352, 448, 1404. See above, No. 289, (page 98) and see notes to No. 285, below.

13 *Siddhiyar*, 3, 5, 6. The Tamil சேட்டை is not brought out in Mr. Nellaswami Pillai's translation, (page 214).

14 *Sivapragasam*, 18.

117. Tāyumānavār. (Page 49, No. 114).

See above, Note 61, page 159.

118. Friend. (Page 48, No. 117).

"Kinsman......good friend give strength and life to those who praise Thee". Thus in the *Rigveda*[1] is Indra addressed. So in other places in that Veda.[2] The closeness of God to the soul in spiritual relationship is expressed by Tayumanavar in terms of friendship in passages other than the verse under comment.[3]

When the soul counts God its nearest and dearest Friend—the Friend of whom nothing in life or death can rob it—this effect follows by a beautiful necessity: the chief and all-inclusive friendship being secured, we are at leisure from ourselves to sooth and sympathise; we are able to extend our thoughts and our ministries of love to all around us, and to reflect in our relations with men that exquisite relation which God has designed to establish with us. Our own private friendships then produce no exclusiveness but rather they become the types of our feelings to others and the ever-springing fountain-head of friendly thoughts and courteous deeds; while these private friendships and our wider relations alike are all brought up into the lofty and purifying friendship which we hold with our God and He with us.[4]

"There is a friend that sticketh closer than a brother."[5] The Greeks had a saying, "The wise are the friends of God and God of the wise,"[6] but the Jews of our Lord's day had a saying about Him, "He is the Friend of sinners."[7]

119. Dry Leaves, etc. (Page 50, No. 118).

See above, note 77 page 171.

120. Soma-Drink. (Page 50, No. 118).

See above, note 79 page 172.

121. Breath. (Page 50, No. 118).

See above, note 79 page 172.

122. Captive. (Page 52, No. 121).

See above, note 103 page 178 on "Booty"

---

[1] R. V. 3. 51. 6.

[2] See references in my *Foregleams of God*, ch. v. § § 3, 4.

[3] See above, No. 47.

[4] Horton, *Proverbs*, 238.

[5] Prov. 18: 24.

[6] Charles, *Apocrypha and Pseudepigrapha of O. T.* i. 547, note.

[7] S. Luke, 7: 34.

123. ONE FAITH'S TEACHING. (Page 54, No. 123).

.From different angles of vision God is beheld, says the poet, and the result is divergency of opinion. God is said to be (1) Female, (2) Male, (3) Everything, anything, (4) Light, (5) Abode of Sound and the primal causes, (6) Ultimate Atom, (7) Time. God is all, it is taught, and yet not all. See above, page 161.

124. VEDAS, ETC. (Page 55, No. 124).

See above, note 20 page 138 on Āgamas. Purāṇas are the eighteen works chiefly dealing with cosmogony and the gods. The Mahābhārata and the Rāmāyana are reckoned as histories.

125. DUAL, NON-DUAL. (Page 55, No. 124).

See above, *Introduction*, part v, Advaita.

126. I SHALL NOT NEED THE STAGES FOUR. (Page 53, No. 124).

On the Four Stages see above, page 174. A rendering corresponding in sense to mine is, "Enough! no more of discipline I want."[1] Quite the reverse meaning is given by Shanmuga Mudaliyar's, "So I shall only pin myself to the *Sadhana*[2] of Sariya, Kiriya, Yoga, Gnana."

127. THAT WHICH I WOULD BE. (Page 56. No. 124).

See above, *Introduction*, part v on the nature of the soul to become that to which it is attached.

128. BE LEAST OF ME AND MOST OF THEE. (Page 56. No. 124).

The Tamil உன்னை நானென்று பாவிக்கில், literally, 'By the considering of Thee as me,' refers to the *Sōham Bhāvana*, the practising of 'I am He', or *Sivōham Bhāvana*, the practising of 'I am Siva.' One of the great texts[3] of the Upanishads is *Brāhmāsmi*, 'I am Brahma,' 'I am God.'[4] Upon this text is based the *Sōham Bhāvana* religious exercise. There is a great difference between what the Vedanta has built on this text, and what the Siddhanta understands by *Sōham Bhāvana*.

[1] A. K. in *Prab. Bharata*, Nov. 1914, p. 215.
[2] Practice.
[3] See above, page 165, footnote 9.
[4] *Brih. Aran. Upanishad* 1, 4, 10.

The Vedanta view is best stated in the words of Swami Vivekananda :

> Your godhead is the proof of the God Himself.............If you are not God there was not any God and never will be. This, says the Vedanta, is the ideal to follow. Every one of us has to become a prophet and you are that already, only know it. Never think there is anything impossible for the soul. It is the greatest heresy to say that. If there is sin, this is the only sin, to say that I am weak or others are weak. [1]

Relating the instance of a man who lived in a forest and kept saying day and night, '*Sivōham*,' '*Sivōham*,' even when he was being crushed in the jaws of a tiger, the Swami observes :

> There have been many such men. There have been cases of men, who, while being cut to pieces, have blessed their enemies : "I am He, I am He, and so art thou". I am sure and perfect and so are all my enemies. You are He, and so am I......Saints and sinners, men, women and children, great and small, why not teach it with the voice of thunder, teach it to every man that is born and ever will come into the world, the man on the throne or the man sweeping the streets, rich or poor. I am the King of kings; there is no king higher than I. I am the God of gods : there is no god higher than I.[2]

The Swami's view-point is unmistakable, it is that of the Vedanta. "The Muhammadan says there is no God but Allah. The Vedanta says there is no God but man." [3] The Christian's "Nearer my God to Thee" becomes to the Vedanti "Nearer my God to *me*." [4] There is thus no doubt as to the meaning of *Brahmāsmi* to the Vedanti—'I am God.'

In the Siddhanta we are in an entirely different atmosphere of thought. The equation 'I am God' is to S. Tayumanavar "the daring of unbridled fancy." [5] He asks,[6] "What is the use of our babbling by night and by day that the ineffable One, the Source of Bliss is we ?." The *Śiddhiyar* devotes a whole section to the refutation of "the confusing statement of the heretic that He is God," [7] and exhorts, "knowing well the distinction between yourself and the Supreme, practise *Sōham bahavana*." [8] The practice is enjoined in these words :

---

[1] *Practical Vedanta*, part i, page 18.

[2] *The Freedom of the Soul*, pp. 10, 11.

[3] *Practical Vedanta*, part ii, p. 13.

[4] *Maya and Freedom*, p. 11. "You are the only gods to be worshipped." (*Practical Vedanta*, part ii, 17). One or two Muhammadan mystics are said to have expressed themselves in terms almost Vedantic. Thus Bayazid of Bisham, "I went from God to God until He cried from me in me, 'O thou I'!" (R. A. Nicholson, in *J. R. A. S.* 1913, p. 65.)

[5] Above, No. 43, p. 26.

[6] N. M. 484.

[7] *Siddhiyar*, 2, 5, *Refutation* (1).

[8] *Siddhiyar*, 2, 5, *Refutation* (18).

When the soul realizes, 'I am not the world of seen things', and 'I am not the unseen Supreme One,' and is in a state of humble devotion so that He has communion with it and if, in that state of communion, the soul meditates,' 'I am He' (*Soham*), the Lord will manifest Himself in union with the soul, one with it. As by the charmer's charm snake-poison disappears, even so the soul's impurities will disappear and purity will be attained. This is why the Vedas (Upanishads) exhort us to practise *Soham*.[1]

The soul is not to be mistaken for God.[2] The identifying of the soul with God is like identifying a crystal with the light reflected on it.[3] Darkness does not disappear (thus a learned Tamil writer observes)[4] by fancying the eye to be the sun, nor will there be sweetness by fancying the tongue to be sugar—even so are the limitations of the practice of *Soham*. The basic principle of the *Soham Bhavana* in the Siddhanta is the conception of *the soul's capacity*[5] *for becoming what it loves*. What has been written in a similar context on Sūfi mysticism may be illustratively noted here:—

God is conceived as transcendent, and the soul cannot reach Him without taking what Plotinus in a splendid phrase calls "the flight of the Alone to the Alone.' Jalaludin says:

> The motion of every atom is towards its origin;
> A man comes to be the thing on which he is bent.
> By the attraction of fondness and yearning, the soul and the heart
> Assume the qualities of the Beloved who is the Soul of souls.

'A man comes to be the thing on which he is bent': what then, does the Sufi become? Eckhart in one of his sermons quotes the saying of S. Augustine that man is what he loves, and adds the comment, "If he loves a stone, he is a stone; if he loves a man, he is a man; if he loves God—I dare not say more, for if I said that he would then be God, ye might stone me.".[6]

The gift of God's power, it is taught in the *Siddhanta*, transforms the soul into "God's purest gold."[7] The mere exercise of *soham*, as a religious practice, is meaningless and the exercise is efficacious only when there is the grace of God, indeed the grace of God will achieve union with Him.[8] It is to this union, attainable by the

---

[1] *Siddhiyar*, 3, 9, 7.

[2] *Siddhiyar*, 3. 6. 7; 3. 6. 9.

[3] Nalla. *Siddhiyar*, page 240, note.

[4] K. S. Mudaliyar, *Tayumanavar*, page 204.

[5] See above, *Introduction*, part v.

[6] Nicholson, *The Mystics of Islam*, 117. 118. In Islam man is not permitted to say *Ana L-Haqq*, 'I am God.' (See Nicholson, *Mystics of Islam* 155; *Studies in Islamic Mysticism*, 79, 80, 108. 182. 230)

[7] Above, No. 37, page 21.

[8] *Sivapragasam*, 86. *Siddhiyar*, 3. 8. 30. Sabaratna Mudaliyar in his *Essentials of Hinduism*, page 102, has his remarks so worded as to make grace an *effect* of *soham bhavana*. Perhaps he does not intend this.

efficacy of grace, that Tayumanavar refers in the hymn under comment and elsewhere.[1] Manikkavachagar speaks of this state of spirituality in the words நாம் ஒழிந்து சிவமானா, 'we have ceased to be and are become Deity,'[2] and the process of reaching that stage is described by the same poet[3] as a gradual wearing away of self:

It is Thy mercy that to-day,
Has driven from me far away
    The darkness of my heart;
And lo! belike the rising sun
Beholden, O most Holy One,
    Within my soul Thou art,
While I, unthinking, thought of Thee
The sun so risen bright in me,
    I saw me drawn anigh,
To where besides Thee there is none,
O Peruntural's Holy One,
    Nearer, yet no more I,
Yea, closer, until all of me,
Worn to an atom, worn to be
    No longer I, was one
With Thee, Siva, who art not aught
And yet without whom there is naught—
    Who claims to know Thee? None!

The Siddhanta has been very tersely contrasted with the Vedanta in the famous line of S. Tirumalar நானென வேதாந்தம் தான் என்னும் சித்தாந்தம், "the Vedanta postulates 'I am God,' the Siddhanta 'One alone.'"[4]

Among Christian mystics deification of man was a doctrine long held. Modern Christian writers on Mysticism refer to it as "the old doctrine"[5] which "to modern ears sounds not only strange but arrogant and shocking."[6] On the other hand it is possible to

---

[1] N.M. 742. 1012

[2] *Tiruvachagam*, xi. line 16. Pope (*Tiru.* p. 153) translates less accurately "I in Bliss was lost."

[3] *Tiruvachagam*, xxii. verse 7. I have departed materially from Dr. Pope's rendering (*Tiru.*, p. 222) and find myself in subtantial agreement with Sir P. Arunachalam's (*S. Deepika* i. 51) except for my grouping நீயலாற் பிறிது மற்றின்மைசென்று 'drawn nigh to where besides Thee there is none.' On 'unthinking thought' may be compared Hilton's words (*Scala* iii. Ch. 5), "The less that it thinketh that it loveth or seeth God, the nearer it nigheth for to perceive the gift of this blessed love."

[4] *Tirumantram*, 2372. See above, *Introduction*, part v. on the text. The English rendering is from Nalla. *Studies*. p. 253.

[5] Fleming, *Mysticism in Christianity*, 245, 246.

[6] Inge, *Christian Mysticism*, 396.

think of "deification" as a term intended to express in an intense manner the inexpressible experience of what the mystics call the "unitive" stage.

Such a word as 'deification' is not of course a scientific term. It is a metaphor, an artistic expression which tries to hint at a trancendent fact utterly beyond the powers of human understanding, and therefore without equivalent in human speech: that fact of which Dante perceived the "shadowy preface" when he saw the saints as petals of the Sempiternal Rose......... The blunt and positive language of the contemplatives concerning deification has aroused more enmity amongst the unmystical than any other of their doctrines or practices. It is of course easy, by confining oneself to its surface sense, to call such language blasphemous......yet, rightly understood this doctrine lies at the heart, not only of all mysticism, but also of much philosophy and most religion.[1]

Dean Inge, at the close of a full treatment of "deification", says that the three views—essentialisation, substitution and transformation—of the manner in which we may hope to be partakers of the Divine Nature[2] are all aspects of the truth, and are not mutually exclusive.[3] The man-becomingness of God as an act of infinite love suggests the possibility, within limits, of the God-becomingness of man. Man becomes Godlike in proportion to his responding to the Love of God. "Some may ask, 'What is it to be a partaker of the Divine nature or Godlike man'? Answer: he who is imbued with or illuminated by the eternal or divine light and inflamed or consumed with eternal or divine love he is a Godlike man and partaker of the divine nature."[4] In the light of the Incarnation, from the viewpoint of love, S. Athanasius may be deemed right, "God became man that we might be made God",[5] and likewise S. Augustine, "He was made partaker of our mortality that we might be made partakers of His Divinity."[6] It has been asked:

If Jesus Christ could say with absolute truth, 'I and the Father are one,' is not the goal set before every man that he too should attain to

---

[1] Underhill, *Mysticism* 500, 501.

[2] 2 Pet. 1:4.

[3] *Christian Mysticism*, pp. 356-368 forming Appendix C, "The doctrine of deification." See Bishop Laneau's *De Justorum Deificatione per Jesum Christum* 1.1.2, 1.1.3, where he discusses if the just are sons of God only in a figurative sense. He devotes 1.1.5 to the meaning of 'partakers of the Divine Nature.'

[4] *Theologia Germanica* (Winkworth's translation) p. 155. In ch. 40 (Winkworth, p. 145) there is warning against the False Light which says "The more like God one is, the better one is, and therefore I will be like God, *and will be God*."

[5] *De Verbi Incarnatione*, 54. *Contra Ar.* ii. 59.

[6] *Enarratio in Ps.* 138.

consciousness of the same truth about himself? From the consciousness of man should he not strive to attain the consciousness of God [1].

Yes, the Christian is enjoined to strive to reach the measure of the stature of the fulness of Christ [2], his every endeavour towards this goal transforming him from glory to glory into the image of the Divine [3], and he, already a son of God, has the hope of something more than being like the Lord.[4] . The Christian, however close he may get to God in character, never does, never can, become God. What the mystics mean by 'deification' is no arrogant claim to identification with God but a transfusion of their selves by His Self.[5] The sobriety of the *Theologia Germanica* insists, in contrast to the extravagances of less famous mystical treatises, on the falsehood and unreality of the light that leads a man to think he is God.[6] The believer does not become Christ. "Christ is more precious to us by what distinguishes Him from us than by what identifies Him with us." [7] At the same time love deifies the human :

Happy is he who hath been worthy to rise to the fourth degree of love and hath advanced so far as to love himself only for God's sake. When shall my soul, enthralled with divine love forgetful of herself, having made of

---

[1] Cobb, *Mysticism and the Creed*, 117, relying on Clement of Alexandria, Athanasius, Origen, Hippolytus, Irenaeus and Augustine. The words of Clement Alex. in *Strom.* iv. 23. 152 are nearly like those of Tayumanavar in the hymn under comment: "In a man's own contemplative life whoever diligently worships God also through his own sincere self-purification beholds in holiness the holy God. For continence abiding carefully in its place watching over and considering itself unceasingly is made like unto God according to its power." This is moderate by the side of Hippolytus quoted by Dr. Cobb: "Thou hast been made God and art become immortal. This is the meaning of the saying 'know thyself,' that is, 'know that thou hast become God.'" On the Tamil equivalent of 'know thyself,' taken from the Upanishads, Mr. Nallaswamy Pillai (*Siddhiyar*, page 198, note) observes, "The expression is very often misunderstood and misinterpreted. It simply means 'understanding oneself,' 'understanding his real nature,' and does not mean 'understanding oneself as God' or as anything else......The Vedas ......postulate the knowledge of God and such passages are misinterpreted to mean that the soul sees God as himself ...The words 'as himself' are nowhere found in the texts."

[2] Ephesians 4 : 13.

[3] 2 Cor. 3: 18.

[4] 1 John 3: 2. S. Augustine's note. His *Tract. iv. in 1 Epist. Joan* is significant: *Nunc filii Dei sumus ; jam nunc ? Quid est ergo quod expectamus, si jam filii Dei sumus ? Quid autem erimus aliud, quam filii Dei ?*

[5] Underhill, *Mysticism*, 503.

[6] Winkworth's Translation, p. 149.

[7] Dr. Forsyth in *Hibbert Journal*, April 1908, p. 486.

herself only a vessel of little worth, be filled with this longing for God, advance towards Him, and lose herself wholly in Him?......O pure and stainless effort of the will! assuredly more stainless and pure in that naught is left in it mingled with the thought of self; tenderer and sweeter inasmuch as the soul is thrilled with a feeling divine! To be thus affected is to be made divine ...... As a small drop of water, poured into wine, seemeth to lose its own self entirely, while it taketh upon itself both the taste and the colour of the wine ......so is it that with saintly souls every human affection in a certain ineffable manner melteth away and is transfused entirely into the will of God.[1]

This God-becomingness of man is possible not so much by reason of the soul's origin and its affinity to God as because of the soul's capacity for assimilation to demon or divinity. The soul has the choice, and where the treasure is there will the heart be also.[2]

129. That Thou Becomest Unto Each. (Page 56, No. 124).

God is understood by the poet as manifesting Himself to the worshippers in the different religions,[3] the one God in all the creeds,[4] and the very difference in the creeds.[5] The reference is mostly to "the six creeds."[6] With this Siddhanta 'catholicity' may be compared the claims of Krishna in the *Gita*:

> They also who worship other gods and make offering to them with faith do verily make offering to me, though not according to ordinance.[7] If any worshipper whatsoever seeks with faith to reverence anybody whatsoever, that same faith in him I make steadfast.[8]

130. A Babe. (Page 56, No. 125).

The soul in the state of primal darkness (see above page 150) is of itself not able to help itself and must receive impulses from without.

---

[1] S. Bernard of Clairvaux, in Grimley's *S. Bernard* 218, 219, 220. "Holiness is conformity to type and the one standard of perfection is God Himself. Set the soul at liberty and its history will be a perpetual approximation to God." (Watson, *The Mind of the Master*, ch. vi.)

[2] S. Matthew 6 : 21.

[3] N.M. 69 1103. 1210. 1211.

[4] N.M. 140, 182, 1088 and above, No. 179.

[5] Above, No. 146.

[6] See above, *Introduction*, part ii.

[7] *Gita*, ix, 23.

[8] *Gita*, vii, 21. Ibn al-'Arabi a great mystic of Islam says, "Do not attach yourself to any particular creed exclusively, so that you disbelieve all the rest . . . God the omnipotent is not limited by any one creed, for He says (*Koran*, ii. 109), 'Wheresoever you turn, there is the face of Allah'. . . . If one knew Junayad's saying, 'The water takes its colour from the vessel containing it,' he would not interfere with other men's beliefs, but would perceive God in every form of belief." (Nicholson, *Mystics of Islam*, pages 87, 88.)

The soul who cognises through the external senses dreams in sleep, and sleeps soundly with but bare breath and without action or enjoyment; and waking again recalls its dreams, and feels its sound sleep, and then enters into eating and exercises. This is the way the soul cognises through the five *avasthas*, with the aid of its physical vestures." [1]

131. THE WORLDS SEVEN-FOLD. (Page 56, No. 125).

These are said to be seven conditions of the soul's existence, (1) when the intelligence is stirred, (2) consciousness, (3) waking state, (4) dreaming in the wakeful state, (5) dream state, (6) watchfulness in dream, (7) dead sleep.[2] See last note.

132. MIND. (Page 56, No. 125).

See above *Introduction*, part v,

133. THAT THOU ART ONE WITH ME. (Page 60, No. 130).

See above, Note 128, page 184.

134. PRIMAL TAINT. (Page 60, No. 130).

See above, page 150.

135. SAKTI. (Page 61, No. 132).

See above, *Introduction*, part vii.

136. TILLAI DANCER. (Page 62, No. 133).

See above, Note 82, page 174.

137. TREE OF LIFE. (Page 62, No. 135).

See above, Note 18, page 136.

138. FORM AND FORMLESSNESS. (Page 63, No. 137).

God is said to have form, (*rūpa*), has no form (*arūpa*) and has formless form (*rūparūpa*.)[3] As *rupi* God is said to be *para*.; as *arūpi*, *apara*; as *rūparūpi*, *parāpara*.[4]

---

[1] *Siddhiyar*, 3. 4. 30. On *Avasthas* see *Siddhiyar*, 3. 4. 33-40, and *Brih. Aran. Upan.* 4. 3, on the various conditions of the soul.

[2] Shanmuga Mudaliyar, in *S. Deepika*, i. 276.

[3] *Siddhiyar*, 3. 1. 38, 3. 1. 55, *Sivapragasam*, 13.

[4] Nalla. *Siddhiyar*, page 155.

139. Yaman. (Page 65, No. 139).

This is the god of death. He is named or alluded to elsewhere by the poet.[1] It is in post-Vedic literature that Yaman is identified with death and is conspicuous as the god, judge and tormentor of the dead. In the *Rig Veda* he is distinguished from Death (*Mritya*),[2] is praised as the first to find a path for men to the lofty heights,[3] and is a benefactor of the devas, having died for them.[4] Yama's world is a heaven the home of heroes.[5] The souls rejoice in Yama's company.[6] There is a Vedic passage which suggests the thought that Yama has power over the dead, and from his hold the dead could be redeemed.[7] In the *Upanishads* Yama is the god of death.[8]

There is a legend in the *Kanda Puranam* [9] of Siva granting the boon of a son to a sage long childless. The son grew up to be a great Siva-devotee. He had been granted to his father with the condition that he would be claimed by Yaman the god of death in his sixteenth year. While the lad, when sixteen, was one day engaged in worshipping Siva as usual, Yaman claimed him. Siva kicked Yaman down dead. Death was latterly restored to life. This victory over Yaman is alluded to by our poet elsewhere.[10]

140. My Evil and My Good. (Page 65, No. 142).

See above, page 143 and *Introduction*, part v.

141. Wearer of White Ashes. (Page 65, No. 144).

Siva is described as an ascetic with his matted hair, and wearing white ashes on his forehead where shines the third eye. In his hair is the river Ganges, and there gleams the crescent moon. Such descriptions of Siva occur in our poet's hymns.[11] They are found in Tamil religious literature generally.

---

[1] N. M. 96. 119. 437. 441. 502. 557. 619 and above No. 214, 225.

[2] R. V. x. 18. 1, speaks of *Mrityu*, not *Yama*.

[3] R. V. x. 14. 1. 2.

[4] R. V. x. 13. 4.

[5] R. V. x. 315. 7.

[6] R. V. x. 14. 9. x. 135. 7.

[7] R. V. x. 60. 10: 'Spirit I have brought from Yama.' In x. 58. 1, we read "Thy spirit that went far away to Yama we cause to come to thee again."

[8] See *Katha*. 1. 4. i. *Kaush*. 4. 14.

[9] The section called *Markanda Padalam*, at page 87, in Arumuga Navalar's prose edition.

[10] See above, No, 225, page 83.

[11] For instance in N. M. 168. 483. 487.

142. MADEST, KEEPEST, CANST DESTROY. (Page 66, No. 145).

Creation is Brahma's work, preservation is Vishnu's and destruction is Rudra Siva's.[1] To Siva is assigned the power of doing all three acts.[2]

143. RED, EIGHT-ARMED. (Page 66, No. 146).

In the *Tiruvachagam* Siva is "the gold-red one the brightness of whose body is shaded with white ashes"[3]

A Hindu, South Indian, convert to Christianity recently drew my attention to a theory which associates, and identifies, Siva as conceived in Tamil literature, particularly as the red one, with Adam of the Bible. He connects the Hebrew word *āhdāhm* which means 'man,' with *āhdam* 'to be red.' I refer here to this ingenious theory merely as introductory to what a Saivite scholar has himself suggested[4]:

> Siva is represented as a man of fair colour with tangled locks of hair. He has three eyes[5], wears a tiger's skin and, armed with a battle-axe, rides a bullock.[6] His appearance, except as regards the three eyes, corresponds exactly with that of a primitive inhabitant of the Himalayan region. The people of this region are fair in colour and have red hair and ride on bullocks when travelling in the mountainous country. His abode was the snow-capped Mount Kailasa situated north of the Himalayas near the sources of the great rivers Ganges,[7] Indus and Brahmaputra.

'Eight-armed,' literally 'eight-shouldered,' is descriptive of one of the many forms in which Siva is represented. Images of Siva are known to exist, from early times, with four, eight, ten, eighteen or sixteen arms. The four-armed figure is a *Sāntamūrti*, 'the pacific one.' In an anonymous manuscript which gives directions as to the making of images of Siva there is no mention in what aspect Siva should have eight arms.[8]

---

1 N. M. 166, 167. The superiority of Siva is asserted.

2 N. M. 178 A famous hymn of Sundaramurti (*Tevaram*, Tiru Vajai Kalam section, stanza 7) begins, "I shall say that Thou art creation, destruction, and preservation."

3 VI, line 44. Also Sundaramurti, *Tevaram*, Tirumārlappādi section 1, பொன்னார்மேனியனே 'Thou with the gold-bright body.'

4 Kanagasabai Pillai, *The Tamils Eighteen Hundred Years Ago.*

5 See above, Note 112, page 180.

6 See above, No. 202, page 79.

7 See above, No. 194, page 75, and notes at page 198.

8 Gopinatha Rao, *Elements of Hindu Iconography*, ii, part i, p. 114 and 115. The learned author refers to the manuscript.

144. Gain, etc. (Page 69, No. 153).

The Tamil of the first line in English means literally 'gold, women, lands.' The same words in the order 'women, gold, lands' are rendered elsewhere [1] 'wealth and beauty's snare.' In the opening words of the well-known *Kaivalya Navaneetam*[2] reference is made to 'those whose attachments are towards gold, earthly possessions and love of women.'

145. Longings Old yet are Tormentful. (Page 69, No. 154).

The Tamil means literally, 'if trouble be yet allowed to come to me.' Although the soul had been surrendered to God, says the poet, troubles and sorrows by way of the old tendencies cease not. In the *Siddhiyar* [3] is this statement:

> The pot smells for a time even after the assafœtida is removed, and the wheel turns round for a time after the potter has taken his hands off it. Similarly the effects of past karma may affect the *jivanmukta* (the sanctified) for a time but all will vanish with his body.

It is well to remember that this analogy is in the immediate neighbourhood of the reference to the state in which the soul is said to remain untainted by any act, even of sensuality [4]; indeed in the text where the wheel analogy occurs it is stated, "Good and evil will not attach to the *jnanis* even though they may perform *all kinds of acts.*" The *praraptha*, effects of past Karma, are believed to last in the case of the sanctified, only so long as the body lasts.

Tayumanavar in the passage under comment may or may not be referring to the experience mentioned in the *Siddhiyar* 'pot and wheel' analogy, but his words express the common consciousness of all who strive for perfection and confess their failures.[5] The cry of the earnest soul has always been, "O wretched man that I am! who will deliver me from the body of this death?" [6]

146. Saintly Garb. (Page 69, No. 156).

The externals of institutional religion have their value.

---

1 No. 316, at p. 105. See also N.M. 319, 453, 569.

2 Preface, stanza i. in Ponnambala Swamy's edition, p. 3

3 3. 10. 6. See notes in Nalla. *Bodham*, 90, 102.

4 3. 10. 5. See notes, above, p. 143—148.

5 Compare the experience of Catherine of Genoa (*Myst. Elem.* i. 266. 267).

6 Rom. 7 : 15.

147. He, She, It. (Page 70, No. 157).

The poet speaks elsewhere of God as "the great one who is male and female, and neither."[1] God is not limited by sex.

148. Their Name. (Page 70, No. 158).

The saints belong, the poet says, to the class அருள் வர்க்கர், *arul varkar*, 'the grace-given ones', and to call such 'mortals' is not right.

149. Words. (Page 70, No. 159).

He laments he had been a hearer and not a doer of the word spoken to him by the Guru.

150. Hands of Worship, Bands of Faithful Ones. (Page 70, No. 160).

In the Tamil கையு மெய்யுங் கருத்துக்கிசையவே தந்தற் கையமினி யுண்டோ (Is there any doubt about my having yielded hands and body in all intention?), the word கை (hands) stands for the lifting up of the hands in an attitude of worship, and the yielding of the body; மெய் means going round the god's temple in the company of devotees. The two English lines give this sense of the original. These religious acts,[2] the poet deplores, have not wrought in him internal change.

151. By Creation. (Page 70, No. 161).

The Tamil word நடுவே is rendered by the commentators as "the Being who is the centre of the great acts[3] of creation, etc." The translation in the text follows this interpretation, according to which the words mean that so great a Being as such a God is enshrined in the human heart. Another translation is perhaps possible:

> See within the sky-space of my heart I hold
> Thee O flame of grace for ever to be there—
> There is nought to this mid-state comparable
> Wherein me thou hast ill-less and good-less placed.

In this alternative rendering the word நடுவே is not taken as an address, as in the other rendering, but as meaning 'the middle state between good-lessness and ill-lessness'. The sense given to நடுவே in the first rendering is that adopted by all the commentators, but the second rendering has its merits.

---

[1] N. M. 334, 1212. See *Tiruvachagam* iii (line) 134, v. 113, 166.

[2] Enjoined on the devout in many writings, e.g. *Tirukkaruvai*, Hymn 73.

[3] See above, note 142, p 193.

152. Deeds Thine. (Page 71, No. 164).

The poet presents a balanced view of the doctrine that God is the doer of all a man does. If God is the doer of all a man does, man should walk worthy of such Divine co-operation and high energizing.

153. Lust, Hate, Delusion. (Page 71, No. 164).

These are the three great sins of the soul. They are named in the same order in *Tirumantram.*[1]

154. Pearl. (Page 71, No. 165).

The original refers to a pearl that had not been bored for the string, "the unpierced pearl." The possessory என் is interpreted into "found of me."[2] God is the Persian mystic's "Pearl of Truths,"[3] and Boehme's "Bright crown of pearl, brighter than the sun."[4]

155. Men Would Praise Thee Not. (Page 73, No. 172).

Thoughts of like import occur in the *Tiruvachagam*:[5]

> If Thou bid me not come to Thee who is there here to calm my fears?
> "This is unmeet," will not men say?

Again:[6]

> If Thou show not Thy gracious fellowship, I die—
> And then will not men scoff?

156. Steel Magnet. (Page 73, No. 176).

"As a magnet attracts a piece of iron, so God draws unto Himself the soul and converts it into His own form."[7]

157. Other Than Teacher. (Page 74, No. 177).

The saint having transcended the spiritual stage in which God was seen by him as Guru (Teacher) desires now to know God as only Light.

158. First World. (Page 74, No. 178).

The Tamil சற் பூமி is translated here 'World of Grace', and is interpreted as 'first in word-revelation'. It is taught that there are seven methods of knowing, *gnana poomikal*, 'wisdom worlds.'[8]

---

1 2436.
2 *Cf.* S. Matt. 13: 46.
3 Davis, *Persian Mystics*, ii. 28.
4 *Three-fold Life*, c. 6.
5 li. line 22 (Pope's Tr.)
6 xxi. line 32 (Pope's Tr.)
7 *Siddhiyar*, 3. 11. 12.
8 *Kaivalyam*, Ponnambalam edition, pp. 315, 317. *Cf.* the seven divisions of Logic in *Siddhiyar*, 1. 1.

159. SIX FAITHS. (Page 74, No. 179).

See above, *Introduction*, part ii.

160. EVER NEW. (Page 74, No. 180).

The Tamil தூக்கமைய் denotes 'uncloying freshness.' The more the Bliss of God is tasted the fresher it is. It palls not with the soul's repeated blendings with it. 'Uncloying freshness' of Bliss is often referred to in terms of sexual union.[1] On being 'plunged in Deity' one may quote Jacoponi Da Todi :

> O great Love, greater than the great sea! O the man who is drowned within it, under it, and with it, all around him, whilst he knows not whe e he is.[2]

So S. Catherine of Genoa :

> I am so placed and submerged in His immense love that I seem as though entirely under water and I could on no side touch, see, or feel anything but water.[3]

161. THIS, THAT. (Page 74, No. 181).

"They who say He is this or He is that know not Him," says the great Tirumular.[4] He had also said, before our poet, "Get rid of the desire to distinguish God as This or That,"[5] and "Waste not life in differentiating as This or That."[6] "It is the property of God," says the author of the *Theologia Germanica*, "to be without *this* and without *that* and without *self* and *me* and without equal and fellow."[7]

162. PEARL-SKINNED FRUIT. (Page 75, No. 103).

The fruit நெல்லி, (*nellie*) of the *phyllanthus* has a transparent skin, and so is a type of Siva whom the saints know with clearness.

---

[1] *Tirukovayar*, 8. The whole section '*Iyatkay Punarchie*' is devoted to this subject of the soul's association with God in spiritual union. The *Tirukovayar* passage may be thus paraphrased :

> Flows joy afresh as oft as I
> My sweetness, dearest, draw from Thee;
> Grows sweetness sweeter as the more
> Bliss blends with bliss all one to be.

[2] Hügel, *Myst. Elem.* ii. 106.

[3] Hügel, *Myst. Elem.* i. 274. See ii. 108.

[4] *Tirumantram*, 1154.

[5] *Tirumantram*, 1186.

[6] *Tirumantram*, 1231.

[7] Winkworth's Translation, page 8.

It is so mentioned in other places by our poet.[1] Other Siddhanta writers make similar mention. Thus Sundaramurti speaks of God as "the *nellie* fruit to those who thoughtfully meditate on Him."[2] Manikkavachagar refers to Him as "the ripe *nellie* fruit in the palm of my hand,"[3] "milk, honey, balm, ambrosia and the *nellie* fruit."[4] It is to Deity that the anonymous writer of *Gnanakummie*[5] refers when he says, "In the forest is the *nellie*, in the house is the *nellie*."

163. GANGES. (Page 75, No. 184).

Siva is described in the *Siddhiyar*[6] as "the Lord with the braided hair, adorned with the Ganges, the crescent moon and the cassia flowers." A king, so runs the legend, once prayed that the heavenly Ganges should be sent down to this world to restore to life his ancestors whom an angry sage had burnt to ashes; the prayer was granted, but Siva, wishing to avert a deluge of the earth, caught the river on his head and held it in the locks of his matted hair.[7] See above, *Introduction*, part ii.

164. SNAKE. (Page 75, No. 184).

When Siva, according to a legend, entered a forest to inflict chastisement upon certain sages, they, by their powers, conjured up a serpent to swallow Siva who was then in the disguise of a mendicant. Siva thereupon seized the serpent and wreathed it round his neck.

165. CRESCENT MOON. (Page 75, No. 184).

It is said that the moon had been cursed, and in its waning condition it appealed to Siva who protected it against all evil by placing it, crescent, on his head.[8]

---

1 N.M. 105, 106, 478, 645.

2 Tēvāram, *Tiru Vanjay Kalam* 3.

3 *Tiruvachagam*, iii. 162 (line).

4 *Tiruvachagam*, xxvii. 15.

5 Stanza 134.

6 *Invocation.*

7 Dr. Pope (*Tiruvachagam*, page 71) suggests that Siva is a personification of the Himalayas whose tangled forests are his hair, and from the midst of them, as from the very heaven, flows down the Ganges, while the crescent moon gleams brightly on the mountain's brow.

8 The story is told at length in *Skanda Purana, Sandirc Sāpā Padalam*, at p. 436 in Arumuga Navalar's (prose) edition.

166. Form. (Page 75, No. 185).

In this verse and in the next following the form of God is the theme. All things are a manifestation of Deity, says the poet, in a sense, and this leads him in No. 186 to a statement of the duty of reverence to all images and symbols of God. The images in temple are taught to be God's form ;[1] even the form of a devotee is God's image ;[2] and further "they perceive God who perceive His form placed in temples as Himself, and they perceive Him too who meditate on Him in the mantric form, and they who worship Him in their hearts perceive Him likewise."[3]

167. Power of Grace, Motherlike. (Page 76, No. 189).

The original உள்மனத்தலமே means "the resting place of *Sakti*" and *Sakti* is the 'motherlike power of grace.' See above, *Introduction*, part vii.

168. Unliving the Life of the Soul of Old. (Page 77, No. 193.)

The Tamil பசுத்துவம் போய் may be literally rendered 'soulness gone', that is, when the soul has outlived its original condition of taint (see above, page 150), and put on newness of nature. The four lines may according to sense be freely rendered thus :

> Bid me come to Thee, Lord, that my soul which is
> Hid in ignorance, see Thee with eyes of faith,
> See Thee as Thy saints, seeing Thee, live ever,
> Be as blest as they, mindless and birthless be.

There is a whole psalm in the *Tiruvachagam* in which each verse ends with the prayer, "Be gracious, bid me come to Thee."[4] There are also the lines in the same poem.

> Thy saints around Thee throng where Thou and they
> In happy sport commingled ever dwell ;
> That I may thither rise to join the band
> Our only Bliss, in grace O bid me come.[5]

---

[1] *Siddhiyar*, 3. 12. 1. *Bhodham*, xii.
[2] *Siddhiyar*, 3. 12. 2. See below, notes to No. 227.
[3] *Siddhiyar*, 3. 12. 4. This refers to those who need images, to those who worship in prayer, and to those who realize greatness in Yoga.
[4] xxviii.
[5] xxi, lines 20, 21 (Pope's Tr.).

169. Mindlessness. (Page 67, No. 193).

The mind is the source of births and re-births.[1] See *Introduction*, part v.

170. Mouth, Hand. (Page 77, No. 194).

The ideal ascetic posture, as may be seen in pictures of devotees, consists, among other things, of keeping the mouth shut and spreading out the hands in such a way that the thumb touches the tip of the forefinger, forming a circle. The poet refers here to a state of false silence, mere form of silence.[2]

171. Nightless, Dayless. (Page 77, No. 194).

See above, page 130. There are two possible states of meditation. In one the man is conscious through his senses he is in a state of meditation, and through the same senses he is aware of distracting influences. This is 'day' (சகலம் *sakalam*). The state of unknowing is 'night' (கேவலம் *kevalam*). The ideal state is where there is neither night nor day. That it is not a state of numbness is evident from expressions, of which the following is typical, of a longing for the activities of praise:

> Grant me to know nor night nor day,
> And in that state unceasing say,
> 'Praise be to God'.[3]

An analogy is furnished by Sufism in regard to the practice of *dhikr*, 'recollection', in the words of Ghazali:

> Let him reduce his heart to a state in which the existence of anything and its non-existence are the same to him. . . Let him see to it that nothing save God Most High enters his mind. Then, as he sits in solitude, let him not cease saying continuously 'Allah, Allah.', keeping his thought on it. At last he will reach a state when the motion of his tongue will cease, and it will seem as the word flowed from it. . . . . Then the light of the Real will shine in his heart.[4]

Another Sufi says:

> The first stage of *dhikr* is to forget self, and the last stage is the effacement of the worshipper in the act of worship, without consciousness of worship, and such absorption in the object of worship as precludes return to the subject thereof.[5]

---

[1] See above, No. 242, at page 87.

[2] See above, No. 126, at page 57. See N.M. 424, "Mere saying 'silence' is not enough."

[3] *Kanthar Alangaram*.

[4] Nicholson, *Mystics of Islam*, 46.

[5] Nicholson, *Mystics of Islam*, 48.

172. NUMBERLESS SOULS. (Page 77, No. 195).

"The number of those who have been freed, and of those who have yet to be freed will equal the number of the days that are past since creation and of the days that are yet to come."[1]

173. JOURNEYED ONES. (Page 77, No. 196).

The original conveys the idea that by pilgrimages the devout acquire "the secret of the Silence." Perhaps the principle of pilgrimages is not to enhance, but to exhaust, the idea of localizing Deity within the limits of 'here', 'there', 'this', 'that'. In spiritual worship God is not localized.[2]

174. TILLAY'S SACRED COURT. (Page 78, No. 199).

See above, note 82, at p. 174. The dance of Siva believed to be materialised at Sidambaram which is Tillay has been esoterically explained.[3] It is said to symbolize Siva's acts in the universe. Thus Tirumular:

> Move all the *tatvas*, the powers and all functions;
> Moveth Sathasiva moved thus;
> Moveth the will of the Willer;
> Moveth the Sakti of Siva;
> Moveth the universe;
> Danceth the Lord this dance of delight.[4]

175. MAID OF THE MOUNTAINS. (Page 78, No. 200).

This refers to Uma the spouse of Siva. See above, *Introduction*, part vii. "By the light of grace, God reveals Himself to us......This Light and Love and Grace, and Will or Power of the Lord is what is symbolized as His Spouse, His Half, Uma, Parvati, Sakti, our Mother."[5] In the *Tiruvachagam* are numerous references to Uma:

> Uma the bride...the mountain maid.[6]
> Thou art in form half a woman.[7]
> Father whose half the Mother is.[8]
> O half of her with eyes of glistening jet.[9]
> Half of whose form the Lady shares.[10]
> Her form who by his side grows as a tender bough.[11]

Tayumanavar refers frequently to "her who is half of him."[12]

---

1 *T.A.P.* 2. 1.
2 S. John 4:21.
3 *Siddhiyar*, 3. 5. 7.
4 *Tirumantram*, 2789.
5 Nalla. *Siddhiyar*, Introduction, page xxxiii. *Kanjipuranam*, 108.
6 V. line 217; xxiii line 39.
7 IV. line 152.
8 V. line 118.
9 V. line 365.
10 VIII. line 38.
11 XII. line 37.
12 See Nos. 142, 211, and N. M. 279, 299, 328, 332, 507, 1089.

176. Lord of Melody. (Page 79, No. 202).

Siva as Lord of the Sama Veda, the Veda of melody, is peculiarly the lord of melody. The Sama Veda consists chiefly of Rig Veda texts set to music for ritual chanting. The Sama is the essence of the Rig Veda, and its essence is Ōm.[1] The author of the *Gita* makes Krishna claim to be of the Vedas the Sama Veda.[2]

177. Sea of Delusions. (Page 79, No. 204).

The original is *விகாரமாந்திரை*, and may be rendered (1) curtain of differentiation, delusion or, (2) sea of differentiation, delusion. Mr. Nallaswamy Pillai prefers "curtain."[3] Personally I favour "sea" as in keeping with the context. A sentence in Cynewulf's *Christ*[4] may be apposite here:

> A perilous way is this of boundless waves and these are stormy seas, on which we toss here in this feeble world, o'er the deep paths.

It was this Christian passage which predisposed me in favour of my translation.

178. Spakest the Vedas Four. (Page 79, No. 205).

There are other references to Siva as having uttered the four Vedas, and as the crown of the Vedas.[5] The claims of Krishna may be compared, "I am the framer of the Vedas' end and knower of the Vedas."[6]

179. Joy of the Homing Soul. (Page 79, No. 205).

The words *கலந்தமுத்தி* may be literally rendered 'the blending, or blended *mukti* state.' Now, *mukti* is 'release,' it is Heaven as the soul's home. The joy here spoken of is the joy of what mystics refer to as 'the unitive stage,' the Siddhanta 'two-less state.' The English preserves the meanings of 'joy,' 'home' and 'the two-less state.'

180. Amidst Thy Saints. (Page 79, No. 266).

Without any test as to fitness, says the poet, he had been accorded the great privilege of the society of the saintly. In our poet there

---

[1] *Chandogya Upan.* 1. 1. 2; 1. 1. 5.

[2] *Gita*, x. 22.

[3] *Studies*, 14.

[4] Prof. Gollancze's translation, V. lines 849—851. See above, No. 111 page 47.

[5] See No. 116, and N.M. 381, 425, 475, 563, 1410.

[6] *Gita*, xv. 15.

are references to love of holy society.[1] There is a section of six verses in *Tirumqntram* on 'the society of the saintly.'[2] There are f. ur classes of godly men whose society in covetable—the devotees whose piety is seen in their pilgrimages to shrines; those who love to sing God's praises; those who in yogic practices seek God; and those who associate themselves with God in the two-less state.[3] "It is heavenly bliss to be a companion of the godly."[4]

181. Speechless Joy. (Page 80, No. 210).

The saints "silent, seek the silence, silent to find the Silence-grantor."[5]

182. Sign and Seal. (Page 80, No. 210).

On Siva's manifestation to the faithful a sign is given them. "The moment my Lord showed me the way of knowing the mark without knowing it, I lost my bonds."[6]

> And with the ancient servants of the king
> Taking His sign alone for a guidance
> Shake falsehood off.[7]

It is the sign of the Silence. See below, p. 221.

183. Time. (Page 81, No. 213).

"God alone possesses the splendour of ever-tarrying eternity...... incomparable with never-tarrying times.........The three times are the three affections of the soul."[8] The soul has to break away from the trammels of the convention we call time to realize God.[9] In prayer time sometimes ceases to be:

> I have observed that during the prayer of passivity and especially in the state of union the soul loses all sense of the duration of time.........There is one single moment only.........the soul being roused to that state lives according to the mode of life in Eternity, where time is no more, neither past, nor present, but one eternal Now.[10]

---

1 N. M. 457. 497, 579, and see above, Nos 74, 75, 115, 119, 128, 217.

2 513—548.

3 *Tirumantram*, 543.

4 *Tirumantram*, 545.

5 *Tirukalit*, 28.

6 *Kantar Anupooti*, 43.

7 *Tiruvachagam*, xlv. 10.

8 S. Augustine, *Confessions* 11. 27. 3. This idea finds expression in *Tirukalittuppadiar*, 30.

9 See Inge, *Philosophy of Plotinus*, i. 173, ii. 92, 98, 99, 100.

10 Lucie Christine, *Spiritual Journal*, 52.

The New Testament passage[1] usually rendered, "Time shall be no more ' and seemingly appropriate to the present context, is interpreted by modern commentators to mean, "There shall be no more delay."[2]

184. Fate, Free Will. (Page 81, No. 215).

In the *Wisdom of Ben Sira* occurs a passage suggestive of a line of thought different from what the Siddhanta teachers teach :

> Say not, 'From God in my transgression,'
> For that which He hateth made He not.
> Say not, 'It is He that hath made me to stumble,'
> For there is no need of evil men................
> God created man from the beginning
> And placed him in the lands of his yetzer (nature)........
> He commanded no man to sin.[3]

185. Lord of the Herd of Souls. (Page 81, No. 215)

See note at page 162, above.

186. Untouched by Counsel. (Page 82, No. 217).

Compare the Biblical, "Who hath directed the spirit of the Lord, or being His counsellor had taught Him? With whom took He counsel?"[4]

187. In this Body. (Page 82, No. 218).

See above page 115. One of the most arresting features of the Siddhanta is the insistence of salvation in the present life.

188. Flame Unflickering. (Page 82, No. 219).

God, it is taught, ever knows and does not forget to be startled into remembrance. "On Him never night of forgetting falls, dawneth nor day of remembering."[5]

189. Court of Gold. (Page 82, No. 220).

See above, pages 174, 201. Siva's acts are said to be manifested in five courts, namely, at Sidambaram, Madura, Tirukkuttalam, Tiruvalangkadu, Tirunelvēli (Tinnevely) all in S. India. Each court has a

---

1 Rev. 10 : 6.
2 Swete, *Apoc*, 129. Charles, *Rev*, i ,263, 264.
3 xv. 11, 12, 14, 20.
4 Isaiah, 40 : 13. 14.
5 See above, p. 3.

special name. The first, at Sidambaram, is the most excellent and central, and is known as Kanagasabai. It is the Court of Gold. The others in the other places above named, respectively, are Court of Silver, Court of Statues, Court of Rubies, Court of the Lotus.

190. My Tamil. (Page 83, No. 222).

The last two lines of the original represented by the last two English lines may be literally rendered, "When wilt Thou who art servant of Thy servants come to me that I may sing Thee in my Tamil psalms for everybody's praise?" The poet's desire is so to realize God that his psalms may set forth God's praises in such Tamil as will, by its sincere piety, command the esteem of men. Elsewhere[1] the poet deplores that his Tamil is not comparable to that of well-known saints, and says:

Unlearnéd I weave many a string
Of pearls of tears and, Lord, I bring . . .
Word-garlands woven for Thy praise.[2]

He speaks of Tamil as an ancient language sanctified by the psalms of the saintly;[3] knows that Siva delights to hear Tamil psalms overlooking the faults of the psalmists;[4] longs to sing like the saints;[5] laments he has not piety enough to sing as the holy or to read what they have sung[6], and is conscious that many men think of his psalms as made of words as light as cotton.[7] See, above, *Introduction*, part iii.

The word 'Tamil' in the lines under comment has been taken by some commentators to mean the Tamil Agamas.[8] If so the third English line, in Tamil fourth, may run, "Come delight of the Dravida Veda-lore."

Another interpretation of the fourth Tamil line, a rather strained one, is, "O strong-armed one whose name is praised in the lofty psalms of the holy."[9]

191. Humble Servant. (Page 83, No. 222).

Elsewhere our poet speaks of God as 'the Servant of those who have passed above the trials of births and re-births,'[10] and addresses Him, "Siva, the Servant of Thy saints."[11] Other Siddhanta writers

[1] See, above, p. 95.
[2] See above, p. 116.
[3] N. M. 581.
[4] N. M. 327.
[5] N. M. 64.
[6] N. M. 102.
[7] N. M. 115.
[8] K. S. Mudaliyar's edition of *Tayumanavar* p. 162.
[9] V. V. Series edition, p, 255.
[10] N. M. 318.
[11] N. M. 1337 சிட்டர்க் கெளிய சிவனே.

nake similar allusions to Siva. Thus Sundaramurti calls God, "the humble One to longing eyes,"[1] "the Servant of His devotees."[2] In all the references and in the verse under comment the word rendered 'servant,' or 'humble one,' 'humble servant that servest,' is எளியான், literally, 'the one in a low position.' The idea is expressive of intense humility. The Christian is reminded of the "Son of man coming to serve and not to be served,"[3] and how "He took upon Him the likeness of a slave."[4]

192. Datura. (Page 83, No. 223).

Datura or cassia is a poisonous flower. On Ganga and moon see above, pp. 198, 199.

193. Yea, Nay. (Page 83, No. 224).

The thought is the same as in No. 166, above and No. 320, 350. The sentiment is the same as S. Pattanattar's, which I freely render thus:

The cry is loud, the cry is long,
  The cry of creeds, "Yea, this He;"
The cry comes back, the cry as strong,
  The cry of creeds, "Nay this is He."
Thus cry all creeds, all creeds as wrong,
  Which cry, "Yea this, nay that, is He."
The truth indeed all creeds proclaim
  That God in very sooth is He
Who evermore remaineth same,
  Not this, not that, but One is He,
Held in the heart's own holy shrine,
Homed in the soul, the Guest Divine.[5]

194. Twain of the Trinity. (Page 83, No. 225).

Brahma and Vishnu, says the legend, were once disputing about supremacy, when Siva appeared before them as fire. The two were unable to discover its beginning or end. They gave Siva praise.[6] On another occasion they could not discover Siva's crown or feet.[7] Although Siva is not dissociated from the acts and attributes belonging to him in the Puranas yet he is considered not identical with the Siva of the Triad but *the* Supreme Being. See above, *Introduction*, part iv.

---

[1] *Tevaram*, Tiruneedūr section, 5. 9.
[2] *Tirukkānapper* section, 8.
[3] *S. Matthew* 20 : 28.
[4] *Phil.* 2 : 7.
[5] *Tiruvidaymaruthūr Mummanikkōvay*, 17.
[6] *Tiruvachagam*, xvi. line 25, xxvii, line 10.
[7] *Siddhiyar*, 3. 1. 49.

195. They are God. (Page 84, No. 227.)

The translation given in the text has been arrived at after many misgivings. A different understanding of the Tamil was possible, as more in accord with average Christian pre-possessions, on the authority of a learned Hindu commentator. "He who is manifested to the eye and to the senses is Siva, and He is the God I worship." [1]

Indeed, in the early proofs of p. 84 the first four lines had actually run in the following form :

Sight of eyes Who is, sense of my senses too,
Light of truth in the sky of the soul is He ;
Day and night are my thoughts of Him, ceaselessly,
Yea ! I draw near Him : God of my worship He.

The rendering had to be abandoned on grounds of grammar.

There is clear Saiva authority for the view that in sainthood is God :

> As God dwells as the life of life in each human soul, the form of His devotee is His form. As he dwells in Sivoham Samadhi [2] he is even God Himself. As he reaches Him in his heart, following the direction of the guru, he is God Himself ; when he and his vision fail altogether, he is without God. If such is the greatness of God's devotees worship them with love to get rid of the bonds of sin.[3]

The saints, according to this, are the media of God and the God in them is worshipped through them. They are God-bearers.[4] My

---

[1] K. S. Mudaliyar, *Tāyumānavar*, p. 365.

[2] See above, Note 128, p. 184.

[3] *Siddhiyar*, 3.12.3.

[4] S. Ignatius was named 'God-bearer.' (Farrar, *Lives of the Fathers*, i. 34). See above, *Introduction*, part v. § 34.

The words of Dean Inge (*Philosophy of Plotinus*, ii. 160) in a slightly different context may be quoted here :

'What would Plotinus have said to the plain question, "He that loveth not his brother whom he hath seen, how can he love God whom he hath not seen?" I believe Platonism can answer this challenge better than Indian mysticism, though in practice nothing can be much more beautiful than the gentle and selfless benevolence of the Oriental saint. . . . Love for Plotinus . . . becomes depersonalised, more so than many of us would think desirable ; but when a Christian teacher bids us to love the Christ in our brethren, when he repeats the famous saying, "When thou seest thy brother thou seest thy Lord," he is saying very much what Platonism says in other words'.

Eckhart (*apud* Jones, *Studies in Myst. Rel.* 223) says, "That person who has renounced all visible creatures and in whom God performs His will completely, that person is both God and man. His body is so completely penetrated with Divine light and with the soul-essence which is of God that he can properly be called a Divine man." The Christian may safely go thus far.

revered friend, and early Tamil tutor, the learned and devout Mr. D. S. Nallatamby of Neervēli, Jaffna, taught me that this verse had the sense that saints are to be worshipped as God. I have had the good fortune to be confirmed in this view by Mr. J. M. Nallaswami Pillai, and Mudaliar R. C. Kailasa Pillai to both of whom I refer above, *Introduction*, part v, § 34 *ad fin.* The next following verse is a corrective of any idea of man being equated with God.

196. Saiva Faith. (Page 84, No. 228.)

The Tamil is நற்பர தற்பர சைவ சிற் சிவனே (*natpara tatpara Saiva sit Sivanēy*) literally 'highest good, God over all, in the Saiva faith of saving Wisdom, Siva.' The sense is adequately contained in the first two English lines. I have, without dissociating 'Siva' from the Saiva faith, rendered 'Siva' by one of its best-known meanings, 'Bliss,' that is, 'the blissful One.' This has been done with the purpose of linking this verse with 'Bliss' in the next two following verses.

197. Alien Faiths. (Page 84, No. 230.)

See above, *Introduction*, part ii.

198. Asat, Sat. (Page 87, No. 240.)

Asat, the Sanscrit *asad*, means 'non-being.' It is the negative form of *sat*, 'being.' In the sense of 'unreal' the words occur in the oft-quoted, and often misapplied, Upanishad line, 'From the unreal (*asat*) lead me to the real (*sat*).'[1] The 'universal mind' is said to 'experience the real (*sat*) and the unreal (*asat*).'[2] *Asat* is not 'nothingness' but an absence of 'being' or 'reality,' as one may gather from the line, 'In the beginning the world was just non-being (*asat*), one only, without a second; from that non-being (*asat*) being was produced.'[3] The mind, says our poet, is in reality, *asat*, but, from its activities in men and gods, he is obliged to recognize it as *sat*.

---

[1] *Brih. Aran. Upan.* 1. 3. 28. The Upanishad itself explains the words to mean 'from death to immortality.'

[2] *Prasna Upan.* 4. 5.

[3] *Chandog. Upan.* 3. 19. 1. *Tait.* 2. 7 criticized in *Chandog.* 6. 2. 1. 2. see N.M. 481 and Nalla. *Siddhiyar*, p. 108; Nalla. *Bodham*, p. 76.

199. GRACE, THEE, ME. (Page 83, No 246).

Pattanattu Pillayar, in a psalm of some length, refers to and depicts what seems a realized experience. The concluding portion of the psalm may be thus rendered:

The grace of God came unto me
And slew delusion's might.
Thereafter I obtained
The longing for high wisdom's holy light;
Obtaining, I beheld Thy Deity;
Beholding, gained
The vision of my very soul,
And lo! the moment I attained
To such high knowing, I began to see
All men, all things, as truly they should be,
And saw Thee in Thy fulness, no part but whole.[1]

This is the soul's three-fold seeing, of Grace, of God, and of its own self. A modern thinker has these remarks on this:

The gradual elimination of thought 'atom by atom' from consciousness, while drawing it closer and closer to God, leads first to a stage at which all trace of thought is "worn off." Then and there the purified consciousness (*sakshi*), or the soul which lay hidden behind the veil of thought, becomes visible to itself or appears in its "own proper form" in unspeakable repose. This is called *anma-darsanam*, or knowledge of the soul. Next is realized *Siva-darsanam*, or knowledge of God who rises from the bosom of the soul in the glory of the sun. This is "His way"—*His usual method* of manifesting himself to those men who worship Him in a purely subjective manner. Just as the soul enshrined in the body "rises" or manifests itself from the body, God enshrined in the soul "rises" from the soul and manifests Himself to the soul. These are the two fundamental experiences of human nature. ... After attaining it there is nothing to attain here or elsewhere.[2]

The subject of *ânma-darsanam*, the soul's vision of itself, is dealt with in most Siddhanta writings.[3] Tayumanavar speaks of it in other places.[4]

In Plotinus we have reference to God-seeing and soul-seeing, and of the soul raising itself to the realm of the spirit:

It will see God and itself and the All; it will not at first see itself as the All, but being unable to find a stopping-place to fix its own limits and determine where it ceases to be itself, it will give up the attempt to distinguish itself from the universal Being, and will arrive at the All without change of place, abiding there where the All has its abode.[5]

---

[1] *Tiruvitaimaruthur Mummanikkovai*, 13.

[2] Sir P. Ramanathan, *Mystery of Godliness*, 9, 10.

[3] *Sivaprajasam*, 72; *Irupavirupaktu*, 7; *Siddhiyar*, 3, 8, 28.

[4] *e.g.* N. M. 768, Nos. 305, 310, at pages 103, 104.

[5] *Enneads*, 6. 5. 7, translated in Inge's *Phil. of Plotinus*, i. 203.

So again Plotinus:

In knowing God, the spirit knows also itself; for it will know what it receives from God, what God has given to it and can give. In knowing this it will know itself, for it is one of God's gifts, or rather the sum total of them.........If it cannot see Him clearly, it is because seer and seen are the same. For this reason spirit will know and see itself, because to see is to become oneself the thing seen.[1]

Catholic theology on soul-seeing and God-seeing is best summarised in Devine's words. "Spiritual progress depends on two things in general, to know ourselves and to know God. Bishop Ullathorne teaches us how to know ourselves when he quotes the words of S. Catherine of Siena, 'Know yourself not in yourself but in God, and God in you.'"[2] Devine quotes and endorses the following from a classic on Catholic mysticism.

When the soul is so gathered into herself and so separated from the sight of all earthly things, and from the use of her bodily senses, that she feeleth herself as she is in her own nature—that is, without a body. If then thou desirest to know and see what thy soul is, thou must not turn thy thoughts upon thy body to seek it by imagination there, and to feel as if it were hidden within thy heart as thy heart is hidden and contained within the body............Withdraw thy thoughts from all bodily things, and from the care of thy own body, and from all thy five senses, as much as thou canst, and think upon the nature of a reasonable spirituality........... It is very hard for a soul that is ignorant ever to have this sight and knowledge of itself, or of an angelic nature or of God......All spiritual things are seen and known by the understanding of the soul and not by the imagination......Nevertheless, I say not that thy soul should continue to rest in this knowledge, but by means of it shall it seek a higher knowledge above itself, and that is, the nature of God. For the soul is as a mirror, in which thou shouldst behold God spiritually. And therefore thou must first of all find thy mirror and keep it bright and clean from fleshly filth and worldly vanity, and hold it up well from the earth that thou mayest see it and our Lord therein also.[3]

200. Tears, Love-tremor. (Page 89, No. 249).

Devotion leads to physical consequences like tremor and tears. The poet frequently refers to these signs of inward feelings.[4]

---

[1] *Enn.* 5. 3. 7, in Inge, *Phil. of Plot.* ii. 89. 90.

[2] *Mystical Theology*, 277. cf. the words of S. Irenaeus (*Adv. Haer.* iv. 34, 6). "As those who see the light are within the light and partake of its brightness, so those who see God are within God, and partake of His brightness."

[3] Hilton, *Scale of Perfection* 249, 250. Father Dalgairn's edition of the Rev. Walter Hilton's *Scale of Perfection* is the best known.

[4] N. M. 83, 176, 190. 295, 498, 513, 556, 558, 976.

The passion of devotion in the matter of praising God has been found by Catholic saints to be physically overpowering :

Alas! this poor nightingale would wish to raise its notes ever higher, and to perfect its melody the better to sing the praises of its well-beloved. In proportion as it praises, so does it delight in praising, and in proportion as it delights in praising it is dissatisfied at not being able to praise better; yet to find what content it can in this passion, it makes all sorts of efforts, and in the midst of them faints and falls, as it happened to the most glorious S. Francis, who amidst the delight that he took in praising God and singing his canticles of love, shed abundance of tears ....remaining quite exhausted and often losing respiration through the effort of aspiration after the praises of Him whom he could never praise enough. [1]

201. THE LOTUS OF THY FAIR FEET. (Page 90, No. 253).

Initiation at the feet of the Teacher imparts great wisdom, and it is the initiation into saving wisdom at the feet of the God-man Guru that is meant here. This is referred to by S. Sundaramurti in "the longing for the laying of His feet upon my head," [2] and in S. Manikkavachagar's, "They learn the meaning of their song beneath Thy holy feet." [3] When grace is so manifested that thoughts of 'I' and 'mine' cease to be, the stage of initiation is *Tiruvadi* (of the holy Feet); when all is seen as God it is *Tirumugam* (of the holy Face); when ecstasy of bliss is realized it is *Tirumudi* (of the holy Head). [4] It is taught:

Learning at the feet of God
  Godlike maketh mortal me:
Learning at the feet of God
  Granteth heaven my boon to be;
Learning at the feet of God
  Bonds unbindeth, maketh free;
Learning at the feet of God
  Powers bestoweth, victory. [5]

Tayumanavar refers to the Feet in various contexts. He offers adoration to the Feet; [6] he is the slave of the Feet; [7] he is at the Feet, takes refuge there and clings to them; [8] he prays for the Feet to

[1] S. Francis De Sales, *Love of God*, Book v, ch. 6.
[2] *Tevarom, Tiruvatikay Veerattanam*, 1.
[3] *Tiruvachagam*, i, lines 92, 93.
[4] Tiruvilangams' *Sivapragasam* (Tamil), p. 142.
[5] *Tirumantram*, 1598.
[6] Nos. 27, 136, 206, 254, 274, above, and N.M. 303, 304.
[7] No. 152, above. N.M. 358.
[8] Nos. 135, 169, 176, 223.

be placed on his head;[1] the Feet are to be won in some future time;[2] ... longs to rest beneath the shadow of the Feet.[3] It is explained that "the feet of God stand for the light of His wisdom, and grace,"[4] and that" reaching the feet of God is final liberation and beatitude."[5]

202. SEEING, SIGHT, SEEN. (Page 92, No. 260).

That God is the seer, the vision and the seen is stated elsewhere also by the poet.[6]

203. THOU BECOMEST I. (Page 94, No. 265).

See p. 184 and see No. 298. What is meant here is the *advaita* relationship, for which see *Introduction*, part v. What is *not* meant is that the soul becomes God.

204. TWO-FOLD TEST. (Page 94, No. 266).

Want and fulness occasion likes and dislikes, that is, attachment.

205. TAMIL OF THE THREE. (Page 95, No. 274).

The three are Appar, Sundarar and Sambanthar, more fully dealt with in *Introduction*, part iii.

206. WE LIVE, THOU LIVEST. (Page 96, No. 277).

Souls, it is taught, are co-eternal with God. See above, *Introduction*, part v.

207. SPORT. (Page 98, No. 289).

See above, pp. 143, 182. In No. 285 the original means that the differences in the creeds are due to "the sport of God."

208. THE BELOVED. (Page 100), A REVEL (Page 100).

The use of love-language to express the soul's relationship to God is very ancient. The poet in this section of thirty verses employs erotic figures. The mystic experience is represented as being narrated by a soul to a fellow-soul, by one maiden to another. See, above, *Introduction*, part viii. for a fuller treatment of the erotic

[1] N. M. 177, 379, 507.

[2] Nos. 229, 275, 366, above.

[3] No. 379, and N.M. 408.

[4] *Siddhiyar*, 3. 9. 4, see *Bodham* 8 and 11.

[5] *Siddhiyar*, 3. 8. 12. 16.

[6] N. M. 309, 1290.

element in mysticism. The words of the Sufi mystic Jalaludin Rumi refer, for a like reason as S. Tayumanavar's, to a spiritual revel:

> I have put duality away, I have seen that the two worlds are one;
> One I seek, One I know, One I see, One I call.
> I am intoxicated with Love's cup,
> I have no business save carouse and revelry.[1]

209. SECRETS UNSAYABLE. (Page 100, 107, No. 291, 292, 321, 322).

S. Teresa, speaking of a stage of spiritual experience called "the flight of the spirit," says:

> With the swiftness of a bullet fired from a gun an upward flight takes place in the interior of the soul—I know no other name for it but "flight." Although noiseless, it is too manifest a movement to be an illusion and the soul is quite outside itself; at least that is the impression made upon it. Great mysteries are revealed to it meanwhile .. ..[2]

In the chapter on Spiritual Matrimony she says, in a manner suggestive of thoughts not dissimilar to those of our poet in this section of thirty verses:

> All the graces here divinely bestowed on the soul come, as I said, through no action of its own, save its total abandonment of itself to God. They are given in peace and silence, like the building of Solomon's temple where no sound was heard. It is thus with this temple of God, this mansion of His where He and the soul rejoice in each other, alone, in profound silence.[3]

S. John of the Cross gives us the vividness of his experience:

> In that soul wherein abides no desire neither images, nor forms, nor affection for any created object, the Beloved dwells most secretly, and the purer the soul and the greater its estrangement from every thing but God, the closer and most intimate is His embrace. This dwelling is secret[4]

Even if a writer, observes the latest expounder[5] of S. John of the Cross, possessed the experience himself, as S. John of the Cross possessed it, and S. Teresa when she wrote her *Interior Castle*, he could not reveal that experience to those who have never enjoyed it themselves. S. John of the Cross speaking of the communication of the Holy Ghost to the soul says:

> This breathing of the Holy Ghost in the soul, whereby God transforms it in Himself, is to the soul a joy so deep, so exquisite, and so grand that

---

[1] Nicholson, *Mystics of Islam*, 96.
[2] *Interior Castle*, 6. 5. 10.
[3] *Int. Castle*, 7. 3. 9.
[4] *Living Flame*, Stanza, 4.
[5] Watkin, *The Philosophy of Mysticism*, 300.

no mortal tongue can describe it, no human understanding, as such, can conceive it in any degree; for even that which passes in the soul with respect to the communication which takes place in its transformation wrought in this life cannot be described.[1]

The "secrets" of Love are part of Rabbinic mysticism. "In one of the most mysterious and most exalted parts of the heaven, there is a place called the palace of Love; profound mysteries are enacted there; there are assembled all the most well-beloved of the Heavenly King; the Holy One (blessed be He!) lives together with these saintly souls, and unites Himself to them by kisses of love."[2] Of a rapturous experience of his St. Paul writes how he was "caught up into paradise and heard unspeakable words, which it is not lawful for a man to utter."[3] A mystic of the East makes mention of "ecstasy and words beyond all ecstatic words,"[4] reminding one of Faber's thought, "There have been words said which could never mean to others what they meant to us; there have been works which needed not words and were more than words."[5] When Coventry Patmore showed his friend, Father Gerard Hopkins, the manuscript of *Sponsa Dei*, the latter returned it to the poet with the remark, "That is telling secrets."[6]

210. In Stillness be. (Page 100 No. 292).

In No. 322 the same expression occurs as "seating me by His side." The original சும்மாவிருக்கி recalls what the poet tells us his Guru had told him, சும்மாவிரு, 'be still'.[7] What writers on mysticism call 'introversion'

begets a great stillness in the soul which is technically termed *Quiet*, or the *Orison of Quiet*......It is not only an integral part of mystical religion; it is the necessary condition of God's deep self-communication to the soul. "Be

---

[1] *Spiritual Canticle*, xxxix, 2.

[2] *The Zohar*, quoted by Dr Abelson in *The Quest*, July 1913, p. 729.

[3] 2 Cor. 12 : 4. Of S. Francis of Assissi it is said that "several things had been manifested to him in vision which he would never discover to anyone; secrets (says S. Bonaventure) which perhaps could not be expressed in words" (Butler, *Lives of the Saints*, x. 136).

[4] Davis, *Persian Mystics*, i. 94.

[5] *Creator and Creature*, 80.

[6] Champneys, *Coventry Patmore*, i. 318. The *Sponsa Dei* was destroyed by the poet himself on receipt of the letter of Father Hopkins.

[7] N.M. 38, 40, 100, 116, 118, 162, 353, 416. 436, 464, 510. 5·1, 537, 538, 631, 685, 705.

still and know" is the great rule of the mystical life......It is that "busy rest" in which the soul abandons all superficial activity for the supreme act of stretching towards God......Father Augustine Baker, in a metaphor of thrilling effect, describes it as the soaring of an eagle in mid-air which, for a good space, can cleave its way through the blue "with a great swiftness but withal with great stillness, quietness and ease, without any wavings of the wings at all or the least force used in any member, being in as much ease and stillness as if she were reposing in her own nest."[1].........The soul on tip-toe, waiting in a tense rigour of expectancy to know, to feel, to experience, to taste as much life as its quivering palate can assimilate—such a conception is essentially modern and makes a strong appeal to a generation which delights in giving itself up to the impression of each moment.....There is also a negative element in the mystic quiet. The soul that would hold the Divine word as the shell holds the ocean must be empty, not only of vagrant thoughts and superficial interests, but of its own darting inclination towards whatever seems to it Divine. It must no longer go out to seek; it must wait.[2]

211. NAUGHT TO HINDER. (Page 100, No. 292; Page 107, No. 322).

Literally "with nothing in front of me," that is, every hindrance to clear vision and close union being put out of the way. Albertus Magnus exhorts:

Do not think about the world nor about thy friends, nor about the past, present, or future, but consider thyself to be outside thyself and alone with God......Let nothing come between thee and God.[3]

When the soul turns to God, by making itself the passive instrument of spirit, it finds that "there is nothing between."[4] This is Ruysbroeck's "to be God with God, without intermediary or any difference that might become an intermediary or an obstacle."[5]

212. CLING TO ME. (Page 100, No. 293; Page 107, No. 323).

Closeness of the soul to God, its attachment, is thus expressed. It is bidden:

Cling thou to that which He, to whom nought clings, hath bid thee cling,
Cling to that Bond to get thee free from every clinging thing.[6]

---

1 *Holy Wisdom*, 3. 3. 7

2 Herman, *Meaning and Value of Mysticism*, 120, 121.

3 Quoted in Jones's *Mystical Religion*, 219.

4 Inge, *Philosophy of Plotinus*, ii. 89.

5 Underhill, *Ruysbroeck*, 88.

6 *Kurral*, Bk. i., ch. xxxv. 10.

Father Beschi in his notes on this Kurral couplet says, *Dei amorem tenaciter prehende, et, ut sensibilium amorem extinguas, illum ipsum Dei amorem quotidie tenacius prehendere, atque augere stude*, which may be rendered, "Lay hold of the love of God firmly, and, that you may kill the attachment to the things of the senses, cultivate the practice of daily grasping that very love of God more and more firmly, and of being fruitful therein."[1] The same thought, of there being nothing between the soul and God, is thus expressed by Scupoli:

> You are not to do your own will, but to let God do in you what He wills. Let your will be always so freed from self as to have no desire of your own; and if you have a desire concerning anything, desire it only in such a manner as not to feel regret if you should be thwarted in it, but that your peace of mind may remain as undisturbed as if you had entertained no wish in the matter. This is true liberty of spirit, not to bind one's self to anything. If you yield up your soul to God in this state of detachment, free and alone, you will see the wonders God will work in you. O wonderful solitude and secret chamber of the most High, where only He will give audience, and speak to the inmost soul.[2]

The whole spirit of the interior life, says Jean Nicolas Grou, is summed up in the words, "God only."[3] God, it is a commonplace of mysticism, is the Lover of the soul, and "verily our Lover desireth that the soul cleave to Him with all her might, and that we be evermore cleaving to His goodness."[4]

213. BEYOND ALL TELLING. (Page 100, No. 293; Page 107, No. 323).

Of the soul and its Bridegroom in the unitive stage S. John of the Cross, after discoursing (see above, p. 213) on the breathing of the Holy Ghost in the soul states, as a reason for the ineffableness of the resultant experience, that.

> The soul united with God and transformed in Him breathes in God that very divine aspiration which God breathes Himself in the soul when it is transformed in Him.[5]

This condition of ineffable association of the soul with God is

---

[1] Quoted in Pope's *Kurral* p. 246. *Augere* has the sense of 'increasing' as well as of 'being fruitful.'

[2] *Interior Peace*, ch. v.

[3] *Hidden Life* (Hutchings' edition), p. 114.

[4] Mother Julian, *Revelations of Divine Love*, Ch. vi. She says elsewhere, "Till I am substantially united to Him, I may never have full rest, nor very bliss, that is to say, till I be so fastened to Him that there be right nought that is made between my God and me." Ch. v.

[5] *A Spiritual Canticle*, xxxix, 2.

the secret of His countenance where there is no shadow but a privacy of glorious light.

It is light that lives. It is a photosphere, within which opens upon the happy inmate the sweetness and the response of a personal while eternal smile. It is not it, but He. It is not a sanctuary, but a Saviour, and a Father, seen full in Him, giving to the soul nothing less than Himself, indeed in vivid intercourse. It is the Lord coming to manifest Himself, and to make His abode with the man and to dwell in him, and he in Him. It means the spirit's sight of Him that is invisible. It means a life lived not in Christianity but in Christ, who is our life. [1]

214. Joyous Silence. (Page 101, No. 225, Page 108, No. 325).

The Tamil is capable of being so rendered as to make the speechlessness a result of the union.[2] My renderings "in joyous silence" (page 101) and "(joyous in silence)" (page 108) are intended to make the silence simultaneous with the realization of bliss. This would be consonant with the idea of concurrent and yet consequential speechlessness expressed by the words வாய் மடுத்து, meaning, in their context,[3] "drinking to the fullest and up to the throat."

215. Caste, Custom, Birth-mark. (Page 101, No. 296, Page 108, No. 326).

The translation, both here and in other parts of this section and in the next, designedly stops short of conveying the fulness of the erotic realism of the original. By 'caste, custom, birth-mark' being affected the maiden (soul) means that she had been assailed in her virginity. The Hindu mystical significance is that "the soul, losing its characteristic taint, has become divine."[4] The erotic mysticism of Madame Guyon furnishes parallels to more than one thought suggested by this *Revel in Bliss*.

Divulge not such love as mine,
Ah! hide the mystery divine,
Lest man, who deems my glory shame,
Should learn the secret of my flame.
In sylvan shades and caverns rude
I taste the sweets of solitude,
Retired indeed, but not alone,
I share them with a spouse unknown,
Who hides me here from envious eyes.
From all intrusion and surprise.[5]

---

[1] Bishop Moule, *The Secret of the Presence*, 14.

[2] So Arunachalam, *Revel in Bliss*, 37, and Barnett, *Heart of India*, 86.

[3] N. M. 274, 360, 544, 662, 1073 for example.

[4] Arunachalam, *Revel in Bliss*, 37, *note*.

[5] *Poems* (Cowper's Translation) p. 49.

1457—28

216. Cast Away. (Page 100, No. 298, Page 108, No. 328).

Compl te self-effacement is the most fitting preparation for the realization of the Divine. "Our alienation and severance from Thy beauty all proceed from ourselves. Deliver us from ourselves and accord to us intimate knowledge of Thee." Thus prayed Jami,[1] a great mystic of Persia, for, as another, Mahmud Shabistari, says, "In you, void of yourself, will He display His beauty."[2] Detachment is something to be practised, something to be acquired, something in which one should be perfected, so that detachment comes to one without *conscious* effort. "The very essence of prayer is to lose one's self in God which can never be while the soul is gauging and testing itself."[3]

217. His Very Self. (Page 101, No. 298, Page 108, No. 328).

See above pp. 184—196. The Siddhanta teachers clearly lay it down that *the soul is never God.*[4] The same is a fundamental of Rabbinic mysticism:

> There can be no greater truism, as far as the Jew of Rabbinic times is concerned, than that his union with God was......a union "with another than self." He never for an instant forgot that "however self be penetrated by God" yet was God other and transcendently greater than he, his Master, King, Shepherd and Guide. In fine the "God-within" idea coalesced with the "God-without" idea......Where mysticism is liable to run amuck is, in its mistaking the *contact* of man with God for the *identity* of man with God.[5]

The extravagant statements of Christian and other mystics must be taken to be intense forms of expressing the transforming character of the assimilation and association of the human soul with God. Eckhart's, "The Father makes me Himself and Himself me,"[6] analogous to our poet-saint's words, is not unlike the hard saying of the Blessed Angela de Foligno, "It is given unto me to see Christ who draweth me with such gentleness that sometimes He saith, 'Thou art I, and I am thou'."[7] It is the Persian's more balanced, "Thou art become my greater self."[8] He employs in this context

---

1 Davis, *Persian Mystics*, ii, 55.

2 Davis, *Persian Mystics*, ii, 27.

3 Grou's *Hidden Life* (Hutchings' Transl.) 205.

4 *Siddhiyar*, 3. 6. 9.

5 Abelson, *The Immanence of God in Rabbinical Literature*, 354, 355,

6 Quoted by Jones in *Studies in Mystical Religion*, 232.

7 Quoted by Herman in *Meaning and Value of Mysticism*, 157.

8 Jalalu'd Din Jami, in Underhill's *Mysticism*, 510.

the figure of wine mixed with water and asks, " Who can the wine and water part? " More felicitous are the illustrations employed by S. Teresa to explain what has to be experienced to be understood:

> Union may be symbolised by two wax candles, the tips of which touch each other so closely that there is but one light; or again the wick, the wax and the light become one, but the one candle can again be separated from the other, and the two candles remain distinct or the wick may be withdrawn from the wax. But spiritual marriage is like rain falling from heaven into a river or stream, becoming one and the same liquid, so that the river and the rain cannot be divided; or it resembles a streamlet flowing into the ocean which cannot afterwards be disunited from it. This marriage may also be likened to a room into which a bright light enters through two windows—though divided when it enters, the light becomes one and the same.[1]

About the idea of the streamlet and similar analogies see above, *Introduction*, part ix.

218. Elements, Senses. (Page 102, No. 299, Page 109, No. 329)

The soul is above mere " organic " existence.

I reproduce here Sir P. Arunachalam's illuminative note on this stanza:—

> Thou art not " the earth and other elements " i.e., the *sthula sarira* or gross body composed of flesh, bone, blood, etc. which are resolvable into these elements. Thou art not (*a*) the organs of action. or (*b*) of sense, or (*c*) the " internal " which together constitute the subtle body or *sukshma sarira*.
>
> (*a*) Organs of action (*karmendriya*) are hand, foot, organ of voice. organ of generation, organ of excretion.
>
> (*b*) Organs of sense (*jnanendrayi*) are the organs of sight, hearing, smell taste and touch.
>
> (*c*) " internal organs " (*antahkarana*) are chitta mind-stuff, manas, the vibration therein caused by the impact of external objects conveyed through

---

[1] *Interior Castle*, vii, ch. 2, 5. These analogies keep dissolvable union and ' spiritual marriage ' distinct. This quotation and others, from *The Interior Castle*, are from the Bendectine edition revised by the Very Rev. Dr. Zimmerman (London: Thomas Baker, 1912). Father Devine (*Mystical Theology*, 469) thus quotes the above from an earlier edition of *Interior Castle*:

" Let us suppose union to be two *tapers*, so exactly joined together that the light of both makes but one light; or that the wick, light and wax are all one and the same, but that afterwards one taper may be easily divided from the other, and then two distinct tapers will remain. and the wick will be distinct from the wax. But here [in the spiritual marriage] it is like water descending from heaven to a river or spring, where one is so mixed with the other that it cannot be discovered which is the river water and which the rain-water. It is also like a small rivulet running into the sea, whose waters cannot be separated from each other; or as if there were two windows in a room at which one great light entered but which though entering divided, yet makes but one light within.... "

the organs of sense, buddhi the reaction following the vibration, the determinative faculty, and *ahan-kara* the idea of "I" that flashes with the reaction, the I-making faculty.

(*a*) and (*b*) are not the visible organs but brain centres.

(*a*) and (*c*) together constitute what, in English psychology, is called "mind" being however understood to be a subtle form of matter. In verse 2 I have for want of a better word translated manas as 'mind,' but it is of course not correct. When there is no vibration (*i.e.*, thought) in the mind-stuff, deep sleep supervenes in ordinary mortals, in all save the jnani. Therefore the manas is there described as "standing as thought and sleep"

Thou art the Soul, Pure Intelligence or Spirit which by the help of (*a*) and (*c*) is able to know external objects and experiences, pains and pleasures, and stands apart as witness of all these experiences in waking state, in dream, in deep sleep, and in the two further states called *turiyam* and *turiyatitam*[1]

219. His Feet. (Page 102, No. 300, Page 109, No. 330).

See above, page 211. A royal saint among the Vaishnavites is recorded as rejoicing;

> What makes me king is not the crown
> Men set upon my head,
> But king when King of kings doth make
> His lotus-feet my crown.[2]

It is said of the Saivite saint Sundarar that one night, while he was sleeping outside a Siva temple afraid to go in because of its renown for sanctity, Siva, taking the form of a mendicant, lay down in the same house and placed His feet on Sundarar's head. "Sir," said the saint rudely disturbed, "wherefore are your feet upon my head?" He received the answer, "Not knowing where your head might be I have done this!" The saint changed his position and was sleeping again, when Siva's feet were on his head once more. The saint asked angrily, "Who are you?" "Do you not know me?" said Siva, and disappeared.[3] Thereupon, so goes the story, Sundarar reproached himself, and praised Siva in the ten stanzas which form the collection entitled *Tiruvatikai Veerattānam.*

220. Self-knowledge. (Nos. 300, 330).

See above, p. 209. This is the soul's coming to itself.[4] On November 11, 1509, S. Catherine of Genoa experienced such a burning love for God that, it is recorded, "This creature, all lost in her own self, found her true self in one instant in God."[5]

---

[1] *Revel in Bliss*, 39. [2] Govindacharya's *Dravida Saints*, 133.
[3] Nagalinga Mudaliyar's edition of *Sundaramurti's Psalms*, p. 16.
[4] *Cf.* S. Luke 15 : 17. [5] Hügel, *Myst. Elem.* i. 188.

221. Died to me. (Nos. 300, 330).

This is not more literal than "died to sense,"[1] or "died to thought."[2] A physical consciousness, not necessarily to be always expected of such 'dying,' is related of S. Teresa. "During the short time the union lasts she is, as it were, deprived of all feelings, and, though she wishes it, can think of nothing . . . She is as it were absolutely dead to the world, the better to live in God."[3] The idea of 'dying to self' so inseparable from 'detachment' is thus brought out by Sacramelli :

> A vase cannot be filled with sweet scented liquid unless it be first emptied of all else ; so, God cannot pour into our hearts the priceless balsam of Divine love, before, by dint of mortification, we have purged it of every imperfect attachment, especially, of that we bear to self, which, being most deeply rooted, is calculated to do us great harm.[4]

222. Linked to Me. (Page 102, No. 301, Page 109, No. 331).

See above, *Introduction*, part vi, and see pp. 130, 200. Births and re-births are a waking and a sleeping.[5]

223. Banyan Tree. (Page 102, No. 302, Page 109, No. 332).

See above p. 169. The exposition of மனதே கல்லால் to mean "my mind being stony"[6] is fanciful.

224. Mystical Mute Show. (Nos. 302, 332).

The posture of the devotee seated with his palms spread out and upward, the forefinger meeting the thumb in a ring, is said to represent the posture of Siva when he was seated under the banyan tree on His appearance there to enlighten His saints, "the Four." The thumb represents God, the first finger the soul, the second, third and fourth stand respectively for "I"-ness (ஆணவம்) karma and maya, the three forming the Siddhanta பாசம் (*pāsam* = bond or attraction). The soul (forefinger), ordinarily in the company of the three attractions, is said to be, in the mystical posture, linked to God (thumb). This is the "mute-show." See above, pp. 200, 201.

---

[1] Barnett, *Heart of India*, 86.
[2] Arun. *Revel in Bliss*, 39.
[3] Underhill, *Mysticism*, 425.
[4] *Directorium Asceticum*, vol. iv, Art. iii. c. iii, § 155.
[5] *Nanjari Vilakkum*, Stanza 95.
[6] K. S. Mudalyar's edition of *Tayumanavar*, p. 713.

225. SEEING. (Page 102, No. 303, Page 109, No. 333).

This stanza refers to that experience in which seer and seen are one.

And perchance we should not speak of sight. For that which is seen—if we must speak of the seer and the seen as twain and not as one—that which is seen is not discerned by the seer nor conceived by him as a second thing; but, becoming, as it were, other than himself, he of himself contributeth naught but as when one layeth centre upon centre, he becometh God's and one with God. Wherefore this vision is hard to tell of. For how can a man tell of that as other than himself which, when he discerned it, seemed not other, but one with himself indeed? [1]

It is an error to suppose, Dr. Rufus M. Jones [2] rightly cautions all, that the mind in ecstasy is *necessarily* a blank. As a Catholic mystic writes, "It is no longer I who am there, it is He. I see myself no longer, I only see Jesus. I am not destroyed, but His life takes possession of me, dominates and absorbs me." [3] The saints of Sufism have expressed themselves in words analogous to those under comment. One says:

When my Beloved appears,
With what do I see Him?
With His eye, not with mine,
For none sees Him except Himself. [4]

Again:

Myself with mine own eyes I saw most clearly,
But when I looked with God's eyes, only God I saw.
I passed away into nothingness, I vanished,
And lo! I was the All-living, only God I saw. [5]

226. DARKNESS. (Nos. 303, 333).

God transcends vision. The more the soul has glimpses of Deity the more does He seem incomprehensible, and greater the light by which He is seen the more is it perceived that He is above sight.[6] In the stage of union there is a consciousness of the fact, which in its utter incomprehensibleness is as darkness.[7] Tauler instructs:

---

[1] Plotinus, *Enneads*, vi. 9, 10.

[2] *Studies in Myst. Religion*, 76.

[3] Lucie Christine, *Spiritual Journal*, p. 237.

[4] Nicholson, *Mystics of Islam*, 165.

[5] *Ibid*, page 59. "The soul becomes a stranger to itself" (Benedict xiv, *Heroic Virtues*, ix, 267.)

[6] S. John of the Cross, *A Spiritual Canticle*, vii. 10.

[7] Watkin, *Phil. of Mysticism*, 344, 345. See Underhill, *Mysticism*, 415. The "dark night of the soul" is a different experience, one of depression and dereliction.

Bear thy foolish and barren heart into the Wilderness of the calm and living Godhead. Then look upon the Divine Darkness, which is dark from its surpassing brighness to the comprehension of men and of angels, as the shining of the sun on his course is as darkness to weak eyes..... ..Bear thereto thine own deep darkness, robbed of all true light, and let the Abyss of the Divine darkness alone be acknowledged while other things remain unknown. The Abyss which is unknown and has no name, is Salvation.[1]

227. UNDIFFERENT. (Nos. 303, 333).

"In the transformation within the unity all spirits fail in their own activity, and feel nothing else but a burning up of themselves in the simple unity of God......If the soul observes itself it finds a distinction and an otherness between itself and God; but where it is burnt up, it is undifferentiated and without distinction, and therefore it feels nothing but unity." [2]

228. NEARED SIVA-LAND. (Nos. 305, 335).

In No. 335, more literal than No. 305, the soul is represented as nearing "Siva-land's sweep of bliss." [3] European mystics speak of "the Wilderness or Desert of Deity, suggesting thus that sense of great, sweet spaces 'beyond the polar circle of the mind' —of a plane of experience destitute of all homely furniture of thought—which seems to characterise a certain type or stage of contemplation." [4] It is the "Divine Ignorance" or "Dark," the "Cloud of unknowing," 'a place beyond uttermost Place, Eckhart's "still wilderness where no one is at home," and Tauler's "quiet Desert of the Godhead." The realisation subjectively described by S. Tayumanavar as "Siva-land's sweep of bliss" is Tauler's "Abyss," [5] and the "dim contemplation" of S. John of the Cross.[6] That the experiences in this stage of "darkness" are not blankly negative we have here the Saiva poet's "I saw His beauty", and the clearer statement of Richard Rolle:

> In the Wilderness......speaks the loved to the heart of the lover; as it were a bashful lover, that his sweetheart before men entreats not, nor friendly wise but commonly and as a stranger he kisses .... soon comes heavenly Joy.[7]

In this context, and as apposite to the effect of "nearing"

---

[1] Tauler, *Instructions* in A. W. Hutton's edition of *Tauler*, 324.

[2] Ruysbroeck, *apud* Watkin *Op. cit.* 320. Underhill, *Ruysbroeck*, 160, 161.

[3] In No. 150 above it is "vastness of holiness."

[4] Underhill in *The Quest*, July 1913, pp. 639, 640.

[5] *Instructions* in Hutton's Tauler, 324.

[6] *Dark Night of the Soul*, i, ii, ch. 17.

[7] *Fire of Love*, ii. ch. 7.

God, may be noted the words of S. Manikkavachagar which I render differently, in point of technique but not in substance, from the version given above at p. 187.

This day Thou gavest me, my God, Thy grace to see
  Thee in my soul, in splendour as the rising sun,
Dispel my darkness, driving gloom afar,
  And I, unthinking, thought on Thee so stand,
O Glory of the grace-lit soul, and, nearing Thee,
  I wore myself away to little, least,
Knowing beside Thee naught, and lo! was one with Thee,
  O holder of the haven of the heart!

229. WITNESS. (Nos. 309, 339).

The poet refers to God in other places as the Witness.[1]

230. UNTOUCHED BY ACTIONS. (Nos. 309 339).

"There is naught in the three worlds", says Krishna, "that I must needs do, naught that I have not gotten or that I shall not get; yet do I abide in work."[2] Again, "These works fetter me not for I abide as one indifferent and unattached to these works."[3] Philo taught, "God ceases not from working: as to burn is the property of fire, so to act is the property of God."[4] The question whether, as Leibnitz held, God works under a moral necessity, or as Plotinus argued, the act of creation is due to God's eternal perfection is briefly discussed by Dean Inge in his *Philosophy of Plotinus*.[5] Compare our Lord's words, "My Father worketh hitherto and I work."[6]

231. BEING, BLISS, WISDOM (Nos. 311, 341).

The original is *Sat-Chit-Ananda*, சச்சிதானந்த, a title of God occurring frequently in Saivite literature. Our poet-saint uses it often.[7] There is an Upanishadic passage, "He who knows Brahma as the real (*satya*), as knowledge (*jnana*) and infinite (*ananta*) obtains

---

1 Above, No. 133 and N. M. 136.

2 *Gita*, iii. 22.

3 *Gita*, ix. 9.

4 Quoted in Hügel, *Myst. Elem.* ii. 80.

5 i. 146, 147. He quotes Eckhart, 'God creates from all eternity and constantly.'

6 S. John 5. 17.

7 E.g. N. M. 279, 415, 570, 1,306, 1,307. In No. 152, above, it is rendered "Pure Light of purest Bliss."

desires."[1] which, if emended, as Deussen proposes, by reading *ānanda* (bliss) for *ananta* (infinite), would yield the customary three-fold definition of Brahma as *sat-cit-ānanda*, (being, intelligence, bliss).[2] God is *sat*, the only Reality; *chit*, pure Intelligence; and *ānanda* pure Bliss. The word "pure" is in the sense of there being no distinction of subject and object.[3]

232. THIS BODY. (Page 104, No. 312.)

See above, *Introduction*, part vi.

233. STRANGERS. (Nos. 315, 345.)

"I beseech you as strangers and pilgrims that ye abstain from fleshly lusts."[4] S. Catherine of Genoa has said:

> I seem to myself to be in this world like those who are out of their home, and who have left all their friends and relations, and who find themselves in a foreign land and who, having accomplished the business on which they came, stand ready to depart and return home—home where they are ever with heart and mind, having indeed so ardent a love of their country that one day spent in getting there would appear to them to last an year.[5]

"Here we have no continuing city."[6]

234. THE GOD OF LOVE. (Page 105, No. 317.)

Kāman, the western Cupid, is the "bodiless." Pope[7] summarizes from *Kamba Rāmāyanam* the legend of the 'bodilessness' of Cupid. Siva was practising austerities, and Cupid, under the instigation of other gods, sought to distract Siva from his devotions. Cupid was punished by being burnt to ashes by fire proceeding from the third eye of Siva. Cupid was, however, given back his life but not his body.

235. SAFFRON. (Page 106, No. 318.)

The rendering of வெயில் மஞ்சள் as "sun-baked saffron" seems to be in accord with its occurrence elsewhere[8] in a description of sensual life as mere glamour. "Yellow sunshine" is Sir P. Arunachalam's rendering.[9]

---

[1] *Tait. Up.*, 2. 1.

[2] Hume, *Thirteen Principal Up.*, p. 283.

[3] Arun., *Revel in Bliss*, 43. Nallaswamy Pillai (*Studies*, p. 301) draws attention to Bishop Westcoft's conception of tri-personality of God in the idea embodied in 'God is Love.' (See Westcott's *Epistles of S. John*, additional note on 1 John 5 : 20).

[4] 1 Pet. 2 : 11.

[5] Hügel, *Myst. Elem.*, i. 274.

[6] Heb. 13 : 14.

[7] *Tiruvachagam*, p. 160, note.

[8] *Pambatti Sittar Pādal*, stanza, 50.

[9] *Revel in Bliss*, 45.

236. JANAKA. (Page 106, No. 319.)

Janaka, King of Videka, famous in an Upanishad [1] for his wisdom and piety is an example with our poet-saint [2] of duty without distraction. The *Gita* holds him up as an illustration of action without attachment. "Fulfil ever without attachment the work that thou hast to do, for the man that does his work without attachment wins to the supreme. For it was with works that Janaka and others came unto adeptship." [3]

237. YEA, NAY. (Page 106, No. 320.)

This verse sums up the teaching of the entire poem—the soul, giving up all distracting contrasts and distinction, should stand indifferent to likes and dislikes, to yea and nay, in quietness and confidence, knowing itself, and so pass on to the knowledge of oneness with Deity.

238. THIS BIRTH. (Page 115, No. 355.)

See above, page 115 and *Introduction*, part vi.

"When we consider the case of a soul which, after passing through eighty-four thousand wombs of four-fold nature, is born in a human body, we can but compare it to the case of a man who with his own hands has swum the white ocean. Was it not to this end namely, of serving God with mind, speech and body that souls are endowed with human birth?" [4]

239. THE SHADOW. (Page 121, No. 379.)

From the oppressive warmth of births and re-births the soul longs to hasten to the refreshing shade of the refuge of the Feet of God.[5] The soul's final resting-place is God. *Fecisti nos propter Te, et inquietum est cor nostrum donec perveniat ad Te.*[6]

---

[1] *Brih. Aran. Up.*, 3. 1. 1, 4. 3. 1, 5. 14. 8.

[2] N. M., 154, 188.

[3] iii. 19. 20. "It was a fault which people were not sufficiently careful over, not seeing how serious it was nor considering that by fostering and allowing such attachments, they let others take possession of a heart that belonged to God alone, and stole from Him what He counted the most precious thing of all." (Stewart's *The Holiness* of *Pascal*, p. 76).

[4] *Siddhiyar*, 3. 2. 89; 3. 2. 92.

[5] See *Tirumantram*, 1600.

[6] Aug. *Conf.*, 1. 1. 1.

I. OPENING WORDS OF THE ENGLISH TRANSLATION

N.B. 1. The reference is to page of this book.

2. The letters A, A.K, C, G, P, S.M, mean translations by Sir P. Arunachalam, 'A.K', Rev. McKenzie Cobban, Dr. Graul Rev. G. Phillips and Mr. Shanmuga Mudaliar, respectively.

II. OPENING WORDS OF THE TAMIL IN N.M. EDITION

N.B. 1. The first column of figures shows the numbering of the hymns in N.M. Edition.

2. The second column of figures shows the page where, in this book, there is a translation.

3. The Roman figures refer to the pages of the Introduction.

4. This Index does not include incidental phrases or passages from Tāyumānavar, or quotations made in Tamil or in translation from other writers.

III. PRINCIPAL SIDDHANTA WORKS

N.B. 1. Bōdham = Siva Gnāna Bōdham.
2. Siddhiyār = Siva Gnāna Siddhiyār.
3. Pattanattār *Padal* is a general term for his hymns particularized where cited.
4 *Tēvāram* means hymns of Appar, Sundarar, etc., particularized where cited.
5. Right-hand figure indicates page of this book.
6. The *Kural* and *Nāladiyar* are not strictly speaking Siddhanta works.

Siddhiyar

(Quoted by book, section, verse)

Siddhiyar—*continued*

IV. GITA, RIG VEDA AND UPANISHADS

N.B. 1. The Gita is cited by lesson and verse.
2. The R. V. is cited by mandala, book and verse.
3. The Upanishads usually have three divisions, some two and some no chapters.

Maitri Upanishad—*continued*

Māndūkya Upanishad

Mundaka Upanishad

Mundaka Upanishad—*continued*

Prāsna Upanishad

Svetasvatāra Upanishad

Taittareya Upanishad

V. BIBLE (AND APOCRYPHA REFERENCES

VI. PRINCIPAL SUBJECTS AND PRINCIPAL WORDS NOT IN OTHER INDEXES

N.B. 1. This Index is not exhaustive.
2. See List of Contents at the beginning of this book.
3. Reference is to page of this book.